1945

1995

FIFTY YEARS OF PUBLISHING

Never the Last Journey

Never the Last Journey

Felix Zandman
WITH DAVID CHANOFF

SCHOCKEN BOOKS, NEW YORK

All rights reserved under International and Pan-American Copyright Conventions. Published
in the United States by Schocken Books Inc., New York, and simultaneously in Canada by
Random House of Canada Limited, Toronto. Distributed by Pantheon Books, a division of
Random House, Inc., New York.

Grateful acknowledgment is made to the following for permission to reprint
previously published material:

American Society for Metals: Excerpt from *Tatnall on Testing* by F. G. Tatnall.
Reprinted by permission of Amy L. Bird for American Society for Metals.
The Beate Klarsfeld Foundation: Excerpts from *Documents Concerning the
Destruction of the Jews of Grodno, 1941–1944* by Serge Klarsfeld. Reprinted
by permission of The Beate Klarsfeld Foundation.
United States Holocaust Memorial Museum: Excerpts from *The Death Camp Treblinka*
edited by Alexander Donat. Reprinted by permission of the United States
Holocaust Memorial Museum.

Library of Congress Cataloging-in-Publication Data

Zandman, Felix.
Never the last journey / Felix Zandman with David Chanoff.
p. cm.
ISBN 0-8052-4128-0
1. Zandman, Felix. 2. Holocaust, Jewish (1939–1945)—Personal narratives.
3. Holocaust survivors—United States—Biography.
4. Jews—United States—Biography.
I. Chanoff, David. II. Title.
D804.3.Z357 1995
940.53'18—dc20   94-41413

Book Design by Diane Kasprowicz
Manufactured in the United States of America

2 4 6 8 9 7 5 3 1

This book recounts many conversations held over a long period of time and reconstructed from my memory. In each instance the substance and tone of these conversations is accurate; the dialogue is as precise as memory permits.

To Ruta,

whose love gave me the strength

for this and so much more.

And to the memory of

my beloved parents, Genia and Aaron,

and my sister, Mira.

Contents

Zog nit keinmol az du geist dem letztn veg.

Ven himlen blaiene farshteln bloie teg.

Kumen vet noch unzer oisgebenkte sho,

S'vet a poik ton unzer trot mir zainen do!

Never say you are making the last journey,

That the leaden heavens have hidden the blue days.

The hour we have prayed for will come at last,

And we will march proudly forward—we are here!

A Partisans' Song

For many years I was simply unable to talk about the Holocaust. It was not until decades afterward that my wife, Ruta, was able to begin drawing the story out of me, making it possible for me to articulate those things I had suppressed for so long. Expressing what I had lived through enabled me to put it into perspective. I began to see those events in the context of the entire life I had managed to live instead of as an inexpressible nightmare that seemed always on the verge of breaking forth from my subconscious.

Once I was able to tell her the story, Ruta began urging me to write it down, but for a long time that was beyond my strength. Then, a few years ago, I was having lunch with a prominent Israeli author. The conversation turned to the war years, and I mentioned that I had been saved by a Polish family, which had hidden me and four others for seventeen months beneath the floorboards in their bedroom. The writer was instantly attentive. Here was an unusual existential situation. How could five people have managed to live together for so long jammed into a grave? How could they have survived physically, emotionally, and morally in such inhuman circumstances? Because the fact was that when the Soviet army finally arrived, the five of us had emerged from our hole in the ground as decent human beings. There was plenty wrong with us physically, but psychologically and morally we were still whole.

The author was taken by what had happened and wanted to write about it. But after several discussions I could see we weren't on exactly the same wavelength. From his point of view, our time in the grave presented an opportunity to explore fundamental questions of human interaction. I wasn't insensitive to that. We all knew that we had survived because we had established rules of behavior, a kind of social contract that we could either adhere to and live or ignore and die. Although I was only seventeen when I got out of the hole, the experience had made me understand in my bones why the Ten Commandments were created. They weren't just ethical precepts; they were rules for the preservation of society. I also knew what it meant to have nothing but the resources of your own mind and spirit to fend off insanity and give yourself a reason to continue living. These things were hardly insignificant. But still, those seventeen months were only one part of my life. If I was going to write something, I wanted it to be complete.

Although we hadn't agreed, my conversations with the author drove me to think more about putting my experiences down on paper. Others talked to me about it as well, including Isaac Zuckerman, one of the heroes of the Warsaw Ghetto uprising. He believed that every survivor was obliged to bear witness, to fill in his or her little piece of the canvas. Despite my anxieties, the reasons for writing began to appear more and more compelling. My parents and grandparents especially were on my mind. Along with most of the other Jews of Grodno, Poland, they had died in early 1943 when the Nazis liquidated the ghetto. Writing a book would enable me to perpetuate their memory—not only theirs but also the memory of the rest of my family and the others in Grodno who had meant so much to me in those days.

I had already tried to do that through other means. I had named my company Vishay, after the little Jewish village where my family had its origins. To many people the name had a strange sound to it. But for me it recalled my grandmother who had been such a pillar of strength to me and others, and it suggested all those other vanished Jewish communities of Eastern Europe. Still, I know that businesses, like people, disappear. They are born, they grow, and given sufficient time, they die—even the largest of them. I have had the great good fortune to watch my company develop from nothing into an international corporation of sixteen thousand people spread out over eleven countries. I hope and expect that it will go on for a hundred years after I am gone. But I know for certain that books exist forever.

I had other reasons for writing. Like all survivors, I am driven by the Holocaust. That catastrophe transformed my life and in many ways shaped the person I was to become. But by no means do I consider my experience on this earth a tragedy. I was an adolescent when those terrible events happened, and since then I have lived through intense and interesting times. I became a scientist, an inventor, and an entrepreneur. I have ridden a sometimes breathtaking adventure through the world of international business and finance. I have experienced the immense pleasures of scientific discovery, of finding new things, and bringing abstract concepts to life. Even when I was young, I had the idea that I would love to create something that would make a contribution to the way people live. I count myself among the lucky few who have seen their youthful dreams turn into reality. Most satisfying of all, the social and spiritual isolation that accompanied me for so long after the destruction of my home and family have eventually led me to realize my essential identity as a Jewish man in the land of Israel.

Of course, as an adult, I have experienced my share of normal human sorrows, but I also live with the love and comfort of Ruta, who has been a true life partner; my three wonderful children, Gisele, Ariele, and Marc; and their families. I consider myself a happy, fulfilled person. That is why I thought that if I was going to write anything at all, I had to write everything. To do otherwise would be a distortion.

Yet when all is said and done, I am a person who should have been dead in 1943. Four or five times I escaped death by a hairsbreath—why me rather than the twenty-nine thousand other Grodno Jews who did not escape I cannot begin to say. I did live in a cramped black hole for almost a year and a half, from which my companions and I got away only by a miracle. I sometimes lecture at business schools and universities, not on the Holocaust but on industry and trade. Along with my talk about economic life, I try to impress on my audiences a sense of optimism and hope. The young people I am addressing come to hear about business, but they are hearing it from someone who has more right than most to convey the message that they should never feel everything is lost, no matter what the adversity or how grim the circumstances.

"Never say you are taking the last journey" is how the famous Partisans' Song put it. I took that conviction away with me from the devastation I lived through. Isaac Zuckerman felt we should all bear witness. Hope is an irrevocable part of the witness I have to bear.

Felix Zandman

Philadelphia and Tel Aviv

November 1, 1994

Never the Last Journey

The lull ended on June 23. A month and a half earlier, the Red Army's 1944 Winter Offensive had run out of steam, but now the Soviets had rebuilt their forces and prepared the next attack. All along the eight hundred miles from the Gulf of Finland to the Black Sea, the Soviet armies stood poised. Against them were arrayed 180 German divisions, three fifths of the Wehrmacht's entire order of battle. But these were not the robust, confident units that had poured into the USSR almost exactly three years before. These German divisions were bloodied and exhausted, their numbers shrunken and their armored strength depleted. They knew the blow was gathering, and they knew that when it came there would be no help. Three weeks earlier the Allies had landed in Normandy, and the best of Germany's armed might was struggling to hold back the tide in the West. The Eastern armies were on their own.

As the Soviet strength grew, German military intelligence labored to identify the focus of the imminent assault. The Red Army's Winter Offensive had bitten off vast gouges of territory in virtually every sector of the front, but nowhere was the Soviet advance more threatening than south of the Pripet Marshes toward the Black Sea. There Soviet units already stood on the foothills of the Carpathians. If that barrier were breached the Germans would be facing an irruption into the Hungarian Plain, at whose western end lay Vienna and beyond it the German homeland.

North of the Pripet the situation was marginally more promising. A string of fortified cities, the "Fatherland Line," guarded the approaches to northern Poland and the Baltic. In this sector the 850,000 men of Army Group Center, under the command of Field Marshal Ernst von Busch, faced a total of 1 million Soviet troops. The numbers favored defense, and the fortress cities constituted a formidable shield. To German intelligence all signs pointed to an attack—not here, but in the South.

The Soviets nurtured that perception. In late May and into June they carried out one of the most elaborate deceptions in military history, building thousands of mock artillery pieces and tanks, creating bogus communications networks, defensive fortifications, and false troop concentrations. The Soviet General Staff worked in the strictest secrecy; nothing was written, and only the top commanders knew the true picture. But behind the mask the Red Army was on the move. At night, under blacked-out conditions, two entire armies streamed northward. Twelve rifle divisions and a tank corps took up positions in the Byelorussian sector, ready for a surprise assault.

On the twenty-third the Soviet offensive erupted with overwhelming power. Late that first day, a double flanking assault sealed the fate of Vitebsk, a vital Fatherland Line fortress that had beaten back two attacks during the Winter Offensive. Three days later the Soviet vise clamped shut, annihilating the battered remnants of five Panzer divisions. Three hundred miles from the old Polish border a gaping hole had been torn in the German front.

Other strongholds of the Fatherland Line were also borne away before the Soviet avalanche. Just north of the Pripet Marshes General Rokossovsky's First Byelorussian Army broke the German lines and crushed five more divisions at Bobriusk. Behind the front, partisans played havoc with rail lines and bridges. From north, south, and east the Red Army converged on the military hub and communications center of Minsk.

On July 2 the horns of the Soviet thrust met behind that doomed city, encircling 100,000 German troops. A few units escaped southward through the tractless forests. But most were caught in the great pocket and either died there or surrendered. Army Group Center was collapsing. In ten days Germany had lost almost a quarter of a million men.

Reeling back toward Poland, the Germans struggled to put together a stand, but there was no natural line of defense, and the speed and power of the Soviet offensive gave them no time to regroup. Molodechno fell, then Baranovich, then Lida. On July 13 the Soviets reached the previously Jewish city of Grodno, on the Polish side of the old border.

In the early morning hours of July 15 the final assault on this strongly fortified city began under cover of a thick mist. An SS tank division put up fierce resistance, but by 2:00 A.M. the next day Soviet troops had overrun the post office and the railway station. Before midday the last Panzers were fleeing northwest, where a bend in the Nieman River offered a barrier they could use to good advantage.

There on the Nieman, just above Grodno, the scattered German units gathered for a stand—tanks, artillery, mechanized infantry—even a division of field police. In the tree-covered hills above the riverbank, remnants from all the region's overrun German strongholds frantically dug themselves in under a rain of Soviet high explosives.

On the German side of the river lay two villages, Losossna proper and Lesser Losossna. Not far from Losossna proper, in a wooded area that had once been known for its lovely summer dachas, sat a two-room cottage in which lived Jan and Anna Puchalski and their five children. The Puchalskis were deeply religious, and they had been praying that the front would wash over them and move quickly westward. They were heartened by the news that Grodno had fallen, and by the huge explosions that told them the Germans had blown the Niemen bridges.

But now thousands of troops were moving in and digging trenches all around their house and through the surrounding woods. As they realized the Germans had resolved to make a fight, the Puchalskis' anxiety skyrocketed—for themselves and for the guests they had been caring for since the liquidation of the Grodno ghetto a year and a half before. In a tiny pit underneath the floorboards of their second room five Jews lay jammed together—two men, two women, and—a seventeen-year-old boy named Felix (Feivel) Zandman.

"**F**EIVEL" said my grandma Tema Freydovicz. "Feivel, tell me, whom does this house belong to?"

    We were standing together on the balcony of our big house at 28 Brygidzka Street, where my family occupied one apartment, my uncle Grishka another, my grandparents and my as yet unmarried uncles and aunts Sender, Kushka, Fania, and Lisa a third. Part of the first floor was given over to the offices of the Freydovicz construction and building supply company whose shops, storerooms, and stables were housed in other wings and outbuildings that extended around the large courtyard. It was a trick question; the house was packed with Freydoviczes and Freydovicz enterprises.

    "It's our house, Grandma. We own it."

    Tema's voice was soft but strong, like the hand that held mine in a gentle yet firm grasp. Her broad face and blue eyes conveyed a sense of power as well as love, at least so it seemed to me at the age of nine.

    "No, Feivele. It's not ours. Tell me [she pointed to the flowerbeds blooming alongside one of the warehouses], whose garden is that?"

    "It's ours, Grandma."

    "No, Feivel, I'm sorry, the flowers aren't ours either. But what about those stores over there?" We looked across the courtyard to the row of shops that also belonged to the Freydovicz company.

    "Ours."

    "No, Feivel, not ours."

    "What do you mean 'not ours,' Grandma? I know they belong to us."

    "No, Feivel, they don't. They could all burn down tomorrow. The government could take them away from us. The whole thing might vanish. They aren't ours."

"Ah, ha!" I caught on to the trick. "I know what's ours, Grandma. Papa told me. He told me that the only thing we really have is what we learn. He said that is the only thing that's important. Everything else they can take away, even your clothes. But they can't take away what you know."

Tema's deep blue eyes gazed into mine. "You know," she said after a moment, "even that is not ours."

"Why isn't that ours, Grandma? Don't I know the things I've learned?"

"Well, Feivele, now you know it, but maybe tomorrow you'll find out that you don't know it. How many things were right yesterday that today we know are wrong?"

This was most frustrating. "Grandma, tell me. What is ours, then? Don't we have anything at all?"

"Yes, Feivele. We have a great deal. But the only things we own are the things we give away. That's all we really have. If you help a person, if you give of yourself—that no one can ever take away from you."

I should have guessed. As far back as I could remember, Grandma Tema had been taking me around with her to visit hospitals, old age homes, and orphanages, both of us hauling bags of food or clothes for those less fortunate than we. She was an endlessly energetic, one-woman philanthropical enterprise. From the time I was five she had me standing in front of audiences at charitable events, playing the violin or declaiming a poem I had memorized for the occasion. In these places big lights would flood down, practically blinding me to what always seemed an immense crowd of people swaying in front of me. Choking down my fright, I would launch into my poem or my sonata while she stood there, beaming. My grandmother was a charitable institution all by herself.

Grandfather Freydovicz was not a charitable institution. He was a businessman, just but hard. Also a teacher. "Feivel! Go and buy me a box of Plaski cigarettes," he told me once. But at the corner store there were no Plaskis. Now I had a dilemma. I could just hear him. If I came back and told him there were no Plaskis, it would be, "What? You dummy. So why didn't you buy some other kind?" But if I bought the other kind and gave it to him? "Feivel, why did you buy these? Who asked you to? Why can't you ever follow orders?"

Maybe I hadn't gotten Grandma Tema's riddle about what we owned, but this one I could figure out. I bought the other brand and put them in my pocket. "Grandpa," I said when I got back, "there were no Plaskis." "You dummy, so why didn't you buy another kind?" I put my hand in my pocket, took the package out, and handed it over. "I did, Grandpa, here they are." "Well, well," he said, taking them. "You're okay, Feivel." Getting a compliment from Nahum Freydovicz, even one as modest as this, felt like winning the Medal of Honor.

That was a strict man. With Grandpa Freydovicz you obeyed the rules and didn't expect compliments just because you did something okay. And if you broke the rules, you took your punishment. I remember my uncle Sender smoking a cigarette at the age of twenty or twenty-one. Smoking was an offense; none of the children was allowed to do it, even one as big and strong as Sender. Grandpa walked with a cane, the lasting result of the "Spanish grippe" he had caught during World War I. He took the cane and beat Uncle Sender across the back until the cane broke. Sender never budged, although he could have run away just like that. But he took his beating without moving a muscle. He had broken the rule, and he was ready for his punishment. What was fair was fair.

But as stern as he was, my grandfather was also very loving. I knew he loved me, his first grandson, very much. On Sabbath I always walked hand in hand with him at the head of the family procession that wended along Brygidzka Street and over the bridge to the Slobodka Synagogue: the two of us first; then my uncles Grishka, Kushka, and Sender; then my father; then the ladies. Later that day, after the big meal, Grandpa Freydovicz would always take me aside and tell me stories. One of his favorite was the story of the beaver, which I heard repeatedly (the story may have saved my life when the Nazis liquidated the Grodno ghetto; unfortunately it did not save his).

"A beaver lived in the forest and went fishing every day in the lake. He always went by the same path, never deviating. Now, the hunters who wanted to catch him knew his route and knew he never changed it. So they put a trap right on the path. That day the beaver went down the path as usual and saw the trap. He stopped in front of it and started to cry and lament. He knew it was a trap and that he shouldn't get in, but he didn't know what else to do. The path was too familiar, and he couldn't think of anything but staying on his regular course. Eventually he got in, the cage slammed shut, and that was the end of the beaver.

"Feivel," said my grandfather, "what would you do?" "He's stupid," I said. "I would go around." "You're a good boy. Don't get into the trap."

Next *shabbas* it was the same thing. "Feivel," he said, "I have a story for you, a story about a beaver." And so it would go. Training according to my Grandfather Freydovicz. In other words, if you have a trap in front of you, don't cry about it, don't mourn over it, don't get into the trap. Just go around it. Don't be stupid.

Each of the families in our big house had its own apartment, but there was constant travel from one to the other, and I could often hear things that took place in my relatives' lives. Real commotions were rare, though, which made the shouts coming from my grandparents' home one evening especially startling. "Help!" yelled my grandfather. "Help! Somebody stole the money. Thieves! *Gonovim!*" There was a great rush upstairs. Everybody ran—me, my mother, my father, my uncles. When we got there, Grandpa and Grandma Tema were in their bedroom, where a massive yellow safe stood against one of the walls, the safe that was locked and unlocked with two long keys my grandfather kept in the night table next to his bed. Each day the money from the stores would come in, be counted on the big dining room table, then locked in the safe. I had seen it a hundred times.

"Somebody stole my money from the safe," announced Grandpa when we were all standing there. Everyone was excited. Such a thing had never happened before, and how could a thief have gotten up there with the house full of Freydoviczes?

"Who took the money?" said my grandfather, eyeing me suspiciously, then turning his angry gaze on the others. "Somebody in this room took it. Only the family knew where the keys were. So it had to be one of you."

At this unexpected accusation everyone became agitated and started proclaiming their innocence, though in the midst of the hubbub I noticed my grandmother standing calmly near the wall, unaffected by the uproar.

When the noise died down a bit she said in her soft voice, "I did it. I took the money."

"You?" My grandfather stared at her in disbelief. "Why did you take the money? "What did you do with it?"

By now everyone was staring. "I gave it away," she said. "I gave it to people who needed it."

"What?" Grandpa couldn't believe what he was hearing. I could, though; I had had a lot of experience with Grandma Tema. If she saw someone in need she would find a way to help. I could easily imagine her unlocking the safe and putting the money in her big brown handbag. I could even picture some of the likely recipients.

"Who did you give it to?" said Grandpa, quieter now but still wide-eyed. He must have forgotten the Jewish law about charity, though I was sure Grandma Tema hadn't. If possible the giver should not know to whom he is giving nor the receiver from whom he is receiving.

"I can't tell you," she said. "It's not your business."

My father, Aaron Zandman, universally called Archik, had married into the wealthy Freydovicz family and was a junior partner in the family business. But he himself came from a very different background—a family of impoverished scholars who had moved to Grodno from the Jewish towns of Lida and Olkienik, eighty miles toward the Russian border. His father, my grandfather Zandman, was an Orthodox Jew who spent his life in studies.

Grandfather Zandman taught me to pray and put *tefilin* on, but he spoke to me strictly in Yiddish, never Hebrew. "Grandpa," I'd say, "we speak Hebrew in school. I'm proud of it. Let's speak Hebrew." And I'd carry on my part of the discussions in that language. But he refused. "The language of the Torah," he told me, "you shouldn't talk."

Conversations around the Zandman table spanned the Bible, the Talmud, prayers, but also philosophy and contemporary affairs—Zionism, for example, a subject that engrossed the entire Jewish community of Grodno. At the age of nine I already knew I was a Zionist; in my school, the Tarbut, it wasn't a question of whether one was a Zionist, only what kind of Zionist.

But Grandpa himself didn't feel comfortable with the idea. After all, the Messiah had not yet come, and he didn't know if Jews ought to be returning to the Holy Land before that blessed moment arrived. "I'm not sure about this question," he told me. "I'm still weighing it." When I stayed with my Zandman grandparents I always slept between him and my grandmother Rifka. I asked him once why he wore his socks to sleep, a habit I had been curious about for years. "When the Messiah comes," he told me, "and he can come at any time, Feivele, it will be faster to go to Jerusalem."

In the manner of many pious scholars of those days, my grandfather Zandman did not work, but spent all his time studying—which was, of course, the essence of life. Meanwhile, his wife, my grandmother Rifka, supported him and their three children by selling cloth out of a tiny store and winter shoes from her home. But even though Rifka kept the family's body and soul together while her husband devoted himself to piety, she was not exactly a typical Orthodox woman.

In the first place, she was the daughter of the Kelmer Maggid, an itinerant holy man famous throughout Poland in the latter part of the nineteenth century. The Kelmer Maggid's sermons were legendary. Chanting in a characteristic singsong, he excoriated the rich from one end of the country to the other, thundering the need for compassion and exhorting them to give, give, give, and give to the poor and to provide jobs for those in need. In each synagogue on his route he damned the wealthy while at the same time urging and commanding and shaming them to donate, to endow, to build hospitals, orphanages, schools, and clinics. At one point in his travels a group of merchants were so afraid of his attacks on false weights and measures that they denounced him to the authorities and had him thrown in jail before he had a chance to deliver his sermon. He himself was utterly destitute, but he never gave that a thought. Money for his own necessities didn't engage his attention.

Both in our own house and in Grandfather Zandman's the Kelmer Maggid was a regular topic of conversation. For us it was a *yiches,* a glory to the family. Whenever I was called on in the synagogue to say a prayer it was always mentioned that I was the Maggid's great-grandson. Many years later, when I was a student in France, I was invited to lunch in the house of a local rabbi. He asked where I was from, who my parents were, my grandparents. When he got to my great-grandparents and heard that the Kelmer Maggid was my ancestor, he instantly got up from his chair and made me sit down in his place, blushing with mortification that he had taken the head chair in front of the Maggid's direct male descendant.

How exactly such a personage as the Kelmer Maggid could ever have had a daughter like my grandmother Rifka puzzled me then and still puzzles me. Rifka was learned; she knew the Talmud inside out at a time when girls were neither expected nor encouraged even to read. When years later I saw the movie *Yentl,* it seemed to me that Isaac Bashevis Singer might have modeled his heroine on Grandma Rifka. Her erudition made her a revolutionary all by itself. But Rifka did not stop there; she was also a real radical who took part in the 1905 revolution against the czar. When I knew her she still liked to sing the "Marseillaise," the revolutionary anthem before the "Internationale" became popular.

But even Rifka's radical politics paled before an act of hers so extreme that it scandalized everyone who knew of it. She refused to cut her hair and cover her head with a *sheitl,* the wig every Orthodox woman wore so as not to immodestly display her natural hair. Didn't it say in the Shulhan Arukh, the compilation of laws, that a married woman could not expose her hair to the sight of men? To religious Jews such a revolt was inconceivable. But Rifka was stubborn as granite, and because she was, it struck the spark of revolution in all the other family women. If Rifka wasn't going to wear a sheitl, neither were they. Even though all this happened two generations before mine, the reverberations were still shaking the family when I grew old enough to know. Exactly how my pious grandfather Zandman had married a woman who wouldn't wear a sheitl was a phenomenon no one could fathom.

At the Freydovicz dinner table conversation generally went to business and practical affairs, but Grandfather Zandman's home glowed with the give and take of ideas. My scholarly, Orthodox grandpa had three sons: Archik, my left-wing Zionist father; Moshe, an apolitical Zionist; and Yosef, a non-Zionist Marxist who belonged to the Jewish Socialist Bund. When they and Grandma Rifka, the Orthodox, radical, women's libber, all got together over a table loaded with borscht, challah, flanken, gribbines, and tsimmes, the talk would make my head spin. I adored listening. There was a joke that said if you had two Jews you'd always get three opinions; but the person who made that up had never had *shabbas* dinner at the home of Rebbe Berl Zandman, where opinions sped through the air like warring angels.

As the first grandson of both families I was showered with affection. Both wanted me for the holidays, and I was vaguely aware of fights going on over who would get me, also that a compromise was reached, which was why I would have the first

Passover seder one year with the Freydoviczes and the next with the Zandmans. I was besieged by love, and I loved both my families dearly.

Although my father had been taken into the Freydovicz family business, he was a businessman neither by training nor inclination. He was actually a chemist who had received his Ph.D. from the University of Vienna, where he had also taught. But on one of his visits home he had fallen in love with Genia Freydovicz, and his heart had persuaded him to marry and stay in Grodno.

In Poland, though, Jews were unable either to find teaching jobs in universities or to hold research positions. Nor did northeastern Poland have much in the way of industry. All of which meant that my father could not find work doing the things he loved and so had to be content with the junior partnership my grandfather Freydovicz offered him in the building and supply company.

That my parents loved each other deeply I had no doubt. But I also sensed that there were areas of friction. My father spoke to me only in Yiddish, never Polish. He considered that Yiddish was at the root of what Europe's Jews were and what he was. He took pains to imbue me with a love for the language and its culture, holding me on his knee and reading to me from Sholom Aleichem and other Yiddish writers. He had a beautiful singing voice, too. Often when the whole family gathered, people would say, "Archik, please sing." And he would go into a corner and sing melodious Yiddish folk songs. My mother, on the contrary, spoke to me exclusively in Polish, which was considered by her family more upper class. So already there was a kind of a schism.

Then, too, my father was a Zionist Socialist. Each May 1 he took me to see the illegal demonstrations. We didn't participate, but we always found a good place to see the workers come marching down the street. I would watch, enthralled by the crowds and noise. Then the mounted police would charge in and scatter the marchers, which was especially impressive. Sometimes my father and I would listen in to Radio Moscow together. He wasn't a Communist himself, he told me, but he was certainly in favor of social change.

My mother's family, on the other hand, were business-people with firm conservative convictions. That difference could have dramatic results, as it did when my father became embroiled in a strike against the company.

The Freydovicz firm built large projects—army barracks and bridges, among other things—though their main business was supplies: lumber, cement, piping (which they manufactured), and other construction materials. They had a considerable number of employees, both Jewish and Polish, though mostly Jewish. Grandfather Freydovicz had made his three sons, Kushka, Sender, and Grishka, junior partners. Then my father had come into the firm, and his younger brother Yosef had been taken in as well.

Yosef Zandman was an accountant, which was good for the company. But he was also a Bundist, which was not so good. The Bund was a Jewish-Socialist organization, fiercely committed to workers' rights. I even heard dark rumors that Yosef might have been a Communist, though at the age of ten I hadn't the vaguest notion of what the difference between a Socialist and a Communist might be.

I was all too aware, though, of the turmoil that seized the family when my uncle Yosef organized a strike against the Freydovicz Company. Grandfather Freydovicz's reaction was volcanic: He demanded that my father talk to his brother at once and have the strike broken. But my father refused, whereupon my mother left my father and went to live upstairs with my grandparents.

The days that followed this trauma were filled with tension. I navigated between the first and second floors of our house, listening to my father explain the strike and why he could not agree to pressure his brother to stop it; namely, because he believed it was justified. On the other side my grandfather and my mother were appalled. "How can you defend such a thing" they asked him, "when we do so well by our workers?" Besides, you're breaking the company—you, a member of the family, and a partner on top of it! You are disloyal!" Even the police got involved; they came around wanting to know who instigated the strike, and were they perhaps Communists?

Eventually the employees went back to work, my mother moved back downstairs with us, and life resumed its former peacefulness. But I was left thoroughly confused about whether the strike really had been justified, or if my father had been disloyal to the family, or if maybe both things were true.

The strike made me aware that the conflicts and divisions in Grodno's Jewish community weren't limited to arguments around the dinner table. There were rich Jews and poor, business owners, and Socialists. Among them there could be real anger. On my Freydovicz side we were rich; on my Zandman side, poor. In Grodno differences were a way of life; they electrified the atmosphere. I sensed it, though I had no way of understanding the extent to which my city throve on its groups and factions: orthodox and secular, Zionist and internationalist, Yiddishists and Hebraists, Communists and conservatives—a dozen varieties of leftists and another dozen of Zionists. Jewish Grodno was alive with intellectual, political, and cultural ferment. It was hectic and fragmented, like a noisy, argumentative family, full of conflict, yet still a family.

Jews had lived in Grodno since the late 1300s, when they were granted a charter by the Grand Duke Vitold of Lithuania. By and large, Poland had proved an attractive place, especially considering the alternatives. Despite occasional periods of suffering and even temporary expulsion, over the centuries the city's Jewish community made Grodno into a commercial and religious center. In 1939 Grodno had a population of fifty thousand, of whom thirty thousand were Jewish, and the most profound division in the city was not among the Jews, but between Jews and Poles. They were two nations living on the same land, Jewish people and Polish people—which meant Catholic people. A Jew could not say the words "I am a Pole," because that would be the same thing as saying "I am Catholic." The two communities lived together as neighbors, some hating each other, some liking each other, but always with an edge of uneasiness and, on the Jews' part, an underlayer of anxiety.

Not that there was much in the way of organized pogroms in Grodno, though in 1935, when I was eight years old, a riot swept through Poland. In Grodno gangs of Poles ran wild in the streets, breaking down windows and doors, destroying property, and attacking whatever Jews they could find. From my window I saw people throwing rocks, and one big stone landed in the courtyard. Later I heard that some people had been killed.

That was unusual; in Poland anti-Semitism was a fact of life, but community relations were usually more peaceful. I had to worry about my own private pogroms, though. Our house was near a Catholic church that ran a day school. I would start home from my own school with a big group of friends, but by the time we got to my neighborhood there were fewer of us, and when I turned onto Brygidzka Street I was usually alone, walking right into a crowd of Polish kids who had just gotten out of the Catholic school. I often came home bruised, and sometimes I feared for my life. On one occasion I found myself running in terror to the door of Mrs. Starowolski just ahead of a mob of attackers who I was sure were going to kill me. She let me in, then walked me to my house. My mother wanted me to learn to box so I could defend myself better, though I never seemed to get around to it. As close to the church as we were, I would listen to the singing that welled out during Mass, so beautiful it entranced me. I loved to hear the angelic voices of the choir, especially during the nighttime prayers, and I used to wonder how it was that the same bastards who were beating me up could make such ethereal music.

For Jewish students in Grodno there were several religious schools, including a well-known yeshiva. The Bund had its own primary school, where they taught their mix of Yiddish culture and socialism. Then there was a Polish-language school where Hebrew was taught once a week. My own school was the Tarbut primary school and gymnasium. Tarbut was a secular Hebrew-language school, part of a Zionist educational movement that established itself in Lithuania and Poland at the beginning of the century.

A few Jews also attended the regular Polish public schools—a few because the government-sponsored schools would take only two or three Jewish students per class. This despite the fact that 60 percent of the city's population was Jewish. To add insult to injury, graduates from a regular school qualified for university studies, but not graduates of a Jewish gymnasium. The Jewish secondary schools frequently gave a higher level education than their Polish counterparts, but the universities wouldn't recognize them. So Jews who wanted to attend a university in Poland had to spend an additional two years at a Polish gymnasium—if they could get in. Either that or go to a foreign university instead, which was how my father ended up at the University of Vienna, my uncle Sender at the University of Danzig, and my uncle Moshe at the University of Grenoble.

From early on I wanted to be an engineer. I was always interested in machines and how things worked. Constructing things appealed to me, maybe in part because of the Freydovicz building enterprises that surrounded me. I wondered how one might construct a bridge or an airplane, and I was impressed when my uncle Sender went off to Danzig to study engineering. At school I really started to like mathematics. Whenever I solved a difficult problem I would get a feeling of peace, as if now everything was right with the world. I never seemed to follow exactly the route laid out by the teacher; I was happier trying to find my own way to the answer. Teachers generally didn't like that, but I did. It was an internal triumph. There was one answer (unlike questions of politics or religion). I knew it was true, and I had found it myself. Despite my grandma Tema's philosophy of ownership, this, I felt, was mine.

In a way Tarbut was another home, a place for intellect and rigor, and also a place for pride. We were imbued with Zionist ideals. Israel was our Jewish homeland, and Hebrew was our language. Eventually we would go there and build the country. Except for Polish language and history, all the subjects were taught in Hebrew. We even prided ourselves on speaking Hebrew outside the classroom rather than Polish or Yiddish, which would have been more natural.

Among Tarbut's students almost every different Zionist movement had its adherents. Even the Tarbut elementary school had a political life. By the time we were eight or nine we were thinking about these things, influenced by the Zionist longings of our parents and teachers. Each of the major parties that exist in Israel today was embodied in the movements that gripped Poland's Jews, and each of them was bent on winning the young people of Grodno to its banner, from Hashomer Hatzair on the left to Betar on the right.

I was attracted to Betar, the organization that eventually evolved into Israel's Likud Party. They wore uniforms and they trained with rifles. They weren't just Zionists, they wanted a Jewish state. I liked that idea. But my Socialist father was horrified. "You cannot join them," he said. "This is the wrong approach. You absolutely will not be with them!" He tried to explain; like many left Zionists he considered the idea of a separate Jewish state anathema. "What would you do with the Arabs, Felix? Whatever we create in Israel it has to be together, it has to be binational, a binational entity. Not a state, Felix." But I wouldn't accept it. "If together, who needs Palestine?" I argued. "I have together here in Poland. Why do I have to go there for it? Don't we deserve a state?"

"It's our country, Felix, the place where our forefathers were. But that doesn't mean a state. That doesn't mean we can push out the Arabs. Besides, even if you wanted to, there are millions of them. You can't."

My father's objections to Betar made some sense, even though I really thought we should have a state. But I respected him. "You're too small to make up your mind like that, Felix. Listen to the others. Look around." And since I was determined to join something, I went to see the others. The first was Hashomer Hatzair, the extreme left. They wore very nice gray uniforms, and I was impressed. But at the first meeting the leader looked at me and said, "Who's the new guy? What's your name?" "My name is Felix," I told him. "What's your name in Hebrew, Felix?" "In Hebrew it's Shrage Feivel."

"Shrage Feivel? What a strange name. We'll give you a new name. From now on you're Yehuda."

I was so offended, I got up and left. The guy didn't like my name, so he tried to get rid of it, my perfectly good Hebrew name, Shrage Feivel. Schmuck, I thought. So that was the end of Hashomer Hatzair. Eventually I joined Akiba, which looked like a more moderate Hashomer. In the meetings we talked about Israel, emigration, building the land, exactly the same subjects the other movements were talking about, although without the sharp edge of Hashomer's Marxism or the military overtones of Betar.

These Zionist organizations were fighting for our souls. Tensions among them ran high. In school the kids even had fist-fights, especially between Hashomer and Betar. Betar wanted a state, which was enough for Hashomer to accuse the Betar kids of fascism. That's crazy, I thought. Hashomer wanted to improve social conditions, which in the Betaris' minds made them all Communists. That seemed equally crazy.

But the times didn't encourage moderation. As the thirties wore on, events in Germany sent pulses of anxiety through Poland's Jewish community. The spellbinding orator Ze'ev Jabotinsky toured the country's Jewish centers with his message of crisis. "Leave everything you have," he preached. "Leave it! Hitler is coming. Go to Israel—by foot, by car, by boat, any way you can. Do it now! We are on the road to catastrophe. It doesn't matter what you have here. Just leave it and get out. Go!"

Every time he was in town my father would go to hear him. Coming back he would tell me, "Felix, the man is an extraordinary leader, a tremendous speaker, but I don't entirely agree with his ideas. He's causing a panic, and nobody's going to go anyway." Generally speaking he thought that what Jabotinsky was saying about a coming crisis made sense, but he didn't share his conviction of extreme urgency. Still, Jabotinsky was the most magnetic personality he had ever met.

My father was a Zionist, but he never talked about actually going ourselves. Zionism was right philosophically; Israel (Palestine at that time) was our homeland, where someday all the Jews would be. Didn't we pray, "Next year in Jerusalem"? But that hardly meant that we were going to actually pull ourselves up by the roots and just take off. A few, of course, did go. In 1938 there was a big panic after some violent anti-Semitic event in Germany, and five kids disappeared from school. They were last seen riding their bicycles out of town; their friends knew they were going to try to ride all the way to Palestine. Two weeks later the police picked them up on the Romanian border (a thousand miles to the south), and they were brought back—only to perish a few years later with the ghetto.

Even people from our family went. My father's brother Moshe went as a participant in the 1933 Maccabiah athletic games. Like most of the other athletes, he stayed on illegally, trying desperately to get an immigration certificate for his wife and son. He never succeeded, and they, too, died with the ghetto. My uncle Kushka Freydovicz went to Palestine to study at the Technion for a year. But love brought him back to Grodno, and he and his wife were also swallowed up.

So it wasn't as if we didn't have examples in front of us. But still we never gave the idea serious consideration. Palestine itself was mostly a barren desert broken by malarial swamps, impoverished villages, and struggling farming communities. In essence our lives were too comfortable. As well tell a contented American today that he should go to live in the Sahara. "Go to live in the Sahara?" He'd think you were crazy. "What are you talking about?" That's the way many Polish Jews looked at it. Adventurous young pioneers might go, devoted idealists might go. But in my immediate family, with the exception of Moshe and Kushka, it got no farther than ideas and talk.

That left me unsatisfied. At school we were filled with a love of Israel. I was utterly sure that one day I would go there and build something. I daydreamed about living in a kibbutz and helping to plow and plant and harvest. But in 1939 I was twelve years old and, as strong as they were, what did those dreams mean?

As the situation in Germany worsened, the Yiddish newspapers were filled with incidents. My grandmother Tema would take me into her bed in the afternoon after tea and read to me out of the papers. As she related the atrocities and the desecrations in Germany, tears welled in her eyes and trickled down her cheeks. I thought these were terrible things. But at the same time I could see that my father seemed even more worried about the war in Abyssinia, where the Italians had attacked, and then the war in Spain.

When the Ribbentrop-Molotov pact was signed in 1939, my father said immediately, "This means a new partition of Poland." There had been three historical partitions of Poland, as we all learned in school, until eventually, toward the end of the 1790s, Poland had disappeared entirely. So "partition" sounded ominous. But even this kind of talk didn't particularly affect me. I heard it, but life was still life. I was eating, drinking, studying, sometimes being beaten up by bullies. Life was not different from how it always had been. Danger was around the corner, but when had it not been? There would be some pushing and shoving, perhaps even a war. The Freydovicz business might get worse. Maybe there would be more pogroms.

But things might get better, too. Maybe Hitler would be happy with a piece of Czechoslovakia, or a piece of something else. After all, the French and the British were strong, and behind them stood America. They would never let anything really terrible happen. And how about the Soviet Union, Germany's blood enemy despite the pact? What was this little German really going to do? Mainly it seemed like hot air. Trouble had never been far off, but the Jewish way of life had persisted in Grodno for six hundred years, a tremendous continuity. In 1939 extermination was not a thought that had yet entered anyone's mind.

2

AT the end of August 1939 my bicycle was requisitioned by the Polish Army, along with all the other bicycles in Grodno. Mine was special, a half-size bike that had been made by the Staro-wolski bicycle factory for one of my birthdays. I wondered what the army would do with a bicycle like that. Who would ride it?

I knew it was a bad sign, the army wanting all the bikes. There were a lot of other signs, too. At school they began teaching us what to do if war came. They taught us about gas masks (though we weren't given any). If you don't have one, they said, you should soak your handkerchief in water, press it against your nose, and run. If bombing started we should go to our bunkers, as-suming we had a bunker. If a grenade landed near us we should throw it away fast.

We listened, never thinking for a moment that any of this might become real. It seemed to me about as serious as the sci-ence lecture that proved that at the present rate of combustion the sun would burn itself out in a thousand years (this was before any-one knew about the sun's atomic reactions). In fact, I didn't see what difference it would make to me if the sun was around in a thousand years or not.

Still, August was a nervous month. Almost every day my father came home from work agitated, with stories about Hitler and what he was saying. After dinner he would sit down with me and try to explain what the Nazis were doing in Germany and Aus-tria and Czechoslovakia. We read that the French and the British were telling the Germans that if they attacked Poland, there would be war.

But despite the nervousness, nobody packed up and left. We discussed it, we talked about it all the time. Visas were available to Australia, and Shanghai was an open city. Even Amer-ica was on our minds. One branch of Grandma Tema's family had left for Oklahoma at the end of the nineteenth century, and two of our relatives had visited from there in the twenties. My great-grandmother Chaya had even gone there to live. But in Oklahoma there were no Jews and no synagogue and no kosher food, so she had come back. Still, the family had done well there; America was obviously a good place. Should we maybe consider going? But during all the discussions I never once heard a serious proposal that we should get out.

In the background was the fact that the family had been through wars before. This wasn't necessarily anything new. World War I had ended only twenty-one years earlier, and the Germans had occupied Grodno for the last year and a half of it. During that time the Freydovicz family had evacuated to far-off Tsaritsyn in the Ukraine. Their exile had been unpleasant, and I had heard many stories about it. Food was scarce, and they had had to eat potatoes all the time. For Pesach they had been unable to get any matzohs. After they returned, the Russian Civil War had come to Grodno, and Trotsky's Red Army had bombarded the city. During the fighting my grandparents had gotten separated from their children and, as the oldest, my mother had taken care of the other five. Some of them were sick, and during one of the shellings she had run through the streets to the apothecary for medicine. That event had stayed in her mind.

But my grandfather Zandman's family had stayed in the Grodno area during the German occupation, all except my father, who had been evacuated east with his high school class. The Germans, they said, had been quite civilized, much nicer than Russians, not anti-Semitic at all. Generally speaking, life in German-occupied Grodno had been quiet and easy.

Of course, the Russians had tried to frighten people into leaving with scare stories about the Germans, but nothing had happened. Anyway, in the end nobody in the family was killed, no one had starved, and they were all reunited. Everything had ended up okay. A world war had been fought, the Russian Revolution had passed through, but in essence these events had not changed life for the Jews of Grodno. Obviously the best course now would be to sit tight and hope for the best.

•

Early on the morning of September 1 the radio announced that school classes in the city would be postponed for several days. "Skirmishes" were taking place with the Germans along the border. Fifteen minutes later, the sirens began wailing and we heard the drone of airplanes. Then came explosions as bombs began raining down on Grodno. In Brygidzka Street people were hit, and some of them came to our door bleeding and asking for help.

My grandfather immediately decided to construct a shelter in the basement. Cement sacks were laid across the floor above where we would stay, and food was brought down. For the next week, whenever the sirens went off we hurried into the shelter, listening to the thud and roar of the bombs.

France and Great Britain now declared war on Germany, and we hoped that the fighting would be over quickly and Germany defeated. But it didn't happen. Instead the Germans got closer and closer to Grodno. When it was obvious that the Polish Army could not stop them, the family decided to evacuate to Lida, farther to the east. Numerous relatives of my Zandman grandparents still lived there and would be happy to take us in.

I didn't know anything about it until my mother said, "Get your clothes, Felix. We're leaving." By the time we were ready, there was an air of panic in Grodno. We only had time to throw our clothes into valises and pile into the three taxis that pulled up in front of the door, the whole extended family from Grandpa Freydovicz to my four-year-old sister Mira.

In Lida our Zandman relatives made us welcome. My Zandman grandparents had already arrived, and now a horde of Freydoviczes took up residence, too, but nobody seemed to mind the crowding. Whatever minor tensions there might have been in the past between the rich, worldly Freydoviczes and the poor, pious Zandmans evaporated. It seemed—to me, anyway—that we were one big, happy family.

On September 17 the Soviets entered Poland from the east. One day later, they were in Lida. It was obvious what this meant for the Poles. With the Germans in one side and the Soviets in the other, there would be no more Poland. I could see it was a tragedy for them. For us, though, maybe not. At least my Socialist father didn't think so. "Everything's going to be okay now, Felix," he said. "There won't be any more persecution of Jews. No more fighting in the streets for you. It will be a good life, you'll see."

We moved back to Grodno immediately; it was also in the Soviet zone. By now the Red Army was arriving in force. I watched the tanks rumble in and the strange soldiers in their strange uniforms who spoke a language I only half understood. My father was enthusiastic about the possibilities now that eastern Poland was about to be annexed to the Soviet Union, and he took me with him to speeches and political rallies. At the first one we attended, a Soviet political officer had harangued a huge crowd. I struggled to understand the words. "There is no need to fear Hitler," he said. "Hitler is dead. We have killed him." Even I knew that was a lie. But my father didn't seem to care that the speeches were all propaganda. He believed that the war was now over and that our part of Poland was on the verge of becoming a much better place. All the wonderful things we had heard about for years on Radio Moscow were about to come true.

But before long, something changed his mind, though I wasn't sure what. One day about a month after the Soviets arrived, he came home despondent. "It's all a big lie," he said, sitting down with me as he did when he had something serious to discuss. "What I told you earlier, Felix, it's all a lie. The biggest deception of my life. Can you forgive me? If you possibly can, please take out of your head what I have told you." That wasn't hard. Not much of it had stuck in my head in the first place.

Whatever it was that disillusioned my father, I didn't see it. In fact, many of the changes in Grodno seemed for the better. Best of all was that the Soviets put a stop to the overt anti-Semitism that had always been part of our lives. Many Jews were

Socialists or Communists, and all of a sudden they began taking important positions. The possibility of having a Jewish judge or a Jewish mayor had never occurred to anyone before. Nobody would have dreamed of it. But now it was happening.

Many Poles hated that, of course. It was disconcerting that anti-Semitism was now officially outlawed. They were even forced to change their language habits. No one, for example, was allowed to say "Zhid" anymore, the common term for Jew that carried with it an offensive connotation, like "dirty Jew." All of a sudden one was not permitted to pronounce this standard vocabulary item upon pain of a visit from the NKVD. How, then, to indicate a Jewish person? It was a problem you could hear some Poles struggling with. "He's a Zhi . . . a Zhi . . . a . . . you know, he's one of those who pray in a synagogue."

The Poles detested the Soviet occupation and everything about it. It was understandable; their country had been taken away from them. But for me at the age of twelve, Soviets meant no more pogroms, no more beatings on the street. I felt free as a bird. All the things I had been doing before I still did, even more of them, because the Soviets loved to organize youth activities. I went to school—although Tarbut was now forbidden to teach Hebrew and had switched over to Yiddish. Later I transferred to a Russian-language school. I played in the orchestra, competed in olympiads, and took up the accordion in addition to the violin. The youth authorities gave ski classes and established young people's paramilitary groups. Our parents might have been worrying themselves sick about the future; after all, the Germans were only a few miles away now. But many of the youngsters were having the time of their lives.

Among other innovations, the Soviets instituted a new school system, open to everyone. Before they arrived, there had been four secondary schools in Grodno. Overnight there were nineteen. Everybody in town seemed to be enrolled in some kind of school. Teachers were so busy they worked two shifts. My father, who had been unable to teach before this because of the prohibition against Jewish professors, suddenly had not one teaching job but three—two in high schools and one at the teachers' college. He had never liked business; teaching was his true vocation. Now he was constantly on the move, running from one school to the other. He loved it.

My mother didn't love it; she would rather have had him at home. But then she went back to school, too, for medicine. She had been a medical student in Berlin for a year before she met my father, and now there was an opportunity for her to train as a medical technician in the newly opened feldscher's school. My sister Mira, now five, was also in school. Everyone was busy, everyone was learning.

Shortly after the division of the country we had a visit that shook us badly. The Glass family, old friends and business associates of Grandfather Freydovicz, arrived from their home in southern Poland, an area now controlled by the Germans. They pulled up in front of our house in two limousines filled with children and suitcases.

At dinner that night they told us about life in the German zone. We listened in shocked silence as they described the confiscations of Jewish property that had started. Nobody had been killed yet, but the Germans were talking about the many offenses Jews had committed. Now they were beginning to raise the idea of concentrating Jews in restricted areas. Threats were in the air; the atmosphere was ominous. "One day or another they are going to kill everybody," said Mr. Glass.

The Glasses had escaped, leaving behind their steel factory and everything else they couldn't carry. Somehow they had managed to make their way through the border checkpoints. They were going to Vilno in Lithuania, still an independent country but under Soviet "protection." In Vilno, transit visas were available. In Vilno, they had been told, they could make arrangements to get to Shanghai. They begged us to come with them. "You have money," said Mr. Glass. "You can do it. You have to do it, because I'm telling you, they are going to start murdering people. There's no question. We have room for you in our cars, or you can rent your own." They wanted to get as far away from the Germans as possible, as fast as possible. They were deeply frightened.

That started our family talking. For an hour or so the discussion was more serious than any I had heard before. But nothing had really changed the old reasons for riding it out rather than turning ourselves into refugees. "What are we going to do?" said Grandma Tema. "I can't take my fur coats. It's going to be cold. And what about the children? We don't even speak their language. How would we survive?" As it was, the business was still going on. Who could tell what the Soviets might do, but the war at least seemed to be over. Wouldn't it be safer to stay in the place we had always known than just to abandon ourselves to the winds of fate as refugees? The Glasses stayed overnight, then left the following morning. Without us.

Soon after that, my grandparents became refugees anyway, but from the Soviets, not the Germans. It didn't take long before the Soviets began implementing their ideas of ideology and class struggle. Tarbut, with its Zionist tenets and Hebrew-language curriculum, was closed down. Zionism was prohibited. Zionists and members of the Bund began disappearing, were arrested by the Russians and deported to Siberia.

Everyone was given a new passport, and when people started comparing, they noticed that some passports had a mysterious extra paragraph, paragraph six. Those with passports like that began to wonder about it, including my grandparents and my uncles Kushka and Grishka. When we asked some Soviet soldiers we had gotten friendly with they said, "Oh, you have a passport like that? That means Siberia." They knew instantly. They had seen it before. Paragraph six identified the politically unreliable; it meant "capitalist," or worse—Zionists or other nonconformists.

Afraid of being deported, Grishka, Kushka, and their wives fled, one couple to Lida, another to the village of Mosti. The good thing about the Soviets was that they were not organized. Word had gotten around that if you went from one city to another inside their zone, nobody would know anything about you. You would be a refugee, that's all. They had no system of checking from one place to the next. Many wealthy people left Grodno for Lvov. Others, like our friends the Starowolskis, were arrested and put on trains for Siberia or Kazakhstan (where most of them survived the war). My grandparents decided to go to Slonim, seventy miles to the southeast. One day we were all living together in our house, as we always had. The next morning when I woke up they were gone.

We ourselves weren't in danger, though. Neither was my uncle Sender or his family. For some reason neither Sender's nor my father's passports carried paragraph six. They didn't know why—possibly an administrative oversight, or maybe someone thought they were all right, despite their being members of a capitalist family. Sender and my father thought it was probably the latter. In fact, both of them had been visited by delegations of Freydovicz employees asking them not to leave. They had always been fair, the workers said, and now the workers would protect them. There was no need to worry.

So we were not deported. But the Soviets did confiscate our apartment. In its place we were given a little flat farther down Brygidzka, which had now been renamed Karl Marx Street. There we shared the rooms with a Russian family, so living conditions were very tight. At night our neighbors would walk through our bedroom to get to the bathroom.

I knew that my parents—my mother, especially—missed their belongings and our former way of life. But I didn't mind the crowding, and so many new things were happening that my friends and I felt we were living a kind of adventure. And though my mother was unhappy about having to move, I didn't feel as if she was desperate about it either. There was hardly time to feel sorry for ourselves. Both she and my father were working hard. My father's life was filled with teaching, and my mother was busy with her medical studies. It seemed to me that despite the deprivations, they had a feeling of satisfaction about how their lives were going.

Of course, it was a different story with my grandparents in Slonim, where I was sent to visit them several times. Slonim was a Jewish *shtetl,* an old wooden village of about ten thousand people off in the countryside toward the Pripet Marshes. My grandparents lived there in a rented room in a small house. Their lives had suddenly turned grim. Grandpa's business had been taken away from him, his house confiscated, his children and grandchildren scattered. All of their philanthropies were gone, all the great respect they had enjoyed. In Slonim no one knew them, or knew what they had been.

It was terrible to see my grandfather in this state, this man who had always seemed so stern and powerful. My wonderful grandma Tema was often in tears. In Slonim she prayed a lot, but it wasn't like the prayers I remembered so well. In the old days she loved to take me into the forest with her to recite psalms; being alone outdoors seemed to her the right place for the beautiful psalms, which were her favorite prayers. With the sunlight coming through the trees I would hold her hand and listen to her chanting. But her prayers now were different, full of sadness and anger.

One day in the room she was crying and complaining bitterly about the Bolsheviks. She wanted them out, gone. They were liars and robbers. They had confiscated and destroyed everything. They should just get out. Grandpa might have been a capitalist, but he could see easily enough where that would lead. "What do you mean, Tema? You want the Russians out? Are you crazy? If they leave, who do you think will come in? The Germans will come in. Do you want the Nazis? Is that what you want?"

"No," she said, "I don't want them either. I don't want Russians and I don't want Germans."

"Who do you want, then?" asked Grandpa.

Grandma Tema stopped a moment to think. "Not Russians and not Germans. I'll tell you who I want. I want Roosevelt, that's who. *Ich will Roosevelt!*" She had been praying for Roosevelt all along.

On June 22, 1941, I was in Slonim again, visiting my grandparents. School was out, and I was going to take my vacation with them. That morning we heard Soviet foreign minister Molotov's voice come over the static on the radio. The voice said that early in the morning German forces had crossed the borders. War had started between the Soviet Union and Nazi Germany. The announcement was hardly over when we heard planes overhead and the whistle and roar of the bombs.

In a matter of minutes, Slonim was aflame. Every house in town was wood, and most of the roofs were straw thatch. They went up like matchsticks. We had been bombed in Grodno, but usually we were down in the cellar and the explosions sounded muffled and distant. I had never actually been frightened. Now I was. My memory flashed back for an instant to a fire we had had on Brygidzka Street when I was young. I had grabbed a candelabrum, but my mother had shouted at me to drop it and run for my life. I wanted to run now, too. The whole place seemed to be burning around us. For the first time I felt the word "war." I was now in the middle of this "war" I had been hearing about for so long.

My grandparents quickly packed everything they could into two huge suitcases, and Grandma Tema dragged them down the ladder steps into the cellar one at a time, then came up and closed the trapdoor. Unable to walk without his cane, Grandfather wasn't much help. But as the house across the street burst into flame, the two of them pushed and pulled a barrel of water onto the trapdoor, with the idea that if the house burned, the water would somehow save the things in the cellar. When I understood what they were doing I yelled at them to stop. "Put the valises in the well!" I yelled. "In the cellar they'll burn up!"

"But they'll get wet!" shouted my grandmother. "At least you'll have them!" I yelled back. Finally Tema wrestled the barrel off the trapdoor and disappeared into the cellar. A moment later she struggled up with one suitcase, probably figuring there was a better chance of saving something if they were in different places.

By now I wasn't so afraid, despite the roar of the fire. Sutherland came into my head, the great cowboy hero in Karl May's Wild West novels. I had read dozens of them in Polish, and I knew that when fire swept the prairie the thing to do was counter it by setting a backfire. If for some reason you couldn't set a backfire, your only hope was to make a run for the nearest river.

That was obviously what we should be doing. In fact, there was a little river running right by Slonim. "Let's run!" I shouted. "Let's get to the river!" By now we seemed to be surrounded by fire, even though our house hadn't yet caught. We were in danger of being trapped and burned alive. But my grandparents didn't know what to do. They seemed to be pondering the question, weighing where we should go or what might be best. I was yelling at them that we had to get moving, tugging at their arms. Finally they agreed. Grandma pushed the valise into the well and we headed toward the river.

As soon as we got out onto the main street we found ourselves engulfed in a crowd of people who had the same idea. Instinctively everyone knew that the river was the only safe place. By the time we got there, the riverbank was crowded with villagers standing or sitting in clumps or lying on the grass, panting for breath. Thousands of people were watching helplessly as the town burned down in front of them.

By now the houses nearest the river were on fire, sending gouts of flame and black smoke into the sky. The heat bore down on us, oppressive and frightening. The air was heavy with the stench of burning horseflesh. I realized that I was sweating profusely, and I noticed that many people were removing articles of clothing. Not far away I saw Bella Hirschorn, a beautiful fifteen-year-old girl from Grodno who was now living in Slonim. She was taking off her blouse. I watched entranced as she unbuttoned and slipped it off. I saw something black underneath, her brassiere. I couldn't take my eyes off her or move a muscle, even as the firestorm blasted and crackled toward us.

For a day and a night, Slonim burned. People sat on the grass as close to the river as they could get, talking or sleeping fitfully. In the morning we could hear the distant thunder of artillery, and it occurred to me that it had probably been going all night long behind the roar of the flames. By now, though, the fire had burned down, leaving Slonim a smoldering, charred ruin. Here and there a house had escaped, and a few areas of the town weren't touched at all. But everything else was ashes and embers. Among the debris sat the burned-out hulks of Soviet tanks, the bodies of their crews sprawled on the ground next to them. Some tankers had died trying to get out, and twisted, blackened corpses stretched halfway out of turrets, still wearing their leather tankers' hats.

The house my grandparents had lived in was in ashes. Where it had stood there were now only a few bricks scattered on the smoking ground. We looked into the halfway collapsed cellar and saw embers glowing. Nothing was left.

Pulling our one remaining suitcase up from the well, we walked over to one of the neighborhoods that hadn't burned. There we found somebody who had room and would put us up. Everyone was doing the same thing. Three quarters of the city was gone, but those who still had houses were taking their neighbors in. Every room must have had four or five people staying in it, but that night when I looked around I didn't see anybody sleeping out on the street.

In our new room my grandparents were distraught, Tema especially. She was possessed with anxiety about the fate of her children in Grodno, Lida, and Mosti. Unable to do anything herself or take any steps to find out about them, she cried constantly. "My children, my children, my children." I found it almost unbearable to listen to her.

Meanwhile, we waited for something to happen. For several days people went around trying to collect the remnants of their belongings and find enough food to feed themselves. Then one morning we were suddenly aware that Germans had arrived in town. They materialized suddenly, unexpectedly. We were in our room when Grandma Tema sensed that something was wrong. Looking out the window, we saw people running; then we saw the soldiers.

Tema went into the other part of the house, but in a moment she was back. "They're rounding up men," she said. "They're taking the men away." The Germans outside in their gray uniforms looked to me like ordinary soldiers. No one had ever heard of the *Einsatzgruppen,* the SS units whose special job was to murder Jews. We were about to find out.

Quickly, Tema put my grandfather and me in bed together and threw a blanket over us. I was thinking how silly it was to be in bed wearing my pants when the door opened and a tall German walked into the room; he was wearing an officer's hat with a skull badge on it. Before he could open his mouth, Tema started off. "My husband is old," she said in German, "*Er ist alt.*" "An old man, paralyzed in bed. The little boy is also sick, with a fever." The German looked at us for a moment, then turned and walked out. As he left the house we could hear him order our landlady's husband out in front of him.

As soon as he was outside, I jumped out of bed and looked through the window. Just down from the house I saw the Germans putting the men they had gathered into an army truck. They brought them to the truck, some singly, some in little clusters of twos, threes, or fours, just the way they were catching them. The first truck filled and drove off, and another took its place. The loading continued. Then the second drove off and a third arrived, then a fourth. In the midst of the commotion I saw an old Jew in a black frock coat and hat. Two soldiers were holding him by the arms, and a third was hacking at his beard with a hatchet. The two who held him were punching him and pulling his beard while the third hacked and hacked at it. Suddenly I had the sense I was in the middle of a nightmare. I knew we were in the hands of savages.

3

GHETTO NUMBER ONE

THE women and children left in Slonim were racked with fear. All the men who hadn't run off had been taken. No one knew why or where they were going. Then, late in the afternoon, the local peasants began coming in from the fields, and word spread like wildfire. The trucks had stopped not far from town. The German soldiers had taken all the men out, lined them up, and machine-gunned them. Our landlady broke down in despair. From every side I heard wails of grief and anguish. They filled the air of the burned-out village.

Grandma Tema was beside herself. She wanted instantly to get back to Grodno, to be with at least some of her children. But there was no way to go. Who knew if the trains would start running or when? The few phones in Slonim hadn't worked for weeks. There was no way to communicate with the outside, no way to find out what might be going on elsewhere—in Lida, for example, or Mosti.

That evening three people arrived in Slonim by foot: a gymnastics teacher from my school, his wife, and daughter. They stayed with us in our room that night. They told us that in Grodno, just before the German attack, the Soviets had arrested large numbers of people who were marked for deportation—all those with paragraph six passports who had not been taken earlier. They themselves had been arrested and put on a train packed with other deportees, bound for Siberia. The famous Zionist Nachum Bass and his wife were on the train, too.

They had traveled all night. When morning came, the train had been attacked by German dive bombers somewhere near Baranowicz. After the bombing the planes came back and strafed people trying to escape from the wreckage. Many were killed, including the Basses. The gymnastics teacher and his family had walked more than thirty miles from the site of the attack. Now they were on their way back to Grodno.

Two days later, my aunt Lina appeared in Slonim. Lina was Kushka's wife. They had managed to get back to Grodno from Mosti, and she had volunteered to come and get me and my grandparents. It was a tremendously brave thing. Lina was beautiful; with her light brown hair and button nose she could easily pass for a Pole, at least in front of Germans. Her Polish was perfect, without any trace of a Jewish accent.

After a couple of days Lina finally decided that the only way to get back would be by train—the trains had just started to run again. But getting on a train was almost impossible. The countryside was swarming with refugees trying to get someplace other than where they were. With people mobbing the stations, the railroad authorities were doing their best to give priority to invalids and keep everyone else off. But my grandfather walked with a cane, and somehow Lina succeeded in getting tickets for him and Tema, and also for a young, very pregnant woman named Franye, who was desperate to get back to Grodno.

But for Lina and me there wasn't any room, so we started off on foot. That night we lay down in a field. The mild night and the smell of the new June grass should have made it easy to fall asleep, but we were both too frightened and passed the long hours watching the stars twinkling in the black sky. The next morning Lina overcame her fear and flagged down a German Army truck, part of a small convoy that was passing by. I couldn't get over her boldness, and I struggled to hide my own fright. The truck took us as far as Bialystok, a big city only fifty miles from Grodno. I had relatives there, and we stayed with them overnight. That evening they told us they were packing their belongings. The Germans had posted an edict that all Jews had to move into the ghetto, a closed area where they would live apart. I had heard that word before, in my class on medieval history. It seemed eerie that the Germans were bringing that idea back to life, and vaguely ominous.

The next day Lina and I covered the final fifty miles to Grodno by train. It was already dark when we arrived and the city was under a tight curfew, so together with the other Grodno passengers we had to sleep huddled on the floor of the train station. The following morning we found that the family was back in our old home. After the Soviets left, everyone had gone back to the house. They were all there—my mother and father, my little sister Mira, Grandpa and Grandma, Sender and his wife and two children, Kushka—all except for Grishka and his wife, who had been hiding from the Soviets in Lida. From them no one had heard anything.

The whole family greeted us with joy, but they were also buzzing about what had happened the previous night, while Lina and I were in the railway station. German soldiers had swept through Grodno with lists of people, including my father, Sender, and Kushka. By the time they got to our house word had spread of what was happening, and Kushka and Sender had jumped out the back window and hidden behind one of the outbuildings. But my father had refused to jump and had been arrested. They had taken him to the prison along with 150 others—all of them highly educated people. Then they took the first 100 out to be shot. My father had been only a few places back. When they had taken the 100 they sent him and the others home. My father had just gotten back a few minutes before Lina and I walked up.

The family was in a state of terror, but at least we were all there, except for Grishka and his wife. From Lida there was no word at all. No one knew what to do. They debated sending Kushka to Lida to find out, but in the end they decided against it. Grandma Tema sensed that something terrible had happened there; after all, we saw what the Germans had done in Slonim. She was in anguish. "Where is Grishka?" she kept saying. "Where is Grishka? How is he?" But there was no way to find out.

Tema was spared the news, but as we found out from refugees later, Grishka was already dead. The *Einsatzgruppen* had also been at work in Lida. There, too, they had taken the men out and massacred them. Grishka had been shot along with several thousand others.

It had dawned on me in Slonim the instant I saw the soldiers chopping at that old man's beard that the life I had lived up till now had come to an end. My happy, carefree existence was a thing of the past, and I was now living in a different world. We were filled with foreboding. In Bialystok they had forced the Jewish community into a ghetto. No one was sure why, but the reasons could not be good. And if they had done it in Bialystok, the chances were they would do it in Grodno.

A few days before Lina and I got back, an edict from the German authorities had been posted on the walls. All Jews were ordered to wear an identifying armband, white with a blue Jewish star on it. We made them, and everybody started to wear one. I found that I liked it. I was a Jew and I was proud to show it.

But a month or so later, another edict was posted. The white and blue armbands were no longer permitted. Now all Jews had to sew a yellow star on their coats over their hearts and on their backs. The penalty for not wearing it was death. Also, Jews were ordered to walk in the middle of the street. No Jews were allowed on the sidewalk. If Jews were walking together they had to walk in single file, one behind the other. Whenever they met a German, they had to take off their hats.

I hadn't minded the armband at all, but the yellow badges were a different story. They made me feel humiliated. I hated having to walk in the street, and I had to force myself to take my hat off to the gray-uniformed soldiers who were swarming through Grodno. I knew these people were unlike anybody I had ever met before. Anti-Semitism had been a way of life in Poland, but this was no ordinary anti-Semitism. The Germans had turned our world into a place of barbarism. I understood that they were determined to degrade us in every way they could.

You could see it in everything. My great-aunt Sonja's husband had immigrated to the United States several years earlier and had become an American citizen. He had recently come back to get his wife, but for some reason they had stayed too long and had been trapped when the war broke out. At the German headquarters he told them that he was Jewish, yes, but he was also an American. Here was his passport to prove it. "Good," they said, "you are an American citizen. In that case you don't have to wear a yellow star on your back like everybody else, only on the front." When he described his meeting with them I thought, This whole thing is like having them spit in your face, including an American. I despised them.

As if to illustrate how different the Germans were, one day a Spanish brigade came through the city, sent by Franco to fight against the Soviets. They were in Grodno for about two weeks, and while they were, the atmosphere changed entirely. The Spaniards seemed like decent people, normal people. They associated with the Jewish men without a sign of dislike or hatred. They went out with the Jewish girls. And when they left, it was even harder to face the barbarians who had taken control of our lives.

Thinking about the yellow stars and the degradation, after a while I realized that I really didn't feel humiliated. In fact, I wasn't depressed at all. I was angry. I began to look at the Germans as beasts. It isn't degrading to be attacked by a vicious dog, I thought. You have to find a way to deal with it, but the fact that you are attacked doesn't lower you in any way.

But at the same time, I had started to believe that maybe something really bad might happen to me or my family. I found myself thinking of survival, that we had to find some way to get through this alive. That same feeling infected others, too. Pogroms and killing were on everyone's minds. The Germans might do anything, we thought. We had seen enough to know what they were capable of, or we thought we had. The massacres in Lida and Slonim and other nearby villages had happened just a few months before; then in Grodno the hundred intellectuals had been murdered.

We took steps to protect ourselves against what we thought might happen. Each of the children had money sewn into his or her clothes in case we got separated from the rest of the family. It was also decided to try to hide the family's reserves. We knew that if a ghetto was set up we wouldn't be able to take much with us, so how to preserve at least something was a problem.

Sender the engineer came up with a solution. Across one end of the basement we could build a false wall, leaving three or four feet between it and the real exterior wall. No one would be able to tell anything had been changed without measuring the interior and exterior dimensions of the basement. Between the two walls we could store all the property we had managed to save, the paintings, furs, carpets, gold and silver, the merchandise we had gotten out of the stores before the Soviets confiscated everything.

But building the wall would be a big project; we needed a mason for it. Fortunately, we had one. When the Germans had originally occupied half the country in 1939, hundreds of thousands of Jews had fled into the Soviet zone. Many families, including ours, had taken in refugees. One young man had lived with us through the whole Soviet occupation, and now he was back with us again. He was a bricklayer by trade, and by now we considered him almost one of the family. So we took all the things out of their different hiding places and brought them down to the basement, where the bricklayer built a false wall the width of the house.

In mid-October 1941 we woke up to find that a new edict had been posted on the walls. "From November 1," it announced, "all Jews will be permitted to live only in the following areas." Two different sections of the city were delineated. One was the ancient Jewish Quarter from the Middle Ages. But since there was not nearly enough room there for thirty thousand people, a second ghetto was set aside, in the neighborhood of Slobodka. All the Poles there were expelled, and barbed wire was strung around the perimeter. Ten thousand Jews were assigned to live there. "Any Jew found residing outside the designated areas will be shot," the edict declared.

It was snowing the day we went into the old ghetto. Each of us was wearing as many clothes as he could put on, three or four shirts, several pairs of pants, a couple of jackets. I walked with my parents and Mira; my Zandman grandparents; Sender; his wife, Sarah, and two children; and Sarah's family, who had been living with us for the past several months as refugees. Most of the other Freydoviczes had been assigned to Ghetto Number Two, in Slobodka. In front of us we pushed a little horsecart piled high with our belongings, as did others in the crowd that grew denser and denser as we drew near the narrow street that was the ghetto's only entrance. It struck me that no one in this mass of people was either rich or poor. They were all the same, trudging along with the same slow pace and the same downcast looks. I felt like an animal being herded. Around us as we moved through the entranceway to the Jewish Quarter German soldiers were searching people and beating them, taking whatever they liked from the mounds of possessions passing by.

In Ghetto One a cousin of ours had a large apartment that was now parceled off to various families, a family per room. We lived in one room—my grandparents, parents, Mira, and me. Originally the dining room, it now had four beds in it, which along with the other furniture took up most of the space. During the night it was our bedroom; during the day we folded up two of the beds and pushed things aside and it became our living and dining room. The next room was slightly larger than ours. In it lived Sender and his family along with his wife's mother, three of her sisters, and a brother.

Despite the crowding, it seemed to me that we could get along here. Very quickly a Jewish administration was set up in the ghetto. Called the Judenrat, it organized public kitchens, clinics, and other services, including a Jewish police force. We had a big family meeting about that, all the cousins, uncles, wives, and children packed into one room. The talk was about what these Jewish police would be doing and whether it made sense for one of us to become a policeman. It was obvious that whatever else their duties might be, they would also be working with the Germans and would have to carry out their orders. They would have to make decisions about people, and my father was firmly against any of us joining. "Don't pass judgment on anyone else," he argued (that was to become a constant refrain of his: "Don't make yourself a judge"). "The police will have to do that all the time. But we will not be part of it." The decision came very fast. There would be no joining the police.

At first my father went to work for the Reiffheisen, a German company that had set up operations in Grodno. But he soon quit that and took a job as an accountant in the Judenrat. Then he left that, too. I watched him as week after week he grew more listless and less able to do things. It seemed to me that he was drawing into himself, becoming distant and less interested in what was taking place around us.

But as my father sank into depression, my mother took on responsibility for the family. She started to smuggle. It wasn't difficult to get out of the ghetto. The Reiffheisen and other German companies were doing business in town, and some Jews worked for them. In fact, the Reiffheisen had taken over our old house, and Sender and Kushka were both employed there. So people had work passes. It was also easy to get passes to go from our ghetto to Ghetto Two, where the Freydoviczes were living. Of course, if you were caught outside illegally, you could be put in jail or shot. But that didn't stop people. And once you were outside you could find a way to buy food or other things and bring them in. They searched you at the entrance to the ghetto, but the Jewish police would let you by if they could. It was only when the Germans were checking that the situation could get dangerous.

But then it could get really dangerous. People were shot for it, some of them on the spot, some of them, like my friend Siomka Stuchinsky, after spending time in the Gestapo jail. Siomka was fifteen years old. He had showed up in Grodno one day after somehow making his way alone from Lvov, 600 miles to the south. That's where his family had fled to from the Soviets, and that's where they had (all except Siomka) been massacred by the Germans. One day at the ghetto entrance Siomka had been caught bringing in a pocketful of tobacco. He was thrown in jail and, despite the entreaties of the most important people in the community, he was executed there.

Still, my mother started to smuggle, leaving the ghetto with a permit, then stopping in the city to buy clothes, which she would trade for food when she got back. I smuggled, too. I would get out with a pass to visit my relatives in Ghetto Two; then on the way back I would buy some milk or bread and stuff it into the deep pockets of my long coat. One time the German police stopped me at the checkpoint as I was going back in and ordered me to take off my coat. When they found the two bottles of milk in the pockets they broke them, and one started to club me with his fists. But before he had a chance to hurt me badly, the Jewish police grabbed me and pushed me out of there. When I got home I was taken care of, but Sender was angry. Why had I allowed myself to get caught with two bottles like that? Didn't I know milk was a scarce commodity? I should never have risked more than one.

That time I was saved by the Jewish police. But shortly afterward I wasn't so lucky. Inside the ghetto, Jews were permitted to walk on the sidewalk, but if you saw Germans you had to get into the street and take off your hat. I still hated that. I couldn't stand the idea of taking off my hat to beasts, so I avoided Germans whenever I could. One day I saw a patrol headed in my direction, so I turned around and started to walk the other way. But they had noticed. They ran after me and caught me in the middle of the street. I felt hands grab me, then I was knocked down by a blow from a rifle butt. The next thing I knew I was on the ground thrashing around, trying to protect myself from the rifles they were swinging at me. But I couldn't. The blows smashed down on my arms and body. I was sure I would die from what they were doing to me, if they didn't just shoot me first. Then it started going through my head that that's what they were going to do. Any moment now they would shoot me, and that would be the end. I was aware of the mud and grainy snow I was rolling around in, and that the snow was now turning red.

But there were no shots, and after a while they got tired beating me and stopped. When the soldiers had gone, people came over and helped me to stand up and walk. I finally got home, thinking, My God, my mother is going to be so upset. My clothes are so filthy. In the old days, in my previous life, my proper mother had forbade me to play soccer because I would dirty my clothes. I was supposed to be always neat, always clean. Of course, I played anyhow. But when I would come home dirty, my mother was always very angry. Now it came to me that if I arrived looking like this, my clothes torn and ground with mud, what would she think?

But when I walked in, I was greeted like a hero. My proper mother held me and kissed me. They were so happy to see me alive. All the other adults came and kissed me on the head—a combination of relief that I was alive, and pride. They had already heard what had happened. "We're so proud of you," they told me, "so proud of you." And I understood that resistance was in their minds, too.

The depression that enveloped my father also affected many of the other adults, but not the children. At first I had almost nothing to do. The Germans had prohibited academic schools in the ghetto, and it took a while before trade schools were organized that trained people for the weapons and other workshops the Germans had set up but that also served as covers for more traditional learning. But though I had nothing to do, I wasn't idle.

The young people in the ghetto were together all the time, doing whatever we wanted. I was almost fifteen when we were closed in, just going through puberty. We smoked cigarettes out of the way of our elders and we started experimenting with the girls, and the girls with us. Kissing and touching each other behind closed doors and in alleys, just as I suppose we would have done had there been no ghetto. There was no sleeping together, though, at least not among my friends. With six or eight people living in each room there was simply no place, no matter how much we might have been thinking about it.

Other things were happening, too. I began playing the

violin more, taking part in chamber groups with other musicians. A group of us also went into business. One of my oldest friends was Leon Trachtenberg, who had been a classmate of mine since I started school. Leon was short but sturdy, a boy with a broad smile and an unusual ability to get things done. Among his other skills he was a natural entrepreneur, and he dreamed up the idea that we should go into the tobacco business.

Leon had noticed that tobacco sold on the black market at one price by the pound but at a much higher price in small amounts. Somehow he managed to find a supply of printed tobacco company paper (the Shereshevsky Tobacco Company had a huge factory in Grodno), out of which we could make little tobacco boxes that looked like the real thing. Then he got labels printed up at a shop in the ghetto. Another boy's father owned a store and agreed to sell whatever we could provide. So we got to work, cutting dried leaves into black market tobacco, making boxes, filling them, and labeling them. We were in business.

Leon came by his entrepreneurial instinct naturally. His father had had a good business before the war selling and servicing agricultural equipment. In the ghetto he succeeded in going into the cooking oil business, even though the Germans would never have dreamed of letting anybody open a cooking oil plant. But Meier Trachtenberg not only did that, he even persuaded the Germans to provide the machinery and raw materials for it.

Leon's father knew that the German war effort needed something called "pokust," a kind of water repellent for wood. Pokust was made from vegetable oil, which was unavailable in the ghetto and was sorely needed by people whose diet had been deprived of fat. Somehow Meier Trachtenberg sold the Germans on the idea that he could provide a regular supply of pokust. All he needed was the equipment and shipments of oilseeds. In short order the machinery and presses were brought into the ghetto and consignments of sunflower seeds began to arrive. From then on there was always a supply of cooking oil, not only for the Jews, but for the Poles outside who were also suffering from lack of fat. The by-product of seed pressing was a cakey mash ordinarily used as animal food. But that, too, was eaten by the ghetto dwellers.

In fact, commerce flourished in the ghetto. People found what they could do, and they did it. Grodno was 60 percent Jewish, and Jews constituted the bulk of the tradespeople, craftsmen, and shopkeepers. Without Jews the Polish population would have been hard pressed to keep life going. As a result, commerce between the ghetto and the outside sprang up naturally. The ghetto made shoes, clothes, and other necessities. These were smuggled out and traded for bread, butter, and potatoes.

To me, anyway, life seemed more or less normal. Or maybe I was just getting used to the conditions. Food was in short supply. People were beaten and tormented. Occasionally someone was killed, as happened to an escaped Russian-Jewish prisoner of war who had taken refuge in the ghetto. The Germans announced that if he wasn't turned over they would hang twenty people from the Judenrat. He was given up and shot. But incidents like this didn't threaten the life of the ghetto. If they don't do anything worse, I thought, we can live like this for a hundred years.

Occasionally representatives of the Judenrat would come around to collect money. They would announce that the Germans had a list of people they were going to arrest unless a bribe was paid. Each family would be called on for a contribution of gold or zlotys. We gave, as did everyone. And like others, we eventually ran out of money—though people found it hard to believe that the Freydoviczes had nothing left.

To get more money for the contributions, Grandpa Freydovicz decided we had to take some things out of the basement of our old house. So one night Sender and Kushka stole out of the ghetto and sneaked into the basement of 28 Brygidzka. But when they knocked out some bricks in the false wall and opened up a hole, the hiding place was completely empty. Everything was gone. Thieves had broken in through the outside wall and cleaned the place out. They had known exactly where to make the hole.

The hiding place had been one of the great family secrets. I was questioned closely about whether I might have told one of my friends about it, but I hadn't. Neither had anyone else. We knew it could only be one person, the refugee mason who had lived with us. He was in the ghetto, too, and the next day we took him before the rabbi. The rabbi made him swear on a Bible and generally put the fear of God in him, and eventually he confessed. He had done it one night with the help of a German civilian. But the German had then gone back on his agreement and had taken everything for himself. The long and the short of it was that the bricklayer had neither the goods nor the money, which meant that we were now destitute. My mother and grandmother each had a ring. There might have been a watch or two. But the cache was gone. We had almost nothing left to barter or sell to the Poles. It was a catastrophe.

News from the outside was also increasingly grim. In the winter of 1941–42 the information we got from German-language newspapers and the rumors that came in through the grapevine were only bad. All of it spoke of German victories. The only exception came in December 1941, when we heard that the United States had entered the war. The whole ghetto rejoiced. Now, we thought, the Germans can't possibly win. Only Mrs. Rajgrodski, Sender's mother-in-law who lived in the next room, reacted differently. While everyone else was celebrating, she was crying bitterly. Her son Nachum had gone to Cincinnati three years earlier, and now she was sure he would be drafted into the American army. We were all sitting in the ghetto with our fate on the line, but she was still overwhelmed by a mother's anxiety at the thought that her son might possibly come into harm's way.

News was one of the things we hungered for. We lived on rumor. Someone had heard some Gestapo officer say something. Another one had overheard some snatch of conversation between two soldiers. The hero of the moment was the one who had information, any information. Leon Trachtenberg lived in a house whose inhabitants included a Farbindungsman—one of the ghetto's three Jewish liaisons with the Gestapo. This was the most powerful position in the ghetto; the Farbindungsmen were much more influential than the leaders of the Judenrat. They had daily contact with the Gestapo.

Sarnatsky, the Farbindungsman who lived with the Trachtenbergs, would talk at the dinner table. Leon would bring the news to me, and I would tell my parents. Another friend of mine with whom I played quartets often had news from the battlefront. I didn't know where he got it from, but I suspected he had a secret radio. Of course, all radios had been confiscated, and it was strictly forbidden to have one. From time to time I would come home and very proudly announce that this or that had happened on the front. "How do you know?" my father would ask. I wouldn't say. But one day my friend disappeared, arrested by the Gestapo. The regular war news stopped, and our quartet became a trio.

We had been living in the ghetto for nine or ten months when a new spate of rumors started. In Warsaw, we heard, Jews were being removed from the ghetto and transported somewhere. Where, nobody knew. Vague stories were circulating that the ones taken were being gassed and their bodies burned. But nobody really believed it. People thought it was panicmongering. I heard it one day in late summer from my friend Lolek Kabak, who had heard it from his mother. "Come on," I said, "what are you talking about? Be serious." Slonim had happened. Mass shootings in Lida had happened. But those were men; they had shot the men. To take out women and ch8ildren? To murder old people? Gas? Burning? It was unbelievable, as if someone had said, "You know, there is a city in Siberia where the people are cannibals. They eat people, but first they drain the blood and sell it to Mongolia." These were bizarre horror stories, Gothic tales. Killing we could understand, we had seen it. But gas chambers and ovens—that was from a world of fantasy.

•

On November 1, 1942, exactly one year after the order for Jews to move into the ghetto, a woman came running into our house, the best friend of Sender's wife, Sarah. A minute later Sarah came into the room, her face deathly white. "They're closing the ghetto today," she said. "The deportations are starting."

WE had heard stories about what was happening in Warsaw. Now something was starting here. This night. The rumors hadn't been believable, the tales of deportations to God knew where for who knew what purpose. But Tania Prenska knew what she was talking about. She worked for a Volksdeutsch—an ethnic German—who had connections with the German Army. In fact, he told Tania that he was helping to organize the Volksdeutsche to help surround the ghetto. The Grodno Gestapo office had only five people. This was going to be a big operation, and they would need all the help they could get.

After a hurried family discussion, my uncle Sender decided that he would try to escape from the ghetto with his wife and two children. My mother was also determined to get out with me and my sister Mira. But my father refused to come. "I can't leave my parents," he said. "I absolutely can't do it." My mother begged him. "Please come with us, Archik, please!" "No," he said. "But you go. You should try to survive. Do whatever you have to. But how can I leave them?" "But you have a brother," she said. "Let him stay." "No, it has to be me. I'm staying with them." I couldn't believe my father wasn't coming with us. How could he let us go alone? But on the other hand, my poor grandparents. While all the commotion was going on in the house, I couldn't seem to think right. I was angry at my father but heartbroken for my grandma and grandpa.

I kissed people good-bye, the thought flashing through my mind that this might be the last time I would ever see them. But there was no time to think. Outside it was dark already and my mother was pulling at me to come. Sender and Sarah had already bundled up their three-year-old Haim and their baby Abrasha. The next thing I knew we were sneaking through the alleys to a place we knew where it was possible to slip onto Dominikanska Street and out of the ghetto.

We made our way through the city to our old house,

keeping in the shadows and avoiding the few people who were out. Twenty-eight Brygidzka had been taken over by the Reiffheisen company for use as an office and warehouse, but there was nobody living there. When we got there, Sender opened up one of the apartments and told us to stay put and wait for him. Then he took the children and disappeared into the night. He was going to bring them to their old nanny, Sarah told us; she had already agreed to take them in.

An hour later, Sender was back. Now the five of us— Sender, Sarah, my mother, Mira, and I—climbed up to the attic above my grandparents' old apartment and closed ourselves in, waiting to see what would happen.

For the next three days we lay there, nibbling on the bread we had brought along, and waiting. From the street we heard a constant racket of horses and wagons. Ordinarily Grodno was quiet. With a partial curfew during the day and a full curfew at night, not too many people were around, especially since 60 percent of the city's inhabitants were cooped up in the ghettos. Now it was obvious that something unusual was going on, though we couldn't tell what. Our plan was to wait until it seemed that the streets were normal, that whatever was happening had happened. Then we would climb down and try to get back to the ghetto.

After the third day of noise, Sender decided the attic was no longer safe. Late that night we crept downstairs and outside. Across the courtyard one of the warehouse buildings had a storage attic, like a hayloft in a barn. Sender knew where to find a ladder, and the five of us climbed up to the outside door of this second-floor storage space and crawled in, pulling up the ladder behind us.

The next morning we heard the sounds of the Reiffheisen employees coming to work. A short time later there was a scraping noise on the wall of our storeroom, as if a ladder was being put up. We froze. I felt as if I had stopped breathing. Other sounds came through the wall; somebody was climbing the ladder. Then hammering started on the outside of the door, and in a moment we realized that the door was being nailed shut. A rough voice shouted in Polish, "I caught the Jews! Go get the Germans!"

Sender didn't waste a moment. The outside door was the main access to the storage space, but there was also a trapdoor which opened onto the ground floor. Sender pulled the trapdoor, open, and we all dropped down onto the straw-covered floor below. Picking ourselves up, we ran out to the courtyard. Polish workers stopped what they were doing and stared at us. Then I heard boots pounding on cobblestones. Soldiers were running along Brygidzka Street toward us, their weapons clanking as they came. We had been headed for the street; now we turned and ran for the far end of the courtyard. There was no way out. We were like mice in a trap. In another moment the Germans would turn the corner, and there we would be. Instinctively we ducked into our house and raced down the cellar stairs to get as far away from them as possible.

At the far end of the darkened cellar we came up against the wall—the false wall I suddenly remembered. And yes, right there in front of us was the opening Sender and Kushka had made when they came looking for our things. We squeezed through, into the space between the false wall and the outside foundation wall. It was dark there, too, except for a patch of gray daylight that played in through a hole in the outside wall—the hole the thieves had made when they robbed the cellar. I crawled through it first. Then my mother came, pulling my sister behind her. Then Sarah poked her head out. But halfway through, she got stuck. Sender pushed her from behind, and I grabbed her arms and pulled with all my might, but she was wedged in tight. Sarah was slim and graceful; we couldn't imagine how she had gotten caught. But she couldn't move. I felt like I was in a nightmare where you have to run but you can't. By now the Germans had to be on their way into the cellar. Any second I expected to hear their voices.

Finally Sender gave her a powerful shove, and something let go; Sarah was free of the hole. She scrambled out, and we ran through the gardens of the next-door house and suddenly we were on the sidewalk. When we finally stopped to catch our breath

I noticed we were on Piaskova Street. I had just been following Sender, without thinking about where he was taking us. Now I saw we were near the house of Mr. Heidemak, a Polish engineer friend of Sender's. A moment later the five of us barged in through his front doorway.

Mr. Heidemak was home, but for a moment he was speechless at this sudden incursion of Jews. The Germans were hanging anyone who helped Jews, along with their families. But Heidemak was married to a Jewish woman, and we knew he was a friend. "People saw you come in," he said. "You can't stay here. We have to do something else—maybe Konopnicki can take you." I knew that Mr. Konopnicki owned a large plywood factory in Mosti and had been a friend and business associate of the Freydoviczes; he lived on the outskirts of Grodno. "Let me check," said Heidemak. "You stay here."

A while later he was back with the news that we could go to Konopnicki's. With Heidemak leading, we walked, all of us together, trying mightily to look like normal Polish people out for a stroll. That night we slept in Konopnicki's large apartment. But in the morning Konopnicki said, "Look, Sender and his wife I know. I feel obligated. But I can't hide more than two people. It's too many. The three of you have to go. Maybe you can get back into the ghetto."

In fact, by this time my mother wanted badly to go back. She was extremely upset about having left my father. We had no idea what might have happened to him and the others. We had heard all the street noises, but we didn't know if deportations had taken place or what. And if there had been, had they taken my father and his parents? Or her parents, in Ghetto Two? Neither Heidemak nor Konopnicki knew what had happened either. Both ghettos had been sealed. There was a lot of talk in town that many Jews were being taken away somewhere. Beyond that they, too, were in the dark.

My mother was set on getting back. She had to find out what had happened to my father. But I didn't want to go. As far as

I was concerned, the ghetto was nothing more than a trap, like the trap the hunters laid down for the beaver in my grandfather's story. If there was any way to hide on the outside, that's what I wanted to do. "Yes, Felix," my mother said when I told her, "you stay out. Try to find some way to save yourself. I'm going back to be with your father." Then she kissed me and walked out the door with my seven-year-old sister.

That morning Mr. Heidemak took me to the house of a woman he knew on the outskirts of the city. When we got there they talked for a few minutes and I heard her say, "Okay. I'll hide him." For the next few days I stayed with her. Each morning she went out to work while I stayed inside. One day, to alleviate the boredom, she took me out walking. We went all the way to Ghetto Two, just to look around. When we got there I saw that the gate was closed and barred. Nobody could get in or out. Quite a few Poles were standing in the street looking in at the Jews who stood behind the barbed wire fence. But as we stood there with them someone from inside began shouting, "Oy, there's Felix. Felix, hi. How are you, Felix? Felix!" It was a friend of mine, completely oblivious to what he was doing.

We left quickly. I didn't think anyone had noticed it was me he was yelling at, but there were German police around, and we were both frightened. When we got back to the house I decided I couldn't stay there anymore. I didn't know this woman, and we both understood that she would be killed if she were caught hiding me. Besides, by now I was anxious to get back, to see what had happened to my family.

The next day I walked back to Ghetto One and stood outside the gate with a small crowd of Poles looking at what was going on inside. All of a sudden I saw my mother on the other side of the wire. At the same moment she saw me. Then she was talking to one of the Jewish policemen. The gate opened and he came out and pulled me in, slapping me around—though the blows didn't hurt at all. I could tell he was just doing it for show. Rubinczyk, the chief of the Jewish police, was at the gate, too. I saw him smiling as the policeman gave me a final slap and handed me over to my mother.

When I got back to our house everyone was there—my father, my grandparents, even Sender and Sarah. After what we had gone through I was angry at my father and I told him. Why had he stayed with his parents and not gone with us? "How could you do that?" I asked. "How could you not protect your family?" "What do you mean, my family?" he answered. "And how about your grandparents? You wanted to take them, too? They can hardly walk. Eighty years old. Who was supposed to protect them?"

I had no answer; he was right. But I still wished that he had come. In fact, no one had been taken from the ghetto. There had been no deportations at all, although for three days the ghetto had been shut tight and there had been a lot of movement in and around the city. It was known that the Germans had taken the Jews from all the surrounding villages and had transported them to the Kielbasin camp outside of Grodno. The horse and wagon noises we had heard in the street were the sounds of the village Jews being taken away.

Kielbasin had originally been a training camp for the Polish Army, but after the war started the Germans had used it as a prison for Russian soldiers. We knew that thousands of Russians had died there, many of them from typhoid fever. The Russian Jewish soldier who had hidden for a few days in the ghetto had escaped from Kielbasin and had talked about how horrible the conditions were. Now the tens of thousands of Jews from the *shtetlach* were there. We couldn't imagine the Germans would keep them in Kielbasin; the camp was nothing but flimsy wooden barracks, and winter had already started.

From the sworn deposition of Sonie Lewcowicz, an inhabitant of Dabrowo, a shtetl in the Grodno district, presented at the Bielefeld Nazi trial:*

*Documents Concerning the Destruction of the Jews of Grodno, 1941–1944, edited by Serge Klarsfeld (The Beate Klarsfeld Foundation, 1989), Vol. I, p. 447.

On November 1, 1942, the local administration in Dabrowo announced that we would be resettled. In the morning—it was a Monday—a unit of SS appeared where we were concentrated in the Dabrowo cinema. They told us we would be allowed to take all our valuables and also to bring food and drinking water for two days. The men were formed into a column, but the women and children were loaded into wagons. All were directed toward Grodno. On the way—in the vicinity of Nowy Dwor—we passed many human corpses on the road. It turned out that they were the dead from the resettlement of Nowy Dwor, which was happening on the same day as ours. Our men were beaten on the way to hurry their walking.

Before evening we arrived at a camp near Grodno called Kielbasin. It was surrounded by a barbed wire fence. When we arrived there were already several thousand Jews in the camp. In the course of a few days transports of inmates regularly left for unknown destinations, but resettlers from other areas always took their places, so that the total number never dwindled.

I spent six weeks in Kielbasin camp. Typhoid fever and dysentery reached epidemic proportions. Hundreds of people died and were buried in the surrounding woods. An SS officer by the name of Wiese arrived from Grodno and our group was taken to Losossna station and loaded onto freight cars.

Our transport was under way for a day and a night and in the morning hours we arrived at Treblinka. I was completely stripped and stood in line for the barber. I was then taken out of this line and brought into the work camp. All the ones remaining were murdered on that same day.

I was in my house two days after I got back when we noticed that a crowd was gathering on the street a little way down from our door. I went up to the attic and looked out the window. Below I could see a number of Gestapo officers, including the commandant, Wiese, a man who always brought terror wherever he went. He seemed to take special delight in brutalizing people and was known as a sadistic killer who thought nothing of shooting randomly into crowds and executing people arbitrarily. Always dressed in a black uniform with shiny silver zippers and buttons, Wiese was feared and detested. People called him *Malach haMavet,* the Angel of Death.

There in front of the crowd were also some Jewish policemen and three other people, two men and a young woman. I knew the woman; it was Lena Prenska, the sister of Sarah's friend who had warned us that the ghetto was being closed.

I saw Rubinczyk there, the Jewish chief of police, and Dr. Braver, the principal of Tarbut who was now the head of the Judenrat. Then I saw the ropes and nooses tied to an overhang of the house on the corner. I watched as Wiese made Lena and the two men get up on a wooden bench. Then he put the nooses over their heads. A moment later the bench was kicked over and the three of them were swinging slowly from the building.

The news cut through the ghetto like a knife. Lena Prenska was one of the most beautiful young girls in the city, and the idea of her dying like that was horrifying. She and the others had been caught outside the ghetto at the same time we were hiding on Brygidzka Street. She must have been warned by her sister, too, I thought, and now she was dangling from an iron rod jutting out of the corner house.

Later Leon Trachtenberg told me that Wiese had ordered Rubinczyk to do the hanging himself but that he had refused. Leon had heard it from his brother, who was standing in the crowd. Somebody else had now been made chief of police. His brother had also seen Lena spit in Wiese's face. People had been ordered not to remove the bodies; Wiese wanted them to be a lesson to anyone who might be thinking about escape.

Not long afterward the Germans announced that all the people from Ghetto Two were going to be sent to a labor camp. However, families that were separated would be allowed to reunite. Anyone in Ghetto One could make arrangements (if they had the necessary bribe money) for family members in Ghetto Two to come live with them instead of being transported to a labor camp.

In fact, most of our family was in Ghetto Two. In a couple of days they had moved in with us: Tema and Grandpa Freydovicz; Kushka and his wife, Lina (who had gotten me from

Slonim); my mother's youngest sister, Fania, with her husband, Berko, and their ten-month-old son, Haim, and her other sister, Lisa, with her husband, Mula, and their three children. The whole family was back together.

But the living conditions, which had been tight before, now became almost impossible. As crowded as the ghetto had been, several thousand more people were now squeezed inside. In Sender's room there were twelve; in our room, six. At night the room became one bed. Going to the bathroom meant stepping gingerly among the bodies of the sleepers, trying to find space to plant your toes.

Then we heard that Ghetto Two had been emptied. We didn't know any of the details except that the Germans had loaded everyone onto trains. Overnight a quarter of the city's Jews disappeared. Some people were sure that they all had been sent to their deaths. Others were equally sure it was for labor in the East. Many didn't want either to talk or think about it.

From the sworn testimony of Fenia Rapoport at the Bielefeld Nazi trial regarding deportations from Ghetto 2:

> It was in the late afternoon when a Jewish policeman came and told us to be ready with our baggage in two hours. We stayed in the houses until Jewish policemen came and ordered us to follow them to Jarusolimska Street.
>
> The sights at the assembly point were horrifying. Hundreds and hundreds of people had collected there. There was much crying and screaming. A large number of German police were there. I think that the streetlights were lit. We had to wait about an hour, then we were led to the train station. The wagons were packed with as many people as could be squeezed in. They were regular railroad passenger cars. It was forbidden to speak loudly. No food was issued, nor was there any water. It was very cold.
>
> When we got down from the train at Auschwitz, about two hundred to three hundred people were separated out from the others. I never saw my parents again.*

*Klarsfeld, Vol. IV, pp. 352–353.

From the "Hefte von Auschwitz," the official Auschwitz arrival records. "RSHA" is the *Reichssicherheitshauptamt,* the Reich Security Main Office, an SS agency established in October 1939 that included the Gestapo (Office IV). Initially headed by Reinhard Heydrich and later by Ernst Kaltenbrunner, the RSHA was officially entrusted with implementing the "Final Solution." RSHA transports were trains ordered by the RSHA and supplied by the State Railway:

> NOVEMBER 18, 1942. RSHA TRANSPORT. JEWS FROM THE GHETTO AT GRODNO. AFTER THE SELECTION 165 MEN WERE COMMITTED TO THE CAMP [MONOWITZ, THE AUSCHWITZ LABOR CAMP]. THEY WERE GIVEN NUMBERS 75952–76116. ALSO, 65 WOMEN RECEIVED NUMBERS 25065–25129. CHILDREN, WOMEN WITH CHILDREN, AND ALL ELDERLY WERE GASSED.
>
> NOVEMBER 25, 1942. RSHA TRANSPORT. JEWS FROM GRODNO. 305 MEN WITH THE NUMBERS 77720–78024 AND 128 WOMEN WITH THE NUMBERS 25793–25920 WERE SELECTED FOR THE CAMP. CHILDREN, MOTHERS, AND OLD MEN WERE GASSED.
>
> DECEMBER 2, 1942. RSHA TRANSPORT. JEWS FROM THE GRODNO DISTRICT. 178 MEN WITH THE NUMBERS 79390–79567 AND 60 WOMEN WITH THE NUMBERS 26287–26346 WERE SELECTED FOR THE CAMP. CHILDREN, MOTHERS, AND OLD MEN WERE GASSED.
>
> DECEMBER 8, 1942. RSHA TRANSPORT. JEWS FROM GRODNO. 231 MEN WITH THE NUMBERS 80764–80994 WERE SELECTED FOR THE CAMP. CHILDREN, MOTHERS, AND OLD MEN WERE GASSED.*

After Ghetto Two was eliminated, people seemed to be obsessed with theories of how they would be saved from whatever fate was swallowing up everyone else. One school of thought said that with Ghetto Two gone, Ghetto One would now be safe. Clearly, the Germans had found it awkward and inefficient to keep two ghettos. Now that there was only one, the rest of us would be all right. Others were sure that we would be protected because the Germans were incorporating Grodno into

*Klarsfeld, Summary Volume, p. 128.

the Third Reich. They were even giving the city a new German name—Garten. Now, they said, we are *German* Jews. Obviously they won't do anything terrible to German Jews. They'll probably only deport Polish or Lithuanian Jews. Everyone was clinging to whatever straw seemed most likely to bear the weight of his or her imagined salvation. The ghetto was turning into a world of fantasy.

The little pleasures that had kept life bearable for so long were now a thing of the past, the flirting and long days spent with friends. My music-playing was finished, too. The Germans had gotten into the habit of breaking into apartments at random to terrorize people and steal whatever caught their eye. A few weeks after the elimination of Ghetto Two they had stormed into ours and shoved everybody they found into the bathroom. I was closest to the door, and as I looked through the keyhole I saw Schott, the Gestapo deputy commander, pull my violin out of the closet he was rummaging through. He opened the case, took it out, and plucked the strings. Then he put it under his chin and began to play. It wasn't bad, I thought, he had obviously had some training. Abruptly he stopped, glanced at the violin, then took it by the neck and smashed it against the wall. My heart stopped for a second. I stared in horror as he casually tossed the splintered wood and dangling strings onto the floor, then went back to grabbing things out of the closet. He left with my precious stamp collection under his arm.

By now I was going to work every day, doing hard labor for the Germans. My friend Leon was in the same work commando, which was often assigned to the rebuilding of the Gestapo headquarters. My job was to mix cement and carry it to the bricklayers. At first the cement hods seemed unbearably heavy, and even though I was getting bigger and stronger, I found it almost impossible to carry them on my back up the three flights of stairs. But eventually I learned how to do it.

Every day I would go out and every day I'd bring a piece

of bread home. The work commando wasn't closely guarded, and we often had a chance to barter or buy food from the Poles. We got paid a pittance for our work, but at least it was something. I had become the family breadwinner.

I felt very good about this, and very proud. I was doing something productive to help my family. In fact, by now I was the only one. My father had not been able to work for a long time, and my mother now seemed to me a defeated woman. She had left my father once, and something had happened to her when she did that. She felt she had betrayed him—or so it looked to me—and that thought overwhelmed her. It had broken something inside her, and afterward she was a different person, I knew that she would never leave him again.

By this time my friends and I were thinking hard about escape. We had heard rumors that some people had found their way out to the partisans, though none of us knew anyone personally who had done that. There were even Jewish partisans, people said. But the idea of slipping out of Grodno and joining them had an unreal feeling about it. Already December was here, and the Polish winter was bitter, with temperatures down to minus thirty. The partisans were out there somewhere in the countryside, but where? How could you find them? And how could you survive the forest and the cold while you were looking?

•

Sometime in mid-December, our turn came. The Germans announced that several thousand Jews would be moved to Kielbasin. The ghetto, they said, was overcrowded. By now many stories of Kielbasin had filtered back to us. It was known that people were hanged there and shot. Typhoid was supposed to be raging. It was a terrible camp. On the other hand, there was no talk of gas chambers or ovens, nothing to corroborate the most bloodcurdling rumors.

When the list for transportation came out, our family was on it. So was Sender's. All the transportees were ordered to take warm clothes and a loaf of bread. We would be allowed to have anything we could carry with us. Kielbasin would not be our final destination; from there we would be taken to a camp where we would have to work. But everything, we were assured, would be okay.

When the list came out my father went to Mottl Bass, one of the three Farbindungsmen who worked as liaisons with the Gestapo; he was going to beg Bass to take us off the list. When he came back to the house, he was crestfallen. "Well," he said, "I talked to Bass and Bass said only one thing: 'Whom do you want me to put in your place? We have to give them the number they have demanded.'" "Nobody," my father had said. "Put nobody in our place."

It was nighttime when the police showed up at our door to take us—two Jewish policemen and a Gestapo man. The two Jewish policemen we knew. They were card-playing friends of my uncle Sender. The Gestapo man was Commandant Wiese himself, wearing his black suit sparkling with zippers and carrying a sub-machine gun in the crook of his arm.

The Angel of Death came into our apartment. I stood behind him watching as Sender spoke to him in German and showed him a big piece of paper, his engineering diploma from the University of Danzig. "Okay," Wiese said, "you stay. Stay with your family." Then my father took out his Ph.D. from the University of Vienna. Wiese tore it up. *"Du gehst!"* he barked. You go! I was standing behind him when he said it. Leaning up against the closet wall was the ax we used for chopping wood. I was looking at this ax, staring at it. Wiese's long, skinny neck was right there in front of me. What if I pick up this ax? I thought. With one swing I could cut off his head. The urge was singing inside me. Just pick it up and swing it at his neck. I could see the exact place where I would hit him. But I didn't do it, and the next moment it was too late.

Snow was falling heavily as my mother, my sister, my

father, my Zandman grandparents, and I joined many other people walking toward the Grand Synagogue, all of us carrying our belongings in our hands. When we got there, the synagogue was already half full. They had taken the pews out, and the main room looked cavernous, a huge open space with the *bimah* and the Ark of the Torah in front. The room was bathed in a glare of lights. People were sitting on the floor or on their things. Others arrived continuously, all night and into the early morning—old people, men, children, women carrying infants. Sometimes they came in a slow trickle, sometimes in groups, all of them crowding into the chamber.

From time to time Gestapo men came in, and a commotion would start as people tried to get out of the way. Now and then I heard volleys of machine-gun shots, and sometimes I could make out one or another of them shooting at the walls and ceiling. A few times they shot into the crowd, and screams and shouts raised above the general noise as people milled around frantically. I saw Wiese walk up to one man and shoot him, right across from where I was standing. The body slumped to the floor, and two Jewish policemen dragged the body out.

Sometime in the early morning the crowd began to move out of the synagogue into the frigid air. Snow was still falling out of the gray sky; the ground was blanketed with white. Grandma, Grandpa, and other old people who couldn't walk were put into horse-drawn wagons that were waiting on the street. The rest of us were lined up four abreast in a long column. It looked to me like thousands of people. I heard that Rubinczyk, the former police chief, was at the front of the column with two other members of the Judenrat. People said that they had put some kind of clown hat with bells on Rubinczyk's head.

Mother, Father, Mira, and I walked together. On either side of the street stood Germans with rifles and whips. As we moved along I was aware that people were being whipped and clubbed, but things seemed to be passing in a blur, and I knew I was hardly registering what was happening to us. I felt a whip come down on my back. From far away in the front of the column a violin was playing. I could just make out the strains of "Yiddl Mitn Fiddl." Then a voice shouted in German, "*Singen sie!*" "Sing, goddamnit! All of you sing!"

5

M AY G OD W ATCH O VER Y OU

THE column moved out of the ghetto and through the streets of Grodno. A few times we stopped, then we'd start up again under the lashes of whips and blows from rifle butts. We walked and walked, German soldiers and Volksdeutsche with rifles moving along either side, like dogs herding sheep. I wasn't tired, but I was worried about Mira, who was only seven. She had always been frail and was often sick. How far she might be able to go I didn't know. The forest was black against the frozen fields. The gray sky was still filled with the snowstorm that had begun the previous night. We had been moving several hours when guard towers loomed out of the snow in front of us and I saw the barbed wire fences. Kielbasin looked just as I had imagined it.

As soon as we had passed through the front gates, we were assigned to barracks. These were flimsy wooden buildings, not much more than sheds. They had been built half underground so that when you entered you had to step down several steps. The floor was bare earth. On either side of a central aisle two tiers of wooden plank shelves had been built, our beds.

Inside the barracks we lay down on the shelves, exhausted, my father and I on top, my mother and Mira below us. Nearby Grandma and Grandpa lay on another bottom shelf. I saw my school friend Lolek on another shelf across the room; our eyes met momentarily. Farther down the tier I made out another friend, Salka Chazan, lying there with his mother. There were no stoves at Kielbasin, though each of us had been given a thin blanket. My father and I huddled together, getting warmth from each other's bodies.

The next morning they had us line up in rows by block and counted us. As they did, I looked around and took stock: A double row of barbed wire fences enclosed the camp, with guard towers every hundred and fifty yards. I could make out the machine guns mounted in the towers, and the searchlights that swept the camp at night. Guards restrained snarling German shepherds in front of us as we were counted, and other dogs walked the perimeter of the fence on short leashes held by their masters.

After the head count came exercise for the men and older boys. At first I didn't believe that they would make us do calisthenics and run around the frozen yard—but I quickly took off with the others, my knees and arms pumping like mad, my breath clouding out in the frigid air. That turned into a morning ritual whose presiding spirit was Rubinczyk, the former police chief. He gave orders and encouragement, his voice powerful and commanding, impelling everybody to move. "Do it!" he'd yell. "It's good for you. Never mind what else is happening, just do it. Keep your spirits up and you'll keep living." He was like a one-man army fighting back a tide of despair.

One of the first days at the morning lineup they announced that they were going to form a police force of Jews for the new arrivals. People from seventeen and up could volunteer. I was only fifteen, but I talked to my father about it. I told him I wanted to join the police. He looked at me, his face full of disappointment. "Don't you remember our discussions?" he said. "Never be a judge. Never. No one in our family will join the police. You are not allowed to do it." I was boiling inside while he was saying this. Kielbasin did not look like a place you could come out of alive, and I wanted to survive. I wanted to live. "No," he was saying. "You can't do such a thing." I didn't answer, but inside my head I was holding a dialogue with him. "I want to live. This is for my skin, okay? Maybe I'll have a chance if I join them." But my father just looked at me, and I knew I couldn't do it.

From the beginning I understood instinctively that Kielbasin was a stop on the way to death. Nobody who put people here had any intention of keeping them alive. These were not circumstances where we, the *heftlinge* (prisoners), were assumed to have some value, even the value of a slave laborer, whose life is at least worth sustaining. We were simply being stored for the next step, which might come at any time.

We were living without heat in the bitter northern Polish winter. Our rations were a watery soup with a few pieces of rotten potatoes in it, which we got once a day, supplemented by two hunks of bread per day. The latrines were off behind the barracks, a hut with a long ditch, which men and women used together. It was no surprise that people were becoming ill and that some were already dying of the dysentery that was sweeping the camp even before we got there. I watched the burial parties digging ditches in the rock-hard ground and rolling the bodies in.

Others were shot, beaten to death, or hanged, often by the chief of the camp himself. This was a huge, red-faced man named Rinzler, a vicious, violent sadist. At one morning lineup he took out my great-aunt Sonja (who was married to the American citizen who had to wear only one star) and beat her with his bead-tipped whip, laying her head open. The next day when we were lined up he noticed a small pile of human feces; at night somebody had obviously been unable to make it to the latrine. Grabbing an old man with a beard, he forced him to the ground and ordered him to eat the excrement with a spoon he gave him. The man ate it in front of everyone.

I had no doubt that we were all going to die, which made me especially intent on the names Rinzler read from a list every morning after lineup. "The following people," he would announce, "are not needed here. They are permitted to go back to the ghetto." Although I didn't know it at the time, these were people whose relatives in the ghetto had managed to bribe the Gestapo to have them sent back. The lucky ones were usually told the day before that their name might appear on the list. So if you knew, you waited to hear your name. But many more waited, too, hoping to hear if by some chance, some inconceivable chance, their names might also be called.

One morning Rinzler called a name. There was a pause, and nobody came forward. Then a second cousin of mine, sixteen-year-old Rifka Freydovicz, stepped out. It wasn't her name, but she had decided to take a chance. Rinzler looked at her, looked at the list, then took his pistol out of its holster, and shot her in the head—my beautiful cousin. The shot rang out. Her body crumpled, and she was dragged away by one of the Jewish policemen. Like all the rest, I stood there staring, numbed by what was happening to us.

The first morning after exercise I was set to work with a group of men digging holes in the frozen ground with shovels they had handed out to us. Then in the afternoon we were ordered to fill the holes back up. The next day we were taken to the same place to do the same thing. It was a peculiar feeling. As stupid and hard as it was, digging the holes at first gave me a sense that at least I was doing something that might be used for some purpose. But then we were told to fill them in. And then we repeated the process, one day, then the next, then the next. Digging those holes, then filling them back in, I began to experience a sense of despair that I had not felt before.

One day a group of us were taken for potato-picking outside the camp. We walked out, surrounded by Germans. The fields had been harvested in the fall, and now they were frozen hard. But we were supposed to dig up whatever potatoes might have been missed in the harvest so they could be used for our rotten potato soup. Scrabbling in the frozen dirt with my hands, I was thinking about escape. And coming back at the end of the day, I couldn't get the thought out of my mind. How could I get out of here?

I was sure now that I was going to die unless I could run away somehow. The talk in Kielbasin was all about how we would be transported to work camps. I would hear people say, "We are strong. We'll be able to survive." But I didn't feel that way. I thought, I can't stay alive even here, let alone in some work camp. In a month I'll be dead from hunger and work.

I felt like a trapped rat. I started arguing with my family that we had to do something, we had to run, the Germans were going to kill us. But I got no support. My father would not even think of trying. He was not going to leave his parents, and as far as he was concerned, that was the end of the discussion. My mother, too, had given up thought of escape. She had left her husband once, and she would not do it again. The experience had traumatized her. I could see in her eyes that she had given up. As strong as she had always seemed to me, I knew she was a destroyed woman.

I thought, Maybe they won't go, but I will. All my thoughts and instincts told me to get out. Of course, actually escaping was another matter, especially given Kielbasin's fences and machine-gun towers. But I was thinking all the time about how I might do it.

The day I dug for spoiled potatoes was my sixth in the camp. The next afternoon one of the Jewish policemen approached me and told me that for a watch and a loaf of bread he could give me a chance to escape—not a sure thing, but a chance. I had a watch. I also had the round loaf of bread I had brought along under my coat from the ghetto. I was saving it for an emergency, but this looked like the right thing to spend it on. This was what I had been waiting for. "What is it?" I asked. "What kind of chance?"

"Here's what you do," he said. "Every day in the morning they bring bread in from the ghetto." I had seen the long, horse-drawn bread wagons. "After they're unloaded the wagons go back. What you could do is jump on the back of one of those wagons. The driver won't see you, or if he does, he won't care—they're Jewish anyway. It will look like you came with the wagons as a helper. When you leave, I'll be standing at the gate with the Germans. I'll let you through, but I can't say what the Germans might do; that's the chance you take. Six others are going to try it. There are seven wagons. You can be on the seventh."

When I talked to my father, he wasn't enthusiastic. "You shouldn't do it," he told me. "It's too risky." But I could tell he wasn't sure of himself. "I want to take the chance," I said. "There might not be another one. I'm going to go." "Felix," he said, and I thought he was going to argue. But he didn't. "*Felix, der Eibershter zohl dir hieten.*" May God watch over you. I hugged him, then I hugged my mother. All of us were crying. I had the strong feeling that I would never see either of them again.

The next morning at about nine o'clock I was waiting behind the barracks that was used as a kitchen. The wagons had delivered their loads of bread and were beginning to move off. As the policeman had told me to, I clambered onto the last wagon as it pulled away. I had seen the others jump onto the backs of the first six wagons, and now they were all perched on the tail ends, looking like they belonged.

Once I was sitting there, I was facing backward. The wagon moved slowly as I watched the camp go by, afraid to turn my head around to see what was happening at the front. When we got near the gate I realized I was praying to God that the Germans wouldn't suspect, that they would just let us through. If they caught me, I was dead, just dead. On either side I could see the German guards and the Jewish policemen. Please God, I prayed. Let nothing happen. Let them not stop us. I felt like I was in a kind of daze. Inside my head my voice was repeating, "I'm dead; one stop and I'm dead. I'm dead; one stop and I'm dead." And then I realized the wagon was outside the camp. The gates swung closed behind me.

We were on the highway leading toward Grodno, and I was flooded with relief. But it didn't last long. About fifteen minutes outside the camp I saw two motorcycles coming up behind us. SS men. They pulled up at the head of the convoy and shouted at the drivers to stop and turn around. I couldn't quite make out what they were saying, but it was something about returning to pick up a load that had to go back to the ghetto. The wagons began laboriously circling around, the horses snorting with the effort, the leather harnesses and long wooden beds moaning and creaking.

I thought, Felix, forget it. You're not going back. You're free. You just got out, why would you go back? On either side of the road were deep ditches full of snow. It looked like an easy landing. I jumped and tried to burrow out of sight into the drift. Out of the corner of my eye I noticed that one of the others had also jumped.

I lay still in the ditch buried in snow as the wagons finished their turns and started back down the road. I didn't get up until they had disappeared into the grayness. Then the other jumper and I stood up, brushed ourselves off, and started walking toward Grodno. We didn't know each other. He was a young man from one of the little towns whose Jews had been transported to Kielbasin weeks before. On the way we hitched a ride in a Polish farmer's wagon. We were afraid he might turn us over, but we thought we could always jump off and run if we suspected he was going to. Besides, it was much safer to be riding in a wagon than walking alone down an empty road. He took us all the way to town and we smuggled ourselves into the ghetto, sneaking through one of the places I knew where there were holes in the barbed wire.

When I got back to our apartment, everyone else was still there—Sender and Sarah, Kushka and Lina, Lisa and Mula, Grandpa and Grandma Tema and the others who hadn't been deported. I told everyone the news, including the terrible story of Rinzler shooting Rifka Freydovicz. Grandma Tema told me that she had tried to get us out; she had bribed the Gestapo driver Niestroy with the diamond ring that was the only thing she had left after the robbery. He had taken it, but when none of us came back, they knew he had done nothing.

That night I hid in a closet in the bathroom when the police came to check identity papers, as they often did at night. I was going to have to hide out until new papers could be arranged for me. The next day there was news from Kielbasin, brought back by the wagon drivers: Five people had been hanged in the camp. I knew it had to be the others who had escaped with me.

At the end of December news hit the ghetto that Kielbasin had been evacuated, that all the people there had been sent to another camp. The place was empty. The same day, that evening a few hundred people returned to town from Kielbasin. Among them were my father, mother, sister, and grandparents.

They told us that the Germans ordered everyone to prepare to leave, for a "work camp." But a few hundred people had managed to hide in the barracks and other places around the camp and avoided being taken. They were eventually all found and rounded up, but not until after the convoy had left. Apparently it had been too difficult to get another train ready. Or maybe none was available. So they had been sent back to the ghetto. My father thought that they hadn't been shot because the Germans didn't want news like that to create a panic in the ghetto. The official story was still that everyone was being sent somewhere to labor camps.

My family returned from Kielbasin on January 1, 1943. By this time there were few illusions—though even now the true facts about Auschwitz and Treblinka weren't known. But the *shtetlach* Jews had disappeared—maybe forty thousand people, vanished as though they had never existed. Ghetto Two was gone—eight or nine thousand more. And now several thousand from the deportation we had just survived. Nobody had heard anything from the ones who had been loaded onto trains. All those people, and not one word had gotten back to anyone. It wasn't natural. If they were alive, they would have found a way to communicate. Somebody would have gotten a peasant or a driver or a workman to carry a message. Somebody would have promised that his brother or sister or father would pay if a message was delivered. And it would come. But there had been nothing.

As the rumors about another deportation mounted, people began searching desperately for ways to protect themselves. Fights began over jobs. It stood to reason that in the next transport they would take the ones who were doing nothing useful—the weak and the idle. But people in the shoe shops and clothing shops were making things the German Army needed. A job there could save your life. Or maybe a job as a policeman, or at one of the German companies that had set up business in Grodno (like the Reiffheisen, where Sender and Kushka worked, or the great Todt organization).

Everyone was also thinking of how to hide or maybe even how to get out. How good were your contacts with some Polish friend or former colleague? Maybe some Pole would be kind enough to take you in, even though he would be putting his own head on the line. One thing was for sure: Deportation meant death.

Jammed together like we were, we had fifteen families living in our building. Like everyone else, we set up our hiding places, two of them. The first no one had much faith in. A false partition had been built across one end of the big attic and a clothesline hung in front of it. To anyone who took a casual glance into the attic it would look like the laundry was hanging against the far wall. Meanwhile, behind the wall there was room for at least fifty or sixty people.

The second place was much better. Above the second-floor kitchen ceiling was a crawlspace that extended under the eaves of one side of the roof. At the side of the crawlspace, where the roof angled down, there was no space at all. But at the other end there was maybe a foot and a half. Here, as we found when we tested it, there was just room to squeeze eight people lying flat.

A cleverly designed trapdoor was made in the kitchen ceiling and a ladder readied. If deportations started, the eight chosen people would climb the ladder and get in through the trapdoor. Then the ladder would be removed and taken somewhere else. There wouldn't be an inch to move, but this hiding hole would be almost impossible to find.

But who would be assigned to this space? After discussion it was decided that each group in the building could send a young person or a young couple to the kitchen ceiling. Meir and Chaya Rajgrodsky would go—the younger brother and sister of Sender's wife, Sarah. Then sixteen-year-old Dodchik Fein and the Efroimson sisters, Mima and Lila. From our family, my mother's youngest sister, Fania, her husband, Berko; and me. We were the chosen survivors. The rest would go to the big attic.

In the middle of January, two weeks after my parents re-

turned from Kielbasin, the ghetto was sealed. Police surrounded
the barbed wire perimeter. A list was circulated with the names of
the essential workers and others who had a *lebens schein,* a dispen-
sation to stay. These were the people judged "worthy to live." From
our family only Sender, Kushka, and their families were on the list.
They were given special passes and told to go to a place near the Judenrat building, where they would stay during the action. The rest
of us were ordered to the Grand Synagogue for transportation.
Everyone without a special pass would be taken—a huge number.
People were saying ten thousand, that this was a transport of ten
thousand. The Germans were beginning to clean out the ghetto.

The transport started at night. Even before the telltale
sounds began, we sensed it was under way. Inside the house everyone made for the hiding places. The eight of us who had been chosen climbed up the ladder into the crawlspace above the kitchen;
then the ladder was taken away and we closed the trapdoor. I was
jammed there in the dark next to Berko on one side and Chaya
Rajgrodsky on the other.

From outside we heard noises, screaming, and the barking of dogs. Shots rang out—single shots, then volleys. Voices
shouted in German. This transport wasn't like the others; people
weren't all going quietly. The crawlspace was close and hot. Nobody made a sound. As tense as I was, I thought we had a chance
here. I knew that Sender and Kushka had taken special precautions
to protect us. They had given ten rubles in gold to Isser Schwartz
and Nyonka Levin, two Jewish policemen who were friends of
theirs. To the extent that they could, they were going to deflect any
searches away from the kitchen.

The day passed. We kept hearing shouts and shooting
from outside as the roundup continued. From the house, though,
everything seemed quiet. We thought we had heard people come
in at one point, but we weren't sure. By now, though, Berko and
his wife—my aunt Fania—were beginning to break down. They
were dying with fear for their infant son, Haim, whom they had
not been able to bring with them into the crawlspace.

All the others in the house were hiding in the big attic behind the partition, except for the young children, who could not be prevented from crying. It had been decided that these children could not be allowed in; they would be too much of a danger to the rest. Fania's baby, Haim, was one. My aunt Lisa had also been unable to take her two-and-a-half-year-old daughter into the attic. She had had three children, one of whom had died in the ghetto the year before. The other was older, but she had had to leave her little girl. Another family, the Dworetskis, also had to leave a child out. They were a couple in their fifties already who had had a miracle child born to them a year earlier. That child, too, could not be hidden.

When it had become obvious that none of the young children could be taken, my grandfather Freydovicz decided that he would stay with them. He refused to go into hiding; he would remain with the babies and take care of them. My wonderful grandmother Tema left her husband and was taken to hide in the attic with the others. But the stern old businessman would not go. He stayed downstairs with the three children, two of them his grandchildren, one not, waiting for the Germans.

In the crawlspace the pain was indescribable. Fania was twenty-three years old, eight years older than I. She had had the baby in the ghetto, and we all lived in the same room. I would see her nursing him, this baby Haim. She had been able to keep her anguish inside at first, but we had been there for a full day now and she couldn't stand it any longer. What was happening with their child? She was racked with sobbing. Berko was whispering to her, trying to console her. "We'll make more children," he was saying. "We love each other. We'll have others. We're still young, we'll build a new life." But she wanted her baby. "Where are they? What's going on? It's already twenty-eight hours we've been here. Please go down. Please look. Please see what happened to him." She pleaded with him, even though it was almost sure that they were already gone. The noises had stopped for some time. We could hear nothing but silence. But Berko wouldn't go. He was scared. He could not physically make himself go.

I couldn't bear it. I was squeezed in next to them listening to every word, every whisper. I just could not stand her pain. My heart was beating. I felt a choking sensation and pressure in my chest. Finally I said I would go, I would go down and see what had happened.

We opened the trapdoor. Fania was lying closest to it, then Berko, then me. I rolled over on top of them to get to the opening. The ladder, of course, was gone, but there was a pipe on the wall that I could just reach. I grabbed hold of it, swung myself over, and slid down.

The house was dead quiet. I made my way carefully through our apartment. But the rooms were empty. There wasn't a soul. I did a quick search through the other rooms, but there was no one.

Then I went back to the kitchen, where Fania and Berko were waiting behind the open trapdoor. "Sorry," I looked up at them. "Sorry. Everyone is gone. There's no one left."

Then I started to shinny up the pipe. I grasped it, wrapped my legs around it, and started to inch my way up. But I couldn't do it. I'd climb a couple of feet, then feel myself begin to slide down, climb again and slide down. I didn't have the strength to keep from slipping. I knew where the ladder was, but I couldn't bring it. It would betray us all. I tried again and got almost to the top. Berko reached down to catch me, to help me up to safety, but our hands couldn't quite reach. We were inches away, but then I slipped again. I was desperate to get up. I had the feeling that a German could come in at any moment.

Finally I said, "Okay, it's no use. I'll go to the attic with the others. You close yourselves up there." Berko and I looked at each other. Then he put the trapdoor back in place.

A GIFT FROM GOD

WHEN I got over to the hiding place in the big attic, everyone was there. The Germans hadn't found them. In whispers they asked why I had come. What had happened? I told them the story. I said that when I searched the house I couldn't find anybody. Grandpa and the three children were gone. When I said this, a muffled sob came from my aunt Lisa, whose little daughter had been with Grandfather. She slumped down to the floor. Off to the side, Mrs. Dworetski collapsed into her husband's arms.

A day passed. Sometime toward evening we heard footsteps on the stairs and German voices. Soldiers were in the attic. Behind the partition no one breathed; there wasn't a movement or a sound, just a perfect stillness in which we could hear with utter clarity the shuffle of the soldiers, the creaking of the floorboards, and the brief exchanges of words. We all knew that in a moment we'd see their faces come around the false partition. But the next minute we heard the boots on the stairs again and the sounds moving away from us. It wasn't until they were well down the stairs that I realized I was breathing again.

We kept ourselves closed up in the attic all that night and through the next day. Then on the third evening the street sounds began to seem more normal, as if the people who had not been deported were coming back from wherever they had been kept during the action. Tentatively we ventured out, absorbing the fact that we had been spared. But when we went to the kitchen to get the others, we stared at the ceiling in shocked silence. The trapdoor was open. The crawlspace was empty. They had all been taken.

In three days the ghetto had been emptied of ten thousand people—the "transport of the ten thousand," as everybody was now calling it. Of Grodno's thirty thousand Jews, only seven or eight thousand were left.

From the sworn testimony of Moshe Notes, given at the Cologne Nazi trial:

My family was taken first. I hid and was brought to the synagogue later, at dusk sometime between January 15 and January 18. When you came into the synagogue there was first a large foyer. Wiese was standing there, between the foyer and the sanctuary. Inside it was already quite full of people and their baggage.

The sanctuary was reasonably well lit and I found my family. We stood a little to the side. Then Wiese appeared, wearing his dark coveralls and his hat. As he entered, everybody began to shout, "Wiese! Wiese! Wiese!" and immediately the shooting began. I saw him holding his pistol in his hand and pulling the trigger, shooting into the mass of people. Among those shot were children. There was a lot of blood.

When we left the synagogue we had to step over dead men, women, and children. We then went to a railroad freight station. From there we came to Birkenau during the night of Friday to Saturday. This was a camp next to Auschwitz.*

From the "Hefte von Auschwitz," the official Auschwitz arrival records:

JANUARY 20, 1943. RSHA TRANSPORT. JEWS FROM GRODNO. 155 MEN WITH THE NUMBERS 90822–90976 AND 101 WOMEN WITH THE NUMBERS 30035–30135 WERE SELECTED FOR THE CAMP. THE OTHERS WERE GASSED.

JANUARY 21, 1943. RSHA TRANSPORT. JEWS FROM GRODNO. 175 MEN WITH THE NUMBERS 91115–91289 AND 112 WOMEN WITH THE NUMBERS 30136–30247 WERE SELECTED FOR THE CAMP. THE OTHERS WERE GASSED.

JANUARY 22, 1943. RSHA TRANSPORT. APPROXIMATELY 3,650 JEWS FROM THE GRODNO GHETTO. IN THE SELECTION 365 MEN WITH THE NUMBERS 92544–93143 AND 229 WOMEN WITH THE NUMBERS 30771–30999 WERE SELECTED FOR THE CAMP. THE OTHERS WERE GASSED.

JANUARY 23, 1943. RSHA TRANSPORT. JEWS FROM GRODNO. 235 MEN WITH THE NUMBERS 92909–93143 AND 191 WOMEN WITH THE NUMBERS 31000–31190 WERE SELECTED FOR THE CAMP. THE OTHERS WERE GASSED.

JANUARY 24, 1943. RSHA TRANSPORT. JEWS FROM GRODNO. 166 MEN WITH THE NUMBERS 93313–93478 AND 60 WOMEN WITH THE NUMBERS 31362–31421 WERE COMMITTED TO THE CAMP. THE OTHERS WERE GASSED.†

*Klarsfeld, Vol. V, pp. 208–210.
†Klarsfeld, Summary Volume, p. 129.

Over the next few days a trickle of people who had managed to escape the transport made their way back into the ghetto. They told stories of having run off from the column as they were being marched to the train station. Many had tried, they said, but most had been shot down.

To our amazement and joy, Meir and Chaya Rajgrodsky showed up among the escapees. Then Dodchik Fein and the Efroimson girls arrived, and Berko. They had all managed to get away before the column reached the train station. So had Fania, Berko said. They had fled together at the bridge out of the city, but in the shooting and confusion they had gotten separated and afterward he hadn't been able to find her. He had hoped she was already back.

They told us the Gestapo had found them in the crawl-space not long after I had slipped down the pipe for the last time. The Germans had been led to the hideout by Isser Schwartz, one of the Jewish policemen Sender and Kushka had paid to keep them away. They had all been taken to the Grand Synagogue and marched from there toward the railroad station. Someone had seen my grandfather in the crowd, riding in a horse-drawn sledge. They had caught a last glimpse of him sitting in the back, bare-headed in the minus-twenty-degree cold, cradling the three babies in his arms.

Berko was distraught over Fania's disappearance, but a day later she walked into the house. I hung on her words as she de-scribed how after she and Berko lost each other she had walked through the forest to Losossna, several miles away. Before the war the Freydoviczes had owned several dachas there, in the woods overlooking the river. I knew the place very well. Most of the sum-mer houses had been rented out, but we always used one ourselves. I had spent almost all the summers of my life in the Losossna woods.

In Losossna Fania had gone to the house of Jan and Janova Puchalski, who for many years had been caretakers of the Freydovicz dachas. Janova Puchalski had taken her in and had said that she could hide with her as long as she'd like. But she had only stayed one night. The Puchalskis had five children and lived in a tiny two-room house; it hadn't seemed to her as if anyone could stay hidden there for long. Besides, Fania wanted to get back to Berko. She was sure he had made it into the ghetto. Together they could make other plans for escape.

While I was listening to Fania and Berko I decided that if I had to hide for one or two nights, Janova Puchalski would probably help me, too. The idea that I might actually call on someone for help was something of a revelation to me. Our experiences with the Poles had mostly been different, including with my sister's nanny. She had nursed Mira and had lived with us for several years. But when we were closed into the ghetto, she had talked with my mother over the barbed wire. Afterward my mother had come in extremely upset. The nanny had asked her for her clothing. "The Germans are going to kill you anyway," she had said. "So why not give them to me?" Coming from a person who had lived with us, this callousness had had an effect on me. Until I heard Fania talk about Janova Puchalski, it hadn't really occurred to me that I might call on someone out there.

•

With the Jewish population about a fourth of its original size, the Germans now contracted the ghetto, cordoning off a small area for the remaining seven or eight thousand to live in. Because our house was in the section turned back to the Poles, we had to change places. We ended up in the large building that housed the Judenrat—in the apartment of the Halpern family, old friends of my mother and father.

Here we had only part of a room. Conditions were so crowded that there wasn't enough space for everybody to sleep. Everyone else was also doubling and tripling up; the Judenrat building and all the other buildings in the shrunken ghetto were overflowing. At night the hallways were filled with sleeping people, though they weren't as packed as the apartments.

With a little more space in the hall, that's where my

grandma Tema slept. I hardly recognized her now. She had been persuaded by the others to hide when Grandpa had stayed in the living room with the babies. But afterward she was a broken person. She had been a tower of strength before; now she was finished. There was no more love in this most loving of people, no more thought, no more anything. She looked to me as if she was among the living dead. Tema had been such a powerful soul. Now she had turned into a husk.

So many of the people around me seemed to be going away, either physically or mentally. My mother, too, was broken, abstracted in her grief. That time she had left my father had ended her thoughts of escape. Now she was defeated, resigned. Like Grandma Tema, she was waiting for death to come to take her.

But others in the family were thinking about Losossna. With Janova the caretaker out there, maybe that would be a chance. After all, she had helped Fania, and she had seemed willing to do even more than she had. If people escaped, maybe she would give them food. Maybe they could hide there for a night on the way to somewhere else. But how long could anyone stay in that tiny place? There had to be somewhere to go. But where? Into the forest, yes, but it was bitter cold. People were talking about all kinds of plans, fantastic thoughts, wild ideas. Not one of them made sense to me.

Ever since I had gotten new identification papers I had been working as a laborer again alongside my friend Leon Trachtenberg, hauling fifty-kilo bags of cement, mixing concrete, and laying bricks. We were both sure that soon the Germans would take another bite of the ghetto, maybe even finish it off this time. We needed a plan of our own. I told Leon I knew a place. If we could get out together we could go to Janova Puchalski's first. From there we could figure out what to do next. It wasn't much of a plan—no better than the others I was hearing. But having a place for one night might save our lives. Since the work gang was sometimes split into groups and sent to different sites, we agreed that if we smelled trouble we would meet back at the main workplace—

the unfinished Gestapo headquarters. From there we would make a run for Losossna.

On Friday, February 12, I got up for work as usual, and my mother cut me a hunk of bread for breakfast. As I ate she came over, took my head in her hands, and kissed me, not something she did very often. I was still thinking about it as I met up with Leon and the rest of our work crew.

At Gestapo headquarters that morning they divided us up, and my group was sent to the house of Errelis, chief of the Grodno area Gestapo. The rest, including Leon, stayed behind to work at the headquarters.

I spent that morning in Errelis's basement, where we were rebuilding a bathroom. But at about eleven o'clock I sneaked off and bought a half bottle of vodka to smuggle back into the ghetto. Getting away wasn't a problem; we weren't guarded. The Germans knew how many of us there were, and they knew we had nowhere to go. But it made buying things easy, and I did that almost every morning. My smuggling was all we had to live on these days.

When I got back to Errelis's place the others had gotten big news: The ghetto was closed; the Germans had started rounding people up for another transport. The work gang was in a frenzy. Everyone was repeating what they had heard. Supposedly the Germans were taking women and children especially. Many had already been gathered and sent off. Nobody knew what was true, but part of it, at least, wasn't rumor. We had been ordered to go back. A truck was being sent to pick us up.

As soon as I heard that, I started walking. I had no intention of waiting for the Germans to come to get me. As fast as I could, I went back to the lady who had sold me the vodka, someone I had bought from before and knew slightly. I begged her to hide me. "Just for today," I said. "Please, hide me for one day. There's a transport right now. Just take me for a day, then I'll leave." "No," she said, "I can't do it. You're a nice boy. I like you a lot, and it's a shame, but I can't do it. My husband would kill me."

I begged, I did everything I could to persuade her. I wished I could offer her something, anything at all. But I had nothing. Even my watch was gone, given to the policeman back in Kielbasin. Finally she said, "No! Absolutely not! Go back to the ghetto." That was it; she just wouldn't do it. I had nowhere else to turn and no idea what to do. Slowly I walked back to Errelis's house, trying frantically to think if there was somewhere nearby I might hide. I needed to find cover; then when things calmed down a bit I would get out to Janova Puchalski's.

When I arrived back to the Gestapo chief's house it was empty. While I was gone, the truck had come and taken everybody. I couldn't go to the main site to get Leon; I was sure his group had been taken before we were. I was utterly alone. As I was wondering what to do, Errelis's Great Dane came up and began to nuzzle my leg. He was supposed to be a guard dog and I was a little frightened of him, but now he seemed friendly. I leaned down to pet him, and I lost myself in thought.

For some reason my mind seemed to be working with a terrible exactness, very precise and ordered. The first thing to do, it told me, is take out the half bottle of vodka and drink it. I opened the bottle and drank the whole thing; the liquid seemed too precious to waste. Now, it said, take the yellow stars off your jacket. I did. Number three, go find Heidemak's lady friend, the one who hid you before.

I walked and walked, the snow crunching under my feet, but I could not seem to find the place. Nothing looked exactly right to me. I thought, Felix, it could be you are a little drunk. I knew it was a small house somewhere near Konopnicki's, but it seemed to have disappeared. Okay, I thought, the next plan is to go to the nanny who hid Sender's children when we tried to escape the first time—the time we got out through the hole in the cellar wall. She had kept them for almost a week then, although afterward she had brought them back to the ghetto. They looked too Jewish, she had told Sender, they're circumcised. People would start asking questions. She had given the children back, but I knew she had a good heart. If she took the babies for a week, I thought, maybe she'll take me at least to sleep overnight.

By now it was starting to get dark. I realized I was on Dominikanska Gasse, the main street of the town. On one side behind the stores and shops that fronted the street was the ghetto; on the other, the Polish area. Among the stores was a barbershop, and looking in the window I saw that one of the barbers was a Polish boy I had gone to school with during the Soviet occupation. I slipped in the door and caught his eye. He smiled at me and came over. For a moment I thought that maybe he would have a place for me to stay. But instead he whispered in my ear that it was too dangerous, I would have to leave.

As I stepped out of the door, two German soldiers materialized in front of me; I hadn't even seen them. They said something to me, and I said something back that I could tell was not too coherent. Then they told me to go home. They hadn't even suspected. What Jewish boy would be wandering around the streets drunk, especially on a day like this?

I crossed the bridge over the Nieman and managed to find the nanny's house. By now it was dark, curfew time. From inside I could hear singing and loud voices. Looking in the window, I saw that there was some kind of party going on. After a while I saw the nanny, and as she came close to the window, I knocked. She turned and looked out; then she saw me through the glass. A moment later she was whispering to me at the back door. "Felix," she said, "here's what to do. Go out back to the stable and sleep with the cow. Then in the morning you can escape. If anybody finds you, I didn't have anything to do with it."

That night I slept with the cow on the straw of its stall, sure that I would wake up to find it kicking me or goring me with its horns. But the night passed peacefully. The next morning the nanny came out to take care of the cow and brought me some porridge. I was ravenous; I hadn't eaten since breakfast the previous morning. When I finished, I left the bowl in the straw and walked toward Losossna, thinking about Janova Puchalski and her husband, Jan.

I wondered why Janova hadn't occurred to me before. She was someone I had known forever. Each summer since I could remember, her older children and I had played together. She herself used to take me with her sometimes when she went visiting or shopping, and on special occasions she would milk her goat and give me some to drink. I remembered that once while she was pulling the goat's teats the milk spritzed up into my face, which made us both laugh. The milk was always foamy, and you were supposed to drink it right away. It had a strong goat odor, which I hated. But on the other hand, it was considered an extremely healthy drink, so I always downed it without complaining.

Janova was a strong, determined woman, big-boned and robust. She used to tell the children what to do in firm tones, but she was also warm and kind to them. I liked her very much, and I knew that she liked me. She would give me a kiss when she saw me and hold my hand when we went out. In some ways she reminded me of my grandma Tema before fate broke her. Although they were so different, there was something similar about their characters. People naturally felt their warmth and gravitated toward them. They were both powerhouses.

Janova's husband, Jan, was a big man with huge, heavy hands. I used to stare at his fingers when I was young. Each finger seemed enormous and powerful all by itself. I knew he had been in the army earlier, and I thought he must have been a good soldier. He was a very handsome man, with a mustache. He never said much to me. In fact, it seemed as if he did not talk much at all. I had the feeling that Janova was the one who ran the family.

It was late in the morning when I came out of the Losossna woods and knocked on the Puchalskis' door. When it opened, Janova was standing there. Her broad face lit with surprise; then she took me in her arms and kissed me. "Pani Janova," I said, "can you let me stay here for a night?" She looked at me.

"Just one night. After that I'll go." "Felix," she said, "you'll go nowhere." Then she took me inside and closed the door.

The Puchalski house had a small kitchen and two rooms. The family—Janova, Jan, the three teenage girls who had been my childhood playmates, and two little ones, three and one—used both rooms as bedrooms. Inside it was steamy and warm, though coming from our life in the ghetto, the house didn't seem all that crowded. I started to talk. I needed a place for a night, but she shouldn't worry. I wasn't going to stay. I was going to go into the forest and find the partisans. "Felix," Janova said when she had sat me down on one of the beds, "that's a crazy idea. It's the middle of the winter, and you don't know where to go. Besides, the partisans would probably just kill you. Stay here with us. I don't want you going anywhere. God sent you to me as a gift. We'll take care of you."

Later that morning, after she had fed me, Janova told me the story of what had happened to her when she was pregnant with her second daughter, Sabina. One night, she said, her husband had come home drunk. Jan was usually a good man, but sometimes he had too much to drink. That night he had thrown her out of the house. She didn't own a penny, and she had nowhere to go. Finally she walked to Grodno and told Grandma Tema what had happened. Tema took her in. She gave her a place to live and made arrangements for her to have her baby in Grodno's Jewish hospital. Of course, I had never heard this story before. It was just one of the thousands of Tema's good deeds, none of which she ever mentioned to anybody.

"So you see," Janova said, "you are a gift to me from God. I will not let you perish, Felix. If you perish, we will all perish together. But there is no question that you will survive. You do not go anyplace."

HOT, FETID, AND BLACKER THAN NIGHT

THAT evening I was lying in bed in the smaller room, half asleep. Suddenly the door flew open and somebody jumped in with me. "Shhh," came a whisper. "Don't say anything." I wanted to shout, but all that I managed was a muffled "Sender!" I threw my arms around him and kissed him. "Sender"—I couldn't believe it—"Sender, what happened?"

Sender's story was hair-raising. He, too, had been at work the day before at a construction site—the Royal Hotel. At about eleven o'clock his group had suddenly been surrounded by German soldiers and marched back to the ghetto. As they got near the entrance gate, Sender saw that people were being lined up and divided into two groups. Wiese himself was doing the selection, sending some to the right and some to the left. It was obvious what was happening: On the right were the saved, on the left the damned. Sender saw his brother Kushka on the right, and as he got near the selection point, he felt confident Wiese would choose him, too.

But although Sender was strong and fit, when it came his turn he was pushed to the left. But he didn't stay there. When Wiese turned his head, Sender moved quickly over to the other group. But Wiese saw him and grabbed him by the collar. "Turn around and walk," he said. Fatal words. One of Wiese's favorite tricks was to question people, tell them to turn around and walk, then shoot them in the back of the head.

Instead of walking, Sender took off down Chasna Street, a narrow alley that led away from the entrance. In his younger days he had been a renowned soccer player for the Grodno Maccabi team, especially famous for his speed. By the time Wiese got his submachine gun unlimbered, Sender was halfway down the street, zigzagging for all he was worth and running faster than he had ever thought about running on a soccer field. The hail of bullets Wiese sent down the alley ricocheted off the walls and the pavement at his feet but somehow managed to miss their target.

Before any of the Germans could go after him, Sender had lost himself in one of the little alleys that ran off Chasna. Picking up a loose brick from the pavement, he found a hiding spot and waited, hoping he could brain whoever came along before they had a chance to shoot him. A couple of minutes later a Jewish policeman came around the corner, obviously looking for him. When he got close, Sender stepped out with the brick in his hand. "I'll kill you if you get any closer," he said. "Take it easy," said the policeman. "I'm not going to turn you in. But you should know they're all looking for you. They're planning to hang you as soon as they get their hands on you. You'd better hide somewhere better than this."

Eventually Sender got into the apartment building where Mottl Bass lived, the Farbindungsman who was one of the liaisons with the Gestapo. In the second-floor corridor he found a toilet room and closed himself in, still clutching the brick. A while later Bass came out, opened the door to the compartment, and there was Sender.

"You know they're searching for you all over," said Bass, startled. "There's an order out for you to be hung. You've got to get away from here." Sender told him that he had a place in mind, but first he needed Bass to go to his brother Kushka, who had been selected out of the transport. He knew that Kushka was carrying a five-ruble gold piece with him. "Tell Kushka I'm alive and get the gold piece for me in case I have to bribe somebody."

When Bass came back with the money, Sender told him, "Look, you know better than anybody what's going on. You know they're eventually going to kill you, too, just like they're killing everybody else. I've got this place I'm going to, at least until the transport is over. I think maybe they'll hide you and your wife, too, for a day or so. If you want, you can come there." Then he told him about Janova Puchalski's.

That evening Sender slipped out through the no man's

land that had been part of the ghetto before the Germans contracted it. By then he knew that the remaining women and children had been rounded up and sent off to the railroad sidings early in the day. Sarah was gone, and his babies Haim and Abrasha. In a state of shock, he had managed to make his way across the Polish area and over the bridge. It was just before curfew, and the streets were almost empty. Nobody stopped him and nobody saw him. When he arrived at Janova's door he still had Kushka's five-ruble piece in his pocket.

On Sunday morning Janova decided that Sender and I should go up to the attic. Neighbors had a way of stopping by unannounced, and she didn't want to take any chances that somebody might walk in on us. Since I had gotten to Janova's I had been in bed, mostly sleeping. But now the shock of the past two days was wearing off and I was experiencing the most violent inner turmoil. I felt I had to know what was going on back in the ghetto. What had happened to my parents and Mira? "They're probably hiding," I told Sander. "I've got to go back and get them." I knew what the hiding arrangements were, and I was assailed by the thought that I could find them and bring them out here. I couldn't stand the idea of leaving them there for the Germans. "Maybe the transport didn't catch them, maybe they've saved themselves, like we did last time. I have to go back for them."

But Sender was having none of it: "You're not going." His voice was a raspy whisper. "You wouldn't have a chance. They'll catch you and kill you. They're gone already. They've taken almost everybody this time. Even if you found them hiding, what makes you think your parents would come out with you? You know your father won't leave his parents, and you think your mother would leave him? Besides, if you got to the hiding place, the others wouldn't let you go back out anyway; they'd be too afraid you might get caught and betray them. You'd just be trapped yourself. Then you'd be dead, too. Forget it."

"But Sender, it's Sunday. You know the Germans don't

do anything on Sunday. I know I could get back. Please let me go. I've got to see what's happening."

"Listen, Felix," he said, "you're completely crazy. Your chances are zero, and you are not going back there. That's all there is to it!"

So I didn't go. I was haunted by it. I knew Sender was right; the chances were terrible, maybe zero, as he said. But it was Sunday, the Germans' day of rest. If ever I could smuggle myself back, it would be today. But the time for it was slipping by. Deep inside I felt that if I didn't go I would never forget it, maybe never get over it. But there was Sender next to me and there was no more arguing with him. How could I get out?

I lay on the attic floor in a state of intense agitation as the day passed and night fell. My black thoughts were interrupted only when Janova stuck her head up into the attic and said, "Come down. Four of your friends just arrived."

When we got downstairs there were Mottl Bass; his wife, Goldie; Borka Shulkes, another Farbindungsman; and Meir Zamoszczanski, one of the Jewish policemen. That made thirteen people in the house, the seven Puchalskis and now all of a sudden six of us. "It's too many," said Janova. "You have to go outside, to the potato cellar."

The potato cellar, out back about thirty yards from the house, was pitch dark and full of potatoes that felt like stones as we all tried to find some comfortable way of sitting or lying down. When we did, Bass told Sender and me what had happened.

After Sender left, Bass had talked the situation over with his wife. They knew Sender was right. Their turn was coming, Farbindungsman or no Farbindungsman. This transport was clearing out most of those who had survived the "transport of ten thousand" a month earlier. After this, Bass thought, only a couple of thousand would be left, and how long would the Germans let them live?

Bass knew where the Freydovicz summer houses were,

and he trusted Sender's word about being allowed to stay at the Puchalskis'. But with all the Germans around and a transport going on he didn't know if he and his wife could get out by themselves. They would have a better chance with the help of a Jewish policeman. So Bass went to Meir Zamoszczanski and told him that they had a place to hide outside the city. If Zamoszczanski could get them out, he could come with them. He also told Borka Shulkes, the second Farbindungsman, who was a good friend of his. Shulkes said that his wife was already in hiding outside the city; he was looking for a way to escape the ghetto and join her. Maybe Zamoszczanski could get the three of them out.

That was how the Basses, Shulkes, and Zamoszczanski had ended up at the Puchalskis'. Now we had to decide what to do. The potato cellar had no future as a hiding place. Food would have to be brought in and out, assuming we could find a way of getting food. The Puchalskis could barely keep their own children fed. There would have to be a way to get excrement out. With six people living there, somebody would be sure to notice suspicious activity. Besides, the place was obvious. If anyone suspected Jews might be hiding at the Puchalskis, the potato cellar would be the first place they'd look.

From an account of the German action of February 13 written by an unidentified Grodno Jew, found after the war in the ground outside Treblinka

The next morning word got out that the ghetto had been closed. Nobody would be allowed to go out to work. However, the Jewish laborers already working outside had left the ghetto as usual between 6 and 7 A.M.

By then we had enough experience to know that a closing meant the ghetto would be liquidated. Indeed, that proved to be true and soon the two henchmen Wiese and Streblow drove in on a sled and started shooting automatic weapons at the workers who were assembled on the Rynek. The people were driven into the synagogue. Operation "Catch a Jew" commenced immediately. The first victims were the members of the Judenrat and their staff, who at that time were staying in the rooms assigned to them, along with the occupants of Number 3 Ulica Zamkowa. I, too, was led into the synagogue.

More and more Jews were pulled out of their hiding places and brought to the synagogue. Around noon the Jewish laborers who had left for work in the morning came back. They were rounded up immediately at the entrance and brought to the synagogue. They had no idea what had happened since they left.

After a few hours even the people who had been living in "isolation rooms" were brought in, those who had particular value, or those who had tried to flee. The whole day I was thinking how to escape from the synagogue. But it was only about 7 P.M. that I had a chance to get out unnoticed and hide in my apartment at Ulica Zamkowa Number 11. That night was quiet because Wiese and Streblow went to rest after their "successful" day of work. In the morning hours a transport of 1,500 people left in the direction of Bialystok.

Sunday brought no change. The ghetto looked lifeless. In the streets only Jewish police could be seen; nobody else dared show themselves. Everybody down to the last person was in hiding. Around noon I took the risk, together with engineer Kuznezen, to leave our hiding place and look for our families.

I found my family waiting for me in our old apartment. We thought about what to do, then went to our hiding place, where we remained until Monday afternoon. Around 5 P.M., however, the chief of the Jewish police, Srebnick, betrayed us to our executioners. They came together with him and led us off to the synagogue.

During the night, around 3 A.M., a transport was assembled of the people who were imprisoned there. We were led to the railroad station at the Poleska siding and loaded onto passenger and freight cars. The train was heavily guarded by German police.

The train made only one short stop, in Bialystok. Then it went on to Treblinka.*

The court noted at the Bielefeld Nazi trial that there were no known survivors of the February transports. The *Documents Concerning the Destruction of the Jews of Grodno* summarizes as follows:

---

*Klarsfeld, Vol. III, pp. 367–370.

AT LEAST THREE TRANSPORTS WERE SENT TO TREBLINKA. . . . ONE TRAIN, NO. PJ (POLISH JEWS) 163, LEFT GRODNO FOR TREBLINKA ON FEBRUARY 14. THIS CAN BE DE-RIVED FROM THE SCHEDULE NO. 552 OF THE *GENRAIBETRIEBSLEITUNG OST* (GEN-ERAL DIRECTORATE, EASTERN RAILWAY). THE TRAIN BORE THE SERIAL ROUTING NUMBER 122. AN ADDITIONAL TRAIN, PJ 165, LEFT GRODNO FOR TREBLINKA ON FEBRUARY 16, 1943. MOREOVER, THE COURT IS CONVINCED THAT A TRANSPORT TRAIN HAD ALREADY DEPARTED FROM GRODNO TO TREBLINKA ON FEBRUARY 13. ACCORDING TO THE SCHEDULE NO. 552, TRAIN PJ 135 WAS SCHEDULED TO DEPART BIALYSTOK FOR TREBLINKA. HOWEVER, THIS DID NOT OCCUR BECAUSE THE PARTIAL LIQUIDATION IN BIALYSTOK HAD BEEN CONCLUDED ALREADY ON FEBRUARY 12, ONE DAY EARLIER THAN ORIGINALLY PLANNED. THE COURT BE-LIEVES THAT THIS TRAIN IS IDENTICAL WITH PJ 135, WHICH WAS REROUTED TO GRODNO AND THEN DEPARTED WITH A FULL LOAD OF DEPORTEES FOR TRE-BLINKA ON FEBRUARY 13.*

From an account by Samuel Willenberg, a Treblinka survivor from Czestochowa, in *The Death Camp Treblinka,* ed. Alexander Donat. New York: Holocaust Library, 1979:

That night brought us further surprises. We suddenly heard the hoot of a locomo-tive. It could only be the arrival of a new transport. . . . After a while I heard a human shriek, a desperate cry for help. Rude curses, and then a shot rang out, then a second and a third. Outside, the shrieks mingled with the sound of feet running. Someone pounded violently on the door of our barracks. The knocking was insis-tent; one could recognize in it the fear and despair which precede death. . . .

Outside the firing went on without a stop. Single shots, the rat-tat-tat of a machine gun, the groans of the wounded, the shouts of the pursued, the calls of sentries—all these frightened us and threw us into terrible tension. . . .

In the morning we learned that a transport of Jews from Grodno had arrived during the night. When they were taken out of the boxcars, the people realized what was about to happen to them. The red glow of the flames, the barbed wire fences, the watchtowers—all that could be seen in the darkness which was illumi-nated by the flames—goaded them into resistance. They were ordered to undress, but they rushed at the SS men with knives and the battle blazed in all its intensity. The Jews defended themselves with the strength of despair. Since they had no

*Klarsfeld, Summary Volume, pp. 121, 122.

weapons, they attacked the Germans with bottles. The transport comprised about 2,000 people, including many women and children. Not all of them took part in the battle. Some of them just prayed. There was never any doubt that the revolt would end with the defeat of the unfortunates. The machine guns reaped a harvest of blood; the new arrivals fell in the roll-call square. Of the Germans, three SS men were mortally wounded. They were removed to the nearby hospital. When we came out of our barracks in the morning a terrible sight met our eyes. The roll-call square was strewn with blood-soaked Jewish bodies. During the night the soft snow had swaddled them in a coat whiter than white.

On the night of Sunday, February 15, Sender went into the house to talk the situation over with Jan and Janova. When he came back, he had an entire plan worked out. "We are going to dig a little cellar," he said, "under the second room." Sender had figured the amount of space we'd need, how it could be dug, where we could put the excavated earth to avoid signs of digging, and how the place could be ventilated. The Puchalskis were nervous about the number of people, but they had agreed. Jan would help with the digging.

The next two nights the men dug into the dirt under Jan and Janova's bedroom floor. Meanwhile, the three teenage Puchalski girls—Sabina, Irena, and Krystyna—kept watch outside, all of us ready to run into the woods the moment we heard the signal that someone was coming. The earth was carried out in buckets and dumped, in the yard, into an unused well that had originally been put in to supply the dachas.

By the end of the second night the hiding place was ready—a hole about five feet wide, five and a half feet long, and four feet deep. To me it looked like a grave. It seemed impossible that Sender expected six of us to get down into it, let alone live there. An air channel had been dug out to the yard where it came up behind the garden. Now the bare bushes partly masked the outlet hole; in spring and summer, Sender said, the cover would be better. We were in mid-February; I looked into the pit again and couldn't believe anyone was thinking about the summer. The

Puchalskis moved the doghouse to that side of the house and tied up Muszka, their dog. If the Germans came, any smells from the hole might seem to be coming from the dog. If the Germans had a dog, it would be distracted by the Puchalskis' animal. On the floor of the hole fresh straw had been spread. The ceiling was the bedroom floor, out of which a small rectangle had been carefully cut under where one of the beds usually was. Once we were inside the hole, the rectangle would be fitted back and covered with shoes or clothes. Then the bed would be pushed back over it.

On the third night the six of us climbed down into the hole and arranged ourselves. There was room for three people to lie on the floor. Two others could sit between their feet. The last could sit on the small tin bucket that would serve as our toilet. I pressed in next to Bass, who was lying next to his wife. Sender, Zamoszczanski, and Shulkes sat between our bent knees, Shulkes on the bucket's wooden lid. I watched as the trapdoor slid into place above us. Outside, the temperature was well below zero. Inside it was hot, fetid, and blacker than night. Not a single crack of light came in through the floor. It occurred to me that if you weren't already dead when they lowered you into your grave, you would probably suffocate to death once you got closed up in it.

In the hole there was no talk, only an occasional whisper. We knew that if somebody else was in the house, any sound could betray us. The little children, Wladek and Wanda, were a terrible danger, too; at three and one they were old enough to give us away but had no way of understanding what the consequences would be for everyone if they did. They didn't even know we were there. They had stared at us when we arrived, wondering at the number of strange people in the house. But we had moved out to the potato cellar quickly, and the digging had gone on at night, while they were asleep. We couldn't afford to do anything that might attract their attention.

I lay there for a while trying to get used to the whole idea. I couldn't. Then I must have slipped off to sleep, because sometime later I was awakened by the flickering flame of the tiny oil lamp Janova had given Sender. "It's time to change," he said.

We had decided that it made sense to rotate positions. That way nobody would get cramped and nobody would develop any attachment to someplace that might be better than someplace else. We moved, squeezing around into our new locations, me on the bucket this time. Then the light went out again.

Before too long a loud snoring sound began to come out of Zamoszczanski. The rest of us were dead still; this danger hadn't occurred to me, and I was sure the others hadn't thought of it either. After a while Sender tried elbowing him a little to see if that would make him stop. It didn't. The snoring rattled through the hole; I was sure he was waking up the entire household. Finally Sender shook him awake. "Zamoszczanski, you're snoring. You have to stop." Zamoszczanski sounded angry. "What do you mean?" he said. "You're offending me. I'm snoring? I never snored in my life." But a few minutes later he was back asleep and snoring just as loudly as before. Now there's this to worry about, too, I thought. I was finding it hard to breathe in the steamy closeness. There were just too many people.

Janova Puchalski thought so, too. After a couple of torturous days she announced that she simply could not keep everybody. First of all, it was too dangerous to have so many people. Second, the space was too small. "You won't survive down there like that," she said. "Some of you will have to leave."

I knew whom she meant. She hadn't said it directly, but her connections were with Sender and me, not the others. I didn't know what to expect. What would happen if she just kicked them out? But the problem resolved itself quickly. "It's okay," said Shulkes. "Zamoszczanski and I are leaving anyway." Although they hadn't discussed it, we understood that they both had contacts elsewhere. Shulkes's wife was in hiding somewhere, and Zamoszczanski had mentioned something about friends near Vilno. They had originally been planning to stay only until the transports were finished and the area had calmed down. Now it had.

Sender went up to talk to the Puchalskis alone, and when he came back, everything had been straightened out. Janova was still nervous. She was placing her entire family in mortal peril; hiding us was literally putting a noose around her children's necks. "But she's agreed that Mottl and Goldie can stay in addition to Felix and me," he said. I was glad to hear it. The Basses had nowhere to go, and I was already thinking how spacious the hole would be with only four people instead of six.

There was another important consideration, which Sender took up with Mottl Bass. I didn't have a penny, and Sender had gotten out of the ghetto with only the one five-ruble piece from Kushka. But Bass had money, a number of twenty-dollar gold pieces he was carrying in a money belt. There wasn't enough food in the house for the seven mouths the Puchalskis already had to feed, and they had no way of buying anything for us. Bass's money would help solve those problems, and he agreed with Sender that it should be given to Janova a piece at a time. We had no idea how long we'd have to stay hidden, so it made sense to stretch the money out as much as we could.

Underneath the numbness and disbelief that afflicted us, we shared a glimmer of hope that at least we might not have to live in the hole too long. The transport action had begun on Friday, February 13. Just a week and a half earlier the German Army had suffered a great defeat. We didn't know the details of what had happened at Stalingrad, but rumor and reports in German papers hinted that it had been a monumental disaster. We hoped beyond hope that it had been and that now the Soviets would break them altogether. But Sender was in no mood for optimism. "Who knows how long we might have to live here?" he said. "The money has to last."

Despite his devastation over the fate of his wife and children, Sender was thinking hard about how we might survive together. "We don't know how long we'll have to be down here," he said shortly after Shulkes and Zamoszczanski left. "We've got to assume it might be very long. If we don't want to tear ourselves apart, we're going to have to have some rules, especially since we're three men and a woman." That thought hadn't occurred to me before, though now that Sender mentioned it, I realized that even though Goldie Bass must have been ten years older than I, she was quite beautiful. I had no way of knowing how much a part this particular subject would play in my fantasy life over the next seventeen months.

But Sender did anticipate it, not just for me but for himself and the Basses, too. The idea of two men, an adolescent boy, and a woman pressed up against each other in the dark for an indefinite time had gotten him thinking. "We have to make a civilized life down here," he was saying. "We want to come out of here alive, and we want to come out as decent people. So the first rule is: No sex." He was speaking directly to Bass. "If you have sex, then everybody has to. But we don't want anything like that, so no sex. If we start to do things of that sort, we'll end up killing each other." Sender was thirty-two, Bass and his wife were in their late twenties, I was fifteen. He was insisting on total abstinence. What Mottl and Goldie Bass were thinking when Sender said this, I didn't know. At the moment it sounded fine to me.

A second rule was changing places, which we had already been doing. Now we put it on a strict schedule. Every two hours we switched, three lying down and one sitting on the wooden lid of the excrement bucket. With everyone exposed to the same conditions there would be no anger and no resentment, at least not on this score.

Not on the score of food, either. The first time Janova handed down the food bowl to the four of us, Goldie Bass divided it up in the weak glare of the tiny oil lamp. She did it exactly evenly, half for Sender and me, half for herself and Mottl. But Sender was thinking about this, too. "From now on," he said, "either Goldie will divide and I'll choose, or I'll divide and Goldie will choose." These were the rules according to Sender Freydovicz—legislation, as it turned out, for maintaining a civil life among four squashed people existing in a grave for what very soon began to seem like an eternity.

Each day, the trapdoor would open once or twice and Janova would hand down the meal. While we ate, the lamp would cast a glow on the food and throw strange shadows across faces and around the hole. But we were afraid of the smell of burning oil and were reluctant to keep the lamp lit much longer than it took to eat, especially at first. Like some nocturnal creature, I began to get used to living in the dark. I also got used to using the bucket when I had to, as we all did. There was no alternative, and our embarrassment quickly passed. Each time Janova handed down the food she also took up the pail to be emptied.

It was harder accustoming myself to some of the other circumstances of our new life, like the worms that were constantly finding their way out of our walls and floor and the fleas that began to plague us after the first couple of weeks. I could never figure out where the fleas came from. I certainly hadn't brought them with me, and I was sure none of the others had either.

The worms disgusted me, but fleas were a real problem. Where they bit a little pimple formed that itched like mad. But if you scratched, it began to hurt and then itched even more, so that you had to redouble your scratching, which turned the hurt into a fiery burn. I wondered if ordinary people with fleas would be driven as crazy as I was being driven. I didn't think so. Ordinary people had other things to do. Lying there in the dark made it easy to concentrate all your attention on itching and scratching.

Eventually I got to be pretty good at killing them. That was something that had to be done while our oil flame was burning. The problem was that fleas didn't crush easily. If you tried, they'd jump away, and even if they didn't, their hard shell was almost impossible to squash. But if you licked your finger, the saliva acted like a glue, and once you had caught a flea you could pinch it by its legs and put it to the flame. It was a laborious business, but that was the only way to destroy them. And the one thing we did have was time.

Lice were a different story. Those you could pop between your nails. I didn't know where they came from either. None of us had had lice when we came into the hole, and I didn't think they had been living in the dirt just waiting for us. But somehow, there they were—body lice, not head lice, which Sender maintained were a different species. These lived in our clothes, especially in hems and corners and other places that were sewn together.

Since we couldn't boil our clothes, we had to delouse them by hand, taking our shirts off and working slowly through the hems and stitches. You could do this in the dark, but it was a lot more effective in the lamplight, when you could see the eggs as well as the adults. You got them one at a time, feeling, searching, grabbing, popping. One and another and another and another. To do your shirt would take an hour or so. Of course, you'd miss a lot of them. But most you would get, and then you'd have the pleasure of relative louse freedom for two or three days, at which time you'd have to start the process over again. It was a constant pastime.

The great problem was that opportunities to wash were few and far between. There was no room for it in the hole, and getting out was a complicated, dangerous affair. Any foray had to be at night, after the youngest children were asleep. Even then there was always the chance they might wake up and see us. Neighbors were another danger. People in these little villages traditionally knew everything that went on in everyone else's life. And this was wartime; people were snooping around for Jews and making rounds to check on things like blackout precautions. Besides, the Germans had turned the whole country viciously suspicious. If someone learned someone else was hiding a Jew, his or her own neck was automatically at risk. Moreover, the chances for blackmail weren't lost on anyone, neither likely victims nor potential beneficiaries.

The result was that we only came up to get washed every few months, Sender and I together, then Mottl and Goldie. When we did go up I was surprised to find that my legs worked, after lying there for months with so little movement. But they did. Janova would fill the round wooden tub with hot water, and Sender and I would wash each other's back while Jan, Sabina, Irena, and Krystyna kept watch outside. We scrubbed fast, alert for the cry of a baby, the dog's bark, or a warning signal from one of the watchers. When we finished, we'd hurry back into the hole and the Basses would come up.

Those moments aboveground were delicious. But they didn't make a huge difference in our state of cleanliness. We had only the clothes we wore, and as month followed month they became less and less bearable. Holes opened up, which we patched as best we could. I soon became an expert at repairing socks, an art my grandma Rifka had taught me. But soon new holes would open and old ones would reopen. We were filthy and we smelled awful. When we lit the lamp and looked at each other we could only laugh. No homeless beggar was ever more ragged.

But we knew we were not alone. Janova's strength conveyed itself to us. She never lost her optimism, and we never for a moment doubted her energy or resourcefulness. One day we were lying there encased in thought as usual when we suddenly heard Janova's foot tapping the signal that Germans were in the house. My heart started beating so loudly I was sure it would give us away. Above us we heard a dog whining—not Muszka, the Puchalskis' dog. They were searching for us.

No one moved a muscle. We strained to hear, but it was hard to make out what was going on upstairs, whether there was one German or several, or if the dog was getting suspicious of the smells that must surely have been seeping up through the floorboards. Outside, Muszka started barking: some kind of dog encounter was taking place out there.

An eternity passed. Finally we heard the tapping signal from above, and we pushed open the door. There in the light was

Janova's face. "It's all right," she said. "He's gone." A German had been here with a dog, so obviously they were suspicious. Fortunately, she had seen him coming and had scattered pepper on the floor to disrupt the dog's sense of smell. When the German started looking outside, the two dogs had gotten angry with each other. Now, thank God, he had left. (It wasn't till after the war that Janova told us the whole story. Jan had had a mistress, and when Janova found out, she had become jealous and angry. Jan had broken off the affair, and in a fit of anger the mistress had told the German police that there were Jews in the Puchalski house. No one knew if Jan might possibly have let the great secret slip or if the mistress had simply denounced him out of vindictiveness without knowing the truth of it. The story surprised me when I learned about it, not that Jan would have had a mistress who had gotten angry enough to kill both the family and the four of us, but that while we were existing there below the floor above us the Puchalskis were living their own domestic life with all its own problems and struggles.)

Each month or so, Bass gave Janova a gold piece, which she would take to Mr. Heidemak in Grodno, who changed it for her. To cover her increased purchases, she discreetly planted the rumor that she was speculating in food. She had been buying for her family; now she was buying for four adults more, and food speculation was an explanation that anyone who noticed could easily accept. She would also get newspapers for us to read, but since she was illiterate she would ask if they had any from yesterday or last week that she might have free to wrap food in.

Every step Janova took was clever and courageous. It was only her planning that was suspect. In the hole we had either feast or famine, though mostly famine. The day she changed the money was a great day. That day she would speculate in meat, and we would see meatballs or lamb or even roast pork. But a week later everyone was back to the usual diet of potatoes and milk or potatoes and water, her own family as well as her guests belowground.

8

A SOCIETY IN A HOLE

THOUGH we lived mostly in darkness, the household noises told us about day and night. The morning turmoil came right through our ceiling, followed by the quiet daytime, when people tended to be out. Evening was announced by another round of voices, scraping, and bumping, and finally came night, when the family slowly fell into quiescence. Time passed and we kept track of it, aligning our own rhythm to that of the Puchalskis.

As the weeks and months went by I became convinced that everybody had fallen in love with Goldie Bass, despite the ban on sex. I felt sure Sender must be in love with her. I knew that I was deeply in love with her. I wanted her more than I had ever wanted anything. How much Sender must have wanted her I couldn't even guess. Mottl Bass went without saying, and he was the one actually lying next to her. In my fantasies she was always there. But there was not a word, not a touch, not a hint from anyone. We were crowded next to each other, but we organized it so that Bass was always between her and the other two. We had strict rules and no one broke them, in part because we sensed how powerful our desires were.

But aside from everyone being magnetized by Goldie, relationships in the hole were cool and distant, the reverse of our physical proximity—even between Sender and me. Each of us was shattered by what he or she had been through. We were absorbed in pain. It took all my strength to say anything at all to Sender. I was always thinking about his wife, Sarah, and the two babies. They were his constant, unthinkable reality, yet it could not be talked of. Okay, I would think, jammed up against him, he lost his parents and so did I. But look what else he lost: He lost his wife. He lost his children.

We couldn't even talk much about the past. Occasionally Sender would tell me something about how the business had been before the war, or about his studies in Danzig, or the soccer team he had played on. But by mutual, silent consent everything that had happened to us in the ghetto was out of bounds, to the extent that Sender never even asked me how it had been in Kielbasin. There was a kind of shyness about everything that had to do with our tragedy, as if we knew we were too fragile to face these things directly. And so between us there was no real connection, no flow of understanding and empathy from one to the other that we both needed so desperately. Instead there was mainly silence.

We did not even know with any certainty about the fates of our families. Despite the rumors, we were not sure by any means that in Auschwitz and Treblinka gas chambers for mass killing really existed. It still seemed so inconceivable. In our hearts we understood that everyone was dead, but we hoped and prayed that perhaps some weren't.

What saved us from being overwhelmed was that our own survival was in the balance. We might have become obsessed by what had happened, especially living there in the blackness with nothing to distract our thoughts—except for *the* great question: Were we ourselves going to live another hour, or another minute? Each knock on the front door, each strange sound in the house, each bark from the yard could mean an informant, or the Germans. Our grief was circumscribed by constant anxiety for our own lives.

On the one hand, I felt like somebody had cut out half my heart or half my brain. I thought, I am amputated. They have amputated me. But I also had hope. I wanted desperately to survive. I dreamed of surviving.

Among my dreams was the black dream of vengeance. I imagined myself going to Germany and killing everyone—men, women, and children, too. I fantasized about it. I swore solemn oaths to myself that I would do it. I not only wanted to kill them, I wanted to shoot and shoot and shoot. I felt I had a duty to do that, I was under the deepest obligation to my mother and father and all the others.

I envisioned revolt. Why had we not done it? The labor

gangs were working in so many places. We knew where German weapons were. We could have overcome them. My mind roamed through the possibilities. We could have killed them. Then we could have taken the Germans' trucks and driven everybody to the forest. Maybe we could have saved five hundred people, or a thousand people. An enormous number, each one a world.

I didn't know, until Bass told us, that there actually had been a rudimentary resistance organization formed by the Zionist Tarbut teachers; the Communists and Bundists had also put together their own groups. But although documents were forged and a few people had gotten out to the partisans, nothing really effective had been done. They talked about breaking out, they talked about fighting. But they had gotten no support from the rabbis or from Braver, the Tarbut director who was also president of the Judenrat. These people, the community's natural leaders, had recommended patience, keeping our heads down. Some would be killed, of course, and that was tragic. But remember, they had argued, this is war, this is what pogroms were. In the end we would survive.

I imagined, too, what it would be like to get out of our hole and live in the forest with the partisans. Or escape to the Soviet Union. There I could become a pilot. Maybe somehow I could even get to England and fight with them against the Germans. Here I was utterly helpless. But if I could only get my hands on a gun and fight. God, did I want that. I could taste it.

I even talked to Sender about it. Why couldn't we just get out of here? Okay, so we didn't know where the partisans were. But they were somewhere, and we couldn't find them by lying in this pit. "Just be quiet," he said. "We have to survive, and this is the best chance we have. What you are talking about is just nonsense." In calmer moments I knew this myself. Sheer nonsense. We hadn't the vaguest notion where the partisans might be. We were a thousand miles behind the German lines in a place where every Jew was being murdered on sight. Sheer nonsense, sheer nonsense.

In my more tranquil periods I thought long and hard about what I wanted to be when I grew up. I savored the possibilities. My old idea of becoming an engineer took hold. What would it be like to invent something? How I would love to make something that would contribute to the scientific world. I knew that these, too, were fantasies, like my fantasy about getting a gun and killing Germans or my fantasy about escaping to the partisans. I was dreaming about what I would like to be when I grew up, but my prospects for ever growing up were not good.

I also found myself with a tremendous yearning for Israel. Of course, I had gotten all that Zionist background at home and in school. For most of us that had been mostly theory and talk, but locked up in the ghetto, the idea had acquired a luminous intensity. Against the terrible story of German victories and the savage march forward of the Nazi Army it had become clear that there was only one place in the world where we had a chance. That was *Eretz Yisrael.* Israel was our country, the one place where if we had to perish, at least we would perish with weapons in our hands. I thought of the deportees shouting as they were led out of the ghetto: "Don't forget Israel. You who are left alive, fight for Israel. *Forges nicht Yisrael!*" Hadn't I heard the shouts while I was marching under the whips and hiding in the attic? Hadn't I heard their last testament to the ones still left alive—their only testament?

We had talked about Palestine in the ghetto, and now we talked about it in the hole. Sender was not a Zionist; he had never been enthusiastic about the idea. The Basses were, and I was. But Sender was by degrees the more practical man. A homeland would be wonderful, but would such a thing be feasible? It wouldn't work. Israel was a dream. Even the talk was a dream. Our business was to face what was here and now. Our job was to live through each day, not to dream about phantasms.

But that didn't stop me from imagining what Palestine was like, what it would look like and smell like. The pictures I had stared at in books were in my mind: farmers guiding a plow with one hand, the other gripping a rifle. I dreamed of working on a kibbutz and building the country, of living together, and having a state. I was always thinking about a state. The Jews would have a state. What a strong country that would be, a country where I would be free, where I could do anything and become anything.

I also had vivid fantasies about how it would be if the Germans were defeated and we walked out alive. I envisioned how our Polish neighbors would greet us, how they would have compassion, how they would open their arms to embrace us with mercy and sorrow. To welcome us back from the dead. Because even though I was dreaming of faraway, impossible places—Russia, England, Palestine—in fact I really thought that if by some chance I got out of this alive I would probably stay in Grodno. That was the only place I actually knew.

I had dreams, too, about the Puchalski family. When this was all over and people learned what they had done, they would be hailed as heroes. The Polish government would present them with the Virtuti Militare, the country's highest medal. I would be forever grateful to them. I would find a way of helping them for as long as I lived. I even began to think that maybe I would marry one of the daughters. First one of them would attract me, then my mind would settle on another, then the third. I was missing affection tremendously. I was missing sex, too, a sixteen-year-old boy in a hole with the same hormones raging through his bloodstream as all those sixteen-year-old boys not living in a hole. My entire world had disappeared, and with it all its girls, all the objects of my desire. They were gone, but the Puchalski girls lived right above us, just inches over my head.

I might have been immobilized and sightless, but the images of my inner world were vividly alive. Girls were there, and violence—love, hate, and unutterable longing. I heard music, too: symphonies and concertos and sonatas—everything I could remember from my violin- and orchestra-playing. Mozart's Turkish March and Beethoven's Fifth and the Boildieu Overture, they all came back. With practice I found I could perform the music and hear the parts in my head. I would lie there and play everything I knew over and over, recalling the attacks, crescendos, retards, and stops. I wondered how Szczuryk would have played them, the great prodigy violinist from Grodno whom I had gone to hear just before the war. The smell and heat of the hole would fade away, and the Mendelssohn violin concerto with all its glorious details would fill my mind. Whatever I knew I listened to in my private concert hall. I kicked myself that I hadn't been a more serious student, that I hadn't learned ten times as much.

I also had a little leather-covered book that Janova had found somewhere, an anthology of poems in Russian. When we were eating I would read Pushkin and Lermontov and try to memorize them a little at a time. Then when the light was extinguished I would repeat and repeat what I had read until the part was engraved in my memory. Next mealtime I'd check what I had done and try for the next stanza.

These things filled my mind in the endless hours. But beneath the dreams and reveries I, like the others, was absorbed by sorrow. Each one of us lived in his own mental world, dreaming his own dreams, terrified by his fears, wrapped in his own pain. And in this universe of ours, this grave we inhabited together, there was not much room for interrelation from one to the other. Among the four bodies lying there, no flow of love bridged our solitude, no intimacies. We did not have the strength to talk to each other about things that were unspeakable.

Like the rest of us, Sender was closed in. The only subjects he and I could discuss with any ease were neutral ones, such as mathematics. In fact, math was ideal—an abstract world of theory and logic that required the full use of your mind. Card-playing was also good. Tracking cards and figuring tactics could keep you busy for hours. When we talked about these abstract subjects, Sender would come alive. I would literally feel that the person lying next to me was returning from the dead.

Sender was nervous about me. Without either of us saying a word about it, he had assumed a paternal attitude toward my well-being. Once in a while he would smoke a cigarette, made from newspaper and a little of the tobacco Jan occasionally brought home from the tobacco factory where he worked. I wanted to smoke, too. I had taken it up in the ghetto, where my friends and I would sneak cigarettes in the alley. But Sender wouldn't let me. "If your father were here instead of me he would not let you smoke. I am not your father, Felix, but I am your guardian. I am treating you as your father would if he were here. I forbid you to smoke."

Sender was especially nervous about math. "What grade are you in, Felix?" (I hadn't been in a classroom for a year and a half.) "How come you don't know more math?" And suddenly there was a subject that demanded complete attention from both of us—Sender to teach and me to learn. "Imagine a triangle," he would say. "A triangle has three sides. Felix, you know what a right angle is?"

"Sure."

"So, one side is horizontal and another is perpendicular. The third one runs opposite the right angle. That's the hypotenuse. We'll call one angle 'alpha,' one 'beta.' The third angle is ninety degrees. Can you picture that?"

"Yes, I can."

"Good. 'Alpha' is on the bottom, 'beta' will be on the top. Understand?"

"Yes."

"Okay. Suppose I take the side opposite angle alpha and divide it by the hypotenuse. Can you picture that?"

"Yes."

"Good. We'll call that number the 'sinus.'"

"I can picture that, Sender, but what the hell is it—the 'sinus'? What does it mean?"

"Never mind what it means. Just do what I tell you."

"I can't, Sender. It doesn't make sense. What do you mean, 'sinus'? Suppose I call it my aunt? What do you mean, 'sinus' is a ratio? What is a ratio?"

"Be quiet. This is the 'sinus.' The other leg divided by the hypotenuse is the 'cosinus.' The 'tangent' is the ratio of the first side to the second side. Now, can you see that?"

"Yes, okay. I can."

"But, you know, if you think about it, the tangent is the sinus over the cosinus."

"No," I said. "That's impossible."

"Come on, Felek, think about it. The sinus is this side over this side, the cosinus is that side over that side. You divide one by the other, the two sides cancel out. All you have left is one side over the other."

"Huh? Sender, you're right. The tangent is the sinus over the cosinus." I started to see some sense to it. There they were, hovering around in my head. The sinus, the cosinus, the tangent. And if you did this and that, why, you were left with the other. Wonderful!

"Now," says Sender, "suppose I tell you that sinus squared alpha plus cosinus squared alpha equals 1. Would you believe me?"

"No," I said. "Prove it."

So he started to talk. Some of what he said I learned by heart. I accepted it. Some I understood the proofs. Hardest of all were equations of the second degree. AX squared plus BX plus C equals 0. Find X_1 and X_2. We did that. Here was a continuous mental exercise, an endless discussion and lecture and dialogue about geometry and algebra. Occasionally when we lit the lamp we'd get scraps of newspapers and a pencil, and Sender would illustrate what we had been talking about.

It was extraordinary training, though, of course, I had no idea how extraordinary, or how much it would help me later. We would also play cards occasionally, if the children were out during the day and we could light the flame. Sixty-nine was Sender's game, a kind of simplified bridge. When he first saw me play, Sender got nervous about that, too. "Son of a gun, Felix," he said. "You don't know how to count cards." He himself kept track of all the cards in his head. Eventually he succeeded in teaching me some of his methods.

I also asked Mottl Bass to teach me a little history and

literature. I was hungry for knowledge. I was thirsting for it. I felt like a sponge. Bass was a lawyer who had been heavily involved in Zionist organizations (his father had represented Poland at the first Zionist World Congress, in Basel). "Tell me Jewish history," I would say, or Greek history or Roman. Anything. But Bass was too upset, too anxiety-ridden to put his mind to it.

I thought about school, where they taught history, of course, but mainly dates of battles and kings that had to be memorized for the exam. Like my friends, I had learned what I had to, then had run off to play soccer. But now I started to think about it. The Battle of Gruenwald—was it 1410 or 1411? And what was that about exactly? I racked my brain to remember. I tried to reconstitute it, bringing the map up in my mind. As a little boy I used to be good at geography. I knew countries and capitals so well that my parents had made a parlor game out of it. "Felix, what's the capital of Albania?" "Tirana." "What's the capital of Bulgaria? of Norway? of Spain? My parents and grandparents would beam at the tiny child reciting the capitals in front of guests.

Now I could see Poland on the map, and Lithuania. Maps from different periods. How come Poland was big like this on one map and small like that on another? When had that happened? Did the Battle of Gruenwald do that? Sometimes Bass knew, sometimes he didn't. Sender, the engineer, didn't know these things too well. He knew math and science, but not history, though he'd tell me what he thought about it. Then I would draw my own conclusions.

I developed an exercise in which I tried to catalog periods of time in my head. What happened, say in 1830? 1848? 1863?— major dates that had stuck with me. What happened in Poland? I knew that. What happened in France? Maybe I knew a little about that. What happened in England? Blank. What happened in America? Blank. So I'd start to ask questions. Sometimes I got an answer, sometimes I didn't. In fact, I had taken the cue from my school during the Soviet occupation. Before the war all we had learned was what happened in Poland; other places were significant only if events there had to do with Poland. But the Soviet schools had taught history by periods, to see when the great waves of revolution had swept through various countries.

Though Bass wasn't able to teach me much history, he was wonderful at keeping the calendar. We tried hard to track the days, weeks, and months; it was a way of fighting the disorientation that constantly threatened. There was also the complicated question of Jewish holidays. The Jewish calendar not only didn't coincide with the standard calendar, the relationship between them changed by the year. We attempted to figure out when Pesach came, and Yom Kippur, and Rosh Hashana. Bass was adept at this, and we came to rely on him as our living calendar. "Aha," he would say after some arcane calculation, "tomorrow must be the first day of Pesach. Let's not eat bread"—assuming we had any bread. Or if there was only bread, we'd pretend it was matzoh and talk about it.

We'd talk about the other holidays, too, always waiting for the times when the children were out of the house and the coast sounded clear. Discussions of these historical and religious events helped maintain a feeling of civilization. We might be living hunched up in a disgusting pit, but we were still a society on a small level, a society in a hole.

Discussions of the holidays inevitably became discussions of morality. It began to dawn on me that our rules, Sender's rules, were enabling us to survive. It was no wonder that the Ten Commandments had been created; they gave people a way to live together. There was nothing abstract about moral rules. They were hard and simple precepts for survival. If we had started to have sex, or if we had started to cheat each other with food, or if we began to quarrel with each other, the results would be fatal. Janova would have had to throw us out, or we would have killed each other. Jealousies and resentment and anger—we had to stamp all that down. The lesson was stark: You have the rules, you abide by them, you survive; otherwise you don't.

The only potential disaster happened early along. The gold pieces we were giving to Janova came from a money belt around Mottl Bass's waist. They were our means to survival—without them the Puchalskis would have been unable to feed us, and very likely unable to feed themselves either. But Bass had been a Farbindungsman, someone of great influence in the ghetto, and Sender suspected that the gold might have been taken for getting people out of transports. Was this money that Bass had accepted to remove someone's name from a selection list? Was it blood money?

Sender wanted to know exactly where the money had come from. Bass told him that it had belonged to one of Goldie's uncles, who had given it to her before he died. Goldie corroborated this, and Sender accepted it. I didn't have an opinion, except that I knew the gold pieces were identical. And there was no way for the pieces to be identical if they had come from many different people. For a while I had been scared. I didn't know what Sender would have done if it actually had been blood money. He might have thrown Bass out, or killed him. I didn't want to think about it. The tension had been almost impossible to bear. But Sender accepted the explanation, and the tension dissipated.

•

We might have been living a varied inner life, but time did not pass more quickly because of it. Occasionally Janova would come back from Heidemak's or from the village with a piece of news. Not long after we arrived, she told us that two bodies had been found in the river, the Alexandroviczes, a Jewish couple who must have escaped from the ghetto at the same time we had. Both of them had had their throats slit. The talk in the village was that they had been hiding with people who had murdered them for the gold and fur coats they had brought with them, though some said the Poles had simply panicked and killed them because they were afraid of being caught. A short time later, Janova heard from Heidemak that Berko had escaped from Treblinka, but that he had been recaptured by the Gestapo and sent to the Bialystok prison. In April 1943, when we had been in the hole for three months, she told us the rumors about a Jewish uprising in Warsaw.

Janova had also heard that the few Grodno Jews who had been left over from the February deportation had been shipped to Bialystok. Since February they had been living enclosed in a tiny section of the former ghetto. Now they, too, were gone.

From *Documents Concerning the Destruction of the Jews of Grodno*:

> AFTER THE SECOND OPERATION IN MID-FEBRUARY 1943, THERE WERE STILL SOME 1,000 JEWS LIVING IN GHETTO ONE. THESE INCLUDED SEVERAL HUNDRED ARTISANS AND OTHER SO-CALLED USEFUL JEWS, AS WELL AS SOME WHO HAD FLED OR HIDDEN DURING THE DEPORTATION OPERATIONS. THEY NOW LIVED IN THE DRASTICALLY REDUCED GHETTO, WHICH CONSISTED ONLY OF A SMALL NUMBER OF HOUSES AT THE ENTRANCE TO THE GHETTO.
>
> IN MID-MARCH 1943, THESE JEWS WERE TRANSFERRED TO THE BIALYSTOK GHETTO. AT THIS POINT, GRODNO GHETTO ONE WAS COMPLETELY EMPTY—IN THE LANGUAGE OF THE GESTAPO, GRODNO WAS NOW "JUDENREIN."*

As time passed, Mr. Heidemak continued to prove himself an invaluable friend. One day Sender developed a toothache. Despite his stoicism, he began to talk about it. We prayed that it would go away, but instead the pain became worse and worse, and when his jaw began to swell, we knew it was infected. Then Sender began to complain that his head was hurting. Then his eye started to hurt. Something had to be done. Janova went to town to see Heidemak, to ask if he could somehow lay his hands on some dental equipment. One day she came back with an entire kit.

We were thankful beyond words when Janova handed it down to us, but I was also terrified, since I had been chosen as the dental surgeon. We lit the flame. Sender opened his mouth and Bass held up the lamp so I could look inside. With one of the instruments, I touched one tooth, then another. There wasn't any question: It was one of the big molars in back, a wisdom tooth.

*Klarsfeld, Summary Volume, p. 32.

I put in the dental pliers, caught it, and clamped down as hard as I could. Then I started to pull. Sender was in agony; the look on his face was frightful. But somehow he kept himself from screaming. I pulled and pulled, but he didn't let out a peep. Finally the tooth came loose. I wiggled it back and forth, then gave it a final yank and it tore free. Pus spurted out. When I looked back inside, there was a big hole where the tooth had been. Blood and pus filled the cavity. As best I could I cleaned it out with some gauze that had been in the kit, then packed it tight with camphor and more gauze. How it was that Sender escaped an even worse infection I didn't know, but over the next few days the swelling went down and Sender reported that things inside felt fine.

One day not long after this, we opened the trapdoor at the signal and were surprised to find Esther Shapiro Heidemak climbing down into the hole. We made room for her between my feet (when we came down into the hole I could stretch my legs out, but now I had grown so much I had to keep them bent). The news she brought wasn't good. Heidemak had been arrested. The Gestapo had discovered he was a member of the underground and had taken him away. She had been hiding with Heidemak's mother and sister, but as soon as he was gone, they had thrown her out. Fortunately, her husband had told her about us. She had had nowhere else to go.

Esther Heidemak arrived sometime in February 1944, after we had been living in the hole for a year. Now we had another person with us, but we had long ago mastered the discipline for close survival. We adjusted.

The news from the battlefront made it easier. That winter the Red Army was on the offensive everywhere. Northeast of Grodno they were battering at Vitebsk, only three hundred and fifty miles away, and to the south, at Kovel, they were even closer. By now we were past masters at interpreting the several-day-old German newspapers Janova brought us. We loved reading that the front was being "realigned" to shorten the supply lines. Each German "tactical withdrawal" brought the Soviets closer. We knew every move and every date; it couldn't be that much longer before the Soviets pushed the Germans back through Poland.

Then, in early June, we heard that the Americans and British had crossed the English Channel into France with an enormous invasion force. The second front had started at last. I spent hours trying to envision what the fighting was like, and wondering how it must be for the French, who were just now being liberated. There were Jews there, too, I was sure, who had been hiding in holes, maybe just like ours. And now they were free. I tried to imagine how that would feel.

By July the war was marching toward us in earnest. Janova told us that Vitebsk had been taken, then Minsk, then Baranovicz—not far from the old border. Down in the hole I could feel the excitement rising. I began thinking how it would be to get out, what the sky would look like, what the air would feel like. I hadn't seen the sun in almost a year and a half. We began to sense a distant low rumble in the earth—artillery. Now and then a plane roared over the house. Jan and Janova were excited, too; we had grown used to judging the state of the world from the tone of their voices, which had usually seemed stoic and determined. Now there was a new edge in their speech: anticipation.

But as activity around the house increased, we also picked up their tension. One day a car drove up—that hadn't happened before. The little Puchalski children had been playing noisily upstairs, but suddenly they were silent. The dog was barking, and from outside came the slightly garbled sound of German. Our first thought was that we had been betrayed.

We went rigid with fear. Then I felt Mottl Bass shifting around, getting out the razor blades he was keeping, I assumed. He had vowed to kill himself rather than be captured; he thought we all should. But minutes passed, and nobody came into the house. Outside, more automobiles drove up. We couldn't imagine what might be happening, unless this was possibly the German retreat for which we had been praying for so long. All during the day, German noises increased. By now the distant growl of the guns had become louder. Tremors vibrated through our floor and walls. As evening fell, people came into the house, but they spoke Polish. We recognized the voices of neighbors.

Later that night, after they had gone, Jan knocked on the trapdoor and asked Sender to come up. The news he brought back down with him was nerve-racking. The German retreat had reached our area. Units from all over had been seen in the woods, from Baranovicz and Melodechna, even from Vilno. From what Jan and his friends could tell, they weren't planning to make a stand. If we were lucky, the whole thing might even be over in a couple of days. But meanwhile it was more dangerous than ever. Germans were everywhere. So were the partisans, and rumors were going around that some of the partisan units were killing Jews. Jan didn't know how often they'd feel safe opening the trapdoor, so the meals and water might not be coming down every day. Maybe they wouldn't be able to empty the excrement pail. We'd have to sit tight.

The next day started off full of angry engine noises coming from the yard and shouts and orders in German. The trapdoor stayed closed. It sounded as though a unit had settled in right around the house. The firing we had been hearing since the previous day got closer; we made out the cracks of rifles and the budabudabuda of machine guns. Several times nearby explosions rocked the earth and we could smell smoke. Sometime in the afternoon the bed above us scraped and we could distinctly hear Janova talking in a loud voice, obviously to us. It sounded as though she were sitting on the bed. The Germans were retreating in panic toward Augustow. They were blowing up their ammunition and throwing their rifles into the river. They were saying that the Soviets were only ten miles from Grodno.

Friday, July 14, was quieter. We could no longer hear the Germans, and the shooting had died down. When Janova came with food and water, she told us that the Germans had set fire to the Grodno railroad station. The post office and city hall were also in flames. Later that day we were shaken by a succession of giant explosions. "They blew up the bridges," Janova said when she opened the door that evening. "The Russians are near the river." The Neiman ran through the woods at the foot of our hill, no more than a hundred yards away. Freedom was on our doorstep.

We hardly slept that night, we were so eager for the day to come and with it Janova telling us that the Russians had arrived, that it was safe to come out. But in the morning a sound came through the earth that sent my pulse racing with anxiety: digging, a lot of it, very near the house. A short time later Jan's deep voice came through the trapdoor: "They're digging trenches in the woods toward the river. We don't know what's happening."

We lay still all that day and night, sick with worry. The digging had gone on for a few hours, then had stopped. Afterward it had been quiet around the house. The big guns had never ceased firing, but we had grown used to them already; they were the constant background against which we listened for everything else.

On Sunday morning, July 16, it all changed. The house was enveloped with the noise of men and vehicles. We heard heavy things being dragged across the ground and metallic sounds as other things clanked loudly. Motorcycles seemed to be racing across the backyard just feet from our heads. There were shouts in German, and what sounded like an army of people running back and forth. *"Mach schnell!"* we heard, *"Schnell!"* A knocking came from the ceiling, Janova's signal. Her voice cut through the trapdoor, hurried and frightened. "We have to leave. We have to leave. They're going to fight here. They've told us to get out." Then there was another voice, harsh and demanding, *"Raus, raus! Schnell! Raus!"* and Jan in his broken German saying something about a goat.

A moment later the house was silent. But in the room above us something was jumping around. We heard a little bleat, then another; hooves knocked delicately on our ceiling. I was utterly terrified at the realization that the Puchalskis were actually leaving. My mind was racing, trying to think of something to do. Why the goat might have been there I hadn't the slightest idea.

9

JAN and Janova did not come back. The house was deserted. Outside, the fighting raged, but inside, the only sound was an occasional bleat from the goat. We sat there in the sweltering heat. We had a small hunk of bread and a quart of water in our bottle. The excrement pail hadn't been emptied in two days and stank abominably. When the battle started, Janova told us that the Germans had burned down several village houses where they were searching for people, waiting outside to shoot down anybody who escaped from the flames.

We are dead, I thought. After all this we are going to be killed here. The thought was unbearable. Grodno was liberated. Whoever was left there was walking around the streets, free. But we were never going to get out of this hole. The Germans would find us and shoot us, or we would be blown up by a shell, or they would set the house on fire and we would be burned alive. I felt a compulsion to get out. We couldn't wait. But Sender wasn't doing anything. At least I'm going, I thought. Maybe the others want to stay in this grave. I don't.

"Sender," I said, "I've got to get out of here. I'm a good swimmer, I'll get down the hill and swim across the river. Janova said the Russians are on the other side. As soon as it gets dark, I'm taking off."

"You can't," said Sender. "They'll catch you, and when they do, you'll give us up."

"Sender, you know I wouldn't give you up. I'd die before I gave you up."

"Don't talk about it so lightly. You don't have any idea what they can do to you. How do you think you could stand up to it? You're not going anywhere."

I begged. "Please let me. I can't live like this. This is my only chance. Please let me go. What are we going to do here?

There's no food, there's no water. The stink is horrible. There's no plan. Please let me go."

"Absolutely not," he said. I felt sobs breaking out; I struggled to keep them down in my throat so I wouldn't make any noise. All these things I had lived through, and I never even felt like crying. But suddenly I was overwhelmed. After all this we were going to end up as corpses in this filthy grave. And instead I had a chance to get out, and Sender wasn't going to let me? The sobs were coming up like hiccups.

"Stop that," said Sender. "Stop crying. What are you, a child? Are you better than everyone else who was killed? Just stay there and be quiet and that's it."

A few minutes later the panic attack had passed and I felt better. Not that our situation had improved. Germans had come into the house and were talking. We heard one say, *"Was ist das stink hier?"* What's the shit smell here? We knew perfectly well what it was. Did that mean they were going to start looking? Carefully, Sender moved the trapdoor back a little, and Mottl, whose German was good, stuck his head partway out to listen. "They're staying," he whispered back down to us. "They're planning to sleep in the house."

When Mottl pulled back inside and we slid the door closed, he sounded shaken. The Germans had been talking about the fighting, something about orders to hold the line of the Nieman at any cost. He had heard them say that field police and SS troops had joined the army units to try to hold off the Soviets. We didn't have a chance—no chance at all if we stayed down in the hole, hardly any chance if we didn't. It seemed to us that the house must be in the middle of a huge German concentration.

Late that night, Sender sneaked out of the hole to look around. The goat was gone, where to, none of us knew. A German was sleeping on a sofa in the larger room—eight or nine feet from the bed over our trapdoor. Sender was out only a minute or two, and when he came back, he and Mottl made a decision: If nothing changed, we would try to escape tomorrow night.

That night, no one slept. We planned what we were going to do. We could climb out the window and head through the woods away from the Nieman toward the little flour mill on the Losossnianka River. If we could get across we would try for the village just down from there, where Sender thought there might be some people who would hide us. Sender and I knew the paths by heart. Goldie Bass also used to spend vacations out here, so she knew them, too.

If we were stopped, we all had to be clear on our story. Mottl and Goldie had decent papers—authentic-looking Tartar passports that had been made up in the ghetto. Poland's small community of Tartars was Polish in every respect except that they were Muslims—circumcised Muslims. There was actually a big stamp on the passport that certified the bearer was circumcised. Esther Heidemak also had identification, as a Polish Catholic woman. It was only Sender and I who had no documents, but Sender could be Esther's husband and I could be their son. Maybe one document would do for a family.

We would tell the Germans that we were running from the Bolsheviks. We had crossed the river in front of them and had taken shelter with other refugees in the basement of a house. But the house had taken a direct hit, and the basement collapsed. We were the only survivors: we lost everything. Mottl Bass would do the talking. His Polish accent was excellent; nothing about it would give us away as Jews, though if the Germans had a Pole with them we would never be able to save ourselves. One glance would be all he would need.

The next day we shared the bread and sipped the water a teaspoon at a time. Among the five of us the quart went quickly. We dripped sweat. Even in the freezing winter the hole was hot; in July it was intolerable.

The battle seemed to have died down a little, or maybe,

I thought, we've just gotten used to it. At this time of year the days were long. It wouldn't be dark until at least ten. If we were lucky there would not be much of a moon. If we were really lucky no soldiers would come to sleep in the house.

At about nine-thirty the front door opened and someone came in. Our hearts dropped into our stomachs. In the bigger room we heard creaks from the sofa. Someone was lying down on it. The son of a bitch is going to sleep there again, I thought. A while later Sender stuck his head out and listened. "I can hear him snoring," he whispered. "I think he's asleep."

We waited. While we did, Mottl and Esther scraped out a bit of the floor and covered up a few family snapshots they had with them. Sender also had two or three little pictures, but he wouldn't leave them. At midnight we went over for the last time how we would get out so it would go fast and silently. You go there, then you, then you. This, that, then this. You move, you stay. You move, you stay. This is what I do, this is what you do. I pulled off my boots, the others their shoes. Sender whispered "Go" and carefully lifted the lid. Then he climbed up and crawled under the bed, then Bass went, then Esther, then me, then Goldie. The room was dark, but moonlight shone through the window. I could see everything perfectly. When Goldie was out, Bass slid the trapdoor back and pushed the old clothes on top of it. By that time Sender was out the window, and the rest of us were following him. The entire operation had taken maybe a minute.

The night was soft and warm; the light breeze caressed my skin. A powerful pine aroma suffused the air; I felt dizzy, almost as if I were going to faint. I was engulfed by sensations. This was the first time in seventeen months that I had been outside. I couldn't even remember the last time I had been out of the hole to wash.

Quickly we put our shoes on and started to move. It was only then that I realized we were in the middle of a battle. Shells were screaming through the air above us. Explosions rocked the woods. A fireball flared up in the trees to our left, sending sparks in all directions. Here and there other fires were burning. Acrid smoke mixed with the sharp pine scent.

We hadn't gone fifty yards when a loud voice shouted *"Halt!"* We froze. "What's the password?" No one opened his mouth. We didn't know. In our planning we had decided not to respond to anything in German; we were Polish refugees who wouldn't know the language. "Who is there?" demanded the voice. A flashlight came on. Its beam picked us out. *"Hände hoch!"* The flashlight gestured upward. We raised our hands. *"Kom!"*

A minute later, we were in a tent with soldiers and an interpreter. *"Sprechen sie Deutsch?"* said one of them. No answer. "Okay, then. Polish." Thank God, I thought, the interpreter's a German.

"Papers!" he demanded. Mottl, Goldie, and Esther handed them over. "They don't have any," said Mottl, gesturing at us, "her husband and son. When the cellar collapsed, we lost everything. We were lucky to get out with our lives. We were running away from the Bolsheviks." As Mottl went into his speech, we were frisked. I was focusing on Mottl's words, but in the background I could hear the soldiers talking: "What's going on? Who are these people—saboteurs? Parachutists?"

"How come this boy is so white?" asked the interpreter. "And how did you get here? This is a closed area."

I was white because I hadn't seen sunlight since the day of the transport. "He's scared to death," said Mottl. "We crossed the river about three kilometers from here, then we hid in a basement with the others. We're the only ones who survived."

"You walked three kilometers along the front and you weren't stopped?"

"No. No one stopped us."

The interpreter told one of the officers there, a captain who seemed to be in charge. "Three kilometers?" said the captain. "How can that be?" Instantly he was on the field telephone, cursing and yelling at someone about the security. "How?" he shouted into the phone. "How could you let five people walk along the front without being stopped?"

Then he turned his anger on us. "Excuse me, sir," said Bass, after waiting for the translation, "we were running from the Bolsheviks on the other side of the river. We hate the Bolsheviks. Then you blew up the bridges and all the shooting started. So we went in the first house we saw to hide. Now we'd like to go to Losossna—we have some friends there." It didn't seem to occur to the Germans that we might have been among them all along, in the little house just fifty yards away. "Goddamnit!" shouted the officer. "A mouse couldn't move along the front without being stopped."

Right then Goldie fainted, just as we had planned it if we got in trouble. Everyone looked at her. "Sir, we haven't had anything to eat in two days," said Bass apologetically. "Bring her some coffee," the captain ordered. Then he told the interpreter, "Explain to them that we don't have any food ourselves." "We'll take care of this whole thing tomorrow," he said. "Tell them to lie down behind that hill there."

That night we spent on the ground, listening to the whine and roar of the shells. From the soldiers around us we understood that we had been caught by a unit of Schutzpolizei, military police. We were convinced that we would be shot in the morning, as soon as they began to question us again. Goldie and Esther found it difficult to stop weeping. Sender and Bass did their best to comfort them, but they, too, were grim and resigned. Sender had a couple of small photographs with him, our only mementos of the family. There was nothing conspicuously Jewish about the pictures, but we decided to bury them anyway. Lying there, shielding the ground between us from the nearest soldiers, we scraped out a little hole and covered them up with dirt.

At dawn the interpreter was back, asking again for our papers. He looked at them, then said, "It doesn't matter. Papers or no papers, you're not allowed to be here. All civilians have been out of here for days. The punishment for this is death!" But Bass's documents had caught his attention. "Muslims?" He had never run across any Muslims before. "What kind of religion is that, anyway?" Bass instantly began to talk about Mohammed and Allah and the Koran. I was pretty sure he didn't know the first thing about any of them. Fortunately the German seemed to know even less.

In the middle of this discussion the captain walked up. "This whole thing isn't worth the time," he said to the interpreter. "Take them over to the command post."

A moment later we were walking single file through the woods with the Polish-speaker in front of us and another soldier behind. I was sure they weren't planning to take us to headquarters. For what? If we hadn't been worth the captain's time, we certainly weren't worth some higher officer's, which meant that they were going to shoot us in the woods. I looked right and left to see where it would be best to run. I was tense, ready to bolt the moment they told us to stop, or at the first shot. If they didn't shoot me first, maybe I'd have a chance.

But there wasn't any shot. Instead they walked us across the road and into a little wood on the far side, where they made us sit down. A few minutes later, two officers came through the trees, one in a police uniform, one an SS. They talked with the interpreter and glanced at our papers; then they walked around us slowly, looking at our faces from every side. I tried to keep my eyes down and my face set in a look of apathy. Finally the SS officer said to the other one, "No question, those two are Oriental types." He gestured toward Bass and Goldie. "And that one's Aryan." He meant Sender. "Tell them to get out of here," he said to the intrepreter. "And tell them the next time we see them we'll shoot them."

We went down the mountain to the little peasant village called Second Losossna, wondering that we were still alive. All we needed was shelter and food for a couple of days, we thought. By then the Russians would be here and we would be safe. But as soon as we walked into town it was obvious we weren't going to have any luck. The first thing I heard was "Zhidi!" "Jews are in the village!" We must have looked like we had come back from the dead—pallid, filthy, sunken eyes, unshaven, wearing an indescribable collection of winter rags. "No," they said when we asked, "we don't have any bread." I recognized a couple of people, and I was sure they recognized me. But it didn't matter. We quickly decided we'd better get out. The peasants were afraid of the Russians coming in, but that wasn't any guarantee they wouldn't denounce us now. I saw the tight smiles on their lips. "Yes," the smiles said. "We know exactly who you are. What business do you have still being alive?"

Outside of the village, we lay down on the banks of the Losossianka. The July sun baked down, making me lethargic and drowsy. I might have fallen asleep, but my stomach was in agony. We hadn't eaten for two days, and then it had just been a hunk of bread, our last meal in the hole. When I started thinking about it I realized that Jan and Janova hadn't been able to feed us much for several days before that either. Finally, Goldie got up. She was going back to the village to find Zosia, she said, a Polish woman in whose house Goldie's family used to stay during their vacations. Maybe she would help.

Sender went with Goldie; the rest of us lay there, exhausted and famished. Then somebody noticed that the field next to us was full of wheat. Mottl said he was pretty sure grain wasn't edible until it had been ground, but we were starving to death and it seemed like a good chance to take. We began picking stalks of wheat and separating the grains. I ground a few of them with my back teeth, trying to crush them into something softer. Then I took a few more. After half a dozen mouthfuls my stomach began to feel a little better, but my jaws hurt so badly I could hardly open my mouth. Maybe I just should have swallowed it, I thought, rather than trying to grind it up.

When Sender and Goldie came back, they brought news. They had found Zosia. She wasn't willing to hide us herself, but she had told them about a deserted cottage in the field not far off. An old woman owned it, but she was staying in the village now and didn't come out often. We could go there; Zosia would try to bring us some food tomorrow.

That night we slept on the dirty straw that was spread on the floor of the cottage, listening to the shooting, which seemed to have picked up again. That was bad news. It sounded as if the Germans were putting up a hard fight, and we had no way of getting food. But the next day Zosia showed up carrying a pot of chicken soup. From the window we watched her put it down in the grass and walk away quickly, obviously not willing to be seen feeding us.

The next day when I woke up, I felt weak. We could get water from the stream, but I needed to eat. The thought occurred to me that I could go into the village and see Antonin, the former mayor of the village, whom my father had known. I even knew which house he lived in. I wasn't sure he would give us anything, but who knew? Anything was better than lying there waiting to starve to death.

When I got into the village I went to Antonin's house and knocked on the door. There was no answer. I pushed it open and walked inside; standing there behind it was his wife, a scrawny, mean-faced woman who took one look at me and began crossing herself furiously. "Jesus Christ," she said. "Jesus Christ. Get out of the house. Get out of the house." It was as if a horrible apparition had appeared in front of her.

"I want to talk to your husband," I said.

"He's not here. Get out! Get out! Get out!"

I turned and walked out, shutting the door behind me. When I looked up, two German military policemen were standing at the front gate, staring at me.

"Who are you?" said one in broken Polish.

"I live here," I said, trying desperately not to show my fright.

"Let me see your papers."

"I, I don't have them. They're at home."

"Where's your house?"

"I'll take you." I didn't know what else to say. "It's in the forest, not far."

We started walking. I was thinking frantically, What am I going to do? Where am I going to take them? But my mind was a blank. Meanwhile, we were walking out of the village and into the woods, in the direction of the abandoned cottage where the others were. I wasn't going to lead them there, but I had no idea what to do. Maybe if we got into some thick woods I could make a break.

"How far is it?" one of them said.

"Another couple of kilometers, sir. But it's no problem. It's really very close."

"To hell with it," said the other in German. "Leave him alone." He obviously had no interest in wandering off into the forest a couple of kilometers just to check on some wretch's papers. Neither did the first. "Okay," he said to me, "we're going to let you go. Just get out of here."

When I got back to the cottage, I was enervated. But nobody else seemed in much better shape. We were out of ideas. The village was worthless to us. Every time someone went there we were taking the chance of being denounced or arrested, even though Sender had told them that there were other Jews in the area. If we were hurt, the Russians would hear about it and punish the entire village. But no one was going to take us in, that was for sure—which meant we were going to have to stay here, with no food, with a battle going on, and the woods full of Germans.

We were sitting around silently on the straw-covered floor of the front room, trying to digest our situation, when we saw Antonin, the former mayor, coming through the field in front of the house. He was carrying a little sack over his shoulder. I couldn't believe his wife had told him about me. Sender and Mottl went out to talk to him, and when they came back in they had the sack with them. Inside was a loaf of bread and a piece of pork fatback, which we divided and swallowed ravenously. Bass said he had given Antonin a British pound note he had been keeping, a wedding present from an uncle who lived in London. Bass had given him his wedding ring, too. Antonin would see what he could do about bringing more food.

The bread and pork fat did wonders. It was funny—before the war I never would have considered eating anything like pork fat, but now it was a lifesaver. I could feel everybody's spirits rising a little. Maybe Zosia or Antonin would come back with more food. Shells were still bursting in the distance, and we could hear the continuous clatter of small-arms fire. But I was sure we could survive if only we could get even a little more to eat.

Sometime that afternoon we saw three German soldiers coming through the field toward the house. A moment later there was a banging on the door. We were sure that someone in the village had turned us in. Rather than wait inside, as if were guilty of something, we all went out to the porch to talk to them. In bad Polish one of the soldiers asked what we were doing there and who we were. Bass went into the old story of having run from the Russians and being caught in the bombardment, except now he added that we had been questioned by the Schutzpolizei already; they had told us to come here. Now we were starving. No one in the village would give us anything to eat. They were all Communists there. We hated Communists.

It sounded to me as if the Germans were swallowing it, but then the non-Polish-speaking one asked the other: *"Sind die Juden?"* Are they Jews? I felt my legs turn to water. I was on the verge of collapsing. "Oh, no," said the first. "They're only Poles. No doubt about it."

With these formalities out of the way they became quite civil, and Bass brought them inside. It seemed as if they had taken a liking to us because we were anti-Communist. We shouldn't be there, they said. The front was much too dangerous. We could get killed up here so close to the fighting. If we went farther back maybe we could get work from the military and find a way to feed ourselves. Meanwhile, they would be back in the evening, and they'd bring some food.

They were as good as their word. That evening we were all napping on the straw when we heard knocking at the door. *"Pan, pan"*—Mister, mister. It was two of the three soldiers, bringing with them bread and a container of cooked macaroni. They looked at us strangely as we wolfed down the macaroni. Then they gave out the other gifts they had brought along, a red sweater and two pairs of stockings—all of them for Goldie Bass.

As one of them stood in the doorway with his rifle, the other told Goldie to go into the other room with him. Goldie got up and went. The door closed behind them. Mottl, Sender, Esther, and I were sitting on the floor, Mottl was trembling. I could see that he wanted to get up and do something, but there was no help for it. I was praying that Goldie would do what the soldier wanted. Otherwise they might shoot us. What's the big deal? I was saying to myself. Let him do it, Goldie. Don't risk all of our lives for something like that. Just close your eyes and let him do it.

A few minutes later they came out, the German obviously not very happy. When the two soldiers left, Goldie told us that he had offered to give her all the food we would need as long as he was there if she would be nice to him. But she had begged him to take pity on her. Don't you have a wife? she had asked. Don't you have a sister maybe? Now it's me, but tomorrow it could be them. Would you like this to happen to them? And it had worked. He was angry, but he didn't do anything, and now they were gone.

The next two days we stayed in the house, listening to the guns. We went out to get water from the stream, but there was nothing to eat. Zosia didn't come back, nor did Antonin. Mostly we lay on the floor, too tired to move, thinking about food. On the hill beyond the field we could see German soldiers. Occasionally we would see planes, and a couple of times there was a fight between Russian and German pilots.

One morning we awoke and the Germans were gone from the hill. They had left during the night. There was no more shooting either, only silence. On the path down from the house a little group of peasants came walking, driving a few cows and pigs in front of them. It was the morning of July 24.

Esther went out to look around. When she came back, she had wonderful news. She was like the dove coming back to Noah's Ark with the olive branch in her beak. "There aren't any Germans," she said. "They've left. I didn't see any Russians either, but the Germans are gone."

We left the house, walking tentatively down the path toward Second Losossno. The fields were deserted. When the path joined the road, we turned toward Grodno. A little way in front of us we saw a solitary figure walking on the road, a Russian soldier. We tried to run, shambling after him as fast as our legs would take us. When he heard us he turned around, surprised by the hands reaching out to touch him and the kisses that were already covering his hands and jacket.

YOUR PEOPLE

THEN I noticed that the Russian soldier wasn't alone. Men in brown uniforms with submachine guns were flitting through the woods on either side of the road. The soldier smiled, then pulled himself away from our hands. He and his friends were the first Soviets to come through, but the Germans were still close by, and they had no time to pay attention to us. Half an hour later we were back at Janova's, hoping that the family might have returned. But the house was deserted and silent. All the doors had been torn out, and the rooms were a jumble of overturned and smashed furniture. The trapdoor was in place, though; no one had discovered the hole. For the last time we went down, digging around for the family photographs Mottl and Esther had buried there.

Almost without talking, we started toward Grodno. The Nieman bridges were blown up; all that was left were pilings and twisted steel. But on the bank of the river we found a man with a rowboat who offered to take us across. On the Grodno side we sat down and took our shoes off to wash our feet. I pulled at my right boot, remembering that the last time I had had my boots off was two weeks before, the night we escaped from the hole. I had had a little problem getting them back on then; in the last year and a half my feet had grown, and it had been all I could do to squeeze them back inside. Now, as I pulled the boot off and unwrapped my foot cloths, my foot felt strange. While I looked at it the foot began to swell until it was almost half again as big as it should have been. I tried to force the boot back on, but it wouldn't go. I quickly decided to leave the other one alone.

With one bare foot and my boot under my arm, I limped into Grodno. Just inside the city, we were stopped by a Soviet patrol. They asked for our papers and Sender said, "We're Jews. We don't have any papers." When the patrol leader insisted, Sender started telling him about the ghetto. But nothing registered. It was as if Sender were describing events that had happened on Mars. "Come with me," said the soldier and instantly the others surrounded us, gesturing with their machine guns. My God, I thought. What now?

We were marched to the Grodno prison, and the great gates swung open to admit us into the courtyard. Inside, we were told to sit down on the cobblestones and wait. I looked around at the graying brick walls and barred windows. I had never seen the inside of the prison before, but this was the place where the Germans had taken the Jewish intellectuals they rounded up at the beginning of their occupation, including my father. They had shot the first hundred; I wondered if they had done it in this courtyard. Soon a Soviet officer walked up and began asking questions, but in a moment we could see that he understood. His eyes were full of sympathy. He was Jewish himself, he told us. "I'm sorry," he said, shaking our hands. "That fellow didn't know what he was doing. I'm so sorry."

From the prison we walked to Brygidzka Street, where we found that our house was empty. The Reiffheisen company was gone, and no one seemed to be living there. Of the four apartments, the upstairs one that had been Grishka's was in the best shape, so we decided to live there.

With no clothes or belongings to unpack, we went outside again and began to walk through the city, hoping to see a familiar face, someone else who had survived. At first we saw no one. But slowly they began to appear. Here and there we saw haunted eyes glancing around furtively. Other Jews, no question; there was no way to hide the hunted expressions or the gaunt, pallid features. *"Amcho?"* one of these ghosts whispered to me. "Your people?" Am I one of your people? *"Amcho,"* I said. "Yes, your people."

Over the next day or two they came back to Grodno, all those who had managed to hide out in nearby attics, cellars, and barns. Dr. Voroshylski had survived with his family (including my friend Viktor), and Dr. Blumstein with his wife Tanya, and their sons Tolek and Alex—both families hidden by Polish people whose lives the doctors had saved before the war. Salomon Zhukovsky, with a long beard and hair hanging down his back, crawled out of the ruins of a section that had been bombed. He had lived alone in a potato cellar like a hermit since the second big deportation, his food brought to him by a Polish friend. My classmate Hela Tarlofsky also emerged, with her father, two uncles, and a cousin, as did Bolek Schiff and Ania Klempner, good friends of Sender's. Franye, the young woman who had been pregnant in Slonim, was there, and Kushka's friend Hillel Braude. There too were the Winicki family, the Gornickis, and Helenka Szewachowicz and Frumka Halpern, who had studied with my mother in the Russian school for medics. When we saw each other we embraced and wept, none of us able to keep down our emotions. We all wanted to know what had happened, to hear about the others, and to tell the story of our own horrors and miracles.

Jonah Zaretsky survived, too, also saved by a Polish family. Jonah was a year or two older than I, but he had always been slight and small for his age. Now he looked even frailer, wizened and on the verge of starvation. During the transport of the ten thousand, when I had hidden in the kitchen crawlspace, Jonah had escaped by jumping into the cesspool underneath one of the courtyard outhouses. Only his diminutive size had allowed him to get down through the toilet opening. The Germans chasing him had looked inside the outhouse, but not down into the hole, where Jonah was fighting to keep his nose and mouth above the surface.

What Jonah told me about the February transport, when I had run off to Janova, filled me with anguish. It was about my parents and Mira. When the action started, they had gone to the hiding place in the attic of the Judenrat building. I knew the place; it was where I would have gone to look for them had Sender let me get out of the Puchalskis'. Jonah had also hidden there. When he asked my mother where I was, she told him that I had gone to work. "I feel that Felix will survive," she had said, "I don't have to worry too much about him." Tears were streaming down my cheeks when he said this. I could picture them so clearly, huddled there in the attic, waiting for the Germans.

In fact the hiding place was found right at the beginning, and Jonah, my family, and the others who had taken refuge there were marched immediately out to the train siding. On the way there Jonah had watched for an opening and had run off. He was the last living person to have seen my family.

Even though we did not yet know for certain about the gas chambers and crematoriums, as we all talked, the certainty sank in that those who were gone were truly gone. The secret hopes that each of us nursed that somewhere, somehow we would see some of our families again were blown away.

On the second day I was overcome when I saw Leon Trachtenberg at the door of our house. We fell into each other's arms, tears running down our faces. Inside the apartment I told him what had happened the day of the deportation, how I had run off from the group working at the Gestapo chief's house and hadn't been able to go back to the headquarters where he was working, as we had planned. Then the story of the Puchalskis and our life in the hole came spilling out.

Leon told me he suspected that I was at the Puchalskis, that he and his parents had gone past Losossna on the way to their hiding place on the farm of Stanislaw Krzywicki, a friend of his father's who lived in the little village of Dulkowszczyzna, east of Grodno. On February 13, the day of the big transport, Leon had been herded back to the ghetto with the rest of the work gang. I hadn't shown up, and he wasn't able to run off. In the ghetto he had been taken to the synagogue where the Germans were concentrating people for the transport. He knew his father hadn't been taken; Meir Trachtenberg had passed himself off as a master mechanic and was considered an essential worker. But Leon had been thrown into the synagogue with the deportees, and when he tried to tell Wiese that he should be allowed to join his father, the Gestapo commander had taken out his pistol and threatened to shoot him. Finally a Jewish policeman managed to convince Wiese that Leon's father was one of the privileged, and they had let Leon out.

In the following days, five thousand Jews were herded into freight cars and shipped East. "The five-thousand transport," Leon called it. Afterward there were only about a thousand left, all of them "useful" workers who were packed into three buildings on Zamkova Street—like a *klatke,* a cage, Leon said. Less than a month later, these, too, were rounded up, except for the ones like Leon's parents, who had gone into hiding.

Leon himself had been put on the last deportee train, but he had climbed through a ventilation window of the moving freight car and jumped to the tracks. When he got back to the ghetto he went to the secret bunkers where the ghetto's last survivors were hiding, three groups of people who had organized and stocked underground places that were known as Grandiski, Krellman, and Landau, after the leaders. Grodno's Jewish world now consisted of a few bunker-dwellers, some others hiding in attics and cellars, and ten or fifteen special craftsmen the Gestapo had kept for themselves.

Making his way by night through the wasteland of the ghetto, Leon had found his parents in their attic hideout. He had led them out, pushing and pulling them over the eight-foot-high church wall that bordered Zamkova Street. In a nearby alley he had arranged with Polish acquaintances to have a car waiting, and they had driven through Losossna to a village some miles away from the Krzywicki farm so the driver would not know their real destination.

Once he got his parents settled in the farmer's barn, Leon had helped his brother Julek to get to Vilno. Then he went off to search for his other brother, Oska. In the Bialystok ghetto he was told that Oska and several others had been shot trying to jump off the same freight train Leon had escaped from. Then, before the Bialystok ghetto itself was liquidated, Leon had found his way back to the farm, where he spent the rest of the war living with his parents in a little enclosure inside the straw bales stacked in the farmer's hayloft. When the front came through, they found that their knees wouldn't work and that they could hardly walk. Their hiding hole had been so small that for the sixteen months they lived there they had been unable to stand up.

The next day I met Zamoszczanski and Julek Trachtenberg, back from the partisans. We also found Lisa Chapnik, Anja Rudd, and Haschia Bielitzka, three girls from Grodno who had escaped to Bialystok using forged Polish documents. Under assumed Polish names they had gotten jobs, working in German Army mess halls and SS kitchens. They had also worked as domestics, cleaning German houses. All the while they had gathered information on German troop movements, plans, and military installations. Together with other Jewish and Polish young women (there were even a few German girls involved, they said) they had hidden stolen weapons and provided intelligence for partisan units operating in the Bialystok region. The spy ring was assisted by a Schindler-like German businessman named Busse. During the day they were poor working girls, so deferential and timid they were virtually invisible. At night they would take their Walther 35 pistols and slip into the forest, carrying the latest news to the guerrilla leaders.

That day, when I got back to our house, who was waiting but Janova Puchalski, who swept me up in her wonderful, strong embrace. She had been frantic with worry about us. When the Germans threw them out, they had been sure we would be caught. There was no way to avoid it. That would be the end of us, and since we would be caught in the Puchalski house, that would be the end of Janova, Jan, and the children, too. Just because the Germans were busy fighting the Soviets was no reason why they wouldn't take time to hunt down those who had hidden Jews.

Afraid for their lives, they had gone to stay with a brother of Janova who lived ten or twelve miles away, far enough, they hoped, for safety. Then, when the Soviets arrived, they had rushed back to their house, only to find that we had disappeared without a trace. Janova had asked around among the villagers and heard that we had been seen. After that she had come searching for us in Grodno.

When I asked about the goat, she laughed. She had been

in a panic, and the only thing that had come to mind was to put the goat in the room. She explained to the Germans that if she left the goat in the yard it would certainly disappear, that's why she wanted it inside. But with the goat in our room, she thought, maybe the soldiers wouldn't go in there to search, and maybe the goat would mask the smell.

With the Puchalskis back, Sender decided I should go to live with them for a while as a kind of emergency fattening measure. I was seventeen years old and I weighed ninety pounds. According to Sender I looked like a walking skeleton, and I was amazed myself when I looked at my arms and legs and saw how the knobs of my elbows and knees stuck out. A refugee physician , Dr. Resnik, who examined me said that I had had tuberculosis, which had left scar tissue on my lungs (Sender, he said, still had active tuberculosis). "This boy has to eat," he told Sender. "You must put some weight on him."

I stayed with Janova for a week or so, eating butter and eggs and drinking milk. Soviet soldiers coming through gave food to us, too, sharing cans of American corned beef and something they called *tushanka,* another American product that seemed to be half fat, half meat. Whatever it was it was delicious, and the corned beef was the best thing I had ever tasted in my life, even better than my grandmother's. I would begin to salivate just thinking about it. Everything the Russians had seemed to be American. They ate American food, drove American Dodge trucks, and even drank American vodka—which they also shared with us. It was all American. (Later, in Danzig, I asked an American sailor for a light, and he flipped me the entire book of matches, leaving me speechless at this offhand demonstration of America's wealth.)

While she was stuffing me, Janova told me about things that had gone on in the house while we were living under the floorboards. The family had lived in constant fear. Every time they saw a German they were terrified that they had been found out. Sabina, the second daughter, said that soldiers used to come around the factory where she had been conscripted to work. When the soldiers had their helmet straps undone the workers knew they were relaxing, but when the helmet straps were snapped shut under their chins, they meant business. People disappeared regularly, and whenever the Germans showed up with their straps shut, Sabina had been sure they were coming for her, that they had already killed the rest of the family and now it was her turn.

The Puchalskis knew there were rumors around that they were hiding Jews, and Janova and Jan had done everything they could to dispel them. They had held parties and little dances at their house (in the hole we had wondered about the extra commotion and what sounded like herds of people trampling around), with the idea that if they invited people in, suspicions would be allayed. Jan even befriended a German officer, whom they had over regularly for tea—another way of guarding the great secret. Would anybody hiding Jews bring a German into his house?

They had also prayed a lot. The whole family went to Mass each Sunday, and they stopped into the church whenever else they could to offer more prayers—for our survival and theirs. At confession the only thing they never talked about was the Jews under the bedroom floor. Janova had laid down the law, Sabina told me. No mention was ever to be made of the subject under any circumstances whatsoever, not even in church. And when Janova said something, none of them thought for a moment about disobeying. Besides, it was said in the village that the Germans had planted priests to spy on people.

After a week at Janova's I went back to Grodno, which by now was filled with Soviet soldiers as the Red Army swarmed after the retreating Germans. But this wasn't the same Red Army that had occupied Grodno from 1939 to 1941. Then anti-Semitism had disappeared as if a magician had conjured it away. The NKVD had made sure of that. Now, I thought, they would be more than just, they would be compassionate. How could they not be? Of Grodno's Jewish community, so far maybe fifty people had come back—fifty survivors out of almost thirty thousand people. How could a tragedy so huge fail to touch these people who had saved us?

But my naive and sentimental expectations died quickly. I would strike up conversations with young Soviet soldiers my age or a year or two older. "Where are you from?" I'd ask. They would tell me, and often they were from some far-off village in Siberia or Central Asia. Everything would be fine until I told them that I was Jewish, that I was a survivor. Then I would feel the scorn and rejection, as if I were somehow contaminated. I'd hear the same kind of words some of the Poles had used for Jews.

But some of the Soviets were themselves Jewish, and with them we had an instant bond. In one way or another they were as devastated as we were. These Jews from the Soviet Union had gone through their own hell during the war, as did all the Soviet people. But they had not witnessed the full force of the Nazi extermination machinery. Now they were in Poland, the heart of the European Jewish community. And they found that the Jewish world was dead, except for a few souls here and there popping up from wherever it was they had managed to hide themselves. These soldiers were in horror at what they saw, and they clung to us. We clung to each other.

Not that the Soviet Union had been spared. Wherever the Germans had gone they had brought their organs of annihilation with them. Minsk, Smolensk, Vitebsk, Kiev, Kharkov—none of the population centers in Byelorussia or the South had escaped. Jews in these places had not been deported to death camps. Those were too far away. Instead the Germans had killed them on the spot, slaughtering everyone they could lay their hands on.

But many of the Russian Jews had had the chance to survive. Nothing happened instantaneously. Depending on where the Jews were, it had taken the Germans a week to get there, or two weeks, or two months. Whoever stayed and waited died, but many had time to run away, to become refugees, moving east behind the front.

Now their sons had come westward through the Jewish graveyards, and they were overwhelmed. Many of them became Zionists and deserted, dropping their uniforms and smuggling themselves to Palestine. Others said, "Let's finish the Germans off first; then we'll go."

In our apartment these Russian Jewish soldiers were always there, either staying with us or just stopping by to visit. You could feel their love; they were the same as we were. We felt that Jews were a single people. The differences that had been so significant in earlier times, capitalist or Socialist or Communist, no longer mattered. Now we were just Jews.

Polish Army units began to come through, too. The Poles in the Soviet Union had formed their own army under General Anders, which had fought in the Middle East, North Africa, and Italy under the British. But Stalin had also succeeded in creating another Polish Army, under Communist control, and many of the troops in that army were Jewish. Some of my older friends and acquaintances had fled to the Soviet Union when the Germans attacked in 1941 and had fought throughout the war with these units. Now they began to filter back, people such as Josef Szwarc and Jashka Jonas, who had lost his wife and daughter in the ghetto.

Partisans were also in Grodno, from groups that had operated in the vicinity and had helped spearhead the Soviet offensive. Now many of these units had been disbanded, and on the street you could come across Jewish partisans, some of them quite young. Boys who had actually done the things I had dreamed about doing.

One of these was my classmate Noah Berezowski. Zeydl Asch had also been fighting. He was an orphan who remembered Grandma Tema bringing food and clothing to his orphanage. He had seen, he said, my grandfather Freydovicz riding in the sled with the children, just before he himself had escaped from the "10,000 Transport." Another partisan was Solomon Polachik, whom Leon Trachtenberg found wandering around the streets one day utterly alone. Solomon had broad shoulders and a smiling, open face. We took to him immediately. He was from Lida, where my uncle Grushka and his wife had lost their lives. But before the Einsatzgruppen arrived Solomon's family had fled to Wasilishky, a little town not far away. A short time later the Wasilishky Jews had been rounded up and machine-gunned in front of an open pit. Solomon's mother and sister were killed, but Solomon himself wasn't hit. When night fell he managed to crawl out of the pit and get away—to Grodno, of all places. There he had lived in Ghetto One until he was captured for the transport to Kielbasin at the end of November 1942, the same transport I had marched in with my parents and sister. Solomon, though, never reached Kielbasin. He slipped away before the column even left the Grodno synagogue.

After another series of escapes Solomon had made contact with a partisan group in the forest and at the age of fifteen had started fighting Germans. By sixteen he was a squad leader and demolitions expert who specialized in blowing up trains and bridges. Until he was taken into the partisans he had never held a gun in his hands. Now he became a skilled guerrilla fighter, and when his unit was finally disbanded he had a jacketful of medals.

Back in Grodno he was searching for friends and relatives but finding that they were all dead. When Leon met him he was living in the back room of a bank that had given him work, desperately lonely. They had instantly recognized each other as kindred spirits. Leon introduced me to Solomon, and when I saw where he was living, I invited him to come stay with us.

By this time our apartment had become a kind of way station for survivors, refugees, and Jewish soldiers. Mottl and Goldie Bass lived with us, as did Josef Weiss, a friend of Sender's who had also turned up alive. Then Pela Byelodvorski and her husband, Meshel, emerged from their hiding place in the forest and joined the permanent residents, which was particularly welcome since Pela was a wonderful cook. Others moved in and out, wanderers and stragglers from other Jewish communities, people trying to go to Israel by foot, people searching for their relatives, trying to find traces of their disappeared families. When these

Jewish survivors came through Grodno they would end up either at our house or at the Trachtenbergs'. One would stop for three days, then disappear; then two more would show up, stay a night, and leave.

Usually people would walk from the Soviet Union into Poland. But we also saw some moving in the opposite direction. A few partisans came from Bialystok into Grodno—that is, into Russia. I would ask, "What's going on? Shouldn't you be going the other way?" But these were committed Communists. They were not staying with the reactionary Poles if they had a chance to live in the Soviet Union.

Now Solomon Polachik moved in. Since the apartment was already chock full, he and I shared a bed. By now Leon and I and Viktor Voroshylski, another friend of ours who had turned up alive, were thinking about school. I tried to persuade Solomon that he ought to come along with us. But he refused. Day by day the front was moving west, and he was distraught about having been left behind. "I have to keep fighting," he said. He couldn't stand the thought that there was still a German Army and he wasn't helping to kill it.

"Solomon," I said, "please. Your parents are dead, your brothers and sister are dead. You're alone. Stay with us. We'll go to Poland [since Grodno had now been annexed by the Soviet Union and Sender was considering a move to Bialystok]. Then we'll go to Israel. Stay with us. We've all lost our families. Now we are each other's family. This is our family now. Stay with us. Don't go. You've killed a lot of Germans already. Your jacket is full of medals. You don't have to do it anymore."

But he was immovable. "No," he said. "I can't do it. It would be desertion. I've got to fight them until the end."

His chance came when the Soviet administration decided to draft everyone age seventeen or older into the army. Leon, Viktor Voroshylski, and I decided we wouldn't go. They weren't any stronger than I was; it was all we could do to walk around. Physically and emotionally we were exhausted. Even with the thought of vengeance so powerful, we couldn't imagine how we might possibly be able to train or march.

Before we could be drafted, though, we had to have identity papers, and since so many refugees had none, the Soviets set up a documentation center called ZAKS. With no records available, the ZAKS officials used a time-tested method of estimating age. They made people open their mouths, as if they were horses, and they examined their teeth. They'd look inside, consider carefully, then say, "You're seventeen." And if that was the decision, the next day you'd find yourself in the army.

Since we had been malnourished for so long, our teeth were terrible. One look in our mouths and they might decide we were thirty. But Leon, as resourceful as ever, nosed around and found a way of getting fake identity papers that proved we were sixteen instead of seventeen.

Solomon, though, would have no part of it. He hadn't an ounce of guile in him, and faking a birth date didn't sound kosher to him. But the main point was that there were still Germans out there, and as long as there were, how could he lie around in Grodno? I spent days and nights drinking with him and talking (thanks to our army friends we had plenty of vodka), doing everything I could to persuade him to stay with us. Maybe a dozen of Grodno's young people had survived in all, and the thought of him going off to get killed was unbearable. But it was a lost cause.

Two months after Solomon joined up, a notice came that he had been killed in East Prussia. He had been a gunner in the artillery. His gun had been destroyed by enemy tank fire, and the entire crew had died. I felt guilty beyond words. Whatever I had said to Solomon, it hadn't been enough. If I had only kept talking, maybe I could have found some other argument. Maybe with Sender's help, or somebody's, I could have physically kept him from going. But I had lost him, and now he, too, was dead.

•

By now Goldie and Mottl Bass had left for Bialystok, on the first step of a journey they hoped would take them to Israel. More Russian Jews came and went as the Red Army continued to pour through Poland. But Grodno also had a garrison force, and we had become really close to a number of the Jewish soldiers stationed in town. They seemed to be at our apartment all the time, with their cans of food and their supply of vodka. We would eat and drink; then they'd take out their balalaikas and accordions and sing melodious Russian folk songs about faraway homes and lost loves. We'd join in and get so carried away by the music that we could almost forget for a moment what had happened.

Major Gorchakov was one of the Russians who attached himself to us. Gorchakov and Sender had a special bond, and the Russian officer became a partner in Sender's struggle to keep food on our table. Sender was a resourceful man. As soon as we settled in, he had found out what the scarcities were in Grodno and what goods were in greatest demand. Then he discovered where a person might acquire such things and how he might sell them. So Sender bought and he sold. He and Gorchakov would cross the Russian-Polish border to Bialystok, buy beer, cigarettes, and other commodities, then sell them in Grodno. The money was next to worthless, but it bought us food.

We had been liberated at the end of July. By October the Soviet administration had gotten the schools open. Leon, Viktor Voroshylski, and I had been looking forward to this, and Sender was urging me to start studying again. Of the ten grades in Soviet schools, I had finished seven before the Germans came in. According to my age I should have been in tenth. But like all the other survivors, I had lost three years of my life. There were huge gaps in our learning.

But at least I had learned some math and science in the hole, which was more than Leon and Viktor had done. But we wanted to start tenth grade together, so we studied like mad that summer until we were all prepared to do it. The result was that everyone else in the class was twenty and we were seventeen.

Math class especially was a wonderful experience. The math teacher loved me. He couldn't understand how I could do

complicated equations in my head. He would call on me for an answer, and it would be there. Of course, he didn't know that I had
just spent seventeen months cooped up in the dark next to a gifted
math teacher doing nothing but figuring equations in my head, so
he was very impressed. "You must do a doctorate in math," he said.
"You have to, you can do these things so well."

"No," I said, "I'm not really interested."

"Why not, Felix? What do you want to be?"

"An engineer," I answered.

"An engineer?" he said. "What a shame."

Viktor Voroshylski was a real talent, at math as well as
everything else he touched. Among his other gifts, he had blossomed into a poet. We found him writing poems on any random
subject that came into his head: the teacher, the sun, the girl in the
next row. To Leon and me the poems seemed extraordinary. But
his father wanted him to become a doctor (medicine being a more
promising profession than poetry), and Viktor was struggling to
suppress his own desires and comply.

Among the girls in our class the most beautiful by far
was Klara, a Russian with blue eyes and soft blond hair. As soon as
we saw her, Leon said, "That's mine!" "Wait a minute," I said.
"She's not property. Let's see what happens." In the end Klara's eyes
were drawn in my direction.

Klara turned out to be very kind and gentle. She lived
with her mother in Grodno. Her father was fighting at the front,
and they hadn't heard from him in so long that they didn't know if
he was alive or dead. We kissed—once, then many times. It did not
go beyond kissing, but the kisses were wonderful. She even took
me to her house and introduced me to her mother. She was twenty
and I was seventeen; I was so in love with her I was dizzy. She was
so tender and affectionate, and I was in desperate need. I wanted to
marry her, although I was shy about telling her that.

Sender was a tower of strength to me, but from Sender
there was no affection, no outward signs of warmth. When he
learned about Klara he was beside himself. "Felix," he said, "you

are completely out of your mind!" And since we had declared our-selves Polish citizens instead of Soviets, with the right of repatria-tion to Poland, before I knew it I found myself on the train to Bialystok, sent off to live with the Basses, who had now taken an apartment there.

An Incomprehensible Treasure

THE Basses' house in Bialystok was another way station, just as ours had been in Grodno. It didn't appear on any map, but people coming through on all sorts of business knew about it. Partisans stopped in, organizers for Aliyah Bet (the illegal immigration to Palestine), gun runners for the Haganah (Palestine's underground Jewish army), refugees of all sorts. They all knew the house and stayed there when they came through the city.

One day one of the transients said, "Felix, you want to earn some money? Here's what you do. I've got twenty dollars in gold. You sell it for me and I'll give you a commission." It sounded good. "I don't know where to do that," I said, "but I'll ask around."

It didn't take long to find someone and agree on a price. When I gave the Polish money to the house guest, he gave me 5 percent. For the first time in ages I had money in my pocket. I did it a second time, then a third. I could already see a little business opening up. But when Sender came through on one of his buying trips he put a stop to it. Was he angry! "Felix, I don't want you getting involved in any speculations. You understand? It's dangerous. It's not for you. You have to study, you have a head, a *kopf*. So study, you hear me? That's your job. Forget this *chazerai!*"

"But Sender, I can make money. Why not?"

"Absolutely not! You go your own way, and your way is studies. Swear that to me."

So I had to swear to stop, but I didn't like it at all. Here I could bring money home, doing the same kind of thing Sender himself was doing. And now I had to stop? What business did he have?

But I couldn't keep Sender from trying to protect me. I understood it well enough. I was the only young person left from the family, and he could not help treating me like a jewel that needed safekeeping. Not that he was always able to keep me out of trouble. One day Sender's partner Gorchakov took me with him on a collection trip. He and Sender had been selling beer, and a restaurant owner owed them money. When we got there the owner paid up, and we sat down to enjoy some of the fruits of Gorchakov's labor. We ate and drank. And drank. I had never seen anyone drink as much as Gorchakov was drinking, and by then I had been around a lot of Russian soldiers. He was drinking like a fish, like a pig. He was pouring rivers of vodka down his throat. He was so drunk I began to despair about getting home. "Look," I said, "there's a curfew, and it's getting late. What's going to happen?"

"Don't worry," came the slurred reply. "I'm an officer of the valiant Red Army and you're with me. Nobody's going to bother us."

"But I'm a civilian."

"It doesn't matter. I'll protect you."

When I finally dragged him out of the restaurant, he could barely stay on his feet. On the way home we were stopped by two patrols, but when they saw Gorchakov's rank they let us go, despite the hour. But just before we got to our house we were surrounded by four young soldiers who were obviously ready for anything. All they saw was a couple of people who shouldn't have been out on the street, one of whom was staggering around trying to keep from falling down. They saw prey.

I had a black-face Cyma watch at the time, which I had gotten from Josef Weiss, who lived with us in Grodno. Weiss had been a watchmaker and had buried a case of watches under his house before the ghetto days. During the war the house had been destroyed, and Weiss couldn't figure out where the case was buried. Sender helped him reconstruct how the house was laid out, where the kitchen had been, the living room, the chimney, and finally he pointed out where they should dig. When they did, there was the case. Some of the watches Weiss sold and some he gave away to our group. I got the Cyma, a famous and expensive Swiss make.

By the end of the war the Russians were using watches as money. You could see them wearing their wealth on their wrists and forearms. Some of them had four, five, or six of them strapped on. These young soldiers spotted mine instantly, and they wanted it. But I wouldn't give it up, and a free-for-all started. They were pounding me and I was swinging back for all I was worth, and there was Gorchakov leaning against a wall, oblivious to everything. I was shouting at him to pull his gun out and do something when one of the Russians smashed me in the face with his pistol butt and broke my nose. I was bleeding all over the place but I kept fighting and yelling, and they finally grabbed Gorchakov's gun and ran off. But they didn't get my watch and they didn't get the pouch of money Gorchakov had tied to his belt either.

When we got into the house we were a mess. I was covered with blood, and Gorchakov looked like he had spent the night in a gutter. When Sender saw us, he was horrified. "I saved the money," I said. "Schmuck!" he shouted. "Who cares about the money? To hell with the money. Give them the money, give them the watch. What's wrong with you?" "No!" I shouted back. "I'm not helpless. You think I'm just going to let them beat me up?" Sender was so mad I thought he was going to beat me up himself. "You're risking your life, Felix. Your life! What are you doing?" He was roaring, he was so angry. Franye Braude was staying in the house then, too, the young woman from Grodno who had been pregnant in Slonim that terrible day when the war started. She had lost her first husband, and her baby had been given to a Polish family for safekeeping. She had remarried while she was in hiding and now was pregnant again. Franye started to laugh. "Sender, he's bleeding like a pig, and you're yelling about watches and money. Look, his nose is smashed over to the side of his face."

Sender was so strange. He never showed any outward affection, yet he guarded and protected me like a mother hen. I tried to convey my feelings for him, but it was very difficult between us. We were so closed up in the armor of our defenses. We never hugged or touched each other. Not that he didn't want it or I didn't want it. But it was not done.

In March Mottl and Goldie Bass left Bialystok for

Lublin, where the Bricha—the chief organization that smuggled Jews out of Europe to Palestine—ran one of its main operations. From Vilno, Grodno, Bialystok, all the Jewish areas in Lithuania and eastern Poland, the underground railroads led to Lublin. From there groups were taken across the Romanian border to the Black Sea port of Constanta, where they took ship for Israel. Later, when Germany fell and Romania became Communist, the Bricha opened routes through Austria and Italy, then through France, skirting the Communist embargo and the British blockade of Israel's coasts.

Watching the Basses leave, it suddenly seemed to me that the time had come for me to go to Israel, too, as I had been planning for years. I made the decision on the spur of the moment, without talking to anyone about it. In fact, there was no one to talk to. Sender was off somewhere on a buying trip, and I knew what he would say anyhow. Leon Trachtenberg had also come to Bialystok, but by now had moved to Lodz, where his father had bought a bakery—so he wasn't available either. I was in school, trying hard to finish. But I could do that in Israel, too. I thought. Why stay?

I packed a few clothes and took the train to Lublin, where I found Mottl and told him what I had decided. He introduced me to someone from one of the kibbutz movements, and before I knew it I had joined a group of young people waiting to be smuggled out of Poland. While we waited, we hid out in a basement that had been rigged with bunks, listening to kibbutzniks tell us what to expect and discussing the new life that would soon be ours in Eretz Yisrael.

I had been in the basement for a week when all of a sudden Leon showed up. He had heard about my plans and had come searching for me. Leon had news: Sender had been arrested in Grodno, but not for black marketeering. The NKVD had picked him up for being the son of a well-known bourgeois capitalist. They had thrown him into the Grodno prison, and if it hadn't been for Gorchakov, they would have sent him to Siberia. But

Gorchakov had somehow gotten him out and had spirited him to Bialystok, hidden in the back of a truck. Leon had seen Sender in Bialystok. Soon he would be in Lodz, and he wanted me to meet him there.

I said, "I'm not going back. I'm sorry for Sender, but I've decided to go to Israel." But Leon wasn't the kind who took no for an answer. What was the rush about going to Israel? I could go there anytime. But how could I leave Sender alone? "Besides," said Leon, "you haven't finished school yet." Why wouldn't I come to Lodz and finish high school with him and Viktor, who was also there? We could all study together and finally get it out of the way. Didn't I think I should graduate from high school first? Afterward I could go to a kibbutz.

In the end Leon persuaded me. I said good-bye to my fellow prospective kibbutzmates, telling them that eventually I'd meet them in Israel. Then we got the train for Lodz. Sender hadn't arrived yet. But we met Viktor Voroshylski there, and Josef Szwarc, who had been fighting with Stalin's Polish army. Leon also introduced me to Hillel Seidel, the local head of the Bricha. Seidel was a powerful character who had fought with the underground resistance in the Vilno ghetto, eventually escaping, staying alive by moving from hideout to hideout. Leon, it turned out, had been leading groups for him from Lodz to Krakow, from where they were smuggled into Czechoslovakia. Now, Seidel told us, he was interested in weapons.

Among other things, the Bricha ran homes for children who had lost their parents to the Nazis. Recently they had been having trouble with Polish anti-Semites, and they needed to be able to guard these places. They needed guns. Whatever they couldn't use, the Haganah could. Would Leon and I be willing to buy guns for them in the North—in Grodno and Kovno and Bialystok? Pistols, submachine guns, anything that would shoot and would fit into a suitcase. If we could find sources for bigger weapons, that would be good, too. The Bricha would make other arrangements to pick them up.

On May 7, 1945, I was eighteen (seventeen according to the fake identity card in my wallet). That evening Viktor and Leon were helping me celebrate when we heard over the radio that Germany had surrendered. That same night, with Hillel Seidel's gun money in our pockets, Leon and I took the train to Warsaw. In the capital, Russian soldiers were going wild, firing their rifles into the air and blowing off fireworks everywhere, screaming "Peace! Peace! Peace!" At the house of an uncle of one of our friends we raised a glass of vodka to it, too, though our own celebration was more muted than the one going on in the streets. For us the victory had come much too late.

From Warsaw we traveled to Bialystok, the first stop on our gun-buying mission. There was Josef Weiss, and there was Sender, too, looking odd. In prison they had shaved his head, and the hair was just beginning to grow into a stubble. Of course, I didn't say a word to him about the gun-running. I knew his reaction would have been immediate and decisive. He told me about his arrest for being the son of the capitalist Nahum Freydovicz. (I thought of my poor grandfather riding off in the snow with the three babies in his arms, on their way to the railroad siding.) Gorchakov and another friend, Colonel Bondarenko, had saved Sender by bribing an NKVD man.

But even then it had been touch and go. They were sure the police were going to pick him up again. Gorchakov hadn't been able to make immediate arrangements to get Sender out of Grodno, so he had hidden with Lisa Chapnik, Anja Rud, and Haschia Bielitzka, the partisan spy ring heroines. They were happy to help Sender, but there were only two beds in the room, and that was a problem. Two people could squeeze into one bed, but who would sleep with Sender? Anja Rud, whose husband had been killed, had sworn never to sleep with another man. Neither of the others had ever slept with a man at all, and they weren't about to start now.

Eventually it was decided that Lisa and Anja would sleep in one bed and Haschia and Sender in the other. According to an old Jewish custom, when unmarried people were forced by circumstances to sleep in the same bed, they had to have a board between them. With no boards handy, and no room for one anyway, Haschia and Sender had separated themselves with a towel. Knowing Sender's rigorous approach to self-discipline, I doubted that the towel had been necessary.

It didn't take long before Leon and I began to find sources for weapons. With the German Army having been chased out not long before and the Soviet Army in residence, guns weren't a scarcity. We started asking among likely Jews where we could get a pistol, or a rifle, or grenades, and before long we had acquired enough weapons to fill a big suitcase.

We wrapped all the guns carefully in rags so they wouldn't bang into each other or knock around; then we dragged the suitcase onto the train for Warsaw. In Warsaw we had to change for Lodz, and it was all we could do to wrestle the monstrously heavy suitcase off one train and hoist it into the other. I was still painfully skinny, and Leon wasn't too sturdy himself. When we got to our compartment, two of the seats were taken up by Red Army officers. I knew that if they found the guns the best that would happen would be that we would be sent to Siberia. It was far more likely the Soviet authorities would just shoot us. I was so nervous I began to get dizzy.

We had dragged the suitcase into the compartment, but getting it up on the overhead baggage racks was completely beyond our capabilities. Leon, though, was nothing if not bold. As if it were the most natural thing in the world, he turned to the Russians and asked if they could give us a hand. "This is so heavy," he said. "Would you mind?" No, they wouldn't mind. The blood was pounding in my head. Up went the suitcase while I strained to hear the telltale clink of metal on metal that would have given us away and guaranteed an appointment with some NKVD executioner. I knew that Leon was one of the great chutzpadiks, but this was too much even for him.

In Lodz I took up residence at the Trachtenbergs' house,

and that April we started school again—Viktor, Leon, and I. Leon's parents arranged private teachers for us, but there was a tremendous amount to catch up on in Polish language, literature, history, and other areas we had had virtually no contact with for several years. At least in literature there were abridgements, but we were so far behind we didn't even have time to read the abridgements. So we split them up. Each of us would read some of them, then we'd tell each other the stories. In June 1945 we took the exam. Thanks to my math training in the hole, I got through that section in record time, and I managed to squeeze through the others, too. When it was over, all three of us had our baccalaureates.

Meanwhile, Sender was constantly on the move, doing business all over Poland and taking serious risks. He and Josef Weiss, who had become one of his partners, were smuggling merchandise from place to place and on occasion carrying significant amounts of money. (I had once met Sender walking down the street with a big sack over his back. I asked him if he had potatoes in there and he said, "No, money.")

In Bialystok they were arrested with large amounts of paper currency and gold and thrown into jail. Weiss told me later that they spent the night in a cell before being interrogated by the commandant the next morning. Sender lay down on a bench and started to snore instantly. But Weiss was too nervous to sleep, and after a while he woke Sender up to try to work out a story. "Let me sleep," said Sender. "Tomorrow morning we'll figure out what to say." In the morning they were taken into the commandant's office, where he had the paper money and the gold stacked up on his desk. "Look," said Sender, "why don't we make a deal? You keep the gold for yourself, give us the paper, and let us go." And the commandant accepted, because otherwise he would have had to record everything, and it would all have gone to the state.

That time it had worked out, but Sender's business was constantly nerve-racking, and he was looking around for something more stable. At about the time I graduated from high school, an opportunity came to buy a bakery in Danzig. With food shortages a regular feature of life, bakeries were good business (Leon's father had bought one, too). Sender decided to buy, and I moved to Danzig to join him and some of our other friends from Grodno.

I wasn't prepared for Danzig, at least not for Danzig's Germans. In Grodno and Bialystok I had seen columns of German prisoners of war being marched through the streets by Russian soldiers, on their way to some horrible Soviet prison camp. They were exhausted, filthy, and dispirited; they walked in silence with their heads down, beaten men. But in Danzig there was a big German civilian population walking around free. Since my first gun-running trip with Leon I had always carried a pistol with me. Killing Germans was no crime. The Poles hated their guts, and the Russian occupation troops wouldn't do more than spit on their bodies.

All my black fantasies from the hole flooded over me. I had dreamed of killing. How vivid my visions had been! I could still conjure them up in all their murderous detail. How I would have a gun and go to Germany. How I would shoot everyone I saw. Shoot them until the gun was red hot, shoot them until they were all dead on the ground. I had sworn to my father I would do this. I had made vows to my mother. If I ever got out of the hole I would do this for them and my sister Mira, and for my uncles and aunts and for Grandma Tema. For all of them.

And now I had a gun. Now I could do it. I looked at the Germans in the street—women and children and old people mostly. There were almost no men. I looked at them and I hated them. Look what their husbands did, and their fathers and brothers. My inner voice was talking to me. They would have done it themselves had they had the chance. Nazis, all of them Nazis. When I was lying there with Sender and the Basses I hadn't made any distinctions—men, women, children. I wanted to kill them all. As many as possible.

But now doubts began to come. Maybe I had been deceived about myself. I had sworn the most solemn oaths that I would do it. But I had never asked myself if I was the kind of per-

NEVER THE LAST JOURNEY

son who could perform such an act. Not in the heat of battle, or to defend myself or somebody else—that I didn't doubt for a moment I could do. But could I put a gun to somebody's head in cold blood and pull the trigger? I watched the women and children, these wretched, ragged Germans, and I simply did not have it in my heart to kill them.

As I realized this, I felt guilt sliding in. It sat down, and it stayed. I tried talking to my mother and father about it, and to my grandparents. I felt they were there with me, in my head. "Do you want me to do this?" I asked them. "Do you want me to shoot down these people here to avenge the rivers of our blood that they spilled?" I felt so badly that I was not just taking out my pistol and emptying it at them. But after a while I thought I had my father's approval. My mother I was not so sure about, either then or later.

So I settled down in Danzig on the second floor of a little house on Kochanowski Street, not far from the bakery. Sender was there and our friend Josef Weiss; also Jonah Zaretsky; Korascz, a former partisan; and Pela and Meshel Byelodvorsky, an old Tarbut teacher of mine. We had also been in touch with Jan and Janova. The new borders put Losossna inside the Soviet Union, but the Puchalskis had declared themselves Polish citizens, with the right of repatriation. Under the new agreement between the Poles and Soviets, anyone who was caught in the border shuffle and claimed repatriation had the right to compensation for their house. The Puchalskis' two-room house had been owned by the Freydoviczes; it was part of the summer houses my grandfather had built. But after liberation we had signed it over to Jan and Janova, and now they were able to trade it for an equivalent house in Danzig. So they, too, came to live near us, which gave me the chance to see Janova often and to be welcomed in her powerful arms.

Sender's bakery needed a bookkeeper-accountant, and that became my job, one that I knew absolutely nothing about. Before long Sender and I were squabbling again. The bakery business might have been profitable, but I didn't see the future in it. "Why don't we drop all this and go to Israel?" I argued. But Sender, of course, had other ideas for me. "Felix," he said, "you should enter the university."

"Sender, we have to go to Israel. What do we need this for? There's nothing holding us here."

"No, no, no! Now that you have your baccalaureate, Felix, I want you to do one year at the university. One year, that's all. Then at least you'll know what it is. If you reject it after that, okay. You'll reject it. You won't hear another word out of me. But first I want you to find out what it is. One year, then you'll see."

Needless to say, somebody else became the accountant, and I started classes in engineering at Danzig's École Polytechnicum. For the Jewish survivors it was a shaky time. It seemed incredible, but a current of anti-Semitism was again sweeping through Poland. The remains of the Jewish community was in a state of traumatic shock. People were struggling to reconstitute something out of lives pulverized by the Nazis, and already the specter had returned. The Bricha had sent us out to buy weapons primarily for self-protection. They feared for the safety of their orphanages and refugee centers.

On one level I accepted all this as normal. Hostility was part of the atmosphere I had been breathing forever. You just blocked it out and got on with your business. But at a deeper level my heart refused to accept it. Look, fellows, I wanted to scream— there are no more Jews. We're all dead. What are you afraid of?

Then on July 4, 1946, news came of a violent pogrom in Kielce, southeast of Warsaw. A rumor had started that Jews there had killed a Polish child, the old blood libel. A mob had attacked a group of survivors who were trying to rebuild the city's Jewish community. Forty-two people had been murdered.

The deaths sent a horrible shudder through the Jewish population. For the raw, exposed nerves of the survivors, it was too much. People started fleeing Poland to Czechoslovakia and Hungary—whatever border they could get across. There was a surge of refugees for Israel. All of a sudden, everyone wanted to go. Already Romania had been closed off by the newly installed Communist government. But the routes through Italy and France were choked with people desperate to get out.

In the midst of this hysteria, one night noises began coming up to us from the street outside our second-floor apartment. We looked out the window and saw a crowd gathering in the street. Angry voices reached up. "The Jews killed a Pole. The Jews killed a Pole." There were no other Jews in the neighborhood. This was for us. Then it started. *"Bij Zydow! Bij Zydow!"* Smash the Jews! Let's kill the Jews! More and more people were streaming in. Already there must have been a hundred of them.

We locked the house. We took sheets from the bed, tied them together in knots, then dropped them through one of the back windows. Outside, the mob was gathering steam. We could hear them pounding on the door; then it sounded as if they were trying to kick it down. Jonah was too afraid, so Sender went down the sheets first, then Pela and Meshel Byelodvorsky, Korasz, and I. Last was Josef Weiss, but he was too heavy and the sheets broke, pitching him onto the ground.

Sender grabbed me. "You run for the police," he said. "I'll try to get the Russians." Then he was gone. I ran as fast as I could the block and a half to the neighborhood police station. Out of breath, I gasped, "We're being attacked. Help us. Please help us." "What's that you're saying?" said the officer behind the desk. "What do you mean, you're being attacked?" I explained, but the questions kept coming. Who are you? What's your name? Exactly what is the address where you say this is happening? They were as interested in this as they would have been in something taking place in South America.

I couldn't stand it. I was going to dash back to the house, but they grabbed me and kept me in the police station. A few minutes later I heard shooting, and when I finally got back, the crowd was gone. Sender had gotten to the Soviet Army compound, and they had come running. The police might not have been interested, but the Russians were happy for the chance to roust out a crowd of Poles.

It was a bad time. Even Jan and Janova were scared, afraid to say out loud that they had had anything to do with saving Jews. In their hearts they were intensely proud of what they had done, and no one could have been more courageous than they. But their heroism put them in danger; it could not be spoken of. Talking to them, and realizing what their situation was, the profundity of our own isolation hit home. Poland was nothing more than a cemetery. We decided to leave.

With the pressure growing, I received a letter one day at the Polytechnicum from Josef Rakoch, the president of the Jewish Students' Association at the University of Warsaw. By this time I was involved in several Zionist organizations, and because of my gun-running for the Bricha I had made connections in different parts of the country. One consequence of my activity was that I had been elected president of the Jewish Students' Union of Gdansk (the Polish name for Danzig), and it was in this capacity that Rakoch was writing to me. He had just received a letter from the French Union of Jewish Students, inviting Polish Jewish students to a conference in Uriage les Baines. The French students had arranged for sixty visas.

Sixty French visas were an incomprehensible treasure. All the Jewish student presidents from the main universities met and decided that Rakoch and I should organize this business, together with Hillel Seidel, who was now the head of a youth movement. Rakoch and I were already friends. I had met him while I was in Warsaw for the Bricha and had slept in his room one night. (He had insisted that I take the bed while he slept on the floor.) Rakoch, Seidel, and I decided right away that the visas should be used for what the French students had obviously intended, which had nothing to do with any conference. They knew about the situation in Poland and how difficult it was to get out of the country. Even though Poland was still nominally independent, the Polish secret police were working closely with the NKVD. The Iron Curtain was beginning to drop. But we had in our hands sixty legal certificates to leave Poland. No one using these documents was ever coming back.

We decided that each one who went would be allowed to take family members, parents, siblings, uncles, aunts—anyone who by any stretch of the imagination might pass for a student. With Seidel organizing our strategy, Rakoch and I got to work. Rakoch was a master at manipulating the system. He had connections all over, and I accompanied him to one ministry after another, mostly waiting outside while he conducted the necessary business. When we had made all the official arrangements, we listed the sixty who would be going. On my side, Sender would come, and Josef Weiss, whose fall out of the second-story window had mainly injured his dignity. Many on the list came under assumed names, or took the places of those who couldn't make it for some reason. Relatives and friends and those who owed favors switched papers and passports. Cohens became Weissoviches, Levins became Epsteins. People used all the subversive identity tricks they had learned in the ghettos. Changes and substitutions were being made right up to the last moment on the train platform in Warsaw. The only point was to get out. We were taking risks with all of this, but we had all learned via the method of undergoing major surgery without anesthesia that when you had a chance to leave, you had better grab it.

A QUANTUM LEAP IN CULTURES

As departure time approached, our anxiety levels soared, especially mine. On international trains customs officials did their inspections in Warsaw, then sealed the baggage. But this group wasn't going to bear too much scrutiny. Half of us were well past university age, and everyone had piles of luggage. Some had mountains. There were all kinds of things we didn't want anyone looking at. Not that I had inspected the luggage myself, but I knew for sure there had to be weapons and gold and God only knew what else. This was no collection of students going to a conference, but an emigration of refugees carrying their most precious possessions with them.

A little earlier Rakoch and a few of the others came to me and said, "Felix, you're probably the best at this kind of thing. You talk to the customs guy." Then they handed me a pile of money. By the time the official arrived, I had just managed to swallow my fear. "Listen," I said, "you're very busy and we've got a lot of people here. Why don't you do us a favor. Don't look at anything. We don't have anything you'd be interested in anyway." Then I gave him the stack of bills. He took them without a word, stamped our papers, and left. It wasn't until he moved out of sight that I started breathing again.

We crossed into Czechoslovakia and came to Prague, where we found that the train to Paris was not running. When it might start again they couldn't say. Maybe in a week. Maybe two. Fortunately, the Bricha there was able to make arrangements for us to stay in a camp where they were housing refugees on their way to Palestine.

We ended up visiting Prague for a wonderful week. I loved it. The city smelled different, like freedom—such a change from the anxiety that was always in the air in Poland. I went to concerts and saw my first opera: *Carmen*. It was tremendous. I began to wonder what Paris would be like. Till now I had been so occupied with getting out of Poland that I had hardly had time to think about it.

When we finally arrived at the Gare de l'Est, our sponsors were waiting on the platform to welcome us. As we climbed down from the train we were embraced by Paul Sternschuss, Adi Steg, and Tecucciano, the heads of the French Union of Jewish Students, the ones responsible for organizing this rescue. When we voted for a committee to see who would represent our contingent from here on, I was chosen unanimously, except for my own vote. I was very pleased, even though the group fell apart the moment after the vote was taken. There was nothing to keep us together. Not a single person was going to the conference.

Everybody began to look around for possibilities—the real students for universities, the others for whatever they might do from here on. The French Student Union gave us tickets for a Jewish kitchen that had been set up to feed us. They also placed us in hotels—pass hotels for the most part. These establishments specialized in trade from prostitutes and rented rooms by the half hour. Some of us were given rooms that were reserved for the daytime trade. During the days the whores used the beds; at nights we did.

I was placed at the Hotel Québec on Rue St.-Honoré, but it took a few days to make the arrangements. In the meantime, I stayed with Jonah Zaretsky. Jonah had an aunt in Paris and had managed to get out of Poland before we did. He had heard our group was coming and had been waiting at the train station with the welcoming committee.

Jonah was living at a hotel on Rue St.-Sebastien, and when we came downstairs after my first night there the person at the desk started shouting at him. Jonah had studied French in high school and could get along. I didn't understand anything, except that the desk clerk sounded outraged. It went on for a while, very loud and angry, but in the middle of it Jonah began to laugh. When the clerk stopped yelling, Jonah was still laughing. "You know what he told me?" he said. "He told me that I could take as many girls up to my room as I wanted. But never a man. Men are absolutely forbidden!"

This was a frame of mind beyond my experience. But then Paris was flabbergasting altogether. I hardly knew where I was; it was as if I had made a quantum leap in cultures. The first time I saw people kissing in the streets, I was amazed. Then I noticed that they were kissing underground in the Métro, they were kissing in the parks, they were kissing in cars. When I wanted to kiss a girl in Poland, first of all it took two weeks to get a kiss, then we'd have to hide behind a doorway in the middle of the night. But these French people were kissing whenever they felt like it, wherever they happened to be. Incredible, I thought. Unbelievable! What freedom!

I felt I was breathing clean air for the first time in my life. Wonderful air, air that made me heady. If I had been impressed by Prague, I was overwhelmed by Paris. I could not believe what I was seeing. Museums were lined up one after the other. The Louvre, the Rodin, the Jeu de Pomme. My head was exploding with it. I visited Notre Dame, Versailles, and all the historical places that I had heard something about or read something about. After the wreckage I had left, I couldn't get enough. For the next two weeks I spent every day exploring Paris.

But suddenly it got to be late October, and the university year started in November. I had to begin studying. But that was easier said than done. In the first place, I didn't speak French. In the second, it seemed that the prerequisite to getting accepted by a French university was having a French high school baccalaureate.

I was in despair briefly, but then I found that before the war the Polish high school baccalaureate had been considered equivalent to the French, for diplomatic reasons. The two countries had been allies and had made it possible for high school graduates to study in each other's universities. The French had exempted the medical faculty and the famous École Polytechnique from the exchange; for that you had to be French. But all their other schools were open to Polish graduates, including the schools of engineering.

The entrance requirements, though, were daunting. Applicants to the most prestigious engineering institutions—the so-called *grandes écoles*—ordinarily attended special preparatory courses for two or three years to learn the necessary math and physics. Then they took a legendary entrance exam, the dreaded *Concours*—of which it was said that 90 percent failed.

I didn't know where to turn. I had already lost too much time, and I felt driven to get my life on track. I couldn't spend three years in preparation. But then I learned there was a way to get around the *Concours*. As an alternative, the French authorities would allow students to study for a degree in general physics and applied mechanics at a university simultaneously with their studies at an engineering institute. If they succeeded in getting a bachelor's degree in physics and applied mechanics, that would be considered the equivalent of passing the *Concours*. But there was a catch: The course of study at both the university and the engineering institute was three years. If at the end of that time you passed them both, you would be awarded a degree in engineering. If you failed one, you got nothing.

There was no alternative. I had to take the chance. So in November I was admitted to both the University of Nancy in physics and applied mechanics and ENSEM (École Nationale Supérieure d'Electricité et de Mechanique) one of the *grandes écoles,* in engineering. I was full of hope. After all, I had done extremely well on the math section of my high school exam (I had finished a two-hour problem in fifteen minutes, and the teacher had asked me to stay in my seat so as not to embarrass the other students). And I had had Sender's special one-on-one course in cerebral mathematics. I felt up to the challenge.

But when classes started I understood nothing, neither at the university nor at ENSEM. Not a single thing. I was attending lectures in French, and I could not make out a word the professors were saying. I wasn't even sure which subjects they were talking about. But what I could see, with great clarity, was that the other students knew far more mathematics than I did. They had all the tools necessary to move through the courses. That was the reason the program was only three years instead of five. They had been through the math and physics already.

After three months I spoke French, or something that passed for French. I had devised a method, which I stuck to religiously. I read through the dictionary and memorized thirty words a day. Most I forgot. But some I remembered, which meant that each week my vocabulary grew. In addition, I started going out with French girls, which had a wonderful effect. I found myself talking, haltingly at first, then more and more fluently.

I was also coming to feel at home in Nancy, where people seemed eager to help with problems. The first person I had met there was a Jewish student from Bialystok, Boris Hirschowski. I had been wondering what to do about my room at the university dormitory, on which a five-hundred-franc deposit was required before I could move in. Boris, whom I had just been introduced to, told me not to worry; he had a thousand francs, and I could use half of that. A few days later, when I presented myself at the *préfecture* to change my visitor's visa to a student visa, the police inspector had refused. I was probably, he told the interpreter who had come with me, not a legitimate student at all but a speculator. When I told the rabbi of Nancy's synagogue what had happened, he said that he would help. And when I tried again at the *préfecture,* the same inspector simply stamped my papers without batting an eye.

At school they left me alone for six months. But then examinations started. At ENSEM they were compassionate. My grades were bad, but slowly they got better. But the university was a different story. At the physics faculty, they did not know you. Some classes had three hundred students in them, some five hundred. Each student had a number. You took the exams and either passed or failed. First you took the four-hour-long written exams. Then you went for your equally rigorous laboratory exams. Finally you underwent three separate oral exams. Your examiners didn't even know your name. They knew nothing about you, which was more or less what I knew about the subjects. I failed everything.

Fortunately, they did not flunk you out after a year of failures. The course of studies was three years, and the French system incorporated its own brand of mercy. At the University of Nancy you could fail repeated exams without being thrown out (though not at ENSEM). I was working as hard as I could for the first time in my life, and I was getting help from two French friends, Armand Sarazin and Joseph Pellet. Eventually I began to catch up—first in math, then in physics. The second year was a little better. I wasn't exactly swimming, but at least I was keeping my head above water.

I was living on a small stipend that the Jewish Students' Union was sending me. But sometime during my second year my relatives in America found out that Sender and I were alive. They had been writing letters to the Red Cross, and eventually my name and Sender's had come through. They immediately began sending help, a hundred dollars a month, which was such an enormous sum that I didn't dare touch it. I sent it all to Sender. Then they dispatched a family representative to check on us personally, a Hollywood lawyer named Morton Garbus, who was married to the daughter of Grandma Tema's sister, Molly (years later I was told he had reported that I seemed bright enough but that I was living terribly). That branch of the family had originally moved to Oklahoma, but now it seemed that at least some of them lived in California. For Sender and me that was extremely exotic.

When Morton Garbus arrived in Paris to meet us, he more than fulfilled whatever fantasies Sender and I might have had about Hollywood. He was the most elegant person I had ever seen. He dressed immaculately and was so refined that he couldn't bring himself to come upstairs to the room I had rented in one of the prostitute hotels I knew from my first days in Paris.

Morton Garbus turned out to be as cultured as he was refined. He spoke to Sender and me in both beautiful Hebrew and

Yiddish and needed little urging to turn the conversation to poetry or classical drama or Greek architecture—or radical politics. Morton was a salon Communist who loved talking about revolutionary theory, even though it was pretty clear that his own life was far removed from any brand of practical Marxism we had ever heard of. To top off the impression he made on us, Morton Garbus apparently knew every one of the great Hollywood movie stars, many of whom seemed to be his clients—Marlene Dietrich, Cary Grant, Rosalind Russell, and Vivien Leigh, among others. I wondered if that could really be true, but later, when Morton's wife, Grace, and daughter Marcia visited, they took me to meet Edward G. Robinson, who also happened to be in Paris at the time. He took us out driving in his raspberry red Buick convertible and spoke Yiddish to me (his family was from Romania). But he shied away from my political questions—back in the United States the McCarthy era was already under way.

That summer after Morton Garbus's visit I went to Paris to stay with Sender during school vacation. After liberation he had made a living by smuggling goods from Russia to Poland. Now he was doing the same kind of thing between Germany and France, traveling regularly between Munich and Paris. He was living now on Rue St. Sebastien, in Jonah Zaretsky's old room at the hotel. The room was filled with items that Sender had brought in and was trying to sell.

Sender's problem was that he didn't speak enough French yet, so he was limited to selling his goods in the Jewish community, where he could communicate in Yiddish. When I arrived, he had two Swedish Facit electronic adding machines that nobody wanted to buy.

"Felix," he said. "I got stuck with these two machines. I can't seem to sell them."

"How do you usually do it?" I asked.

"I go to the Jews," he said. "But they don't want them."

Maybe some French retailer would buy them, I thought.

I spoke French; perhaps I could find somebody. "Why not try?" said Sender. Fifty thousand francs would be an okay price.

So I took the smaller machine with me and found a store near the hotel that sold business machines. I went in and said, "Would you like to buy this machine?"

"How much do you want?"

"One hundred thousand francs."

The store owner examined the machine. "Fine," he said. "I'll take it. Do you have another one?"

"Yes," I said. "But it's more expensive."

"Let me have a look at it," he said.

I went back and said, "Sender, there's something going on here that we don't know." I gave him the hundred thousand. "I think I can get more for the other one." I took the second one down and brought back a hundred and fifty thousand.

When he saw that, Sender asked me to take him to the store and introduce him to the owner. Shortly afterward he began to specialize in business machines, and eventually he became legitimate. In the course of time he went into partnership with another French business machine dealer, then opened up his own company and eventually became one of Paris's major importers of adding machines, calculators, and later, electronic equipment.

By my third year at ENSEM and the University of Nancy I was not a bad student. I had started to love physics by this time, and if I was not excelling in my classes, at least I was passing all the exams. But I was not completely through my trials getting accustomed to the French university culture.

Because my French was not good enough to take lecture notes effectively, I had developed the habit of learning from books. In the big electricity course I had bought a book by Georges Bruhat, a renowned professor of physics at the Sorbonne. My own professor at Nancy, Chevalier, was also extremely prominent. Among his other achievements, Chevalier had developed a special notation in differentials, for which he was famous. Chevalier's notations provided the same answers as the standard system, but there was apparently a vast philosophical divide between his notation and that used by Bruhat in his textbook. In the world of physics at that time it was well known that the two men hated each other passionately.

I, of course, had no idea of any of this. I had never heard of the battle over notation and knew nothing whatsoever of the professors' fierce mutual dislike. When the electricity exam was given, I did well in the written part. In Nancy it was a foregone conclusion that if you passed the written exam, which was mind-boggling, you were home free. Anyone who knew enough to pass the written had to know enough to get at least part of the laboratory and oral exams, and the only way to fail would be by scoring a zero in one of the other parts. I passed the lab exam, too, and then went in for the oral with Professor Chevalier.

The first question Chevalier asked was about Pointing's vector, which required the use of differentials. I knew the subject and gave a clear demonstration of the answer—of course, using Bruhat's notation, which I had learned from my electricity text. Chevalier stared in horror and said one word: *"Sort!"*—Out! I went numb. "What?" I said. "What is it? What's wrong?" "I do not want to see you," he said. "Get out!" When the grades were posted I got a zero, which meant that I failed the whole thing. I had to take it over again in October, by which time I had learned the story. This time I used Chevalier's notation and passed with distinction.

In Nancy I also studied with the famous mathematician Laurent Schwartz, one of the founders of topology and winner of the vastly prestigious Field Prize. Prodigiously brilliant, he already had several theorems named after him and was one of the world's leading mathematicians, although he was only in his early thirties. Schwartz knew that I was a survivor, and he befriended me. He would invite me to his house to eat, which I loved. I still seemed to be starving all the time. When I came to class he would make a point of shaking my hand in front of everybody.

Laurent Schwartz was a Trotskyite, and he tried hard to

convince me that Zionism was wrong. Political discussion with him was an endless enterprise. Despite (or maybe because of) his militance I told him I was thankful to Stalin for my liberation. Stalin might be a murderous dictator, but I had been saved by the Red Army. That was a fact. About Zionism, I insisted that eventually I would go to Palestine. I might be here in France, but I felt deeply that Israel was my homeland.

Laurent Schwartz passed me on the exams, but he told me I wasn't very good at math (I agreed). My head was okay, he thought, but I didn't know enough. He understood why, though, and he tried to incite me to become a mathematician, even asking me to do a doctorate with him. By that time, though, I was more convinced than ever that engineering was my field. I told him I wanted to do a doctorate, yes, but in some aspect of physical engineering, not mathematics.

Nevertheless, Schwartz was inspiring. His lectures were extraordinary. On the driest of subjects he would have the entire lecture hall sitting on the edge of their chairs with their mouths open. People who weren't in his class would come to his lectures just to hear him. Some came who weren't even in the school.

My relative from California Morton Garbus might have thought I was living terribly, but to me it didn't seem that way at all. My intellectual life was intense, and after a while I developed a large circle of friends and acquaintances. I saw the French generally as wonderful people. In the first place, they looked like Jews. Coming from Poland, where distinguishing friends from potential enemies as fast as possible was a necessity, I was constantly on the lookout. At first I would wonder how come there were so many Jews around. But it turned out there weren't. They were just French. With time I began to distinguish a few specifically Gallic characteristics, but most of them still looked like Jews. More importantly, despite one or two ugly incidents, I didn't sense any general anti-Semitism.

In fact it was there, but it was subtle. I didn't pick it up at first, but when I became fluent in French and began to read the newspapers and the literature and understand nuances, I began noticing a kind of intellectual anti-Semitism at work, also an antiforeigner sentiment. The French had their own brand of chauvinism.

But I rationalized it. Look, I thought, this is their country. They can do with it what they want. I'm a foreigner. I'm here by their grace, because they opened the door for me. How could I be such a pig as to expect more? Maybe they did have some prejudices—but if so, they were of a completely different order than the bestiality I had seen among the Germans and among some Poles. A quantum difference. Like one of my professors who at an academic meeting one day told an anti-Semitic joke. I got up, put my coat on, and walked out. Afterward the professor apologized. "Look," he said, "I cracked a joke I shouldn't have. I'm sorry. I forgot that you are Jewish." If he forgot that I'm Jewish, I thought, how big an anti-Semite could he be?

My French girlfriends didn't seem to care either. In Poland the very first thing you had to know was whether you were a cow or a horse. Here it didn't matter. I would be seeing a girl for a while and a moment would come when I'd tell her I was Jewish. The response was usually: "That's interesting." Or more often: "So what?"

So the French were mostly wonderful. And the Jewish community in Nancy took the students to their hearts. They set up a kitchen for Jewish students. (At first they didn't allow Communists to be admitted, only Zionists. We all refused. If it was for Jewish students it would be for Jewish students, Zionist, Communist, or anything else. They gave in quickly.) They invited students to their homes, they put on get-togethers for us. The rabbi made himself available. The community gave us a feeling of warmth.

Among the people I got to know in Nancy were a few Israelis—Palestinian Jews. The first was Elisha Roih, a student in agricultural science at the university, or so he said. Elisha was tall and rawboned. He had a slightly Slavic cast of features, high cheekbones, and an instant smile. He was one of the friendliest, most sympathetic people I had ever met, and I took an instant liking to him. There was something different about Elisha, something I couldn't quite define. He was brash; in his bearing and in the glint of his eyes he exuded self-confidence, even a hint that he could be dangerous if provoked.

Elisha's demeanor was strikingly different from that of the Polish Jews I knew, most of whom had a fearful, wounded air about them. I attributed the difference to the fact that he was an Israeli, born and raised on a kibbutz. I looked up to Elisha. He seemed a symbol of something that had come to have great meaning for me—a strong, self-sufficient Israeli man. I had met a few Israelis in Poland while I was running guns, but only fleetingly. Elisha was the first I actually got to know.

In fact, Elisha's bearing wasn't only due to having been raised on a kibbutz. Before long I learned that he was no ordinary agricultural science student either. Elisha was one of the first contingent of Israeli secret agents in Europe—forerunners of the Mossad. Most were members of the Palmach, the strike force of Israel's underground army. During the war they had fought with the Jewish Brigade, which had been raised by the British Army. When the brigade was disbanded at the close of hostilities, 150 Jewish soldiers had remained in Europe under new identities, their places in the demobilized unit taken by refugees they had trained to assume their old identities.

The agents bought and smuggled arms, organized and escorted refugee boats, and gathered intelligence. For a while Elisha had traveled under a Canadian passport, according to which he was a Québecois (his French wasn't perfect, nor was his English). Now he was an agricultural student. But what he really did was smuggle guns and immigrants across the German border, keeping his eye out for talent—potential candidates for the clandestine Haganah camps that were training Jews in Europe for the coming war with the Arabs.

I didn't know any of this at first. What I did know was that here was an engaging Israeli I could speak my Tarbut school Hebrew to. I sensed there was something else when one day I invited Elisha to take a shower at the Cité Universitaire, where I was living. Hot water in Europe was in short supply at the time (soap was in no supply), and showers were rationed. Elisha was living in a small rented room with no bathing facilities at all, so when it was my dormitory's turn for showers, I invited him over.

We stood in the long line waiting our turn, but when mine came someone pushed me rudely aside. It was a rough-looking older student. "This is my turn," he said. "Excuse me," I said politely, "it's my turn." *"Merde,"* said the French student. Suddenly Elisha was standing between us. "Sorry," he said, "actually it's my turn, and I've given it to him." He gestured at me.

"Your turn?"

"Yes, my turn. And I've given it to him. So he's going to take a shower now."

"You?" the French student looked at him disdainfully. "What are you, some kind of Jew-lover?"

I couldn't believe how calm Elisha was. My own heart was beating a mile a minute. "Listen," he said, "I'll forget what you just said. But it's my turn, and I've given it to my friend. So he's going in now. Is that plain enough?"

"Not only are you a dirty Jew-lover," said the French student, "but you're a liar, too."

This was too much for Elisha's patience. His voice got very quiet. I was riveted. "I come from a place," he said softly, "where if you call somebody a liar, he'll kill you."

"Oh, and where's that?"

"I come from Palestine," said Elisha.

"So," he said, measuring his words. His body tensed, ready for a fight. "Then I guess that makes you a dirty Jew, too."

The next thing I knew, the rough-looking Frenchman was lying on the floor. Elisha had done something to him, though I wasn't sure exactly what. I walked in to take my shower. Then

Elisha took his. The long line of students simply moved up, as if this kind of thing happened every day.

It wasn't much of an incident. In terms of what Elisha had done in his life, it wasn't something that he would remember more than five minutes. But to me it was extraordinary. I had seen a Jew standing up for himself and dealing out punishment to a bully. It struck a chord so deep, I thought about it for days. Later I thanked Elisha for what he had done, mumbling a few embarrassed words about "protecting Jewish honor when I didn't feel that I could do it." The words were awkward, and I wasn't sure he understood what I meant. How could anybody understand who hadn't lived through what I had? But then again, I thought, maybe he did.

Elisha was worried about events in Palestine. We were now several months into 1948. In November the United Nations had voted to partition the country into two parts—one Jewish, one Arab. The Jews had accepted the resolution; the Arabs had rejected it. Since then, violence had been increasing. We heard about attacks by the Irgun and skirmishes and battles between the Jewish underground army—the Haganah—and Arab forces. Pressure was building in anticipation of May 14, the day the U.N. resolution was supposed to go into effect. Everyone knew what would happen then. The Jewish community would declare its independence; then full-scale war would break out. The fight for Jewish survival was coming on.

In early March Elisha suggested to me that maybe I should be part of the Haganah. The way he said it I knew he was telling me that if I wanted to, he could arrange it. His confidence overwhelmed me. I wasn't even quite sure who he was, but what he was saying was clear enough. The Haganah needed people. Elisha thought I had the right stuff for it.

I told him I was interested. I had wanted to go to Palestine for years. I wanted to fight. What did he mean, he could arrange it?

"We have a camp," he told me, "a training camp for Haganah squad leaders. I've already recommended you for it, and you've been accepted. When the time comes, we'll get you over to Israel. If you want to start training, you can leave tomorrow."

The next day I was on a train for Lyons. At the railroad station someone was waiting for me. He said little as we drove off toward the mountains. In the early spring the French countryside looked idyllic, dotted with farmland and pastures and small herds of brown and white cows. The sign at the gate where we stopped said "Colonie de Vacance"—Vacation Colony.

Beyond the fence and low hills that separated the camp from the road, the Haganah had built a full-scale training facility, with barracks, obstacle courses, and firing ranges. The basic training course I started the moment I put my bag down was short—I'd be here only a month—but it was intense. Our instructors went under code names; they were all Aries and Jehudas and Avrams. They were British-trained and had fought with the Jewish Brigade or had served in the British-sponsored Jewish Settlement Police back in Palestine. The whole system was British.

Training with weapons came first, taking them apart, cleaning them, putting them together again. I was already pretty good at this before we started. After the war I had sworn to myself that I would never be without a weapon, and once I got involved in the Bricha, I wasn't. In Poland I always carried a pistol. My instinct for survival told me not ever to leave myself helpless again. The upshot was that I knew guns. The most difficult to put together was the Belgian FN automatic pistol, a very complicated piece of equipment. But I quickly became expert with it, and with all the other weapons they trained us on.

My fellow trainees included girls as well as boys. We were taught weapons handling, how to use a compass and maps, how to navigate at night. We learned grenades and hand-to-hand combat—knife-fighting and basic jujitsu. The instructors, the Aries and Jehudas, were young, and there was something uncomfortable about the idea of Jewish youngsters being expert at killing. But to my surprise I became pretty good at the techniques myself.

Our instructors built up our stamina fast. We went on thirty-mile hikes with backpacks. We climbed in the low Alps that started near the camp. The pace was fast and brutal, designed to take people with no training and harden them at breakneck speed. Every minute counted, and once the course began, no one left camp for a moment.

Meanwhile, in Israel the fighting was heating up. By early May everyone knew that armies from the surrounding Arab countries would attack the Jewish community the moment the British formally gave up their mandate.

Our Homeland, Yes

I GOT back to Nancy in April. Elisha Roih had disappeared, no one knew where. We had hugged each other good-bye before I left the camp, promising to meet again in Israel. I wondered if he was there already.

On May 14 the British mandate ended, and David Ben-Gurion declared the establishment of the State of Israel. I remembered the fierce arguments that used to excite everyone in Grodno before the war. A state or not a state? Hashomer calling Betar fascist, Betar calling Hashomer Communist, fistfights in the Tarbut schoolyard. But the war had cured all that. There were six hundred thousand Jews in Palestine. They needed to protect themselves against their neighbors. They needed a state. The Arab armies were on the march.

My own call came the next day. I was to go to Paris to meet the group I had trained with. I was to carry as few things as possible. The Haganah would make arrangements to get us to Israel. I packed my backpack and took the train to Paris. Before I joined the group I stopped at Sender's to say good-bye. Sender wasn't there, but our close friend (and Sender's business associate) Josef Weiss was. Sender was off on a buying trip, he said. He wouldn't be back for a couple of days.

When I told Weiss why I was in Paris, he almost had a heart attack. He grabbed me and started talking and pleading. He didn't stop for the next thirty-six hours. "Felix, you can't do it. You absolutely cannot do it. You can't do it to Sender. You can't do it to yourself. You will break Sender's heart. If you do this, you will destroy him. If you go and get killed there, he will never recover. This is like a death sentence for him. You must think of your family, Felix!"

Weiss was hysterical. I couldn't get him to stop. "Josef," I said, "I have to go. Who else is going to defend the country if we don't? This is my duty. I have to do it."

"Felix, it's not just Sender. It's the memory of your family. You're the last one, Felix. You're the seed. Everyone is dead. All those children, everyone! You are the only survivor. You can't do it to the memory of your family. The seed of Zandman has to create a family. YOU CANNOT GO TO ISRAEL AND BE KILLED!"

Weiss kept talking and talking. The rendezvous time came and went. Then the time for my train to leave passed. There must be other groups going, I thought. I'll just have to hook up with one of those. I was exhausted from arguing, but Weiss's voice never stopped cajoling and wheedling and begging and ordering. I dropped off to sleep, but he shook me awake. Finally I promised to stay until Sender got back.

Sender told me to finish my studies. "Look," I said, "the war won't last forever. I'll be there for a year, then I'll come back."

"No. If you drop out of your program, they won't take you back (which was true). Your engineering profession will be finished. You have to understand that."

"So I won't be an engineer. I'll work on a kibbutz."

"Well, maybe. But you know you'll be much better off being an engineer. You'll also be much more useful to Israel as an engineer than giving your life in this way. They're sending so many youngsters who don't have your capability, your possibilities to really help the country."

"Sender, these are all *bubba meises*. I have to go."

In the end I did not go. Instead I went back to school. I was in love with school. I was in love with finishing my studies. But it felt hollow. I wanted to be in Israel. I had betrayed myself, and I knew it. I followed the news from Israel day by day. Word came that one of the Israelis who had been studying in Nancy had been killed. I felt I had betrayed my country.

What was it with me and Israel? I didn't go when Leon Trachtenberg dissuaded me in Lublin. I didn't go now, when it was so much more important. Was I just not fated to go to Israel? Or was Israel something that existed mainly in my mind, as it did for so many Zionists in Grodno like my father? Our homeland, yes, and one day all Jews will live there. But in the meantime, the best idea is to stay where you are and do what you're doing. Was that me, too?

I felt a wave of guilt. I knew I had done things wrong in my life. I did not go back to get my parents and sister on that fatal Sunday when I was up in Janova's attic. That gnawed on me. I had not taken revenge for them in Danzig, when I could have so easily. But those things, hard as they were, I could rationalize. I could argue with myself about them. Could I really have rescued my parents then? No, not really. Jonah had told me they were taken early. Probably it was best to have stayed where I was. Did I really think my parents would have wanted me to murder those people in revenge? But this thing that I had just done, that I had just not done. This was morally wrong. I should have gone, I should have risked my life. This time it had been absolutely necessary. If I were killed, I would be killed, and so what? I would have died for something. The Zandman seed, my uncle Sender, my studies? They were pretexts. In the balance they meant nothing. Here was a guilt I could never assuage, a black mark on my conscience that could not be washed away. Nobody could pardon me, because I had done the offense to myself. And it was irreversible.

•

At the end of the third year, I passed all my exams. I received three certificates: an engineering diploma, a bachelor's degree in physics, and another in applied mechanics. I was twenty-two years old (most French students didn't finish until they were twenty-three or twenty-four—*lycée* plus three years of special preparation plus three years of university work). I was very happy, because time was of the essence. I wanted desperately to make a living and to start a family, to establish myself in a normal life.

In fact, I was on my way to doing both. One day in a café in Nancy I had met a girl. We talked for a while and I learned that her name was Ruth. She was a piano student at the conservatory. A few days later at the Student Union, we met again. After that we began seeing each other often.

I had had a number of French girlfriends, but none of those relationships was serious. This was the first time since Klara, the Russian girl in Grodno, that I had met someone I thought I could marry. Ruth played the piano beautifully; she had her heart set on a career as a concert pianist. I loved the music. I had always loved it. Music had helped keep me sane down in the pit. But since the war my life had not had room for it, even though I had bought myself an old violin with the first money I had got hold of after the liberation. Her father, it turned out, was a *chasan*, a cantor. When she took me home to meet her parents in Metz, I heard him sing— music that carried me back to the happy days when I would sit in the synagogue next to my grandfather Freydovicz.

I yearned for a family. I had my diploma as an engineer, so I could earn a living now. The next step was to get married, then have children. I was only twenty-two, but I wanted it all. I needed it. I pushed matters fast, and in December 1949 I proposed.

Ruth's family was not completely pleased. I was a refugee, an alien in the country, with no parents of my own. I took Sender to Metz to meet Ruth and her parents, but he was skeptical, too. "This isn't for you, Felix," he said afterward. But he wouldn't tell me why he thought so. He may have believed I was too young for such a step, but I was sure that wouldn't be a problem. The main thing was to settle down, now that I was able, and start my own family.

Despite Sender's and Ruth's parents' lack of enthusiasm, in March 1950 we were married. Sender found a job for Ruth as a secretary to one of his business acquaintances, and I went to work for CEM, a company that manufactured electrical generators and other equipment. A few months later, though, I was awarded a grant by France's National Center for Scientific Research. They were pleased, they said, to sponsor my work for a doctorate at the St.-Cyr Laboratories under Professor Foch, a well-known Sorbonne physicist.

While I was studying at Nancy I had heard a number of lectures on Sir David Brewster's nineteenth-century discovery of a phenomenon called photoelasticity. It seemed that if you subjected a piece of glass to pressure, then looked at it through polarizing filters, different colors would appear in the glass. Sometime later a German physicist had developed a mathematical theory for this phenomenon, which made photoelasticity into a science. By observing the colors and applying the mathematics, a researcher could determine how much stress the glass was undergoing at any given point.

That had caught my attention. I wondered about the accuracy of the calculations and if maybe there was a key here to measuring stress on other materials, too, such as the steel in bridges. Some interesting but not particularly successful work had been done on this in the 1930s. The idea had taken root that this was a subject I would like to explore for a doctorate.

The moment I started working on photoelasticity at St.-Cyr, I was captured. The phenomenon engrossed my attention. But while my work life was thriving, my home life wasn't. It didn't take Ruth and me long to discover that our attraction for each other was not based on any real community of feeling or understanding. In fact, our basic views of life were quite different, something neither of us had seen before we were married, or perhaps we had not given ourselves time enough to see it. Despite the conflicts, we tried to make the marriage work, but it was a struggle that got no easier as time went on.

Three years later, I was ready to throw in the towel. Neither of us was happy. We had continuous fights, many of them over trivial things, though the basic difference in outlook that was behind them was not trivial at all. This was anything but the harmonious, loving family life I had dreamed of. I wanted a divorce, and so did Ruth.

When I talked to Sender about it, he was as decisive as ever. "No," he said. "In our family we don't divorce. You make a choice, Felix, you live with it. Who says you have to be happy in everything you do?" Sender was a man of rigorous, stoic morality. Monumental morality. "Happiness" was not a word in his vocabulary. Duty, family, endurance—these were his terms of reference. And as far as he was concerned, they ought to be mine as well.

Maybe they were mine, to some extent, anyway. After our talk I thought, maybe Sender's right about this. Maybe I'm taking the wrong approach. He was certainly right about happiness; I had absorbed that lesson well enough. Happiness was not a value that deserved much attention in how you conducted your life. "Are you happy?" was not a question I remembered anyone in my family ever asking anyone else. The idea that Grandfather Freydovicz or Grandma Tema or my parents or any of the rest of them might have guided their lives by the star of their own happiness was beneath consideration. Maybe it will be better after we have children, I thought. I wanted children. Ruth did, too. We started thinking in that direction, and the idea of separating slid into the background.

Meanwhile, my research was bearing fruit. If my emotional life at home was confused and distressing, at the laboratory my mind was roaming through a fascinating, endlessly absorbing universe. In this universe immutable laws of force and resistance held sway, laws that could be persuaded to yield up their innermost secrets if only you could find the right way to ask.

In the 1930s Belgian, French, and German scientists had started asking some of the same questions about photoelasticity that I was asking. Brewster had noticed the phenomenon in glass; his successors discovered that other transparent materials exhibited the same properties—plastics, for example. If plastic was subjected to stress, the same display of colors could be seen through polarized filters.

They then took the next step and began to make plastic models of bridges and other structures that routinely underwent stress and could be weakened in the process. They simulated the stress these parts were subjected to (e.g., the weight of traffic a bridge had to bear) and conjectured that if the stress patterns showed up in a particular way in their Bakelite plastic models, maybe it would happen the same way in the original structure.

And if it did, perhaps you could figure it mathematically. You might be able to tell from your Bakelite model what the metal in your engine part or bridge was doing. You could see how much stress the original was under and where the danger points were. That would be an immense help, for example, in estimating how much weight the steel skeleton of a skyscraper could bear, or the extent to which drilling holes in a cement slab might affect it, or where an airplane wing might weaken.

Of course, the problem was that bridges and engine parts and wings are not made out of plastic. Steel doesn't necessarily behave like plastic when it is stressed, and it was impossible to simulate in the laboratory all the forces a real bridge might be subjected to—storm winds, for example. In addition, joining points like welds and rivets were impossible to duplicate in Bakelite. As a result, I discovered that all the equations I was writing to translate measurements on models to measurements on real structures were full of speculation and subject to major errors. Whenever I talked to designers of bridges and airplanes about what I was doing, they always said, "That's very interesting, theoretically. But there's not much we can do with it. We can't rely on it; plastic isn't metal."

Then I had an idea. Maybe I could take transparent plastic and cement it to the metal, or coat the metal with it. Then if I put the metal under stress, the stress would equally affect the plastic. The plastic would stretch or bend or contract in the same way as the metal it was bonded to. Its surface would assume the same deformation as the surface of the metal. At that point I could measure what was happening to the plastic and in fact also be measuring what was happening to the metal. The plastic would become a sensor for changes in the metal surface. Instead of speculating on equivalencies, I could look directly at the real thing.

That was the theory. In fact, though I was unaware of it at the time, someone had already thought of it, a French physicist named Mesnager, who had done his work a half century earlier. His problem was that he couldn't implement the idea. The idea of coatings had not occurred to him; instead he had tried to embed glass pieces in concrete. Plastics hadn't been available, nor had the necessary instrumentation techniques. But he had envisioned the basic concept.

I did not know that, but I did know that if I wanted to translate the idea into reality, I had to resolve a variety of practical problems. There were no plastics that would do precisely what I wanted them to do; so I'd have to develop them. I'd have to devise cements and bonding techniques that would allow me to apply the plastics to complex structures. I needed to create the instrumentation to take and measure readings and work out the mathematics that lay behind the concept. As I became increasingly immersed in the work, I realized I was involved in developing not just an invention but an entire technology.

The effort to do this took many months. Finally it came down to this ultimate question: Would the bonded plastic actually deform in the same way as the metal surface it was bonded to? To determine that, I began doing field tests. I would go to a bridge, cement plastic on at key points, load the bridge with trucks, and measure the stress optically. Then I would use other methods to calculate the same stress and check the results. And in my tests the optical measurements always worked very precisely.

Some of my work on photoelasticity went into my dissertation and was published as a book, which was immediately acquired by all the libraries. That felt wonderful. I knew I was on the road to making some serious contributions—an old dream. It felt even better when I was given an appointment as a lecturer at the École de l'Aire, the French Academy of Aeronautics.

The Academy of Aeronautics was an elite government-run institute whose students came almost exclusively from France's most prestigious technological universities—the École Polytechnique and the École des Mines. All the students from these institutions who wanted to specialize in aeronautical engineering did their postgraduate work there.

I was excited by the appointment, but I was also nervous. These elite students had been through the most rigorous scientific training available in France. They were simply the best in the country, the *crème de la crème,* and the Aeronautical Academy took only the best of the best. Among other things, they knew more mathematics than I did, which scared me more than a little as I considered how best to approach the course on stress analysis that I had been assigned to teach.

I decided that since my students were such math wizards. I would load my lectures with mathematical descriptions. I would prepare my presentations very, very thoroughly, so there would be no mistakes. And then I would pour the math down on their heads.

I think I did it because I was so scared. As a result, I decided to impress them with how much I myself knew. This was hardly the most effective way of teaching students, which I found out to my chagrin when I examined the class at the end of the first year. The test results were appalling; almost everyone in the group failed.

I was very upset. Over the vacation I thought about it at length and concluded that I was a fake. I had not discharged my duty as a teacher. Instead of teaching my students, I had spent the year showing off. The conclusion was clear: Either I had to resign, or I had to figure out a different way of teaching.

I decided not to resign but to continue the second year. But I did it differently. In the first place, I made sure I understood thoroughly all the areas I felt shaky about. Then I told myself that I should make it simple, and I figured out methods of doing that—which stood me in good stead later, when I began to lecture at universities in the United States.

This time around all the students understood, and they passed. Before, the class had been uniformly grim. Now the students were happy and smiling. That first year had been a disaster for me, but at the same time it was a self-revelation. I went through an internal crisis. I thought, From now on, no more of this monkey business. You are not there to show how much you know, you are there to convey what you know. And what you don't know, tell them you don't know it and talk about it.

This was another subject on which I could hear my father's voice. I remembered so clearly when I would occasionally come home from school frustrated that I didn't understand something, he would tell me not to worry. "It's normal, Feivel. Next time after the lesson, go up and ask the teacher. He'll explain it to you. But if you don't understand a second time, don't ask him a third, because he doesn't know it himself." Now I was the teacher, and I was the one who hadn't known. I felt that if I had been able to face my deficiencies, it was largely due to the simple honesty with which my father regarded every problem. My own tendencies may have led me to the right or left, but I could usually hear this moral bell ringing somewhere inside my head. I had no doubt that that was he.

•

In 1952 Ruth and I went to Israel. We went by boat, in steerage along with a large group of students, all of us spending the nights in hammocks somewhere deep in the hold. The aching back I acquired sleeping down there disappeared the instant I saw Haifa. I walked down the gangway, through the gate, and there waving at me was my uncle Moshe, my father's brother who had gone to Israel in 1933 for the Maccabiah games. He had been a young man then and I was only six, but we recognized each other instantly from the photos we had exchanged by mail. When we embraced I could not stop the tears I felt welling up, nor could he. I had such terrible news to tell him. Of course he had known for years that his wife and son had perished along with the rest of the Zandmans, but I was a direct link to what had happened, to the details he had never heard.

We walked through Haifa together, my head overflowing with impressions. The streets were crowded with children on their way home from school. They all seemed to be skipping or running, bursting with enthusiasm and life. And all I heard was

Hebrew, shouting and laughing and singing in Hebrew. I, so used to judging people from the look in their eyes, looked at these children and saw freedom. It was tremendous. The free children of Israel. "Are they all Jews?" I asked Moshe. I couldn't quite get my hands around this reality. Hordes of Jewish children, so alive they made your head spin. The world here was Jewish, not only the children but the adults, too. I had stepped into the middle of a Jewish universe, a landscape where I myself was not something self-conscious and alien.

We stayed in Haifa for a couple of days, then we drove to Jerusalem to visit Uncle Moshe at home. Moshe had married again, and his wife, Laura, a beautiful, vivacious Sephardic woman, had given him a son. It seemed to me as he showed me around the city that whatever might be going on in his inner reaches, Moshe had managed to rebuild a reasonably happy life for himself.

I didn't see Jerusalem as much as I felt it. I felt the ground under my feet as I walked on it. I needed to touch everything with my fingers. I needed to know what this Jewish nation felt like.

My uncle took me to see the Old City, which you could only stare at from a distance, since it was in Jordanian hands, and the Arabs would not permit Jews to visit. He told me stories of the War of Independence (I couldn't bring myself to tell him how close I had come to being in it). He had been in the Irgun, Menachem Begin's fighting organization. Moshe was a sharpshooter. He was also the chief engineer for all Jerusalem's electrical substations. Whenever the Irgun needed a blackout, he would arrange it for them. He told me he had not joined the Haganah because prior to the war they had not done enough. The Irgun was more active. He hadn't cared one way or another about the politics. The main thing was to kick the British out and establish a state, and he had seen the Irgun moving toward that end. After the war, though, he had dropped his affiliation with Begin's party. For Moshe it was enough that the state existed.

Two of my old friends lived on a kibbutz, Kfar Menachem, in the South: Franye Braude and her husband, Hillel (also a survivor from Grodno). I had first met Franye in Slonim, then after the liberation she had lived with us for a while in Bialystok. At that time the baby she had been carrying when the Germans invaded had become part of a tangled legal case. Her little girl was born in the ghetto, and when the deportations started, Franye had given her to Alex Blumstein, who deposited the infant on the doorstep of a Polish house. It was known that the couple who owned the house had no children, and Franye hoped that they would take the baby as their own and save her life. They had, but when liberation came, the Polish family had refused to give her up. A complicated court fight had ensued, and eventually the judge had decided in favor of Franye. Now she and Hillel were raising two children in the kibbutz: Ilana, and their son, who had been conceived while she was in hiding.

Our first morning at Kfar Menachem we were served an egg for breakfast. Mine was so small I thought at first it was a pigeon egg. It was so pale there looked to be no yolk inside. But the kibbutzniks were extremely proud of these eggs. "You know," said one of the agricultural managers, "it costs a hell of a lot to produce an egg like this. You wouldn't believe how much we have to pay for imported feed for the hens."

"But this is crazy," I said. "You could have an egg much better and twice as big for a third the price. Why don't you just import them?" The suggestion took him aback. "No, no." He shook his head vigorously. "It's very important for us to build up our poultry industry. Eventually we will export eggs!" I looked at him and said, "What chutzpah!" But in fact, that was exactly what the Israelis did. In a few years their agriculture blossomed. But when I saw it in 1952, it didn't look promising. Maybe it was just the contrast with what I was used to among the produce-happy French, but the agricultural effort I saw was worse than dismal. There were food shortages all over the country (in fact we had brought with us a valise filled with sausages, which we shared among delighted friends and relatives).

But the Israelis were scratching for every little thing, any fingerhold, any toehold. And that spirit struck me. The whole country was austere, bare. There wasn't a luxury in sight. But I felt utterly at home, especially in the kibbutz. The social and political issues that so exercised the Israelis, which were the fabric of their lives, didn't particularly engage me. But the kibbutz was a little, tight-knit community, like a noisy, squabbling family that was pulling together for all it was worth. Here was a group of people who had sunk their roots into the soil and were building their lives together. To me it seemed the re-creation of the Jewish family, and my heart longed to be a member of a family like that. Instead of the free-floating electron I was, the palm tree in Alaska, the stranger in someone else's household.

As it was I had Sender, of course, and he had me. But still I was alone. As Sender was alone. We were together, but we were two alones, he in his world and I in mine. We shared an unbreakable emotional bond, but in front of each other we were tongue-tied. Between us there was mainly silence.

I mentioned to Ruth that I would like to live in the kibbutz, but the idea did not attract her. She did not have the same background I did; she didn't share the same attachment. Besides, we were on shaky emotional grounds as it was, and the practical problems would have been immense. Her dream was to be a concert pianist, and Israel in those days was not the place for that. Nor were there any engineering jobs. It was not to be.

We stayed in Kfar Menachem for three days and three nights, loving every minute. Over the next three weeks I explored the whole country, from Eilat to the Negev to the Sea of Galilee. I visited other kibbutzim. I tried to look up everyone in the country I knew—Jonah Zaretsky, with whom I had stayed in Paris; Joe Szwarc, my older friend from Grodno who had fought with Stalin's Polish Army; the Starowolskis, who had spent the war in Kazakhstan, to where the Soviets had exiled them as capitalists. There was little to eat in Israel. Parts of the country were dangerous as hell.

Old Jerusalem with the Temple Wall was off-limits. But I was exhilarated. I couldn't get enough.

•

By now I was working as a laboratory engineer for Snecma, the government-owned company that designed and manufactured airplane engines for the French military. Here I became a full-time test engineer. I also calculated stresses on planes in flight, wearing a parachute on my back and an oxygen mask, since the test models were not pressurized. We wanted particularly to measure the stresses where the wing is attached to the main frame. Ordinarily the wing is attached with bolts, and all the stress from the wing is transmitted through the points of attachment. It is at those points that the wing has the potential to break off from the plane.

To see what was really happening, we applied plastic coatings to the attachment parts. Then we flew. Looking through the optical viewer, I could see vivid, patterned colors glowing here and there along the attachment points. Back on the ground, some of the colors did not disappear, which meant that certain deformations were not temporary; the metal was permanently affected. There was mortal danger there. If the wing were subjected to the same pressure many times, it would become fatigued and break off.

At Snecma I was able to test thoroughly the theories I had developed. Along the way I improved the precision of the mathematics and developed additional measuring instrumentation. In the end I had a highly accurate optical stress testing device. When I demonstrated it to Snecma's managers they seemed impressed and sent me off to their laboratory at Villaroche to do further refinements and testing.

Villaroche was a center near Paris where Snecma developed and designed its new jet engines. There, to my surprise, along with French researchers I found myself working next to a group of German scientists and engineers. Just as the Americans and Soviets had packed their missile programs with German rocket scientists, so the French had brought in German jet engine specialists. Most of them had previously been in Ratisbon, where Germany developed its jet engine, and in fact the French engine they were working on was code-named ATAR, for Atalier Technique d'Aviation de Ratisbon.

At first I was shocked to find myself in this situation. But I saw that the French researchers were getting along just fine with their German colleagues, and I decided to accommodate myself to what I obviously couldn't change. Once I swallowed my discomfort, I discovered that the Germans made excellent professional colleagues. They were friendly and easy to work with, which was fortunate, because Snecma wanted to use my stress analysis techniques in the development of the ATAR engine.

I quickly became familiar with the engines the Germans were working on, but one day I noticed some features in a new series of designs that puzzled me. One of the new engines was obviously being developed for flight at extremely low altitudes. In fact, when I examined the specifications, it was apparent that this engine was meant to perform below sea level. "What's going on here?" I asked them. "The only place these efficiencies would be worthwhile is over the Caspian Sea. Are we preparing for war with the Soviet Union?" "Well," said Weber, the chief of the design team, "there's also the Dead Sea."

I was startled for a moment. What Weber was telling me was that the French were secretly developing this engine for Israel, as indeed it turned out they were (years later in Israel I was able to confirm this). The first Mystère jets the Israelis bought had been especially designed to function in Israeli air space.

Meanwhile, my own research was concluding. With photoelastic measurement technology thoroughly worked out, I took patents on the procedures. (In fact I didn't have enough money for a patent. But André Netter, the patent attorney I approached, understood the process and said he would waive his fee. I told him he would never regret it, and I meant it, though I had no idea at that point when or how I might be able to show my gratitude.) Then I began publishing my results.

The first papers that appeared on the process hit home in France's engineering community. Almost immediately I was flooded by calls from people who constructed bridges, ran railroads, and built engines. Photoelastic coating measurement obviously satisfied a need, and it seemed that the demand for it was far larger than I had anticipated. It occurred to me that there was a possible business here in building instrumentation, conducting tests, and consulting.

Snecma loved the process, but when I started talking to them about a business, they weren't responsive. I pointed out the excitement the idea was generating and the potential for profit, but they were simply not interested in it as a business. If it worked on planes, that was fine, but they didn't care about anything else. Snecma was a bureaucracy, and the kind of entrepreneurial venture I was suggesting was outside their scope of vision.

By now I was more or less gripped by the thought that I might be able to create a business. Jean Avril, one of Snecma's laboratory directors, encouraged me. Even if the company wasn't enchanted, he thought the concept had wonderful prospects, and that lifted my spirits. I had not felt any great entrepreneurial instincts stirring in me in the past. What I had wanted was to become an engineer and make scientific contributions. Already I had been luckier than I ever imagined in that regard. I had published a book and scientific papers. I still didn't feel particularly drawn to business, but by now it was pretty clear that the solutions I had come up with were leading me in that direction.

When I was finally convinced that Snecma would not back me, I left to join Jarre Jacquin, a company that sold scientific instruments. The relationship was a kind of joint venture: They agreed to provide me with an office and a secretary in return for half the profits. Then I borrowed five hundred dollars from Sender for supplies and concocted a number of additional measuring instruments. (I first asked Sender to invest the money and become my equal partner, but he said, "Look, either this idea is worth nothing, in which case I don't want to lose the five hundred, or it's worth something, in which case it wouldn't be fair to you. Take the money as a loan and pay it back when you can.") With that I opened my door to the line of people that was already forming. I solved problems, refined my procedures, and wrote papers on new areas of stress analysis that were becoming clearer to me. I was engaged.

•

In the 1950s, American industry and technology were booming. Research was expanding geometrically, and American companies were casting their eyes on Europe to help fill the demand for scientists and engineers. Early in 1956 the Americans showed up in France in the person of Mr. Marc Wood of Marc Wood, Inc., headhunters and talent scouts. Marc Wood was searching for French scientists and technical experts to sell to Americans. He was a middleman, but sophisticated and astute. Among his contacts was my friend at Snecma, Jean Avril. Jean told Marc Wood what I had been doing, and the next thing I knew Mr. Wood had made me an offer to go to the United States with him.

Nₒₜ many months before this, in February 1956, my wife had
given birth to our first child, a beautiful little girl we named
Gisele, after my mother, Genia. But having this child, whom we
both loved dearly, did nothing to improve our life together. On the
contrary, issues of child rearing now added themselves to the series
of problems we had been experiencing for so long.

But at the same time, having a child made divorce seem
even more out of bounds than it had been previously. Gisele was
not a responsibility either of us took lightly. Besides, there were
other big developments to think about. I had accepted Marc
Wood's offer to come to the United States. He had already completed all the arrangements to showcase photoelastic coatings
stress measurement to the American business and scientific communities.

•

When I arrived in New York, Mr. Wood himself was waiting for
me at the airport with his secretary and a Cadillac limousine. But
he wasn't the only welcoming party. I had written to my mother's
uncle Jake Slaner in Oklahoma (the one who had sent me the
monthly stipends) that I was coming to America for a visit. He
wrote back that his son, my second cousin Alfred, lived in New
York. He would be at Idlewild International Airport to pick me up.

Although the details were a little sketchy in my mind, I
knew that Alfred was ten or fifteen years older than I and that he
was an important business executive of some sort. I had never seen
a picture of him, nor he of me (though I distinctly recalled a photograph we had had in the house on Brygidzka Street of his brother
David, who had died in his teens after a tonsillectomy). We would
find each other at the airport.

Because I was carrying some measuring instruments
that needed a special check, I was the last passenger to emerge from
the customs area. By then all my fellow travelers' friends and rela-

tives had gone. The only people left were Mr. Wood and his secretary and my cousin Alfred, whom of course I did not recognize. As Alfred told me later, he had struck up a conversation with Mr. Wood while they were standing around. "Who are you waiting for?" asked Alfred. "We're here to meet a prominent visiting scientist," Marc Wood answered. "What about you?" "Me?" said Alfred. "I'm picking up a poor French relative of mine."

When I finally came out, Marc Wood put on a full-scale reception. Alfred backed off, scratching his head. He had been sent to pick up his refugee cousin whom the family had supported for years, and all of a sudden there were roses, champagne, and secretaries. He watched the goings-on for a bit, but when no one else appeared he asked if he could inquire what the name of this party might be. "Dr. Zandman," he was told, to his considerable surprise. We had a few minutes together, but Marc Wood's limousine was waiting to whisk me off somewhere, and that evening Alfred drove home to Scarsdale alone

The next day, though, we were in touch. He was very curious about the business aspect of whatever was going on. It turned out that he was not just a business executive, he was president of Kaiser Roth, one of the largest women's clothing companies in the country, makers of Supp-Hose (which Alfred had invented) and other well-known brands. When I described what I was involved in Alfred said, "Wait a minute, Felix. Please let me help you with this."

So Alfred sat down with Marc Wood and worked out the contract for me. He told Marc, "Look, businessmen like you and me are a dime a dozen. But a scientist is something else entirely. Unfortunately, my cousin doesn't know the first thing about business, so I'm going to make sure together with you that he is accorded his proper value." Then he and Marc wrote an agreement that in essence spelled out the terms under which I would be sold to somebody. The first time I read the contract it took me forty-eight hours to get through it. I had to look up almost every word.

Alfred and I became friends quickly. He and his wife,

Luella, welcomed me into their lives, giving me the feeling that I had family in New York, not just relatives. I was still something of an enigma to them, especially having been brought over from Europe because of my work in physics. That was out of the ordinary. They were proud of it, but at the same time they were extremely curious. They were so used to thinking of me as an impoverished student that it was difficult to know how to regard this new development.

They themselves had no way of judging how accomplished I may or may not have been. Whatever Marc Wood had told Alfred about me might have been true, or it might have been mostly a business agent's embellishment. But they had a way of finding out. Luella Slaner's father was Dr. La Mere, a prominent professor of physical chemistry at Columbia University, a friend of Einstein's who had been instrumental in saving a number of leading Jewish scientists from the Nazis. One evening at the Slaners' big house in Scarsdale he was there, and when we sat down together he said, "You know I teach physics, and I understand that you have a Ph.D. Tell me: Do you know what this is?" He drew a diagram on a piece of paper. "Yes," I answered, "it looks like the diagram of Rankin, from thermodynamics." "Yes," said Professor La Mere, "you're right." Then he wrote down an equation. "Do you recognize this?" I looked at it. "No," I said, "I've never seen it before, but it looks like it might have something to do with thermodynamics, too." "That's my equation," he said with a laugh. "It's new. Nobody knows that equation. He's okay," he said, turning to Alfred. That was my first examination in the United States. I thought I had probably passed about halfway.

My first trip to the States lasted ten days, enough time for Marc Wood to take me to a major stress analysis conference and exhibit in Pittsburgh. All the manufacturers were there, as well as the engineers and scientists, many of whose names I knew from the literature. At first I was a bit overwhelmed, but my demonstrations seemed to generate considerable interest, at least among the engineers. Although I couldn't tell exactly, it seemed to me that the academic scientists were a lot more reserved. Still, Marc thought the show was a great success, and we agreed that I would come back for an extended stay in five months, which would give me time to settle my affairs in France.

I arrived in New York for the second time in October, just before the Sinai War started between Israel and Egypt. I heard what had happened, but without speaking English, it was hard to get direct news. I was reduced to relying on secondhand accounts from the one or two French-speaking people I knew. For the first couple of days I was mostly in the dark and extremely agitated. One day I was walking in midtown Manhattan when I heard radios blaring in the street and saw groups of people standing around, listening. The tension was thick; I could read the concern in their faces. I didn't have the slightest idea what the radio voices were talking about, but I was full of worry about the Sinai and what might be happening to that tiny eight-year-old country over there. Obviously something major must have taken place. When I got back to Marc Wood's office I told him what I had seen. "It's so tense outside," I said. "They're all standing around, listening to the news. Please tell me what happened. Has there been some terrible disaster in Israel?"

"What?" he said, "Felix, what's wrong with you? It's the World Series."

"What is the World Series, please?"

"Baseball, Felix. Baseball."

I couldn't believe it. "You're pulling my leg. What do you mean, baseball? Like a sport?"

"Yes, of course. You think they know what's going on in Israel?"

It was like puncturing a balloon. World Series? World? Nobody in Europe had ever heard of baseball. I was in a place where America was the world. A place where what might have been happening fifty-six hundred miles away, in the Sinai, didn't have any undue importance, at least not during the World Series.

But that hardly lowered my anxiety level. I went to the

United Nations General Assembly, where I could listen to the French translation of the debate. There I saw the Soviet and American delegates talking on the same side against Israel, a disturbing sight. But once I got the news straight, I didn't fear for the country. It was clear this was a limited conflict, that the state was not in danger, and that the lives of Israel's people were not at risk.

•

The first thing I did in the United States was publish a paper on photoelastic coatings in the journal *Product Engineering* (Marc Wood translated the paper from French to English). As soon as this paper appeared, hundreds of inquiries started coming in from all over the country. With that, Marc installed me in a luxurious office on the forty-fourth floor of the central building in Rockefeller Plaza. He was pulling all the stops to display me as grandly as he could. I had my main office there and a kind of display space in another building, farther downtown.

Marc Wood's method was to bring all the company executives who were interested in "Photostress" (as Marc had now christened the process) to New York and have me put on a demonstration. Afterward Marc's representatives would wine and dine the visitors. They would never allow me to go to eat with them, though, because of the distinct possibility that I might spoil the deal. I was picking up words and phrases fast, but they were never quite sure what might come out of my mouth. So they were a little wary.

Among those most seriously interested was the Budd Company of Philadelphia. Budd was a giant manufacturer that produced a range of products from railroad cars to automotive chassis. They had recently opened up a division called Tatnall Measuring Systems (after its founder, Frank Tatnall), their first venture into the field of electronic measuring devices. Now they were looking for new ideas in this area that would complement their line of strain gages. Strain gages were the primary instrument for measuring stress electronically, a relatively new and burgeoning technology in its own right.

Frank Tatnall had not invented the strain gage, but he was a dynamic force in its development. He had been in the field from its inception and was an inveterate motivator of people and a gifted promotor. From the moment he saw Photostress work, he wanted it for his business. Sometime later he recalled his first look at the process:

> I called on Marc Wood in the Empire State Building, and he took me to somewhere around Fourteenth Street to see a demonstration. We climbed the stairs of some small building and went into a bare room with tables around the walls upon which was as complete a show of instrumentation as you ever saw. A humble scientific-looking gentleman in laboratory garments was introduced to me as Dr. Zandman. He spoke only French, so Marc Wood translated, as we went around the circle of the operating exhibits. I came alive very quickly; this thing looked good. . . . Though my understanding of its significance was very scanty, and of Dr. Zandman's language still less so, I could see from the light sources, the polarizers, the colored patterns, and the oscilloscopic records from a coated vibrating plate that this was something important.*

Since Tatnall was not a scientist himself, he retained Professor William Murray, chairman of the mechanics department at MIT, to spend a few days with me and give him a report. When I heard Dr. Murray was coming, I was a little taken aback. Murray was president of the American Society of Experimental Stress Analysis and one of the first people to use the strain gage and photoelasticity on Bakelite models. I knew his ideas well from his numerous articles in the professional literature. He was an innovator and one of the great minds working on these problems, a true giant in the field.

Professor Murray did not know Photostress, but he understood the concept instantly, as anyone in the field would. (I always wondered that nobody had come up with the idea before. It was the height of simplicity and absolutely obvious once you

---

*F. G. Tatnall, *Tatnall on Testing* (Philadelphia: Univ. of Pennsylvania, 1979), p. 210

thought about it.) We spent three days together making measurements. "You don't have to convince me," he said, "but I'm an experimentalist. So let's test it against strain gages and weights. Then we'll calculate and compare. Theoretically it should be accurate, but sometimes these things work out differently in real life."

When we finally looked at all the figures he said, "This is perfect." He recommended me to Frank Tatnall, who asked me to come to work for Budd as director of basic research and head of the new Photostress Department. A few days later I was on my way to Philadelphia.

At Budd, Frank Tatnall had brought together the leading ideas and some of the top people in industrial stress analysis: Peter Stein from MIT, and the prominent strain gage scientist, Bill Bean; Jim Starr and Greer Ellis, strain gage instrumentation specialists; Glenn Krouse in fatigue testing machines; and Ed Bowkley for testing machines in the vividly named field of creep, rupture, and relaxation. The world was bursting with new developments in engineering and materials, from advances in jet planes and submarines, to new kinds of industrial equipment and construction techniques, to nuclear reactors—and much of it involved previously unimaginable stress problems.

Tatnall Measuring Systems was intense and competitive. Jim Starr, head of the Strain Gage Department, was a topnotch physicist. He had never finished college, but he had one of the best technical minds I had ever come across. Although we later became close friends, at first we didn't like each other at all and almost never talked. I was pushing the idea that Photostress could replace everything, and he was making his own aggressive claims for strain gages (we were both wrong, of course). But despite, or maybe because of, the competition, the people in Frank Tatnall's labs were an enthusiastic lot. I had landed in a hotbed of research and development.

At first I knew no English (I had only had time for one lesson at Berlitz), so I did the same thing I had in France. However busy I was, I made sure to memorize thirty words a day. If I only remembered ten, in ten days I still had a hundred words; in thirty days, three hundred. Even though I might forget a hundred of those, in three months I was talking. In five months I was giving lectures, though not without trepidation. After my first lecture at Budd I apologized profusely to Frank Tatnall. I was struggling terribly, giving every word what must have been a truly striking French-Polish-Yiddish pronunciation. "Look," I told him, "I can't talk, I'm sorry. I have such a heavy accent." He said, "Felix, first of all, everybody loves you, okay? Secondly, never lose your accent." According to Frank, my way of speaking was "more arresting than just plain American talk"—a considerable understatement. "Make it as heavy as you can," he said. "People will pay more attention. They'll sympathize with you. If you speak like an American, they'll all go to sleep." Frank Tatnall was a marketeer of the first order.

From one of Philadelphia's old-line Quaker families, Frank himself was a committed Christian. There was, in fact, something cherubic and ingenuous about him. He could talk Bible, philosophy, and ethics as well as he could marketing. A man of great warmth and simplicity, he didn't have a prejudiced bone in his body. After we had gotten to know one another he said to me one day, "Felix, you are the best Christian." "Frank," I said, "I'm not a Christian at all. I'm Jewish."

Two months later, after another of my strange-sounding lectures, it was, "Oh, what a lecture! Oh, did people love you! [he was a tremendous ego booster] You are absolutely the best Christian for me, Felix." "Frank," I said, "I'm Jewish. Please remember that." A few months later he said it again, then looked at me sheepishly and mumbled, "I'm sorry, I forgot." My Jewishness was rarely out of my head for a second, but for him, differences of that sort didn't even register.

Frank's opinion notwithstanding, sometimes my language problems were not an advantage. Almost immediately he started sending me around as a consultant. At General Motors in Detroit (where I had brought along a Tatnall salesman who knew

Polish in case I got stuck), while I was having lunch in the cafeteria I excused myself to go to the bathroom. One of my hosts pointed out the direction, and when I got there I saw a door marked "powder room." I couldn't make out what that meant, but when I looked inside, it seemed to be the right place. So I went into the stall, closed the door, sat down, and made myself comfortable. Then the door to the powder room opened and through the crack in the stall door I saw a lady come in. "Oy," I said to myself, "I'm in the wrong one." My feet were visible under the stall door, and I quickly thought about squatting on top of the seat to get them out of sight. But it was too late. She saw them and started screaming, "There's a man in here! What's he doing? There's a man in here!" It was a catastrophe. The stress specialist arrives and the first thing he does is start scaring women in the powder room.

But despite the occasional contretemps, soon I found myself booked for lectures throughout the United States. I was at MIT and Stanford, General Motors and Boeing—the largest universities and corporations. And everywhere hundreds of people would come to listen. The Photostress process was really taking hold in the aircraft and automotive industries. It became a standard tool for teaching.

In addition to lecturing, I began a heavy consulting schedule. I traveled like an itinerant preacher from one company to another, one university to another, usually with Bruce Sutton, a big, strong Budd salesman who drove, carried our equipment, and kept me good company. Budd would send me to help solve problems at particular projects, some of them closely guarded secrets. Among others, I worked on General Electric's ANPD project—for "Aircraft Nuclear Propulsion Division." In the late 1950s GE was secretly building a nuclear aircraft. Powered by an atomic reactor, the plane was designed to fly for years without ever having to refuel. It could stay aloft permanently, just as nuclear subs could sail forever (it was ultimately abandoned when weight problems could not be resolved). The ANPD project was so secret I was not supposed to know what I was working on. "You must be kidding," I said, but they weren't. I had two security people accompanying me every time I had to go to the bathroom.

At General Dynamics I worked on early nuclear submarines, doing component and stress measurements. I was at White Sands and the Redstone Arsenal, where they wanted me to show Wernher von Braun's design group what might be done with stress measurements (missiles have prodigious stress problems). At Redstone they were already bubbling over with talk about going to the moon. That struck me as mad; I couldn't believe they were serious.

My initial experience of the American academic community (with Professor Murray) had been a happy one. Murray was one of my intellectual heroes, and he had had nothing but praise for Photostress. But when as director of research at Budd I began formally introducing the process to the academic scientists, many of them took it badly.

For quite a few of the great names in physical mechanics, Photostress was almost an insult. They had been engaged for years with photoelastic phenomena. They had worked with Bakelite models and epoxy and had striven mightily to solve the theoretical problems. And then, suddenly, Photostress had happened, right under their noses. I had taken a coating of the same photoelastic plastics they were working with, applied it to metal, and said, "Here, with this you can do the real thing. Instead of trying to manipulate models, now you can put it directly on a bridge or an airplane."

For some of those who had invested long years of effort, this simple (but crucial) advance had to be infuriating. To add insult to injury, it had not even been done by an academic scientist, but by someone in the business sector. For university professors, writing papers for professional journals was not a remunerative activity, but the industrial world paid very good wages, and for Budd, Photostress had turned into a significant moneymaker. Nor did it help matters in the least that I was so "French" (in France I had been considered Polish).

The unhappiness over Photostress went to such lengths that a group at Brown University did an involved theoretical study and "proved" that it did not work well. They found that the inaccuracies were enormous—up to 300 percent in certain cases. They did not have physical proof, but mathematically they succeeded in identifying serious errors.

When I examined the mathematics of their proof, I found them a little over my head. I worked with the proof, then gave it to one of my colleagues. Neither of us could find a flaw. Yet I had made thousands of measurements, and I knew that whatever the math said, in the field everything was working out perfectly. How could that be? I was finding errors of 1 percent, 0.5 percent, 5 percent at the very worst (even 5 percent was acceptable), but the Brown University group was showing potential errors of 300 percent. I knew that couldn't be right, whether I could find a flaw in their demonstration or not.

But the professional world loved the paper. It was written by two mathematicians, J. Duffy and T. Mylonas. Their mentor was Daniel Drucker, department head at Brown and a member of the Academy of Engineering, a prominent figure. The authors enjoyed the highest regard of their colleagues, and even more importantly, their proof struck an emotional chord. The academic world began to mock the process.

But strange to say, I kept being invited to Boeing and Lockheed and McDonnell Douglas and all the others to apply Photostress measurements to their airplanes and ships. If anything, my consulting schedule grew even more crowded. God bless America, I thought, when I understood what was going on. The industrial world was saying, "We don't give a hoot about the academic papers. We put a strain gage here; you put Photostress there. We measure one against the other, and it always works." While academic America considered Photostress discredited, industrial America was using the process left and right.

But the theoretical problem bothered me. I knew there had to be a way to prove mathematically that Photostress worked, because the fact was that it did. Either there was something wrong with the math in the Duffy/Mylonas disproof, or there was some other kind of error that was outside my field of vision.

At about that time I hired Alex Redner to work at Budd, a friend and fellow survivor with whom I had studied in Nancy. After his studies Alex had gone to work in Uruguay, but I had begun to pick up distress signals from him about his job and had written that he could join me if he liked. He and his family were now in Philadelphia, which was fortunate for me, since Alex was a brilliant engineer. He and I discussed my dilemma day and night and he brought a new pair of eyes to the problem. Suddenly, with his help, I understood what was wrong with the mathematics. The math was not relevant to applied physics!

What I saw was that the mathematics of the disproof was not wrong, it was just not applicable to any actual case. The disproof was relevant only to a theoretical case that did not exist in practice and that could not be produced in practice. I don't think they were looking for that at Brown University, but that is what Duffy, Mylonas, and the others had found.

Once Redner and I identified the problem, I called Dr. Dan Post, who was one of the clan of professors who claimed that Photostress didn't work properly. Post was a naysayer, but I had read some of his published work and had had a number of discussions with him in the past. I had been taken with both his intellect and his manner. He impressed me as a completely honest man.

Post taught at Worcester Polytechnic Institute in Massachusetts but lived in Albany, New York. I thought he was extremely good, a first-rate optics man who was an exceptionally elegant experimenter. In my opinion (which I kept to myself), Dan Post might have been the best optical physicist in the world.

Telephoning him at home, I said I would like to take a few hours with him to discuss Photostress. He wasn't friendly. "There's nothing to talk about," he said curtly. "What do you want?" I said, "I think I have something new on the situation."

There was a moment's hesitation, but only a moment. "Okay," I heard. "Come up."

So I flew up to Post's home in Albany. We spent the entire evening talking, and I showed him what I had found. When I finally hammered home the last nail, he opened his eyes wide and said, "Damnit, it looks like you may be right." He had a laboratory in Albany at Pratt & Whitney, and in the middle of the night we went over there to look for a book that had some relevant papers in it. We studied the whole night, and in the morning Post said, "Felix, you are right. There's no question. But I can't write the paper. *You* have to write the paper." "Why?" I said. "I need *you* to write the paper. It will be much more credible. I have an ax to grind here; you don't. And anyway, is it true or isn't it?"

"Yes, it's true," he said. "But you know what this is going to do to me, don't you? If I write the paper, I'm a goner, I'm hanging myself. In the whole profession I'm dead." "Okay," I said, "if that's how it is, you decide." "I have to give it some thought," he said, and went out.

When Post came back, he looked grim. I guessed he had talked it over with his wife. "Felix," he said quietly, "I guess I have to write the damned paper with you. There's no way out. It's a trap. You got me into a trap, and now I can't get out."

Dan Post wrote the paper with me. That began what I came to call the Battle of Washington. We presented the paper at the Society for Experimental Stress Analysis's conference in the nation's capital. Everyone knew there was going to be a tremendous clash, and inside the auditorium it was standing room only. There might have been five hundred people there, almost everybody in the entire stress analysis and experimental mechanics world. I had never seen such a crowd or such anticipation at a professional meeting.

Dan Post presented a section of the paper and I presented another section. Duffy and Mylonas, the two leading authors of the disproof, had apparently demonstrated that the flaws in the Photostress technique was its sensitivity to thickness—that is, the thicker the photoelastic coating, the more error you would get. And since it was necessary to use coatings that were 1 to 3 millimeters in thickness, the supposed range of error went from significant to enormous. But after we had figured out what was wrong with their theory Post said to me, "Okay, so let's apply a coating an inch thick [254 millimeters] and see what happens. According to their theory, the error should be gargantuan. But if there's zero error, there's zero error." When we did that, the experiment left not a shred of doubt. The error was so small it could not be measured.

When we finished our presentation, Professor Drucker came up to the podium. "What you've shown here may be so," he said. "But once again, you've proved a particular case. In general it remains true that there are significant errors."

I answered, "I challenge you now to produce one case where there is an error. But I challenge you to produce it experimentally—not on paper. We have shown that there are none. You show me one single case where there is."

Now Duffy had the hot potato. Eight months later I got a telephone call from a friend who was working at the Picatinny Arsenal laboratories. He told me that the arsenal had sponsored additional work by Duffy to prove that there was an error. And Duffy had succeeded. "He's found a case," said my friend, "and this is it." Then he gave me an exact description of the experiment that Duffy was going to present.

When Alex Redner and I duplicated the experiment, we found close to zero error. Almost none. But Duffy had shown a large error. We did it over, then we did it again. No error! I thought, Is this just a gross mistake? Duffy had taken his mathematical theory on one hand and had done his experiment on the other, and the predicted error matched exactly with the demonstrated error. Could this have happened by chance?

The next congress was in Chicago. Duffy was one of the presenters, and I had requested time to say a few words after he had given his paper. I was loaded for bear. "Would you show me slide number three?" I asked. He showed slide three. "Would you show me slide number two?" When I started to point out contradictions he said, "Well, the draftsman must have made an error in the curve."

"Would you show slide number seven?" I said.

That finished it. There was some embarrassed hemming and hawing, then nothing. After that Congress the controversy died a fast death.

No doubt experimental mechanics is considered a dry field by those not in it (to the extent they think of it at all). But like every human endeavor, it can become deeply emotional. This issue was emotional in the extreme. Duffy and his colleagues had developed a mathematical theory, but in their paper they had not adduced a single practical case to support it. When they were challenged, they either had to concede that the theory was irrelevant (which would look very odd) or come up with an experiment that could be duplicated. In the end, Duffy had presented an experiment at the congress which just did not prove the existence of any meaningful error. Those taking my point of view on the controversy included Professor Katz from MIT; Professor Hollister from UCLA; Alex Redner; and, of course, Post. That's where I got involved with the honorable Dr. Dan Post. It wasn't the last we were to see of each other.

•

About a year and a half after I arrived in the United States, I got a call from my uncle Jake Slaner (Alfred's father) in Oklahoma. Although Alfred and I had become close, I had not yet been to see Jake. He invited me to come for a visit.

Jake Slaner lived in Hobart, a town of six thousand people about two and a half hours from Oklahoma City by cab, which was how I got there. We drove over prairieland that seemed to go on forever, the road getting dustier and dustier. What with all the lecturing and consulting, by this time I had seen quite a lot of

America. But what I had mainly seen were cities and universities, never anything quite like this. This was the heart of the American heartland.

We finally got through all the empty space and drove into town, which had one main street, several churches, and some stores. It looked to me exactly like something out of the movies. One of the stores was called "Dixie," and that belonged to Jake Slaner; it was an old-fashioned dry goods emporium that sold men's and women's clothing, fabric, and other domestic items. Jake was waiting for me there, a little, bald spry man with keen eyes and a dynamic manner. He seemed to exude energy and intelligence. He spoke English to me (though even I noticed his accent), which he sprinkled with Yiddish terms and expressions. This was clearly a warm human being. I was already smiling inside as he took me around and introduced me to his salespeople, of whom there were seven.

That evening at Jake's house the door opened and to my shock Frumka Halpern walked in. Frumka was a young friend of my mother's from Grodno who had survived and married a partisan after the war. I had heard they had immigrated to Oklahoma, but we had never been in touch. Although she was very pregnant, I recognized Frumka instantly. Jake had called her with word that I was coming, and she and her husband had made the four-hour drive from their home in Edmond just to say hello for a few minutes. The war had been over for thirteen years, but the feelings Grodno's survivors had for each other had not diminished in the slightest. I suspected they never would.

The Dixie store was about the largest in town, and though Hobart looked sleepy, it was a county seat, which meant that it was also the commercial center for the farmers and smaller towns in the area. Jake Slaner was a good businessman, and he had done quite well over the years. He and his brothers and sister had started the Hobart store more than half a century earlier, and along the way they had opened up several other stores in that section of Oklahoma. For decades they had supplied the people of Hobart and its surroundings with their clothes. The Slaners had integrated themselves into the life of rural Oklahoma.

Still, it seemed odd to me that he and his wife, Jessie, were living there, out in the middle of a dusty nowhere—the only Jewish family in the midst of these cowboy and Indian surroundings. But I also understood it. I remembered vividly that not that many years ago in France, I had been desperate to make something of myself. I remembered telling my wife that if I got a job in the Amazon jungle, I'd grab it (one of my friends had just done exactly that). I'd live in a tent if I had to. All they would have to do is give me a rifle and an injection against malaria and snakebite and I'd go. That was how I talked, but it wasn't just talk. I was determined to build my life.

This other branch of my family was like I had been. They came from the old country to build their lives. It didn't matter where; they weren't spoiled. Oklahoma was a fine place, a place where you could establish yourself, make a living, and raise a family. And when they arrived, late in the nineteenth century, Oklahoma was just beginning to open up.

Alfred had filled me in on the story, which I had heard bits and pieces of when I was a child. His uncle Phillip, one of Grandma Tema's brothers, had immigrated to the United States from the little Lithuanian Jewish town of Vishay in the 1880s. He had arrived, no doubt by accident, in Galveston, Texas. That's where the ship had gone, instead of to New York or Philadelphia. And in Texas at that time, apparently everyone was talking about the opportunities in Oklahoma. He knew nobody in Oklahoma (not that he knew anybody in Texas), and he hadn't any idea what he might do. But that's where people said the opportunities were, so that's where he went.

His travels led him to southwestern Oklahoma, not far from the Red River, which seemed as good a place as any. There he changed his family name from Solnitzky to Slaner (to sound more American), bought a small stock of goods and a horse, and became a peddler, trading with the farmers and the Indians. A few years later he was joined by his sister and two brothers, one of whom was Jake. Of Grandma Tema's seven siblings, four now lived in Oklahoma.

In 1904, at the time of one of Oklahoma's land runs, Jake Slaner got on a horse, and instead of looking for farmland he staked out a location for a store. That was how he acquired the site of the Dixie I had just visited. By then Phillip had died, but Jake, his sister Molly, and his brother Louie ran the store. Louie did most of the traveling and was widely liked by the farmers and Indians, who nicknamed him "Runny Nose." According to the family story, this was because he couldn't stand seeing the poverty-stricken Indian children running around with no shoes or coats in the cold months. He had the habit of giving out clothes and wiping their perpetually runny noses with his handkerchief. When the others told Louie he couldn't do that (after all, clothing was their business), he answered, "The first coat I can give them; they'll buy the next." Whether this was legend or not, it was a fact that Louie was made an honorary Kiowa, and that when he died, his funeral was attended by many of the tribespeople as well as by the townsmen whose families he had clothed.

Meanwhile, Jake Slaner flourished. He married a Jewish girl he met on a buying trip to New York, and in time they became elders in the local community. He was a member of the Masons, the Rotary, and the Elks, he played pinochle regularly with his lodge brothers, and everyone knew that his word was his bond. His wife, Jessie, did well, too, even though coming from a place where they had pianos and opera houses, she found Oklahoma a little rough at first. She was not religious at all (neither was Jake), but she felt she had to do something to maintain their identities in this 100 percent Christian place, so every Friday night she lit the candles, and she did her best to keep the Sabbath.

But Jessie wasn't obtrusive about her religion and she, too, fit right in. She was a Girl Scout leader and played cards with the ladies. Coming from New York, she was attached to books and libraries, so she pushed the establishment of the Hobart library and made it a good one. All Jessie's best friends, of course, were Christian, and they loved her. She used to be invited to give talks on Judaism at the local Methodist and Baptist churches. She and Jake were town fixtures.

To me this was completely fascinating. The idea that an isolated Jewish family could fit in somewhere as apparently alien as Hobart didn't jibe with anything at all in my own experience. I looked around at the rolling prairie and the dust and the white wooden church on the main street and I wondered at it. Yet here they were. Jake and I talked for hours. He told me about the old times, when his mother, my great-grandmother Chaya, came to live with him and his brothers and sister for a while, but wasn't able to deal with no synagogue and the lack of kosher food and had gone back to Grodno. I remembered her well myself. When I was quite young she had had her room in the Freydovicz house, with its own private entrance. When she joined us for dinner the whole family stood up, including Grandfather Freydovicz. She died at the age of a hundred and five, but the family decided to put ninety-nine in the death notices to avoid the evil eye.

Jake told me that he had visited Grodno in 1926, the year before I was born. His mother, who was already quite ancient, had taken him into bed and started asking him questions. (I recalled so clearly Grandma Tema taking me into her bed when she wanted to talk.) "How is it in Oklahoma?" she had asked him. "Do you have a house?"

"Yes, Mama, we have a beautiful house."

"That's nice. And how are your wife and the children you wrote me about?"

"Fine."

"And does your wife have domestic help with the house and the children?"

"Yes, she does."

"That's good. Does her helper come every day?"

"Yes, and sometimes she sleeps over. We even have a second one to give a hand sometimes."

"That's very good. And do you have a piano?"

And a car? And the store? And how many people were working at the store? His mother went on to satisfy herself about the state of life and business over there in Oklahoma, and when she was done, she said, "My dear son, our cousin Rachel from Vishay, has to get married, and I need a dowry for her. Things sound good in America. From you I'd like to have five thousand zlotys." And that's what it had cost him.

Jake also told me to stay close to Alfred. He advised me to put money aside because one day he was sure that I would go into business and that Alfred would be my partner. He was quite clear about it: Alfred and I would be partners. I listened out of respect, but the idea of my going into business was farfetched. "I'm not going into business, Jake," I said. "I love what I'm doing. I have a wonderful job, and they're paying me more than I ever dreamed of making. Why would I go into business?" "Felix," he said, "I know you. I know your character. You will be, you are, a businessman, and you will have a business. I want you to be as close as you can to Alfred now, so that when this happens, he will be able to help you." Neither Alfred nor I was the type to have followed Jake's advice about cultivating a relationship, but the fact was that we were already close friends. When I later asked Alfred whether his father had ever mentioned anything to him on this subject he said that no, there had never been a word.

Jake Slaner was already seventy-seven in 1958. It's possible that he felt we would have few chances to see each other and that he had to get his advice in while he had the chance. In fact, Jake died a year later. All the relatives came in for the funeral, second and third cousins, some of whom I didn't even know I had.

There was no synagogue in Hobart, the Slaners being the only Jews. But the town had taken Jake to its heart, and they found a solution to the problem of where to hold the service. The Presbyterian congregation volunteered their church for the occasion. They removed all the religious imagery and paraphernalia, and for that day the building was converted into a synagogue. In the center pews sat the family, some of the men wearing hats and yarmulkes, and on either side sat the people of Hobart. In the pulpit a rabbi from Oklahoma City conducted the service.

I was moved. I sat there, and during the prayers I thought about Europe. I remembered the Catholic church on Brygidzka Street, which I had lived next to for fourteen years without ever having set foot inside. Would such a thing ever have been possible in Europe, I wondered, for a church to convert itself because there was no synagogue? In honor of a Jew who had died? The idea was inconceivable. Yet I was sitting right in the middle of it, in Hobart, Oklahoma. This was a world I had never imagined when I decided to accept Marc Wood's offer.

THE VISHAY RESISTOR

PROFESSIONALLY, my first years in the United States should have been enough to make me heady. I was fought over by major companies, I battled with giants and emerged victorious. My work was recognized by my peers and valued by the market. America was such an interesting place, too; I liked so much of what I had found. I even felt I was making a place for myself socially. I had gotten involved with a number of Jewish organizations, including a support group for the Technion, Israel's MIT. I had met interesting and warm people in the synagogue, and I had good friends at work.

But at heart these things made little difference. Below the level of daily affairs and intellectual engagement was the level of emotion, and there my footing was precarious. There I walked gingerly.

I did odd things, which I could not help. Instinctively I did not go into places from which I could not get out. I searched automatically for escape routes. If someone came toward me on the street, my mind said, This could be a problem. My eyes went right and left, searching for the best direction to run. Philadelphia was full of parks, but I could not walk through one without thinking how those thick hedges or that little stand of trees might do as a hiding place. I knew just how I would manage it. With a heavy coat and a blanket I could turn myself into a cocoon, stay warm, and survive. First I'd make sure I was invisible, then I'd shut off the world.

At night I dreamed of being chased. Time and again I saw the Angel of Death swooping through the ghetto streets after me, wearing Wiese's face. But I never opened my mouth about any of this. I buried it, covered it over with concrete. One day I was watching a Danny Kaye movie with my wife and I started to laugh. Everybody else in the theater was laughing, too, but my own laugh rang in my ears, startling me. Then I realized why. It was 1958, and

Me and the Colonel had just come out. It was the first time I could remember laughing since the war.

I did not talk about the past. The first time I tried, in Paris, it hadn't worked, and I still could not do it. In Paris there had been a Grodno community, made up of people who had left before the war to study and consequently had survived. Sender, Josef Weiss, and I had attended one of their meetings, and they had asked us to describe what had happened. We walked to the front and stood there, but nothing came out of our mouths. We could not tell it.

When I came to the United States it was no different. One night Alfred and his wife, Luella, asked me if I could talk about my experiences. It seemed to me that they were really interested, and I wanted to tell them. But when I started, a snip here and a snip there, I saw how they closed themselves off. They looked embarrassed, as if this were something one human being should not be saying to another. Luella's eyes had already filled with tears. They could not bear to hear it. When I stopped, they did not ask me to continue. Nor did they (or any of my other relatives) ever ask again, even though in time I came to love Alfred and Luella like a brother and sister.

The only people I could talk to about it were other survivors, like Leon Trachtenberg. Leon and I had never lost touch. After the war he had gone to college in Germany, then had immigrated to America. He, too, had studied engineering, and he had become a specialist in air conditioning and heating. Now he lived in New York and I in Philadelphia, but we saw each other as often as we could. He was one of the few people I felt completely at ease with, with whom my past was not a barrier but a bond.

How could anybody understand who had not lived it? To others it was a horrible curiosity, or just an enigma. When I was filling out my papers for the Budd Company's Personnel Department, they asked if I had ever been arrested, I said, "Yes, during the war by the Germans." They were shocked. "What do you mean, you were arrested? We're putting you in a responsible management position. You can't have been arrested." I said, "Wait a minute. The guys who weren't arrested were the suspicious ones, not me." They had no idea what I was talking about. They lived in a normal world, where I did not fit. I explained and explained but I couldn't tell how my explanations struck them. They weren't sure what to make of it.

In Poland after the war, in France, even in the United States, I was always conscious of my isolation. Imagine, I thought, if a horse were dropped into a kingdom of cows. How would the horse feel? The food is different. The talk is different. The habits are different. That's how I felt, like a completely different animal. A different species. I dressed like everybody else. At a distance, you might even think that I am the same as you. But if I open my mouth and talk about myself, something strange and uncomfortable comes out.

I searched for analogies. You are like a tree, Felix, I thought, a tree that has had certain pieces cut off and has been transplanted. They took you out of the rain forest and replanted you in Alaska, in the snow. With a lot of work and luck you have actually taken root. So here you are, a palm tree in a forest of beautiful pines. You exist, you live. But do you belong?

Nor was I allowed to bring these things up at home. My wife did not want me to talk about it, not to her, and definitely not in front of the children. All that was something best left behind and forgotten. In 1962 our daughter Gisele was already six, and now two more had joined us: our second daughter, Ariele (named for my father, Aaron) in September 1958, and our son Marc (for my sister Mira) in November 1961. I was in love with my children, but they had not helped affairs between Ruth and me. With three children we understood better than ever the commonplace truth that having children does not heal fissures in a marriage. They become instead grounds for further disagreement. There is no question, I would think, the children, too, will be alien from me and my experience. They have been born into a normal world, and I will never be able to convey to them the abnormal world in which I live.

•

Strange to say, the fact that I was closed off emotionally didn't seem to affect my creative side. Sometime in 1961 I found myself playing with an idea for a new kind of resistor. Part of the idea came from my familiarity with bondings, which I had acquired from working with Photostress. Because I was continually engaged with stress problems, I had also come to a thorough understanding of strain gages (Jim Starr's specialty), and other parts of the idea took shape from elements of strain gage technology. Somehow bits and pieces of theory and practical electronics started brewing in my head. I began wondering if it might not be possible to create a resistor that was fifty or a hundred times better than those in use. If I could do that, it would be revolutionary. Resistors were a basic component of every single electric circuit in a world chock full of electric circuitry.

In every electric circuit there is a need to lower or manipulate the current. House current, for example, is 110 volts, but an appliance might require only 10 or 20 volts. This means that for the appliance to work, the current has to be reduced. Ordinarily the major reduction is done by a transformer. After that, the circuit inside the appliance might need a series of different voltages to perform. In a television set, for example, the various components of picture and sound each require a different voltage. Resistors are used to restrict current flow to meet these requirements, much as a valve is used to restrict the flow of water. The bigger the resistance, the less the current.

Resistors are made from materials that resist electric current to different degrees—most often metals or carbon. But metal or ceramic metal resistors have always had a serious problem: They are sensitive to temperature changes. If the temperature of the resistor changes, the level of resistance will also change. If you take a certain resistor of 100 ohms and raise the temperature, the resistance might rise, for example, to 101 or 102 ohms.

In many circuits, especially those used for high-precision applications such as avionics and instrumentation, temperature change can be deadly. Temperature differences will affect the performance of the circuit and consequently the performance of the machine or instrument or appliance. In a toaster that may not be important; in an aircraft guidance system it is. The less sensitivity to temperature change, the higher quality the circuit, the more precise the performance.

What I began to see was a way to make a resistor that would be virtually insensitive to temperature change. That would be something absolutely new, a breakthrough. A temperature-impervious resistor would allow manufacturers of a wide assortment of precision products to upgrade their performance by many factors.

What I was thinking went more or less like this: If you pull on a certain type of wire (as Lord Kelvin had discovered a hundred years earlier), the resistance value of the wire increases. Conversely, if you compress this wire, the resistance decreases. Furthermore, all materials elongate as they get hotter. So consequently, as a resistor heats up, it elongates, and its resistance becomes higher.

All materials elongate when heated, but they elongate at different rates. In general, metals expand much faster than ceramics. If you place a piece of metal next to a piece of ceremic and heat them both, the metal will elongate more. But what would happen, I thought, if you bonded the metal to the ceramic? The metal would want to pull away from the ceramic, but it couldn't because of the bond. In other words, it would be stressed back into conformity with the ceramic, especially if the ceramic is much thicker than the metal. That is, it would undergo compression. If the metal underwent compression, its resistance value would go down. But at the same time, because of the rise in temperature, the resistance value would go up. The trick would be to have one effect cancel out the other. If that could be achieved, I would have a temperature-impervious resistor.

Unfortunately, at just about this time my wonderful friend Frank Tatnall was retired from Budd. Frank was not an expert manager. I knew that, as did everybody else who worked for him. His great talent was motivating others. People loved him and would do anything for him. He had vision; he sparkled with enthusiasm. Maybe this will work, he'd tell you, or maybe that, and you'd begin to think that maybe it would. For many of us he had been an inspiration.

But his weaknesses did make a difference to the company. Tatnall Measuring Systems began to lose money, and Frank couldn't get a grasp on how to turn it around. He was let go and replaced with someone who was supposed to be a good manager but in fact was little more than a bureaucrat. Before long, Jim Starr decided to resign. He said he couldn't work for the new man. "Felix," he told me before he left, "you're going to take over strain gages as well as Photostress. Please take care of my people."

With Frank out and now Jim Starr, too, the atmosphere of the place changed. The excitement of invention and development had fired our offices and labs, but with Frank gone, the spirit was dead. At Tatnall Measuring Systems politics became the order of the day.

It seemed to me, too, that Mr. Budd himself was losing interest in the business. Frank Tatnall had excited him about a new field, but time had passed, and the new bureaucrats had their own agendas. I began to feel that it didn't matter very much to the company if I invented something or didn't invent it. My division was tiny, and Budd was enormous: $600 million a year in sales in those days. They had other things going on that were more important.

I didn't have a common language with the new people. But they certainly did not want me out either. On the contrary, they seemed happy with my work and did their best to encourage me. The only thing I really wanted at this point was to develop my new resistor. I was as consumed by this as I had been by photoelasticity. Budd should fund this idea, I thought. Let them put the money in. If I can do it (I was sure I could), they can set it up as a separate business. The great challenge was to produce a technology with this special resistor that had never existed before, that would be ten times, a hundred times better than anything available. Let the Budd Company take care of the business side of it.

From the moment I went to Mr. Budd with my proposal, he was convinced about the technology. He had faith that I knew what I was talking about. The question was: Would there be a market for a resistor like that? Could the company sell it?

So Mr. Budd put the idea in the hands of his market researchers. When the results came back, they were entirely negative. From a marketing standpoint, apparently, the idea was worthless. Nobody would buy it, they said. It would be far too expensive. The market didn't exist.

I was beside myself. Of course there's no market, I argued. It's an entirely new product. We have to develop the market. But arguing did no good. The decision had been made.

Look what they've done, I thought. They gave my resistor idea to these conventional marketeers, who handled it as if it were some new soap. If you develop a soap that's more or less the same as other soaps and you put the right amount of money into marketing, you get a slice of the soap market. If you build a resistor that's like other resistors and sell it correctly, you'll get a share of the resistor market. That you can assess. But how about if your idea is a complete departure? How about if it doesn't even look like a resistor? How about if it's two orders of magnitude better than anything else? How do they think they can assess the market for that?

In fact I was just venting frustration. I was convinced that if I could develop a resistor so far superior to any other there was bound to be some kind of market for it. But at heart I didn't really care how big the market might be. This was what I wanted to put my energies into, regardless of the commercial potential. It was the second time in my life that something like this had happened to me. Photostress and now the resistor. Now that these ideas had come together, I had to get them worked out. If I couldn't do it at Budd, I'd just have to find some other way. What I really needed was to become my own boss.

That thought, too, had probably been floating around in my head for a while, because as soon as I articulated it, I knew it was the answer. Not that I was interested in it from a business point of view—the challenge of creating a business didn't stir me. In fact, opening a business would be a giant problem. Especially in America, where I had only been for five years and didn't even speak the language well. But if I were my own boss, my creative life would be in my own hands.

The more I thought about it, though, the scarier it seemed. I had a major job at Budd, with a big future. My salary provided more money than I could easily use. And I was being paid to do work I loved. Everything was comfortably arranged; actually, it was almost perfect. I was married with three children. Leaving would be a terrible risk.

But the Budd Company refused to fund the project, and I felt I had no choice. I had the chance here to create a major breakthrough in electronics technology. I needed to do it.

My employment contract still had five years to go, but I went to Mr. Budd and told him that I felt committed to developing my resistor. Would he allow me out of my contract? He was sad about it; neither he nor I was eager to bring our relationship to an end. But he understood and agreed. Mr. Budd was, I thought, an extremely fine man. But I simply had no choice.

When I told Alfred Slaner that I was leaving Budd because they would not invest in a new idea I had, he asked me to prepare a business plan. He wanted to show it to Chester Roth, the chairman of Kaiser Roth Apparel, where Alfred was president. (Chester was Alfred's uncle on his mother's side. Alfred had worked for him summers while he was in college, then had gone into the business full time. By now Alfred and Chester had been partners for many years.) But when I presented the plan to Chester Roth, he was not impressed. It wasn't for him, he said. Why didn't I stick to my job? I was doing just fine as an employee. In the long run that would probably be best for me.

Luckily, Alfred didn't agree. He might not have thought

much of my potential as a businessman, but I knew that at least he trusted me with money. That was because of something that had happened shortly after I arrived in the United States. I had come under Marc Wood's management to demonstrate Photostress and look for a sponsor. But in the interim I had kept my consulting business in France. When I got to know the Slaners, Alfred's father, Jake, had asked me if I could use any money to help carry on the business. In fact, I could. There were some instruments I wanted to buy but didn't have the money for. I had some accounts receivable that would cover them, but there was no cash. So I told Jake, "Yes, I could use $5,000." "Good," he said, and he arranged for Alfred to give me a certified check.

I didn't cash his check, but I did use it as collateral for a loan from a French bank. Nine months later I paid Jake back, the $5,000 plus 6 percent interest. Jake wasn't expecting the interest; he wasn't even expecting the $5,000. I started getting calls from the family. "Felix, what the hell do you think you're doing? Since when do you reimburse family? You don't reimburse! Interest between us? Who ever heard of that? Why did you pay back interest, and why did you pay back anything? That's not the way it was meant. It was a gift, Felix."

I said, "Look, don't tell me gifts or no gifts. Jake asked me if I needed money. I said I'd like to borrow it. Otherwise I would have told him I needed a gift. He loaned it to me, and I used it as collateral. His money was blocked for nine months. So there's the money and there's the interest. It's completely normal. Let's not talk about it."

Later, when I visited Jake in Oklahoma, he told me that during the Depression the store had gone bankrupt. But afterward, when business started up again, he had made it a point to reimburse all the money he owed his suppliers. "You know," he said, "I could have made a lot of money if I hadn't done that. It took me years to pay them all. And after all, I was bankrupt like everybody else. But I paid everybody in town to the last penny." Jake had been intensely proud of that, and that background may have been in Alfred's mind when he decided he trusted me enough to put money into starting a company to develop and produce my heat-impervious resistor.

We both understood what a risk it was. To start off with, it was a technical risk. Even though the idea was more or less fully formed in my head, I didn't even have it completely worked out on paper. No one had to tell me that obstacles always popped up when you tried to translate a concept into reality—often fatal obstacles (in fact, we did have major difficulties to overcome before we perfected the technology). And even if everything did work perfectly, it was still possible that the market wouldn't be adequate to support the business, which is what the Budd marketing people believed. One part of my mind was screaming that this was the least responsible thing I could do. But I was full of confidence and eagerness. I was convinced it could be done and that I could do it. This was my future, and I was going for it.

Alfred had faith in me, too. He helped me sharpen the business plan. Then he loaned me $200,000, for which I signed personal notes. I put $4,000 of my own savings into it, too—so we had our start-up money. "I'll take 40 percent of the company," I said; "you take 60." "No," he answered, "I'll be your partner, but I don't want to be your boss. I want it to be 50-50. This is your business, Felix. Do whatever you think is right. Just tell me about it from time to time."

We decided to name the new company Vishay, after the tiny Lithuanian village where our common great-grandparents Chaya and Sender Solnicki lived, where Grandma Tema and Jake Slaner had been born. I thought about calling it Grodno, but at home I had always heard Tema talk about Vishay, what life had been like there, how she and her brothers and sisters had grown up there. So to me Vishay recalled Tema, which in turn suggested the spiritual connection between Tema and Janova. It gave me the feeling of my family's origins, which were Alfred's family origins, too.

Like all the other shtetls, Vishay's Jews had been wiped off the face of the earth during the war, so at the same time the name evoked the memory of those who had perished in the Holocaust. It might have sounded odd to some people, but to me Vishay had powerful connotations. It expressed the way I felt.

•

Vishay's first employee was Grace Glass, my secretary from Budd, and the first assignment I gave her was to find a building we could use. Driving along Route 30 in Malvern, Pennsylvania, not far from my home, she came across a for-rent sign on a building that housed a Laundromat sales company and some stores. But half the building was vacant, and when I inquired, the price seemed right. I rented four thousand square feet of the available twenty thousand, and asked for an option to buy the entire building. The owner had seen my financial statement, and he laughed when I mentioned the option. I hardly had enough money for the space I was renting. But he gave it to me anyway.

We signed the lease on February 22, 1962, and the next day we started work. From the beginning I husbanded the money. We built our laboratory at night, nailing wallboard and painting and doing everything on a shoestring. I bought furniture and equipment, and a month later we were ready to go.

The beginning was not simple at all, which was no surprise. But it was still frustrating when unexpected problems with no obvious solutions cropped up. We had major difficulties with fabrication. But I was lucky to have two creative technical partners, one of whom was Dr. Dan Post from Worcester Polytechnic Institute.

Several years earlier, Post had sold an idea to Budd about using certain innovative etching methods to make strain gages. It occurred to me that his methods could probably be used in making resistors, too. That would require a good deal of development work, but we both thought it could be done, and I acquired the rights and brought him on board.

Then I hired Jim Starr. After he quit Budd, Jim had

gone to work for Allegheny Instruments, but Allegheny had recently suffered a disaster when a plane crash killed virtually their entire management team. Now Jim was at loose ends. Bill Bean suggested I call Jim and propose to him that we should become partners. I had tremendous faith in Jim's abilities, and I wanted badly to bring him into the venture. Jim was amenable, but he didn't believe in partnerships. "Either I should work for you," he said, "or you should work for me." Eventually he decided to work for me, though I always afterward thought of him as a partner.

Jim was a leading expert in strain gages, and strain gages had the same temperature problem as resistors. A temperature-impervious strain gage would permit new levels of precision in the field of stress measurement. That, too, I was convinced would make a good business. At the same time, Jim could help with resistors, especially in developing cements and foils—advanced kinds of metal resistance surfaces that had advantages over the common wire resistors.

Jim went to work, but not in our rented facility in Malvern. His family was from Detroit, and the automotive industry was a major customer for strain gages. He thought that would be a good area for him, and I agreed. So we rented a little facility in Romulus, Michigan. I wasn't that happy, though, when he said he'd like his own plane to commute to Philadelphia—in his younger days Jim had been a Navy acrobatic pilot. But he soon reconsidered that idea. He'd probably be too distracted by business to fly safely, he said.

With Jim, Dan Post, and I as leaders, we set up three research groups, which divided the main tasks of creating our product. And despite the difficulties and frustrations, after about six months we had a resistor. To my immense satisfaction, it worked exactly as my calculations had predicted. I had had this idea in my head, and now we had brought it into reality.

The resister performed perfectly, but it looked very odd. Resistors traditionally were cylindrical, but the Vishay resistor was flat. The traditional cylinder shape was due to the fact that resistors were usually made by winding wire around a ceramic cylinder. To achieve a given resistance might require a foot of wire. But a foot-long wire would take far too much space. The solution was to coil the wire around a ceramic core that could fit into a very compact space. After that, all resistors were cylindrical, because that was the easiest way to wind wire.

Since I had come to resistors purely from a theoretical standpoint, I saw no reason to use the traditional shape. It made far more sense to create a flat resistor, which would not suffer from inductance, a parasitic effect created by winding wire. Since we were not working with wires but with foils, we didn't have to wind anything. Ours would be flat. The cheapest material we could use to bond our foil to was not ceramic, but glass. So we used glass as our substrate. Then we needed a case to put the resistor in. I found on the market a small, inexpensive flat case that was made for capacitors. We cut the piece of glass to the size of the case; then we attached the leads.

When I measured the power of our now cut-down and encased resistor, I found it was 0.33 watt. The standard resistors at that time were rated at ⅛, ¼, or ½ watt. But I was not a resistor man, and not knowing better, I made our specification .33. The fact was that if someone had told me to make a ½-watt resistor I wouldn't have been able to do it because I would have had to manufacture my own cases, and there was no money for that. The biggest appropriate case that was available cheaply gave us a 0.33-watt resistor.

So here was my new breakthrough resistor—except that it was flat and rated at 0.33 watt instead of cylindrical and rated at the industry standard. Later, after the resistor had become a great success, industry analysts proclaimed that our flat, 0.33-watt resistor had been a marketing coup. Vishay had entered the resistor market with a brilliant ploy, they said, capturing the niche between a quarter and a half watts and forcing everybody else to copy their specification. In fact it was purely accidental. I bought the available components, and whatever came out came out. But it was true that even though the wattage wasn't standard, the characteristics of the resistor were superior, and it was widely accepted. In the end, everybody in the field of ultraprecise resistors was compelled to copy the rating and shape, even though their technologies were different. Even conventional cylindrical resistors began appearing in flat packages that looked like ours.

So we launched the Vishay resistor. We advertised it in trade magazines; I wrote papers on it for the professional journals; our sales representatives made approaches to companies, which I followed up with personal visits. We sent samples out and potential buyers made their own measurements. They didn't believe it at first. But when their tests and measurements proved our claims, they started using it immediately. Sales took off. At the same time, the factory in Romulus, Michigan, began producing our newly developed heat-resistant strain gages, and they, too, gained an immediate place in the market. From almost the beginning, it looked like we stood a good chance of putting Vishay on a reasonable financial footing.

But as the orders poured in, we discovered that we had serious, unexpected trouble on our hands. Often our new customers wanted not single resistors but resistor networks—three or five or twelve resistors interconnected with each other. I had thought we'd be able to produce networks from one piece of metal foil. We'd make a pattern of the twelve resistors, reduce it, print it—and we'd have a twelve-resistor network. If somebody wanted fifteen, we'd produce a pattern of fifteen.

But my assumption here proved to be wildly optimistic. When we got down to the actual production, it turned out that every new pattern had to be engineered separately, with all the costs that entailed. The products we were making for GE or NASA were great, but by the time we delivered them, we had lost our pants. And try as we might, we could not master these costs. Before long it became frighteningly clear that if I couldn't figure out a different way to produce networks, we would soon find ourselves broke.

The idea I came up with was to standardize our production. We would make only patterns of one resistor chip. If we needed a network of three chips, we'd take three and put them together; five, we'd take five. Through the mass production of single chips, all of them the same, we could control our costs. Standardization was the key. It saved us from bankruptcy.

The Vishay foil resistor was the most expensive on the market, but its characteristics made its use mandatory wherever precision was paramount. In the military, for example, the precision of missile guidance depends very much on the stability of resistors. Before the foil resistor, a guidance system might have provided accuracy of plus or minus .6 mile. A Vishay foil resistor improved that by orders of magnitude. Jet fighters, which needed to respond instantly to alerts, were another military use. A fighter plane sitting on a runway in Alaska might be exposed to temperatures of 50 degrees Fahrenheit below zero. If that plane is scrambled and has to take off quickly, with older resistors the pilot would have to wait until his navigational electronics had warmed up. But with temperature-impervious resistors in the circuits, the warmup time was practically zero.

Wherever navigation was necessary—the military, NASA, commercial aircraft producers—acceptance was immediate. Then came the specialty computer makers and instrumentation people. Of course, it was not just the United States. Foreign users were just as interested in the advantages the new resistor provided. The French wanted it, the British, the Japanese, the Germans, and everybody else with aircraft and instrumentation industries.

In fact, soon the big problem was how to meet demand and grow. Since we did not have the money to increase capacity, we needed to sell through licensees. But the problem with licensees was how to give them a license without divulging the secrets of our technology. We had not had that much experience yet, but we understood a basic truth of the technology industry: Once you give someone your technology, you are finished. No matter how good your contracts and protections are, they will steal it from you. It's like a law of nature.

Our production method was to make the chip (consisting of the glass substrate and metal foil), attach the lead wires by which the resistor could be hooked into a circuit, then encapsulate it in our flat capacitor case. I decided that rather than convey the technology to any licensee, I would sell the manufactured chip to them and teach them only the technology of attaching wires, adjusting the resistor, and encapsulating it. That way I would eliminate the danger of someone stealing the technology, or so I thought.

Our first licensee was Sfernice, the largest resistor manufacturer in France. Louis Kaluszyner, a friend of mine and partner in our French strain gage distribution business, suggested I contact them. Sfernice was receptive, and I sold them the license in July 1964, which right away brought in badly needed capital.

After Sfernice started experiencing successful sales, they informed us that they were members of a cartel (legal at that time) together with a British company named Welwyn and a German company. The German firm was owned by Rosenthal, one of the world's foremost manufacturers of fine china. Would we be interested in licensing Rosenthal also?

At Snecma in France I had had German colleagues and coworkers. We had gotten along together without any problems. But that was on a professional level; what was now being proposed to me was something altogether different. This was a question of actually doing business with a German company, in Germany.

Just thinking about it sent my blood pressure up. I didn't know what to do; nothing like this had occurred to me two years earlier, when I was consumed by the desire to produce the foil resistor. This is business, I thought. If Vishay wants to survive and grow we need licensees, and Rosenthal is the largest component manufacturer in Germany. I'd gotten myself into this world, and I had pulled others along with me. How could I turn my back on this, no matter how distasteful? So if they want to pay for the license, I decided, let them buy it. But then came a nagging voice: I didn't know Rosenthal. What if their backgrounds weren't good? Then what? I worried the question. If they were involved in the Holocaust, I wouldn't touch them with a ten-foot pole. But how would I know? Were they going to tell me? I was as tense as a stretched wire.

16

F INALLY I said yes; I would at least meet with them. After that maybe I'd have a better feel for what should be done.

In the late fall of 1964 I met Dr. Kotchi and Mr. Ankele in a Paris restaurant. Dr. Kotchi was the Rosenthal attorney, and Mr. Ankele was the general manager. We shook hands stiffly and sat down, all of us rigid with tension. The atmosphere was smoldering; I felt almost as though the room might explode. I was positive I was not going to go ahead with this.

Then Dr. Kotchi managed the suggestion of a smile. "We have greetings for you from Mr. Rosenthal," he said. "We want you to know that Mr. Rosenthal is Jewish." Those were the first words out of his mouth: "Mr. Rosenthal is Jewish." Then, "Dr. Zandman, we know about your past. We know who you are, and we want you to know that Mr. Rosenthal fled to England during the war. When he returned, the government gave him back his business. He has sent us here and has asked us to convey his warm regards to you." Then he let out a barely audible sigh of relief. So did I.

That began our relationship with Sfernice and Rosenthal, two companies that were to figure largely in Vishay's future (and that I eventually bought). Before long we had also signed a licensing agreement with Welwyn, the British firm in the cartel, and with Kyowa, a Japanese company that had been pursuing us. We had now established ourselves in all the major markets. Very soon Vishay began seeing more profits than I had anticipated in our business plan. Originally I had assessed our market at about $2 million per year, which had seemed more than enough to make the effort worthwhile. Now it began to appear that the potential might be substantially larger.

With Rosenthal and Welwyn the association started well and continued smoothly. Business with Sfernice began harmoniously, too, but within a year warning flags were going up.

Sfernice had hired a new CEO, Jean Schirmer, who had different ideas about how the relationship ought to be structured. "I don't want to buy the chips anymore," he told me. "I want to produce them in France." If the chips were made in France, he said, sales there would increase significantly. But I was leery of transferring the technology, and in the end our discussions foundered. We continued to sell Sfernice the chips, but the relationship was a good deal less cordial. I had the sense that Schirmer believed there were other ways to go that would be more productive for his company. It wasn't long before we were to find out what he had in mind.

•

Not long before Dr. Kotchi and Mr. Ankele appeared in my office, certain events were taking place in Austria that would have interested me deeply had I known about them. On a train bound from Vienna to Belgrade, two Austrian detectives arrested an obscure German businessman whose passport identified him as Hubert Zimmermann. Zimmermann had a warrant out on him for skipping bail while awaiting trial in Germany, but not under the name of Zimmermann. The businessman was in reality Kurt Wiese, erstwhile commandant of the Grodno ghetto.

Since the war, a fair number of Nazis had been captured and prosecuted. The most famous of the trials had been those held in Nuremberg shortly after the Allied victory, when the surviving Nazi leaders had been put in the dock. Other trials had also taken place, many of them of Gestapo and SS men who had participated in the murder of Europe's Jews. But Errelis, the commander of the Grodno Gestapo, had never been tried. At the end of the war the British had taken him prisoner, but he had escaped from a POW camp and dropped from sight. Wiese, master of life and death in the ghetto, seemed to have disappeared altogether.

Their trail, though, was picked up when one of Errelis's deputies, a man named Schott, was denounced to the police by his wife, who was angry about an affair he was carrying on (twenty-one years earlier it had been Schott who smashed my violin against the wall. Before he was arrested he strangled her; then he commit-

Grandfather Berl Zandman.

Grandmother Rifka Zandman.

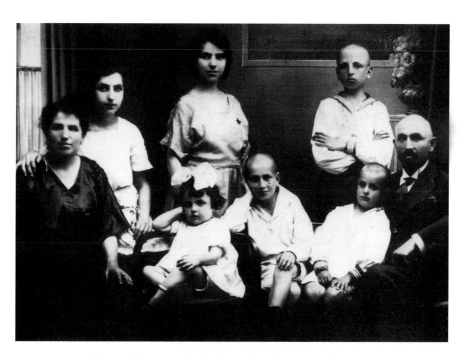

The Freydovicz family, clockwise from left: *Grandma Tema,
Lisa, Genia, Grisha, Grandfather Nachum,
Kushka, Sender, and Fania.*

*Felix's parents, Aaron
and Genia* (left).

*Sender and Felix
in 1935* (below).

 צ 0 ם הכתה ׳ 1 של ״ביהם "תנקות" קאָראָב 6 יו׳ס . תרצ"ח

*Felix's class at the Tarbut primary school.
He is in the first row, second from right.*

Grodno's Jews enter the ghetto, November 1, 1941.

The foundation hole at 28 Brygidzka Street, through which Felix and others escaped in November 1942.

Grodno's Grand Synagogue.

Janova and Felix in Poland, shortly after liberation.

The Puchalski family in 1949, front from left to right: *Wladek, Janova, Jan (with grandson Ryszard), Wanda.* Back: *Krystyna, Irena, Irena's husband, Franek, Sabina* (above).

Sender and Felix in 1946 (right).

Polish-Jewish "students" in Prague on the way to Paris, 1946.

Felix as a young university lecturer.

Felix and tank equipped with thermal shroud.

Ruta and Felix are married, September 10, 1978.

Planting a tree at Yad Vashem in honor of Jan and Janova Puchalski on June 15, 1987. From left: *Moshe Shamir; Beate Klarsfeld; Zdzislaw Kazimierczyk (Janova's grandson); Krystyna, Irena, Wladek, and Wanda (Janova's children); Serge Klarsfeld; Ruta; Felix; Ruta's brother Yitzhak; Supreme Court Justice Beiski; Ruta's brother Yaacov.*

The Puchalski family praying during the ceremony honoring them at Yad Vashem.

Felix, Ruta, and Alfred Slaner at the New York Stock Exchange as Vishay makes its first appearance on the Big Board in January 1984 (above).

Plaque commemorating the Grodno Ghetto, unveiled on March 12, 1991 (left).

A family photograph, taken immediately after the ceremony awarding Felix the French Legion of Honor. From left by couple: Orna Barr and Yitzhak Shoshani (Ruta's brother); Felix's daughter Gisele and her husband, Eli; Felix's daughter Ariele and her husband, Steven; Felix and Ruta; Ruta's brother Yaacov and his wife, Erela; Felix's son, Marc, and his wife, Orit.

ted suicide. But in the course of the investigation the police came across leads to Errelis and Wiese.

I knew nothing about any of this until sometime in mid-December of 1960, a letter arrived from the public prosecutor of Ludwigsburg, in what was then West Germany. My name had been found among those of the survivors of Grodno. The police, he wrote, were in the process of tracking Errelis, Wiese, and other Grodno area Gestapo. Legal actions were being prepared against them. Would I, as a survivor and witness, be willing to help? Could I, for example, provide any specifics on their ranks or official positions? If I saw them now, might I be able to identify them?

I felt as if I had received an electric shock. My heart was racing as I picked up the phone to call Leon Trachtenberg in New York, to see if he had gotten the same letter. Yes, said Leon, he had just opened it. He was going to respond immediately.

I wrote back to the public prosecutor that day. I would do anything I could to help bring Errelis and Wiese to justice. I had been seeing those two in my dreams for years.

Wiese was the particular nemesis of my recurring nightmares. At night he ran after me, sometimes with Errelis or one of the others, often by himself—chasing me down so he could shoot me or hang me. I ran, but in slow motion, never fast enough. Every dream flooded me with terror. I could see his long neck and the pale face and deep-set, glaring eyes under the SS skull hat as he charged toward me, gaining ground, until I awoke, sweating and screaming.

Even in the daytime, Wiese inhabited some inner region of my consciousness. Ever since the war I had gone off to school or to work each day, but in the back of my head Wiese loomed, like some evil mythical figure cradling a machine gun, searching for me, my mother, and my sister. A butcher. But not an ordinary butcher in a bloody apron: a butcher god.

I wrote back to the Ludwigsburg prosecutor, but that was the last I had heard. As far as I knew, the wheels of justice were grinding, and eventually there would be a trial. I did not hear about it when Errelis and Wiese were finally apprehended and indicted. Nor did I know that Wiese had been released on bail and then had disappeared from sight. He had slipped into the underground world where SS veteran circles, the *Kameradschaft,* helped their fellow Nazis with false identities and escape routes to South America and the Middle East.

Wiese, though, didn't quite make it, thanks to Nazi-hunter Simon Wiesenthal. In July 1964 Wiesenthal finally ran him to earth. One of Wiesenthal's best agents was an SS veteran who was the son of a German Jewish father and a Christian mother. "Alex," as Wiesenthal later called this agent in his book *The Murderers Among Us,* had infiltrated the SS veterans' circles and was keeping his eyes open for Wiese after he slipped bail. Alex found him as Wiese crossed the German border into Austria, traveling with forged papers. He was on his way to Egypt, which always refused extradition requests for Nazi war criminals and had become a favorite refuge. Wiese was arrested at the very last moment, just before his train crossed from Austria into Yugoslavia.

Two years later, as part of its final preparations for trial, the German prosecutor's office sent three representatives to Philadelphia to take my testimony. In the West German consulate there they started off by ascertaining if I was a true witness, if I was who I claimed to be, and if I had actually been present in the ghetto. When they were sure of that, they told me where their work stood. In Grodno the main Gestapo officers had been Errelis, Wiese, Rinzler (the commandant of Kielbasin), Schott (Errelis's deputy), Streblow, and Niestroj. Schott was dead by his own hand. Streblow had apparently been killed in the war, and Rinzler had never been found. Wiese and Errelis were now in jail and under indictment. Could I identify them? They spread a series of photographs over the table. My eyes picked them out instantly. "This is Wiese," I said, "and this one is Errelis."

The German courts organized two trials, one for the Bialystok region Gestapo (including Grodno), and one exclusively for the Grodno Gestapo. In September 1966 Leon Trachtenberg and I flew to Germany for the first trial. We needed to go together, Leon said. He had had a heart attack a few years earlier and didn't know if he could stand what we were about to face. I wasn't sure I could either. I was seething with rage.

The court convened in Bielefeld: prosecutors, defense attorneys, interpreters, and a panel of judges. On the defendants' bench sat several Germans. Some I didn't recognize—this trial was for the Bialystok Gestapo as well as ours—but there were Errelis and Wiese wearing drab suits and looking uncomfortable and nondescript. There we were, too, the witnesses: Leon and I and a dozen other survivors. Shulkes, the Farbindungsman who had hidden in our hole for the first few days, had testified earlier. (He was a courageous man. After the war he had immigrated to Australia, but when he was accused of collaboration, Shulkes went voluntarily to Israel for a trial. Go ahead, he said, here I am. Try me. Many witnesses came out, but the court acquitted him. Had he been guilty, the Israelis would undoubtedly have put him in jail.) I knew that another forty or forty-five people were still alive, and I wondered why they had not come, though it wasn't any surprise that people were not up to confronting these assassins of their families.

The court started off by establishing credibility. What were my mother's and father's names, they asked when I took the stand, and where had I gone to school? When did I move into the ghetto, and what was my address there? They asked me to describe the barracks in Kielbasin: how many tiers of bunks there had been and how one entered the bunker—small details that showed immediately if you had been there.

When they were satisfied, they went on. "We are not interested in brutality," they said. "We are not interested in beatings or robbery. We are interested in one thing only: murder. Were you an eyewitness to any murders? If not, you can go. If you were, we want to know about it."

I was an eyewitness. So were others. I described how Wiese had shot Ruwen Kimche in the back of the head one day near the ghetto gate for trying to smuggle in a piece of bread. I had watched the whole incident from Chasna Street. I told about Wiese's random killings in the Great Synagogue and how he had deliberately shot down a man standing next to me, whose body had then been dragged out by other Gestapo. I described how he hanged the beautiful Lena Prenska. Other survivors gave their own testimony about dozens of instances in which Wiese had killed individuals, and dozens more in which he had killed groups of people. Sometimes what they knew was heresay, and sometimes their recollections conflicted. The court winnowed the testimony, dismissing charges wherever the corroboration was shaky or where it couldn't be ascertained if someone Wiese shot had truly died.

Then Wiese himself took the stand. I listened in astonishment as he denied having killed Mr. Kimche. Nor had he shot people in the synagogue. I could not believe my ears when he said softly that he had not wanted to get involved in the hangings of those three people in November 1942. He had only put the noose around Lena Prenska's neck when Errelis's deputy Schott drew his pistol and forced him to do it.

Listening to Wiese talk made me feel strangely disoriented. This was the monster who had haunted my dreams for half a lifetime, an evil god who had brought death and destruction in his wake. And now the ghetto's king of life and death was sitting in the witness stand with his head down, ashamed and broken, mouthing plain, small, sniveling lies. On my way over to Germany I had been unsure whether I would be able to control myself in the courtroom. But now, with Wiese sitting ten feet in front of me, I thought: Could this be the man?

It had never once occurred to me that such a person, such an embodiment of evil, could lie. It had not occurred to me that he would be afraid of the truth. In my mind's eye I could see him declaring, "Yes, I did that. I did that because I wanted to do it. I did it because Jews are nothing, because we were the master race and they were bacteria and microbes who deserved to be erased." I had imagined that he would exalt himself. I expected at least that he would stand up for something he believed in.

NEVER THE LAST JOURNEY

Instead I was listening to him lie and grovel and make pathetic excuses. He didn't do it. He didn't mean it. He was forced into it. I listened and I thought, This man is no Angel of Death. This man is a nonentity, a nothing, a cipher.

Errelis, Wiese's boss, was even worse. I testified that I had seen him at Kielbasin standing next to the camp commandant, Rinzler, when Rinzler shot my cousin Rifka Freydovicz in the head. "I was never in Kielbasin," he said. And though several other witnesses also had seen him there, one thought he hadn't, and the court gave him the benefit of the doubt.

Other incidents also seemed to the judges short on corroboration. Errelis was accused of shooting several groups of people together with Wiese and other Gestapo. But Errelis denied it, and over the years the witnesses' memories had become less than 100 percent clear. He was not even aware, said the commander of the Grodno Gestapo, that Jews in the ghetto were killed at all outside of being convicted in legal proceedings.

During the first recess, people adjourned to the hallways to smoke or talk. Because Wiese had fled prosecution, he was under constant guard and did not appear outside the courtroom. But Errelis was free to come and go, and he walked out to wait on a bench in the corridor, where Leon and I saw him. I paced back and forth, wondering if I should attack him. I even discussed it with Leon. But we didn't do anything. I watched Errelis out of the corner of my eye, sitting there just like a normal person—for all the world as if he were a party in some civil trial, just one more ordinary human being inexplicably caught up in the toils of the law.

In the end it was not proved that Errelis personally had murdered anyone. No one could swear to having seen him pull the trigger. But the court judged him guilty nevertheless of being an accessory in two cases: the murder of at least thirty-five hundred people in Grodno's Ghetto One, and the murder of at least fifteen thousand people in the Bialystok ghetto, where he had been transferred after the final liquidation of Grodno's Jews. For these crimes he was sentenced to six years and six months' imprisonment. He was, in addition, stripped of his rights as a German citizen for five years.

Wiese fared differently. He was convicted of seven counts of murder and ten of accessory to murder. The sentence was seven terms of life imprisonment.*

I had thought that these trials would stir shattering emotions in me. But they didn't. Instead it was as if someone had pricked a balloon—my rage deflated. Watching Wiese and Errelis weaseling and lying disarmed the internal fury that had been my companion for a quarter of a century. Not my fury about what had happened, but about Errelis personally, and in particular, Wiese. He was not worth the rage. They had taken a nothing, given him a pistol and a machine gun, and sent him to terrorize and murder people. There was no ideology behind him, no strength, no belief in the thousand-year Third Reich, no grandiose delusions, no thought or intellect. There was nothing.

I watched these two arbiters of our fate cowering on the defendants' bench and thought, Is this the Nazi Germany that killed us, that wiped us out—these pathetic nonentities? And I felt a transformation. It relieved the tension of my soul. It cleaned me out. From that moment, I stopped dreaming about Wiese. He went out of my psyche. I still had nightmares about Germans and about what had happened (I still do), but Wiese himself exited my dreams.

•

In a sense the trials were a travesty. Almost thirty thousand Jewish people of Grodno had been annihilated by the Nazis. In this massive effort, Wiese and Errelis were two of the chief criminals, yet the court was uninterested in the enormity. The judges wanted specific, detailed facts of bullets shot and bodies identified, exactly as if the two had been common, garden variety murderers. Yet in another sense, the proceedings were exactly right. In the end, the

---

*The separate trial in Cologne exclusively for the Grodno Gestapo was identical to the Bielefeld trial, except that in Cologne there was an incident. During one witness's testimony a man in the audience stood up and shouted, "These lousy Jews are insulting the honor of the German nation. This is a scandal." The judges had him removed.

careful judicial approach to evidence meant one thing: Here was proof of what had happened—legal, documented proof presented in a court of law in which the defendants were protected against hearsay and exaggeration with all due process. Proof that was incontrovertible.

While I was watching the proceedings, the thought came to me that the trial documents ought somehow to be published. After all, this was the only comprehensive and completely credible account of the Holocaust in Grodno. Here a reader would find the examinations and cross-examinations, the meticulous procedural rulings of the judges, the sometimes contradictory and sometimes corroborative accounts of the eyewitnesses. If in the future researchers or other interested persons wanted to know what happened in Grodno, this would be the source to turn to.

After the trials I asked the prosecutor whether the documents would be available to the public. "Yes," he said. "These were open trials. The records will be available." But when I asked to take copies out of Germany to publish them, the court refused. I appealed to them in what turned into a protracted argument. For a number of years my discussions with the German authorities went back and forth. Despite my initial understanding, it turned out that these archives were considered sealed. The courts listened to my arguments, but they did not give an inch.

When it was clear that I wasn't going to make any progress myself, I went for help to Beate and Serge Klarsfeld, whom I had known for several years. The West German government had a healthy respect for the Klarsfelds, for good reason. Some might have said they were even afraid of them. If I couldn't get anywhere, maybe they could.

The Klarsfelds were Nazi-hunters. Beate was a German Protestant woman who had moved to France in 1960. There she had met Serge, a French Jewish survivor, whom she married several years later. Beate heard the story of her husband's family's suffering (Serge Klarsfeld's father had been gassed at Auschwitz), and she became involved. She came to believe that it was the duty of the German people to purify themselves, by which she meant that everybody who was directly involved in the Holocaust should be exposed and prosecuted.

One of the people she went after was Kurt Kiesinger, West Germany's chancellor. Beate Klarsfeld discovered that Kiesinger had been deputy chief of the Nazi regime's radio propaganda aimed at foreign countries, and she began publicizing this. But nobody paid any attention. Then in November 1968 (not long after the Cologne trial ended) she went to a big party rally where Kiesinger was speaking. She found a way of getting close to him, and publicly, in front of thousands of people, slapped him in the face, saying, "You are a Nazi. You deserve to be in jail."

She was arrested on the spot, which was exactly what she wanted, since her intent was to provoke a trial. In a trial everything would come out. Of course that was equally predictable to the government, and in the end the charges were dropped.

But the accusations hounded Kiesinger. He felt them getting closer, and within a year of the incident he resigned. Subsequently the Klarsfelds mounted campaigns against other Nazis, including Klaus Barbie. They pressured the German government to proceed forcefully, and the French government to acknowledge France's responsibility for its Jews who had been deported to the camps.

I had heard about the Klarsfelds, and I read Beate Klarsfeld's book *Wherever They May Be.* By the time I contacted them about the trial records, I had been following their activities for several years.

When I went to the Klarsfelds they agreed to help and threw themselves into the effort. But they, too, had problems. The German judicial authorities simply did not want to give the records out. Their ostensible rationale was that the defendants would be endangered. People might kill them if they knew who they were and where they lived—those who were out of prison. But the Klarsfelds persisted.

Months passed with no progress; then a year, then another. Eventually the Klarsfelds let the authorities know that this case had the potential to draw public attention. People would no doubt be interested in why the German government was withholding records of this nature. Given the Klarsfelds' history, the court authorities understood the implication and moved to strike a deal. In the end the court gave up the documents with the condition that the addresses of the defendants would be blanked out. But otherwise the entire record was verbatim.

By then I had had plenty of time to think about these documents, and I was more convinced than ever how significant they were. I was determined to publish them. I wanted the documentation available for my children and their children, for libraries and scholars and anyone else who wanted to look.

At first I had been glad of the trials for two reasons. Those who had committed the atrocities had suffered, if only a little, for what they had done—and that was a great deal more than had happened to many Nazis. Personally, too, the trials had had a profound cathartic effect: They had helped lift a heavy inner burden. But now I had had time to reflect, and I recognized that something far more important had come out of them.

The court records constituted, I thought, the most owerful witnessing there could be. Readers could pick up many different accounts of the Holocaust. But for the most part these were individual stories, told from a single point of view. Here, though, we had the Nazis' own testimony, the testimony of other German soldiers, of German wives who lived in Grodno, of Poles, of Jews who saw things from different angles. Put all this together with cross-examination, and it became the most precise depiction possible of what had happened there. And in the end this was all that remained of the Jewish community that had flourished in Grodno since the fourteenth century. Only this collection of papers.

•

The final verdict in the Bielefeld trial was handed down on April 14, 1967. The Cologne trial was about to begin. But for the moment my attention was elsewhere. In Israel a potential disaster was developing fast.

Tension along the Syrian border had been building for a while. I had followed the news closely, listening to the reports of terrorist attacks, Syrian artillery shelling from the Golan Heights, and Israeli retaliation. At about the time the verdict came down, there had been a serious air battle, and six Syrian MiGs had been destroyed. It was all troubling. Israel's safety was always an anxiety for me, and when tensions rose, so did my level of worry.

On May 14 the situation in the Middle East took a serious turn for the worse. The news announced that large Egyptian forces had moved into the Sinai and were poised opposite the Israeli border. Rumors of war were everywhere. Supposedly the Egyptians had a hundred thousand troops and a thousand battle tanks poised to invade. As the hysteria built, Jordan's King Hussein flew to Cairo to sign a pact with Nasser. If war did come, it was difficult to see how the Israelis might fight off the Egyptians, Jordanians, and Syrians at the same time.

With her enemies preparing to strike, Israel searched for help. But her longtime ally France suddenly changed orientation, and in the United States, Ambassador Abba Eban was unable to even obtain an interview with President Johnson. From everything I could see, Israel seemed desperately isolated.

We were all afraid that something was going to happen, but nothing did. For three weeks my nervousness increased along with the tension on the borders. Then the Israelis struck. It had never occurred to me that they would make a preemptive attack. They had done that in 1956, but then they had the French and British as allies. Now they were alone.

For the first twenty-four hours I felt like I was underwater. I couldn't seem to catch my breath. Nothing was clear. Nobody had a good picture of what was happening. I had the idea that I would immediately run to Israel, just to be there. Not that I could have done anything, but at least I could be in the country while it was fighting for its life. But then the Israelis began to announce victories. In the Sinai they were taking one position after another; the Egyptian Army seemed to be coming apart. Photographs of beaming Israeli soldiers began appearing in the newspapers. A few days later the Jordanians started to crumble and then the Syrians. My choking sensation alleviated.

A vast sense of relief and happiness followed, which was highlighted for me toward the end of the war when I attended my daughter Gisele's graduation from elementary school. She had gone to a Friends school in suburban Philadelphia, which in the Quaker way was strictly egalitarian; among other things, no prizes or awards were given that might seem to elevate one student above another. But this time, the principal said, they had to make an exception for a person who had excelled in her studies beyond anyone in their experience. Then she introduced Gisele. I watched Gisele walk to the front so modestly, my heart, of course, bursting with pride. What a wonderful day, I thought. Israel had survived, and now I had this *nachos* to celebrate, too.

A week later I flew to Tel Aviv via Paris. The Israeli Aircraft Industry had called me. They needed assistance in certain areas, they said. Would I be willing to talk with them about it? The next day I was on a flight to Paris, where I met with two IAI representatives for a preliminary discussion of what they had in mind. When I told them I was ready to do what I could, we flew on to Tel Aviv.

In Tel Aviv I sat down with Al Schwimmer, the head of the Israeli Aircraft Industry, who described their need for help in certain areas of stress analysis. They also wanted Vishay's precision foil resistors, but these they would like to produce themselves. Precision resistors were a defense product, and France, Israel's strongest ally and chief source of military hardware, had now declared an embargo. Against that background, the Israelis were determined to become as militarily self-sufficient as possible. "We have to create our own industry," said Schwimmer. "What would you think about going into a joint venture with us?"

Without knowing it, Schwimmer had touched a nerve.

Five years earlier, just after I started Vishay, I had gone to Israel for a short visit. One of the people I had seen there was my old Grodno friend Josef Szwarc. Josef was an engineer at a motor manufacturing company. When I told him about Vishay he said, "Felix, why wouldn't you open a company in Israel?" That was an idea that had already been swimming around in the back of my mind for a long time. But I knew it wasn't yet feasible. "I only have fifty people in the States," I told him. "This is a brand-new product. It's much too early." Still, from that moment I had been thinking about the prospect of actually doing it someday.

"Yes, I'd like to," I told Schwimmer. "A joint venture sounds like it might make a lot of sense." After that we started exploring the possibility, looking carefully at the costs and other factors. But the more I examined it, the less it appeared that a joint venture would be the best route to take. It seemed to me that they were looking for two things: One was to locate as much of the defense industry as possible in Israel; but the other was just business expansion. I kept asking Schwimmer, "Why do you want to be a partner in a resistor company? You make airplanes. Why don't you keep making airplanes? I'll set up the resistor business myself."

My thinking along these lines was reinforced by Moshe Shamir, who at that time was head of Sugat, an Israel sugar company. Moshe was a second cousin (my grandmother Zandman and his grandfather had been sister and brother), but though we knew of each other, we had never met. As I was soon to learn, Moshe enjoyed a wide circle of contacts in Israel's business and political worlds. He had somehow heard about my discussions with the Israeli Aircraft Industry, and he called me up. "Felix," he said, "I've got to talk to you." From the moment he got on the phone, he sounded like an old friend. "Look," he said when we met, "you want to set up in Israel, great. I'll help you do it. But you don't need IAI. They'll kill you. They're enormous. They make airplanes. They don't know the slightest thing about your business."

"I've complained about the same thing," I said. "But look, I'm in a delicate situation. I'd love to do it, and they need it.

They also really want it. But I'm not going to be able to work with the people there. The unions, the labor costs they have, their accounting methods—they're baffling me. Vishay is just a baby [Vishay was doing about $6 million a year at that time]. If I'm going to open up here I'm going to have to do it in a way that makes sense for me, not them."

After Moshe and I had talked, I went back to Schwimmer and said, "Look, I will set up in Israel, so Israel will have this industry in the country. You'll have as much use of it as you need, so you don't have to worry on that count. But I don't want to do it as a joint venture. I'll run it myself."

After that I worked with Moshe Shamir to develop a preliminary business plan. By the time we were finished, I felt I had a working knowledge of the many factors that would be part of this equation. I was as excited by the idea of opening up in Israel as I had ever been about anything. The very thought had a sense of fulfillment about it.

When I returned to the United States I had lunch with Alfred at Duffy's Restaurant near Malvern. "Alfred," I said, "I want to set up a plant in Israel."

"Oh, what for?"

"You know, I've looked at it carefully, and on a long-term basis it makes a lot of sense. We'll have lower labor costs there, tax breaks, high productivity. I'll show you the entire breakdown. But it's not that. The truth of the matter is that I want to do it. It will bring money, it will be profitable, no question. But it won't only be good for the company. It will give me a feeling of accomplishing something wonderful. Those things go together."

He looked at me and said, "Go ahead. I agree. If you want to do it, I won't oppose you."

I told him my plan was to put twenty people to work. "If it will work with twenty, it will work with a hundred." I already thought I could see how I might turn this into something really worthwhile.

Over the next few weeks I formalized my plan. Then I

flew to Israel and showed it to Pinchas Sapir, the minister of finance. After that I presented it to several groups in his ministry. I told Sapir I had two days and that at the end of two days I had to leave. On the second day, in the evening, they brought the approved papers over to the Tel Aviv Hilton for me to sign.

With the formalities finished, I hired Mike Arad from the Israeli Air Force to manage the operation. Then I hired Josef Szwarc away from the motor company as our chief engineer. Soon we were training twenty women to make foil resistors on the second floor above a store in downtown Tel Aviv. Vishay Israel was in business.

Israel may have been my spiritual homeland, but conducting business there was truly an experience with a different culture. As I found out almost immediately, Israelis are never content to leave well enough alone. They are an independent lot, inveterate tinkerers and innovators. They want to improve everything. No matter what it is, no matter how good it might be, they insist on making it better. There is no place in their heads for the truism that sometimes the enemy of good is better. I told them, "Look, this is the resistor we produce in the United States today. To be successful, we have to produce exactly the same thing here. I don't want you to make something better than this. I do not want you to improve it. Make it neither worse nor better. I want you to produce the same thing tomorrow as today. Once you know how to produce exactly what we stupid guys over there are producing, then we'll talk about producing better. But don't do it at the same time. Okay?"

And they said, "But it won't work." Already they were bubbling over with ideas for a new, improved resistor.

"In that case," I said, "I won't come to Israel and I'll fire you." They acquiesced. They would try their best.

Then came the equipment. I did not want them looking for or improvising equipment they thought might be better suited. "I'll transfer a section of equipment from the States," I told them.

"Not better, the same equipment. I am even going to send you the tables and chairs. You do not have the choice even to buy chairs in Israel. Everything here will be precisely the same as there." I wanted to get the idea across (although I eventually allowed myself to relent on the tables and chairs, as a compromise).

So we got to work. But it took an entire year before Vishay Israel produced exactly the same product, to the same standards. It was not (and is not) a simple matter. Despite the Israelis' ability and goodwill, they did not understand the production of components, which requires day-in-and-day-out uniformity. You cannot make a product that is a little bit better one day and a little bit worse the next. It has to be precisely the same. And if you do make a change, you have to experiment with that change on 5 percent of production, even after the most thorough testing. Otherwise you can destroy the whole production. The Israelis did not have this discipline naturally. It had to be taught.

And taught. It wasn't a matter of teaching it once and taking it for granted, because self-reliance and innovation are ingrained in their culture. Even later, when Vishay Israel had grown large and had developed world-class management and production skills, we were still dealing with the conflict between this Israeli instinct and the requirements of a precision industry.

That conflict was personified in one of our best managers, Gad Negbi, who had been a paratroop colonel and who was trained to take care of himself no matter what. Along with his other substantial talents, resourcefulness was his stock in trade. Reliance on headquarters may have been in Gad's book, but if it was, it appeared in fine print on the last page.

Whenever we had a breakdown in his factory, which happened on occasion, he was supposed to call headquarters immediately to get it fixed. But he would not do it. He said, "What do you take me for, a dummy? I know how to do it. Why bother you with it?" He wanted to do it by himself. He almost needed to do it by himself. It was in his nature, in his *kishkas*. Eventually we agreed to give him a twenty-four-hour grace period. We compromised with him. And he was a good soldier. At least he agreed to the compromise.

But he was just an example of a general Israeli trait. In one way or another many of our managers there exhibited the same inclinations. I began to think of them as horses, first-class Arabian stallions who had to be broken in. The trick was to do that without losing their magnificent spirit.

In a smaller way, the same problems were evident even at the beginning. Right from the start I could see that Israelis were going to be a challenge. But I loved working with them, and I was absolutely determined to make Vishay Israel a success.

17

LIKE HONEY IN MY HEART

IF the Israelis were keeping me busy, the business in France was also demanding attention. But not for reasons I enjoyed. Our licensee Sfernice was giving us problems. When their new CEO, Schirmer, came in, the relationship began to sour. We limped along with it—Sfernice was France's largest passive component maker—but within a few years it went from bad to worse. Sfernice introduced a new resistor to the market, one that looked exactly like ours.

When we investigated, we found that in fact the technology was not the same. What they had done was to make a wire-wound resistor and put it in the same flat case we used for our chip. From the outside it looked like an exact copy. It did not have the same specifications as ours, but it was the same configuration and could be plugged into a circuit board the same way; it was a potential substitute for customers who didn't absolutely require the precision of the Vishay foil resistor.

As we watched, it began to seem that the Sfernice sales force was trying to move customers from our resistor to theirs. Meanwhile, our licensing agreement gave them the exclusive right to sell Vishay resistors in France. I talked to Schirmer and told him it wasn't right. According to the licensing agreement, Sfernice was obligated to make their best effort to sell our resistor. Instead they were trying to shift the market away from us. What was going on now looked to me like a breach of contract.

I pushed Schirmer on it and even threatened him with a suit. We suspended selling chips to Sfernice, then started again. Eventually we terminated the licensing agreement, which precipitated a suit by Sfernice against us. The legal action proceeded up the ladder of the French court system and then to the European Common Market Court in Brussels.

This long, drawn-out affair was on the verge of being settled when Sfernice took a dramatic new step: They suddenly broke into the market with a foil resistor that claimed the same performance as ours. It was a stunning development. I was so angry I could hardly see straight. Our contract with them had specifically prohibited Sfernice from using foil technology for twenty years after the termination of the licensing agreement. When we took their resistor and analyzed it, we found that they were right: The performance was equal to ours in every way. In fact, the Sfernice foil resistor was not only equal to ours, it was precisely the same as ours.

Vishay's foil resistor had proven to be a true technological breakthrough. Since its introduction, no other component maker had been able to develop anything approaching its performance. Nor had they succeeded in challenging our patents or breaching the security system I had devised to keep our processes secret. But somehow Sfernice had acquired the technology. Worse, they very quickly started selling it in the United States through a subsidiary they set up in Virginia. They began making inroads into our main market, with our own technology, undercutting prices in an aggressive bid for business. Whether we could stop them before they caused real damage was a question I couldn't answer.

While we were considering how to react, a visitor from France, an engineer, showed up at my office in Malvern. He had recently been fired from Sfernice, and he wanted to see me. "Do you know how they got your product?" he asked. Of course we knew that with sufficient time and money our chip could be reverse-engineered and copied. I had assumed that was what had taken place. "No," he said. "They didn't copy it. They got the design from you."

"What do you mean, got it from me? How did they get it?"

"Brannin Boyd gave it to them."

When he said that, my heart sank. Brannin Boyd had been the chief engineer in our Malvern headquarters. I had been so determined to keep the technology secret that together with Boyd and Jim Starr I had set up a security system that compartmentalized production. The materials for our resistor were produced by Jim Starr's Measurements Division in Michigan. Then they were shipped to Malvern for fabrication. In that way nobody who knew the materials would know how to fabricate, and nobody who knew fabrication would know the materials. Only the three of us knew everything.

But a few years earlier, Brannin Boyd had left the company. Of course, he had signed a nondisclosure agreement with Vishay, but apparently he had not considered that an obstacle. According to the French engineer, Boyd had been showing up at Sfernice. Working secretly in a back room, he had apparently helped a few selected Sfernice engineers to duplicate our foil resistor.

Monsieur André Netter was our patent attorney in France—the same man who many years before had helped me take out the patent on Photostress without charging a fee. When I told Netter the story he said, "It's very simple. You have a patent in France. I can go to the judge and get a court order. Then we'll take the police to Sfernice, collect documents and samples, and prove the case."

That kind of straightforward approach wasn't possible under American law, but we were not in America. Netter procured the order, then sent one of his associates to get the police for a visit to the Sfernice factory in Nice. I went along in another car together with Avi Eden, a bright young lawyer I had recently hired. (Avi's father had gone through the Tarbut school in Grodno but had immigrated to the United States in 1938. Sender's wife, Sarah, was Avi's aunt, and Avi's grandmother had lived with us in the ghetto until she was taken in the February transport.) Avi and I waited outside the factory while Netter's associate and a photographer went inside and collected the evidence.

When our attorney went in and presented the court order to the Sfernice management, they stopped all work in the plant so that he and the photographer couldn't see the process in action. Meanwhile, Schirmer ran to a judge to get a cease-and-desist order. But by the time he got back, we had collected all the evidence we needed to show that not only was the product a copy, but also that the methods of fabrication were our methods. We now had a case against Sfernice not only for patent infringement but for theft of trade secrets.

Once we had the proof, a difference emerged among our attorneys as to how best to handle the case. One opinion was to attack Sfernice in U.S. Federal Court on grounds of patent infringement and theft. Another was to proceed against them in front of the International Trade Commission. The preponderance was to take the ITC route. A federal patent case might drag on for four or five years, but the ITC was obligated by law to render a decision within twelve months. The ITC couldn't make a judgment of damages, but they could shut down imports of the Sfernice resistor. With fierce competition from Sfernice's American subsidiary, foil resistor prices were already showing signs of collapse. Speed was of the essence. We brought our charges of theft to the ITC.

At this point we were approached by the Sfernice people. Sfernice had recently taken on a new chairman of the board, Jean-Claude Tiné. Tiné had not been party to our long court fight in France, nor had he been involved in the controversy over the resistor. We agreed to talk to him. Since I was so emotionally involved in this situation, Tiné met alone with Alfred. "You've put us against the wall," he said. "I'm new here, and I don't know exactly what happened; if there has been any wrongdoing on Sfernice's part, I was not involved in it. But I do know that you are giving us no choice. If you persist with your action, you're going to force us to bring an antitrust suit against you. My lawyers tell me that there's a chance you are wrongly preventing people from getting licenses. As you know, that's actionable."

We knew this response was a possibility. The standard defense against a suit for theft of technology or patent infringement is an antitrust countersuit. A patent is a legal monopoly; the corollary of that is antitrust. For such a suit to succeed, the plaintiff has to show that the patent is not valid for one reason or another. "Look," said Tiné, when he and I finally sat down together, "we all know what's going to happen here. Unless you and I can work something out, we're going to move against you on the basis of antitrust." Tiné was cultured and polite, obviously a gentleman. He was trying his best to make a human connection. He knew my background, he said. He thought he could understand some of my feelings. He himself had been in a German prison-of-war camp. "So why don't we all save ourselves a lot of time and money?" he said. "Why don't we settle?"

I listened to our lawyers argue the matter among themselves. Avi Eden tried to make the case that it made sense to settle. There's no predictability, he said, despite the strength of our position. Maybe the laws of physics were etched in stone; the laws of man weren't. Whatever came out of a trial would depend on factors other than the truth. If we did happen to get justice, it would be by chance. Besides, Sfernice was offering us royalties and other inducements that were more or less satisfactory.

Another of our attorneys took the opposite view. "Never," he said. The law was clear, and our evidence couldn't be more conclusive. Now was our chance to nail the bastards to the wall and get them out of the United States altogether.

I decided to nail them to the wall—a major mistake, as it turned out. Napoleon said many times that if you win a battle, keep a door open so the enemy can get out. If you close the door completely, you don't know how he might fight or what might happen. I should have listened.

Instead I listened to the aggressive lawyer and my bruised ego. I was really burning about what seemed to me a personal betrayal. This struck a blow at everything I thought was right. Here was a partner, our licensee, who had a contract with us that prohibited any competition on foil resistors, even legitimate competition. And here was Brannin Boyd, once part of our own company, caught working with the enemy. I felt betrayed. This was terrible, terrible, terrible. I was damned if I was going to back down.

So we sued in the ITC, and as expected, Sfernice brought an antitrust suit against us in Federal court. It was our bad luck that Sfernice sued in Alexandria, Virginia (which was where their American subsidiary was located). In the Virginia court there were two judges who might have heard the case. One, Judge Burns, prided himself on finishing every case in six months. He was a real anomaly; rendering expeditious verdicts was his personal trademark. Six months and no longer.

As luck would have it, Judge Burns was assigned the case, and he said, "I'll finish it in six months, like I would anything else. I don't care how complicated it is." Six jury members were empaneled, and we were under way.

Sfernice's lawyer was William Bittman from the famous Washington firm of Pierson, Ball, and Dowd. Bittman was well known, among other things, for his role in Watergate, where he represented E. Howard Hunt. He had the reputation of being a very clever, very strong litigator.

We, too, had eminent representation. Harold Kohn, from the Philadelphia firm of Kohn, Savett, Marion, and Graf, was one of the country's most highly regarded antitrust lawyers. But Kohn made a serious mistake early on. Given the merits of the case, he decided it was unnecessary to be present in the courtroom himself. Instead, two of his younger associates handled the actual trial work. And they did not do it well.

Bittman, on the other hand, was a master of courtroom melodrama. He engaged in all kinds of shticks. "Is it true," he asked me on the stand "that your cousin, repeat, *cousin,* is Moishe Shamir from Israel? *Moishe* Shamir? In *Israel?*" Just to establish the Jewish connection. (Moshe Shamir had come on as president of Vishay Israel shortly after we started up.)

I felt Bittman was attempting to undercut us through an implicit appeal to anti-Semitism, and I asked our lawyers why they didn't cross-examine me. If the other side was going to play a Jewish card like that, at least we should let the jury know the whole story. But they didn't want to. They felt the case was so strong that they didn't need that kind of thing. In essence they were arrogant young kids who took it too easy. They thought this was a simple, straightforward matter, and that was how they played it. Meanwhile, the other side was exploiting every opening, no matter how tiny, continuously playing covert psychological games with the jurors.

The substance of Sfernice's antitrust case was that our patent on the foil resistor was invalid and that consequently we had no exclusive right to the technology. It was invalid, supposedly, because according to law, from the time a discovery or invention is first publicized, the inventor has twelve months in which to apply for a patent. After that the development falls into the public domain. Sfernice was claiming that we had applied for the patent more than twelve months after we publicized the invention. This was not so. I had had a good patent lawyer handle the process. We had known what we were doing, and we had complied with all the requirements.

But this was Sfernice's case, and their attorney was doing a good job of building a favorable atmosphere. Meanwhile, Judge Burns, in his usual fashion, was hurrying the procedure through to conclusion. That was too bad, because over in the ITC court our case against Sfernice for theft was also moving along, this time in our favor. If that case were decided first, it would have made a strong impact.

But it didn't happen. Burns was as good as his word. He finished the case at speed, and when the jury came back, they had decided in Sfernice's favor. In their judgment there had indeed been patent irregularities. We were ordered to pay $1.5 million in damages, trebled automatically, plus lawyers' fees.

Meanwhile, with the ITC judge apparently in the process of finding in our favor, both Sfernice and Vishay decided it would be best to settle.

At this point, it made sense for both Sfernice and Vishay to settle (which I could have done initially at far more favorable terms and without the agony). We settled by paying them $3 million dollars instead of $4.5 million, and their paying us a royalty of 3 percent for using the process. In the event, we received very little in royalties from Sfernice's subsidiary, primarily because we hammered them hard in the marketplace and they never really were able to get off the ground. On the other side, though, the $3 million was $3 million.

This was my first significant experience with American justice, and it sent me into a towering rage. I was so distraught I had to use my rock-bottom calming methods. "Felix, are you going to die? No. Are you going to jail? No. So what's the big deal, the money? No. So what is it, Felix? Damnit! It's the injustice!"

Since the jury ruled that our patent was irregular, I went back to the U.S. Patent Office. "Look at this judgment," I told them. "You issued the patent, so now you decide. Either annul it or reissue it. Is it a fish or is it a snake? What is it?" They took it under consideration, and after an exhaustive, two-year examination they reissued the patent as perfect. A jury of six laypeople had decided on the basis of ignorance against a valid patent that was revalidated by the U.S. Patent Office. It was vindication of a sort, though not very consoling.

•

On the other hand, I couldn't complain. Slowly but steadily, Vishay was growing. Despite some failures here and there and one or two technological developments that didn't work out, the company was building its sales and becoming increasingly profitable. The foil resistor market was expanding, and Jim Starr's Measurements Group continued to be a mainstay.

Jim had moved the Measurements Group from Michigan to North Carolina in 1979 after being disheartened by too many fights with the United Auto Workers. Though a loner by nature, Jim was devoted to his workers and had introduced a variety of unusual benefits. Among other innovations, the Measurements Group workers enjoyed four-day weeks and profit sharing. But after some years passed, a group of employees mounted a concerted effort to bring in the UAW to protect the benefits Jim had implemented. Their effort failed, but feeling deeply aggrieved and worn out with distractions from his beloved experimental physics, Jim had asked if he could move the plant to North Carolina. He just couldn't work in Detroit anymore, he said.

Jim built the new plant himself. He was involved in each phase, from soil testing to pollution control to the design of the roof. He was a whirlwind, a universal engineer who applied himself personally to every problem. Once he got the plant up and running, he turned his attention to the R&D, which he also did himself. He had a microscope in his office, and he insisted on developing his own products. I sometimes argued with him about his need to keep everything in his own hands, but there was no disputing his success; the Measurements Group was doing very well indeed.

Our licensees were also bringing in profits, and a few years after we established licensing operations in Europe, we expanded to Japan.

In 1968 I got a letter from a Japanese competitor, a strain gage maker by the name of Kyowa. The president, Dr. Watanabe, wrote that he was interested in licensing some of our technology (most of which Jim Starr had developed). Could I come to discuss it?

I had never been to Japan, and I went with pleasure. In talking with Dr. Watanabe, I asked how he had gotten involved with strain gages. The story he told was fascinating. Strain gages, as I was well aware, were an American invention. But the Japanese had neither bought the rights nor stolen the idea in any way. They had shot it down.

During World War II the strain gage had been considered a top secret device that gave the American aircraft industry a significant advantage over Germany and Japan. Before strain gages there had been no way of accurately measuring stress, yet stress was a vital factor in designing effective fighter planes and bombers. Airplanes had to be made as light as possible; the lighter the plane, the more fuel, ammunition, and bombs it could carry. But if you made the airplane too light it would not withstand the stresses and would break apart. So designers were always working on the razor's edge, looking for the optimum ratio between strength and weight. In that endeavor strain gages were essential tools.

In those years Dr. Watanabe had worked for the Japanese Air Force as an aeronautical engineer. His job had been to examine downed American planes to see what might be learned from them. Cemented to some of the fragments he looked at, Dr. Watanabe began finding little red pieces of felt. And when he stripped the felt back he found filaments. At first he had no idea what these odd bits of wire were for. But in mulling the mystery over, it had come to him that they might have something to do with measuring stress. Pretty soon he was experimenting with the wires and hooking up instrumentation. Sure enough, when he stretched the wire and its resistivity changed (as it had to, according to Kelvin's law), he found he could measure the changes precisely. This meant that if the wire was cemented to a material (e.g., a plane wing), he could assess the stress the wing was subjected to at that point by measuring the change in resistance. Dr. Watanabe had rediscovered the principle of the strain gage.

When he went to the air force with his find, they had funded him to develop the same technology. That was how he had started his company, on the basis of a shot-down airplane.

My visit with Dr. Watanabe led to a licensing agreement between Vishay and Kyowa that gave us access to the burgeoning Japanese market for components, to add to our penetration of Europe.

Israel, too, was flourishing. Vishay Israel's president, Moshe Shamir, had exactly the right mix of financial and political talents to navigate the Israeli business waters; and Abe Inbar, a tough, disciplined former air force lieutenant colonel, was running the manufacturing operation with consummate skill.

In 1971 we also had our first contacts with the Soviets. Ever since I had come to America, the Cold War had severely restricted relations of any sort between Soviets and Americans, even professional contacts. But in 1970, Kissinger and Nixon's policy of détente took hold. One offshoot was that I found myself invited to the Soviet Union as part of a scientific exchange. I was asked to present a paper, and I suspected that the Soviets were also interested in licensing our resistor and strain gages.

In a way, Moscow seemed familiar. I had lived in a similar society from 1939 to 1941, when the Soviets had occupied Grodno, and seeing what people's lives were like brought with it a touch of remembrance. On the professional side, I met people whom I knew (and who knew me) from the scientific literature. This was the Brezhnev era of rigid communism, but despite the police state atmosphere I began making friends among my fellow scientists.

At one big banquet where the long tables were overflowing with vodka, the head of the Soviet scientific delegation gave the initial toast to a new era of cooperation. I answered with a few words about peace and understanding, then lifted my glass and said, "L'chaim." That went by most of the people there, but one Soviet scientist, named Poliakov, said, "What did you say? Could you say that again?" So I repeated it. "What is that?" he asked. "It's Hebrew," I said. It means 'To life.'"

Later on during the dinner I asked him why he had asked me that. He said, "I'm Jewish, you know. I knew what it meant, I just wanted to hear you say it again. It was like honey in my heart." At the same time I met Oleg Levin and some other Soviet Jewish scientists. Of course it was impossible for them to get out of the Soviet Union then, but we established contacts that we would take up again in the future.

In the USSR I managed to establish an instant reputation for technical brilliance, which eased my way with the Soviet electronics experts. At one meeting, where the room was packed with physicists, I had asked for a slide projector to help illustrate my presentation. They brought one in, but it didn't work. When the operator couldn't fix it, a nearby electricity professor tried, and when he had no luck, a couple of others looked at it. Soon there was a crowd around the machine, but all the effort was unavailing. Finally they brought in a specialist engineer who performed a variety of operations very adroitly but still got no results. Finally I looked at it. I had no idea what was wrong, and they seemed to have manipulated every possible part already. So I banged it, and instantly it flicked on and started to work. The room erupted in applause and laughter. Later the Ministry of Electronics initiated discussions toward buying a license.

In their pursuit of technological cooperation the Soviets were convivial to a fault. At one point the Academy of Science held a reception for me at which the main attraction was a huge table loaded with caviar and vodka. Each of the principal academicians gave a brief speech—each one, of course, preceded by the obligatory toast. This was at four in the afternoon. At seven that evening I had another meeting at the Ministry of Electronics, so by the time the car came to pick me up I had already been doing my part to further international goodwill for three hours.

At the ministry they started right in on the same thing. I saw a banquet spread out around a small forest of vodka bottles. With very few preliminaries the participants began emptying one bottle after another, drinking and drinking and talking and talking—though by this time none of the talk seemed particularly clear to me. But it did catch my attention when my host, one of the ministry's directors, passed out and slipped under the table. As I watched with interest, two large men came in, took him under the arms, and dragged him out. It was obviously nothing out of the ordinary. As far as I could tell, I was the only one who even noticed.

As the evening progressed I told Yves Dunand, a Vishay France employee who had accompanied me, that he had to get me out of there. "If we don't go now," I said, "I'm going to collapse myself, and I don't want the embarrassment" (although judging from what had happened to the director, passing out drunk didn't involve much embarrassment). I excused myself, Yves took me under the arm, and we walked out. Somehow Yves got me to my hotel room. I spent the next day wondering at the Soviets' approach to negotiations and swearing never to touch another drink as long as I lived. Nevertheless, I was favorably disposed to the idea of granting them a license, a subject I promised to take up with the U.S. government on my return.

•

That trip to the Soviet Union also gave me my first chance to see the Puchalski family since I left Poland for France in 1946. All through the years we had stayed in touch by letter, and in 1951 I had sent them a copy of my doctoral dissertation, which I had dedicated to Janova. From the time I had started working, I did what I could to help them out. I knew that Janova didn't expect it, that she was more than happy just to hear from me. I also knew that she loved me like a son, which in a way I was. She had given me the gift of life.

Over the years all of her five children had married and had their own children, whom I had more or less kept up on. It never left my mind that her children could so easily have died because of what she did, and that large family would have remained unborn. I would look at my own children—Gisele, Ariele, and Marc—and think: You, too, would never have existed had it not been for this magnificent woman.

Jan had died in 1963, and Janova herself had passed away in 1970, a time before détente made East-West visits easier. As a result, I had not gone to her funeral. They had lived in Gdansk since their move there in 1946, and that was where their graves were.

On the way back from Moscow, I stopped in Warsaw. I had been writing to the family, and Sabina and Krystyna, the two oldest daughters, came to meet me. That was a very emotional moment. We stayed the whole night together in the hotel, talking about the past and bringing each other up to date on our families.

I saw the Puchalskis again when I made a trip to Poland two years later. On this occasion I was invited to give a lecture in Poznan, and this time more of the family was able to come, including some of the grandchildren. We met there and had a big banquet and again everyone slept overnight. How wonderful it would have been, I thought, if Janova could have seen us all together.

On another trip I managed to make another connection with my past, this one wholly unexpected. Before the war, my father had told me that we had family in the Soviet Union. I remembered that, and afterward I wondered about them, who they were, and if they had somehow been able to stay alive during the war. But I knew neither their names nor where they lived, so the idea of finding out what had happened to them was nothing more than a fantasy.

But a few years after my first visit to the USSR, I had received a letter from a Soviet mathematician named Simcha Suchovitzky. The letter came to me via Israel. He was, Suchovitzky wrote, my cousin, because according to his calculations I must be the son of Archik Zandman of Grodno, the same Archik Zandman who had stayed with his family during the First World War.

Suchovitzky later told me that he had been heading a Ph.D. examining committee in Vilno, and after the examinations, a reception had been held by a professor of one of the candidates. The professor had gone on at length about a series of lectures on photoelasticity he had heard recently, given by a visiting American scientist whom he had gotten to know, someone named Zandman. "Zandman?" said Suchovitzky. "My mother was a Zandman. Where is he from?" "Well," said the professor, "he lives in America, but he was born in Grodno." At that moment, Suchovitzky said, he knew that at least one other member of the Zandman family had managed to survive.

During my second visit to the Soviet Union we met each other in Moscow, where Suchovitzky was a professor at the university. To my surprise, he spoke to me in fluent Hebrew. The story he told left me wondering at the turns of fate that govern lives, not least the lives of Jews in the Soviet Union.

Suchovitzky's family, like all the earlier generation of Zandmans, was pious, and as a young man in Vitebsk he had trained for the rabbinate (which explained his Hebrew). He was even ordained, but when Stalin came to power, the atmosphere became dangerously antireligious. Afraid, Suchovitzky had moved to Kiev, where nobody knew him, and had entered the university. He liked science, but in the Soviet Union it was also dangerous to be a biologist, or even a physicist. So he went into mathematics, the only subject he could think of that was completely free of political content. And it wasn't only he—almost everybody in his family had taken refuge in mathematics. I met twelve of them, and most were mathematicians.

•

Finding Simcha Suchovitzky and his family was a great joy, a wholly unexpected link to the past. But even while Simcha and I were making connections, Sender, who was so intimately bound up with my emotional life, was slipping away. Over the years Sender had flourished in Paris. His business had grown. He had married again, and he and his wife, Roma, had had two children. Antoinette and Michel. Since I was in Paris frequently, we were able to see each other often. We still never talked about the past; his feelings on that subject were buried as deeply as mine. But the bond between us went far beyond silence.

In September 1972 Sender's wife called me. The instant I heard her voice on the phone, I knew something was wrong. Sender was sick, she said; he had been to the hospital for an operation, and afterward the doctor had told her it was lung cancer. They hadn't taken anything out; they said it had already spread too far. Sender didn't know yet.

I flew to Paris immediately and went with Roma to the American Hospital, where he had been treated. There Sender's doctor explained that the cancer had progressed beyond the point where surgery or any other treatment would help. At first I refused to accept it. I had the idea that if I could get Sender to Philadelphia, the doctors there would find a way of doing something. With that in mind I called Dr. Jonathan Rhodes, a prominent Philadelphia cancer specialist, and put him in touch with the French doctor. But when Rhodes called me back, he offered no hope. "There's no point in bringing your uncle here," he said. "There's nothing we can do for him. He only has six to nine months to live."

When we knew that Sender's situation was truly hopeless, Roma said, "Felix, if you want to go off someplace with Sender, why don't you do it." In fact, I had been meaning to visit Israel with Sender for years. In October we went, taking his daughter Antoinette with us. We had a wonderful time, though for me the trip was charged with emotion. While I knew that Sender was dying, he himself did not. Roma had decided not to tell him. When I asked her if he shouldn't know, so that at least he could face it and prepare himself, she said, "Absolutely not. If he can live one day longer without anguish, that's what I want." And I respected her wishes. While in Jerusalem we visited my uncle Moshe's family—his wife, Laura, and two young sons, Dubi and Dror. Moshe Zandman had died eight years before, the last survivor of my father's family, as Sender, so close to death himself now, was the last of my mother's.

After we returned, I called Sender regularly; then, as the disease advanced, I started flying back and forth to see him. Dr. Rhodes suggested that chemotherapy might delay its progress, but chemotherapy was not well developed then, and no one had any illusions that it might be a cure. Given the terrible side effects, the treatment seemed likely to do little but bring Sender extra suffering.

On May 21, 1973, I called Sender's doctor to see how he was, and was told I had better come quickly. I caught a plane out that night, and in the morning I was at his home. "Poor Felix," Roma said when she opened the door, "Sender died last night."

The funeral was in Paris, at the Bagneux cemetery. Afterward Josef Weiss told me that when we returned from Israel, Sender had asked him if I was all right. "Felix looked at me very strangely when he said good-bye," he had told Weiss, "very strangely and very sadly. I think he must be sick. I'm afraid he's dying." He had had no idea that my sadness was for him as well as for myself. To me Sender's loss was immeasurable. He was my only connection to the family which had nurtured me and loved me; his was the only other presence in the closed-off, private universe I really inhabited. I felt as if I had lost another father.

•

By 1973 I had received permission from Washington to license the foil resistor to the Soviet Union. But on October 6 of that year, on Yom Kippur, war broke out across the Golan and the Suez Canal. Egypt and Syria launched a coordinated surprise attack that found most Israelis praying in their synagogues. Once again Israel was fighting for its life against enemies armed to the teeth by the Soviets. I decided instantly that I was not going ahead with any license. When the Soviet embassy called to ask why, I told them I couldn't give them a license for something that had military applications and might help in killing Jews.

As usually happened when Israel got immersed in war, my nerves were in a state of aggravated excitement. But now I felt more closely bound to Israel than ever.

In the first place, my daughter Gisele was now seventeen years old, and she had decided that Israel was where she wanted to live. I had first taken Gisele with me to visit Israel in 1969, and since then she had been there several times herself. While I had never been able to speak much about the Holocaust, over the years our family life had been suffused with feelings about our Jewishness and about Israel. I had talked to the children about making an *aliyah*—immigrating to Israel—and I knew that some of this, at least, had taken root.

Ariele was only fifteen and Marc twelve, but in June Gisele had graduated from Akiba Academy, a Jewish secular school in Philadelphia's suburbs, where she had learned Hebrew along with the usual curriculum. Serious and intelligent, mature beyond her years, Gisele had a way of reflecting deeply on issues that could surprise even those who knew her well. She had graduated in July, three months before the war, and had left for Tel Aviv to see if Israel was a country where she could really feel at home.

As the war broke, Gisele was not in Israel but in

Philadelphia. I had asked her to come because I was due to go into the hospital for surgery. It wasn't a serious operation, but I wanted her there in case anything unexpected happened. I had had the operation and was back home when news came that fighting had broken out. Gisele wanted to return instantly. But I didn't let her. I told her I needed her to stay with the family, especially since I was already scrambling around for an open seat on El Al myself.

After I left, she wrote a letter (which I found later under my pillow after she herself returned to Tel Aviv):

Dear Daddy,

I love you. I know that we have the same interests in mind, Israel. This war has really shown my dedication for Israel. I saw myself only interested in her welfare. I can't ever relate to people who have no feeling for Israel. So I now know that my place is in Israel and only Israel. I felt so out of place in the U.S.A. (excluding this house) and so helpless. Maybe that's why I was nervous with Mommy. Anyway, I promise to do my best in school—and more than my best is impossible. Please trust me. I won't guarantee everything I do will be right, people learn from their mistakes, but I will use my best judgment. Don't worry, I'm safe physically, but more important—spiritually—in my land. I never felt so strongly Jewish.

Love,

Gisele

If my family was now more deeply involved in Israel, so was I. It wasn't just the business. For two years I had been working on a secret project for the Israeli Army. It was a development that had the potential to give Israeli tanks an important advantage over their adversaries. Right at this very moment Israel's armored divisions were struggling desperately to stem the Arab advance and were suffering terrible losses. My development was just short of being operational, but the war news from Israel was dire. There might still be time to make some kind of difference.

18

THE THERMAL SHROUD

I T had started several years earlier, in Philadelphia, at an Israel bond drive award dinner. General Israel Tal had been there, representing Golda Meir's government. He had given me a plaque and had made a speech; then I spoke a few words about my feelings for Israel. I didn't know Tal except by reputation, which was considerable. He was regarded as Israel's greatest tank commander. In the Six-Day War his division had destroyed the Egyptian forces in the northern Sinai, and until recently he had been commander of the Israeli Armored Corps. He looked the part. Squat, with short black hair and burning dark eyes, Tal gave off an aura of controlled force, like a prizefighter.

After dinner we talked for a while. "I know who you are now," Tal said in his gravel voice. "I understand you're a specialist in stress measurements. We're having some problems I'd like to discuss with you. If you want, you might even be able to help us. Next time you're in Israel, why don't you stop in to see me."

I did. Tal's offices were in the Defense Ministry, where he was busy designing the Merkava, Israel's radical new main battle tank. I was generally aware that there had been a conflict within the Israeli military about whether the next generation of tanks should be heavy or light. Tal had been the chief advocate of heavy tanks and had beaten down the opposition.

Tal's lair was a group of small, drab rooms whose corners and other available floor space were taken up with different types of tank ammunition rounds, engine parts, and sections of armor. Pictures of tanks at rest and in action adorned the walls. The first thing Tal (or "Talik," as everyone in Israel called him) had in store for me was a briefing on where the Israeli tank effort currently stood. A group of respected generals had argued for the light tank approach, he said, but he had been adamantly opposed. You could build more light tanks for the money, but they were more vulnerable. There was a basic principle involved: safeguarding lives. "From a philosophical standpoint," he explained, "we as an army, as Israelis, and as Jews, cannot have tanks that make our soldiers expendable. We must protect our most precious resource. That is the backbone of our military commitment."

So when he started to design the new Merkava, his first priority had been protection. To assist with that he put the engine up front, rather than in back, where it is on the rest of the world's tanks. That switch put extra shielding forward and also opened up rear space for infantry soldiers. As a result, the Merkava was more than a tank; it could transport soldiers into battle or serve as an armored headquarters for a commander and his staff. With its unusual rear hatch, the Merkava also could evacuate wounded from the field. Tal described for me his fire protection inventions, ammunition storage departures, and his novel approach to armor design. These were startling innovations; it was obvious that a tremendous amount of new technology was going into this.

When he explained these things to me I said, "My God, you must have a tremendous scientific staff—just to come up with the concepts, let alone implement them." But no, it was a staff of one: Talik himself. As a career tankman and tank commander, he had had fighting experience with most of the world's leading tanks: American, British, French, even captured Soviet models. He had an insider's feel for what was wrong with all of them.

Tal was the first general in the armored corps who was at the same time a tank constructor. In Israel, as elsewhere, the constructor is usually an engineer and the user a general. Of course they talk to each other, but there is never a single person who really understands in his bones what must be done and also knows how to do it. Tal did.

As he explained what he was doing and why, I was taken by his precise way of describing technical difficulties and the intelligence of his solutions. He must at least be a graduate engineer, I thought, maybe a Ph.D. But he wasn't. Tal, in fact, had his degree in philosophy. Yet he had made himself into a first-rate engineer.

He handled engineering concepts with ease and regularly came up with creative answers to complex problems.

The problem he thought I might be able to help with had to do with the Merkava's cannon. A serious ballistics difficulty affected all tank cannons, he explained, decreasing their accuracy at long range. Now that he had resolved most of his other design dilemmas, he wanted a solution to this one, too.

Since I had never dealt with cannons or ballistics, he started from the beginning, laying out the problem carefully. A cannon is a metal tube. Like all metal, the tube is affected by temperature, expanding in heat, contracting in cold. Ordinarily, the top of a tank cannon is exposed to the sun and heats up, while the underside is in shade and does not. As a result, the tube bends slightly, a small distortion but a crucial one in terms of hitting a distant target. The long tube is so sensitive that wind, cloud shadows, rain, and other environmental temperature shifts affect it, making the cannon a dynamic object, constantly bending in whichever direction the temperature changes dictate—though, of course, none of this is detectable by the naked eye. The result is that when a tank gunner takes aim through his optical sight, the gun is actually pointed off target.

All tanks face this problem, said Tal. A common solution is to protect the tube from temperature shifts by covering it with a protector or sleeve, often made of tin. But isolating the barrel from the environment is only a partial answer, because a sleeve will keep heat in as well as out, and the heat produced by firing the gun won't dissipate. Ammunition can explode in the barrel. As a result, all sleeves were designed to be inefficient to allow for cooling. And this meant that cannon tubes were still affected by temperature changes and firing was still inaccurate. "This bothers me all the time," said Tal. "I'm looking for a breakthrough." The way he said this, it seemed almost like a challenge.

I talked the situation over with Jim Starr, who was (along with Dan Post) the most profoundly accurate technical man

I knew, and the next time I saw Tal, I brought Jim and a mobile laboratory of instruments, strain gages, and temperature sensors of all sorts. When we had done preliminary measurements, we set to work in earnest at Vishay Israel, where we installed a gun tube and subjected it to a spectrum of temperature change situations, simulating environmental conditions. We also carried out field tests, going out with tanks to firing ranges and field exercises and measuring stress and heat distortions there.

Every time I would go out on field testing, it exhausted me; I would come back completely drained. But I wanted to do the field testing in person. I wanted to see it myself. This was, I thought, one of the greatest things that had happened to me in my life. I was so proud and grateful that Tal had come to me. I couldn't express the satisfaction I felt to be able to play a role in Israel's defense.

I also got to know Tal well, which was an experience in itself. I had rarely met anyone with such a quick grasp of technical problems, and I had most definitely never met anyone with as little tolerance for idle talk. He could not bear people who told him they knew something, then turned out not to. If Israel Tal asked you a question and you didn't know the answer, the only course was to say you didn't know. And if you did answer, you were safest answering concisely and directly. Anyone who tried to blow smoke at him was finished forever. He was a killer. He would cut down people in front of me without a thought—fellow generals, professors from the Technion, anyone who had the temerity to waste his precious time.

This characteristic of Tal's flew directly in the face of ingrained Israeli habits. Any time a problem needs solving in Israel, the first thing that happens is that a lot of people begin talking at the same time. "This is the way to do it," says one. "No, it's like this," says another. "No, like that," says a third. They interrupt and shout at each other and make a din that would scare donkeys. It's a national pastime.

When this happens at Vishay Israel (as it still does), I

don't say a word. I give them ten minutes to yell at each other. Then I say, "Now, one by one. What is your opinion?" The first one starts speaking, but he's interrupted by three others telling him he's an idiot and doesn't know what he's talking about. And each one has a different solution. But I am patient. I am not like Talik.

When it's over I say, "Now I've heard you all. I don't understand anything that you said. So no more talking. I want each one of you to write down his solution—one-half page, no more. In writing and signed. So no nonsense."

It's interesting; the majority don't want to write. Only one or two of them actually will do it. And if there are two written answers, I get two viable solutions. All that talk, all that noise, was meaningless. It was just a way of playing a tune or something: Israeli chin music.

By and large, Americans cannot stand that. Neither can Tal. He will not put up with it (in that way he is much more American than I). As soon as this starts, which it always does, like a reflex, he slams the table and rasps, "Shut up! One at a time! And if you don't know, you better say you don't know!" Then everybody gets intimidated, and the only ones who dare to talk are those who actually have something to say. The tumult is finished before it gets started. He has very beautiful meetings this way.

After we had known each other a while, Tal started inviting me to his house, promising to introduce me to interesting people. There I'd find writers, scientists, philosophers, bankers, all kinds. I'd go, but I would never open my mouth. It's difficult to talk in a group like that, because being Israelis, of course they all talk at the same time. A subject gets thrown out, and the place erupts in a hubbub of voices. But since these are Talik's friends and the talk has no consequence for tanks, he refrains from cutting their heads off. I just listen.

I found Tal an excellent sounding board on technical matters; I also came to value him dearly as a friend. Even without discussing intimacies, I felt he understood me, which was an element that so rarely entered into my relationships with people.

"Felix," he said one day, "you are a man who is driven by something. Do you know what it is?" "Tell me," I answered. Then Tal showed me the colors of the Israeli Army's medals for heroism: red; blue; and for the highest level, yellow—the color of our Star of David badges in the ghetto.

He was a person, I learned, of breadth as well as depth. I got used to hearing him quote Kant and Hegel and draw analogies from classical literature. His love affair with philosophers did not end when he graduated from the university. But what impressed me most deeply was the apparent anomaly that this warrior par excellence was at heart a peace-loving man who hated war, one who managed to incorporate his intense patriotism in a deeply humane spirit.

•

As we progressed with our testing, it became clear that we could measure the distortions in the cannon tube minutely. Once I knew we could do that, I was sure we could devise a system that would allow tank gunners to adjust for the deviations. We could, for example, feed the measurements from our sensor to an instrument inside the tank that would tell the gunner how to correct his aim.

The next step was to work out the details, produce the instrumentation, and install it, which we did. It worked like a charm. I was extremely pleased, and when I demonstrated the system to Tal, he got more excited than I had ever seen him. Ordinarily Talik was not given to outbursts of enthusiasm, but this looked like the revolution in gunnery he had been searching for.

Unfortunately, after additional field testing I concluded that even though our mechanism allowed for very significant improvements in long-range accuracy, it wouldn't be usable under real battle conditions. "What do you mean?" growled Tal when I told him. "What's the problem?"

"It works fine in the tests," I said, "but I've been out with the tankers, and they tell me it would be hard to use. They think it would complicate their firing procedures too much." Tal got angry. "I'll teach them to use it," he said. "They are disciplined

NEVER THE LAST JOURNEY

people, and they will learn how to use it!" "I don't feel good about it," I said. "I really don't. I don't like the idea of putting any extra burdens on them when they're in a life-and-death situation." And after we talked it out for an hour or two, Tal said, "Okay, Felix. Don't abandon that, but see if you can't come up with something else."

So I thought, we have to find something that doesn't involve the tank crew at all, that won't provide the slightest distraction, something that does the job by itself. We ran through a variety of possible solutions and concluded that the answer was to put a thermal sleeve on the cannon—which was, in fact, the standard answer. The problem with that was, as Talik had explained, that if the heat can't dissipate, the cannon will blow up. That was the reason all armies were either using nothing or the inefficient tin insulator.

But after a good deal of experimentation, we finally had an idea about how to produce a particular type of material that if wrapped around the barrel would instantly equalize the temperature difference across the tube and at the same time would allow for the dissipation of heat generated from firing the cannon. Instead of trying to protect the gun from external heat changes, we'd go with them. Since distortion came from unequal heating, we'd even out the temperature around the gun barrel. The army christened the device the "thermal shroud," code name "Tampa." When we tested it we found that it reduced inaccuracy at a certain long-range distance from 3 meters to 20 centimeters. Tanks equipped with this invention could pick off enemy tanks like sharpshooters while they themselves stayed well out of effective range. Tal called it a "Copernican revolution."

When all the field testing was complete, Talik went to the U.S. Army with the results. The Pentagon was interested and set up field tests at the Aberdeen, Maryland, proving grounds. This was to be a competition testing, the Vishay thermal shroud against the General Dynamics sleeve in use on American tanks. The same cannon was used, fitted first with one device, then the other.

American and Israeli engineers monitored the tests, and procurement officials and field officers were on hand. When it was over, our solution had outperformed the American device by a wide margin. "Under all firing conditions," the American report read, "the Israeli sleeve is superior."

Yet in the end, the Pentagon did not buy a single Vishay shroud, clearly for reasons other than performance. Meanwhile, the results in Israel have lived up to expectations. During the Lebanon war in 1982 the long-range precision shooting was so successful that the Israelis installed the thermal shroud not just on the new Merkavas but also on their older Pattons, Centurions, and everything else they had.

•

But in October 1973 this was all in the future.

A few days after the war broke out I managed to get a seat on an El Al flight out of New York—only El Al was still flying to Israel. I had never been to Israel before during wartime, but I didn't have to wait to experience the Israelis' anxiety and determination; the atmosphere began right on the plane. Sitting next to me was the wife of the Israeli ambassador to Venezuela. She had received a telegram that her son had been severely, perhaps fatally wounded. Most of the other passengers were young people, anxious to get back to join their units. The tension in the cabin was thick.

In Israel it looked like a disaster was threatening. On the Golan Heights small groups of Israeli tanks were embroiled with a flood tide of Syrian and Iraqi armor. On the Suez Canal, the army's first line of quick-response tank forces had been badly hurt by Egyptian antitank infantry armed with wire-guided Sagger rockets. Then a coordinated counteroffensive spearheaded by one of the vaunted tank charges of the IDF (Israel Defense Forces) had been eaten up by the Egyptian bridgehead defenses.

I felt a compulsion to do something, and I found myself preoccupied by thoughts about the thermal shroud. I couldn't get it out of my head that if the Israeli tank guns could be given a greater range, it might make a difference, even now. But although I had worked out all the technical details of the sleeve, we hadn't yet begun production. Maybe, I thought, we could jerry-rig something and get it installed quickly.

When I drove out to the giant tank plant and depot outside Tel Aviv, I was shocked. The place was always loaded with tanks—some under construction, others being refitted, others in storage. Now it was empty. There wasn't a single vehicle. I couldn't believe my eyes; it was like a ghost town. I needed a tank for experimentation, but I couldn't get one. Everything that had a motor in it and a barrel on it was fighting. They finally dug one tank out of some nether region, and I began trying different possibilities with the cannon. Finally I worked out a kind of modified thermal shroud arrangement, though it took me some days to do it. Fortunately, by then the IDF had a better grip on the situation, but even my experimental tank was taken off to war.

A couple of days later I, too, was on my way toward the front. My uncle Moshe Zandman's son Dubi (whom I had first met as a newborn in 1952) was on alert, but his engineering unit was being reserved in the event that Jordan decided to attack in the East. For days Dubi had been sitting at home with his battle gear ready, impatient and frustrated. When I visited, he begged me for *protectzia,* the Israeli term for pulling strings. I knew people in the Defense Ministry—couldn't I please get him transferred to some unit that was fighting, any unit? I didn't do it, but the next day his own outfit was ordered to report to the Sinai. With no army transportation available, he asked if I would drive. In short order I was hauling a carload of young engineers south, where (though they didn't yet know it) they were soon to be erecting bridges for crossing the Suez Canal.

Meanwhile, at the Vishay Israel plant, all the men had disappeared except Moshe Shamir and one other manager, who was physically handicapped. The war started on Saturday, Yom Kippur. On Sunday all the public transportation buses were requisitioned. Soldiers and reservists (in Israel everyone is a reservist until age fifty-five) were mobilized and moved to the two fronts in masses. All other transportation was disrupted; chaos reigned.

On Sunday the plant didn't work. On Monday the wives of the managers started going around to pick up workers in their cars. The majority of production people were women, and by Monday they were able to muster about a third of the crew. In a couple of days transportation arrangements were organized and the whole place was at work. Engineering stopped, quality assurance stopped—all the primarily male functions stopped. But the women line workers appointed the best people as supervisors and organized production. Shipping was a big problem, since only El Al was flying, but after an initial panic, that was worked out, too. The quality stayed excellent. Everybody paid double and triple attention to what they were doing.

Shamir was working twenty-four hours a day. But he wasn't usually involved in production and couldn't do everything himself. Abe Inbar, our plant chief, would come back evenings. One of the men was transferred from the southern front to the North and was given twenty-four hours' leave. He came to work. When I saw him I said, "What the hell are you doing here? Go home." He said, "No, I have to fix this problem here, I've been thinking about it at the front. I'll go this evening." Joe Szwarc from Grodno and Stalin's Polish Army was mobilized. I said, "Joe, what are you doing? You had a heart attack a few months ago. This is crazy." He said, "Felix, swear to me you'll never tell anyone that." Like Inbar, he was on staff duty during the day, and in the evening he came to work. Under ordinary circumstances the Israelis might have been a bunch of mavericks who wanted to do everything their own way, but in emergencies they knew how to pull together in a way that left me wide-eyed with admiration.

19

M Y son, Marc, was bar mitzvahed in 1974. By then Ariele was sixteen and Gisele eighteen. Gisele was now a medical student at Tel Aviv University, and it was clear that Israel was going to be her permanent home. Whether Ariele and Marc would also make *aliyah* in time I didn't know. Growing up in Philadelphia's suburbs, they were typical American kids, yet they, like Gisele, were imbued with their Jewish identity.

Although I had always felt helpless to discuss the Holocaust with them, I knew they understood they were a survivor's children. How it affected them I wasn't sure (though I yearned to know), yet I was positive that this, too, had influenced their feeling for who they were. I loved them with all my heart, but I was watching even the younger two grow toward adulthood walled off from the core of my own emotional life.

Neither did I know exactly how the long unhappiness between Ruth and myself affected them, though beyond doubt it did. Over the years I had struggled to come to terms with the marriage, but without success. On the contrary, life as husband and wife had become progressively more painful. Twenty-three years earlier, Sender had told me that in our family we did not get divorced. I no longer had the strength for that approach.

The divorce was not an easy one, neither for my wife nor myself. It wrenched horribly to know that my family was being broken up. For better and worse it was the family that had sheltered me, and I could not make out what the future might hold, especially for the children. That was most disturbing of all, and for a time I was despondent about what it might do to them. But even so, I could see no other choice.

Fortunately, for me at least, the demands of work were relentless. Vishay was thriving. We were now doing $15 million a year in sales. Our products had carved out a growing share of the market. Profits were increasing, and we were building up cash reserves. We had also become a public company several years before, and our stock was now traded on the American Stock Exchange. That initial public offering by itself had added several million dollars to our capitalization and had introduced us to a new world of financing possibilities. The process, though, had not been without its trauma.

Our initial stock offering had been handled by Jack Hirsh, a well-known broker who was one of the leaders of Philadelphia's Jewish community. Jack and his wife, Sophie, had become close friends, and Jack had agreed to serve on Vishay's board of directors. When he reviewed our books, he told me he thought the time was right. We were profitable, we were progressing, our accounting was in order; we met all the criteria to go to the market.

In January 1972 all the preparations had been made to take Vishay public. Jack's firm had drawn up a prospectus, introduced us to the financial community, and was busy making the final arrangements for what we believed would be a successful initial offering. A couple of days before the stock was floated I was sitting in my office reflecting on the prospects when George Gerber, our plant manager, raced in, out of breath and shaking. George's face was dead white. "Felix," he said, trying to keep his voice under control, "there's a fire in the primary process!" I bolted out of my seat. "Don't run," he said. "I think everybody's out."

"What do you mean?" I said. "Are they all out or aren't they?"

"I think so," came the answer. "I'm not sure, but I think so."

By this time I was running down the hall toward the primary process unit, which was full of the flammable and explosive chemicals used in the first stage of chip production. Right outside the fire door to the unit a crowd of people was milling around. Black smoke was seeping around the doors, and a woman was lying on the floor being attended by others, her face and hands burned.

I went to open the door to the unit, but hands grabbed

me and I heard people saying, "Felix, don't go in there; you can't do it." But I broke away and rushed in. I felt I had to make sure that everybody was out. As fast as I could I checked all the areas, except one station, where the acrid smoke was billowing so thick it was impossible to see or breathe. I was yelling, "Is anybody in there?" But I heard nothing, and it was impossible to stay.

When I got back to the fire door, it was shut tight. For a moment I thought I was trapped, and I started shouting for them to let me out. But before I had a chance to panic, someone cracked the door open and I slipped through.

When we counted and recounted heads, it was clear that everybody had gotten out. But the fire was horrendous. Fire engine after fire engine arrived, and I watched in horror as the walls collapsed and flames consumed the unit. All around me people were crying as they saw their workplace going up in smoke. One woman kissed and hugged me; another said, "Don't worry, Dr. Zandman. Don't worry, we'll build it back up."

By the time the fire was out, the entire primary processing unit was a charred ruin; whatever hadn't burned down was soaked in water. Our ability to manufacture chips, the heart of the resistors, had gone up in smoke. And all our reserve inventories had gone up with it. We were naked.

That evening all the managers, supervisors, and foremen gathered at George Gerber's house, where we worked until the early morning to get ourselves organized. At eight o'clock everyone reported for work, and the cleanup and assessment began. In the light of day, the extent of the job in front of us was clearer; it would take at least a month to get back into production. That was bad enough, but a few days later I was scheduled to go on the road to help sell the initial stock offering. My heart was in my mouth about that, and sure enough, when the Drexel Lambert representative showed up to look at the damage, he shook his head and mumbled, "This is a disaster."

But our Israeli operation saved us. Not long before, we had opened up our own plant there, in Holon, just south of Tel

Aviv. From a few people working above a store, Vishay Israel had evolved into an efficient, highly organized manufacturing operation with more than three hundred employees. At first they had concentrated on finishing the resistors, the same operation our licensees in England, France, Germany, and Japan were performing. But now the company had begun to fabricate the chip itself, a highly sophisticated process. Not only did they have chips in production, but inventories were available that they could start feeding to us immediately. It did take a month to rebuild Malvern, but with supplies flowing in from Israel, the shipping volume barely suffered. And to my immense relief, neither did the stock offering.

•

With the business in Israel growing, and now with Gisele living in Tel Aviv, I found myself spending more time in that country. As a result, my circle of acquaintances was expanding—new friends, but also people with whom I shared a past. Bella Hirschorn was one of these. Bella was from Grodno, but I had gotten to know her in Slonim, to where my grandparents had fled in 1941 and where I was regularly sent to visit. When I was fourteen I had liked her tremendously, and I had never forgotten the sight of her taking off her blouse in the heat of the firestorm the night Slonim burned to the ground (when I reminded her, she swore I was making it up).

Now Bella lived in Haifa with her husband, Samuel Bornstein. Like my old Grodno friends Lisa Chapnik, Anja Rud, and Haschia Bielitzka, she had emerged from the Holocaust a hero. Shortly after the German invasion, Bella had joined a group of partisans and had spent the war in combat. Among the experiences she had had was one that made me shudder when I heard about it. During one battle she had gotten separated from her unit and had hidden behind a tree as the Germans searched for her in the frozen woods. With the patrol closing in, Bella decided to commit suicide rather than allow herself to be captured. But the only weapon she had was a rifle, and to shoot herself with the rifle she would have to pull the trigger with her toe. As the Nazis got closer, she struggled to untie her boot, but the laces were frozen solid, and her numbed fingers could not undo them. Huddling behind the tree in despair, she watched the German soldiers draw near, then filter by without once looking in her direction.

Bella was now working with Isaac Zuckerman, one of the two leaders of the Warsaw Ghetto uprising. Mordechai Anilewicz had been the inside man, the one who ran the defense. Zuckerman, his partner, was the outside man, whose job was to bring in weapons and supplies and link the fighters with the world outside the ghetto walls. I knew Zuckerman from stories and literature. *Mila 18,* Leon Uris's novel about the uprising, had been dedicated to him. Now Bella introduced me.

Zuckerman lived north of Haifa, in Kibbutz Lochame HaGetaót—"Ghetto Fighters." There he had built a Holocaust museum whose library was underground, constructed to survive direct hits from shells or bombs. He was a man utterly dedicated to preserving the memory of the 6 million who had died; in the museum's library he had gathered a complete collection of books and articles. While he showed me around, he talked passionately about the importance of documentation. I, too, should write a book, he thought.

"But so many people have done it already," I said. "What's one book more or less?"

"No," said Zuckerman, "it would have an absolute value. Each one of us should bear witness. Each one of us lived through part of it and can add to the history. It should not be lost."

Zuckerman's argument had a legitimate sound to it. Talik, too, had urged me to write. But I was reluctant. In fact, I thought, there are so many books already written; every survivor's story is worthy of a book. Besides, I was one of the lucky ones. I was already fifteen when I lost my family. My parents and grandparents had given me a rich background: I had been to school; to a certain extent I had been formed. There were so many who had no memory of their parents at all, whose childhoods were blanked out. Israel is full of these indescribable tragedies, of children who had lost their parents, who lost themselves and still somehow survived. A hundred times worse than my case. Next to these, my story was trivial. If I was a palm tree on alien soil, at least I remembered the palm forest. But they are palms without memory. They dream that perhaps there was something. But they know nothing. And even if my story was worth telling, I wasn't sure it was something I could face—I had such difficulties expressing my feelings about these things as it was. How could I possibly sit down and write them out?

Zuckerman may not have persuaded me to do a book, but we understood each other, and we quickly became friends. One day he came to see me at Vishay with a request. In Warsaw, he said, in the Polish archives, there was certain material about the ghetto and about the Germans, documents that described the uprising as the Poles had seen it. "We need that," he said, "it's unique information." But Poland's Communist government would not give up the documents. Ghoulishly, they were even refusing to provide photocopies. Zuckerman knew I visited behind the Iron Curtain from time to time for lectures and scientific congresses. Would I be willing to smuggle the material out? Someone else would get the documents from the archives and pass them to me. My job would only be to bring them out of the country.

I was scared to death—I could just see myself in the hands of the Polish KGB. But I agreed to do it. I was preparing myself to go, thinking about how I would make the trip and what might be the safest way to smuggle documents, when at the last moment Zuckerman telephoned and said he had gotten somebody else. I had steeled myself for this and was ready to leave, but when he called I felt hugely relieved.

Zuckerman died about a year after I met him, but he was pressing onward right to the end. His final project was organizing the first conference of Holocaust survivors, which drew participants from all over the world. Shortly afterward, he passed away. For me as for others, he had been one of our true heroes.

At about the same time, I met another Jewish stalwart in

Israel, but this one I knew already. I had come back to Tel Aviv after lecturing in China when Moshe Shamir told me he had gotten a call asking about me from an old friend of his named Elisha Roih. Was Elisha Roih someone I knew?

When I called the telephone number a secretary informed me that Mr. Roih was in a board meeting and couldn't be disturbed. I told her who it was and asked her to deliver the message; it was urgent. A minute later a distantly familiar voice came on saying, "Felix, *ze atah?* Is it really you?"

Elisha and I spent the next two days talking nonstop. Neither of us could believe our eyes. Elisha told me what had happened. "I was home one day watching TV," he said, "a program about industrial development in Israel. They were reporting on an enterprise called Vishay. They gave the background, and then they started talking about the founder, someone named Professor Felix Zandman. All of a sudden this Professor Zandman appears on the screen, and my God, Felix, it looked like you! Then Moshe Shamir was on the screen, too. The same Moshe Shamir I've known for years."

The next day Elisha had called Shamir to tell him he had seen him on television with a person named Zandman. Did he know this Zandman? Did he know, for example, if Zandman had studied in Nancy in 1947? "Of course I know Zandman," said Shamir. "He's a relative." But he wasn't sure if I had studied in Nancy, though he knew I had been in France.

Shamir told him I had left for China and was not expected back in Israel until the following month. "Moshe," said Elisha, "it's very important. When you see him, ask him for me if he was a student at Nancy, studying mathematics with Professor Schwartz. And ask him if he remembers a guy named Elisha Roih. If he says he does, give him my phone number."

I listened with fascination while Elisha brought me up to date on his life since we last saw each other. In Nancy I had known something about his work as a Haganah agent, running guns, setting up training camps, smuggling refugees. I had not known that he had spent time in French jails, or that he was an underwater demolitions expert. During the War of Independence he belonged to a secret fifteen-man unit that had specialized in blowing up or capturing ships carrying weapons to Arab countries. Afterward he had been one of the founders of the Israeli Army's frogman unit; then he became the first commander of a special Mossad commando section. Elisha's work had taken him to Egypt during the affair of the German missile scientists and to the Kurdish mountains as part of Israel's support for the Kurd's long rebellion against Baghdad. During the Six-Day War he had been Israel Tal's chief of intelligence in the northern Sinai. Since then, Elisha had retired from the army and gone into the oil industry, becoming head of the Gulf of Suez petroleum industry the Israelis had taken over in 1967. "My life has been one surprise after another," he said. "Whatever I planned, Felix, I never did, and whatever I did was never planned."

We reminisced, and I filled him in on events in my own life. Thirty years had passed, but the chemistry that had originally made us friends was as strong as ever. Before we parted, though, Elisha smiled quizzically and said, "One thing, Felix. I think after all this time you owe me an explanation. It's not why you didn't come with us back then. That I understand. I think you were right to do what you did. But I want to know how long it is since you've been involved in Israel."

"Ten years," I said, "maybe eleven."

"And in ten years, Felix, why did you never call me?"

I hesitated before telling him, "Elisha, it was because I was so ashamed."

•

After Ruth and I had been apart for a time, friends tentatively began introducing me to women. I was free, they thought, so why not? But I wasn't very interested. I was concerned about the children, particularly Marc, who was living with me. He was only fifteen when we separated and more vulnerable than Gisele or Ariele, who were both university students. I had peace and quiet to think through what was going on, and I was not eager to complicate my life with other relationships.

Some years earlier, Moshe Shamir had built a second floor onto his house, and when I was in Israel I liked to stay with him instead of in a hotel. Being in Israel so often, I had come to think of his extra bedroom as my room. I ate with the family and felt at home. One day about two years after the separation I came downstairs at Moshe's and found that he had invited an extra party for dinner that night. We were going out with Leon Trachtenberg (who was visiting in Israel) and two of our friends from Grodno, Moishe Alperstein and Iska Rubinczyk (the son of the ghetto police chief who had marched with my column to Kielbasin). Matasake "Nikki" Nakazawa, the manager of our newly opened business in Japan, was also there. (Not long before, when Nikki was considering the job, he had come to Malvern with his wife. She had dressed for the occasion in a formal kimono and had stunned everybody at the plant.)

So there in the living room were Nikki and Leon and the others, and then this extra person whom Shamir had invited along, an attractive, blond-haired woman named Ruta Shoshani.

After that night, Ruta Shoshani stayed in my mind. Nothing particular had happened between us, but I thought she was quite beautiful, and I had enjoyed our discussion. Shamir told me that she worked for an advertising agency handling the El Al account. Before that she had been the office manager for Yossi Sarrid, a prominent Labor Party politician, and prior to that she had been in the army, where she had worked for then Deputy Chief of Staff Yitzhak Rabin and for my friend Israel Tal.

I was thinking that Ruta Shoshani was the kind of person I would like to get to know better, but that was more or less the extent of it. Moshe Shamir had different ideas, though, and somehow, by accident or design, Ruta and I found ourselves together at

Shamir family affairs and other gatherings. And every time I met her, she got deeper into my head. I started thinking that I really did want to get closer to her, and finally I started to court her.

When we began to talk seriously about things, I went to meet her family at their home in Hadera, north of Tel Aviv. In a way I recognized her mother and father—they were the kind of people Israelis love, pioneers who had come with nothing to build the country and make a life for themselves and their children. In the early 1930s they had immigrated to Palestine from Romania. Ruta's father had started off as a workingman, taking any job he could get, then had succeeded in building up his own road construction business. They were, I thought, strong, modest people.

I found it so interesting how similar these Romanian Jews were to the people I had grown up with in Poland, even though their hometown had been a thousand miles away from mine. Ruta's mother's cooking was the same as my mother's—the same dishes, the same smells filling the kitchen. Their Yiddish was the same Yiddish I spoke. In Ruta's house I found myself in a place that was instantly familiar and comfortable. The way they talked and what they were, their ideals, their feelings about Israel, how they spoke of the past and what they had lost (Ruta's mother's family had stayed in Romania and had perished there)—there was nothing at all strange here. It took me back to who I was.

The impression only deepened as I got to know Ruta's parents better. I loved to go to the synagogue with her father. He wasn't an extremely religious man, but he prayed, and the prayers that moved him were the same prayers that had moved my father and that played so powerful a role in my own memory. "Heneni," for example, in which the cantor asks to be purified so that his sins will not be cast upon the community when he prays for them. Or "N'sana Tokes," a prayer that always brought tears to my father's and grandfather's eyes, written about Rabbi Amnon of Mainz, who was ordered by the local bishop to convert to Christianity. The rabbi asked for and was granted three days to think about it, at the end of which time he refused and was tortured to death for his stubbornness. The prayer is a reminder of how sinful it was of the rabbi to have requested time to think—an obvious thing that should not have been done.

I liked Ruta's brothers as well, the respect they had for their parents and the way they treated their own children. I watched the family together. I saw the feelings they had for each other and the strong attachment Ruta had, not only with her father and mother but also with the brothers and the children. It was even stronger, I thought, than the attachments in our family in Grodno, which were tremendously strong. These were things that had enormous meaning for me. At Ruta's home I found myself in an environment suffused with the values I treasured most, a place where I fit in and where I felt wanted.

With Ruta I was surprised by a wave of unexpected emotions, passion that I had not felt for so long, feelings about re-creating a family with someone who would be bound to my heart. We talked about my children, about my concern for the kind of relationship that would develop between her and Gisele, Ariele, and Marc. That couldn't be predicted, but as I got to understand Ruta's character more deeply I concluded that she would be a wonderful mother for them. They had their own mother, of course, but they needed somebody on my side who was also very strong to protect them and help them.

These, I thought, were reasons to marry someone. But as we grew closer I also began to see something else in Ruta. She was someone with whom I could talk about those things I had never been able to talk about. In all my relationships, my past had been a barrier. Some people were not really interested; others had a morbid curiosity about it or were sickened by it. The Holocaust made people uneasy; no one wanted to get too close to it. But Ruta was not afraid. In her I saw, or sensed, only compassion.

I met Ruta in 1977. Within a year we had decided to get married. "I have a secret for you," I told Israel Tal when we were working together on one of the projects he occasionally asked me to consult about. "I must tell you something." Tal laughed. "You have no secrets from me, Felix. My information system works too well. You are going to marry Ruta Shoshani, right? You know, Ruta used to be my office manager. I've known her for many years. She always had sandals and red toenails. A very hard worker, Felix, a good person. I was always so impressed."

We had two weddings. The first, on September 10, 1978, was in Philadelphia in front of a judge. It was, I knew, a strange idea for Ruta, who had never seen such a thing (civil ceremonies do not exist in Israel). But there were people in both the United States and Israel whom we hoped would celebrate with us, and we wanted to have our Jewish wedding in Israel. Ruta told her parents not to come to Philadelphia. It wasn't a real ceremony, she said, only a formality. Still, it was beautiful. A few close friends came, including Marc Mostovoy, the conductor of the Philadelphia Concerto Soloists, who brought with him a special wedding present—four soloists to play quartets.

Later that month we had a second wedding, at Moshe Shamir's home in Israel. This time we got married under a *chupa,* with a rabbi officiating. A big crowd was there, Ruta's family and all our friends. If the first wedding had been austere and a little formal, this was, we both felt, the real thing.

WHEN I was down in the hole, I used to imagine how when it was all over I would tell people what had happened to me. The fantasy gave me comfort; I'd tell and they would listen with compassion and understanding, though I was never quite sure who these listeners might be.

But afterward I found it wasn't an easy matter. In fact, there was nobody to tell it to. Although we had lived through it together, Sender had never talked to me. Several times I tried to begin a discussion, but each time he had become so agitated that I stopped. The single time we did talk about what happened was once when Josef Weiss started to describe some of the courageous things Sender had done during those days. Sender got involved in the discussion and so did I. But neither of us had really been listening. Each of us wanted to talk about his own pain.

I would see other close friends, survivors, but they, too, were shattered people. Each had his own bitter story, his own never-ending trauma. They, like me, were inward people. If one started to talk, others soon interrupted and switched over to their own story. They were preoccupied by what happened to them. I understood that very well, so I left it alone. In a way we knew each other intimately; we cared for each other. But each of us lived in his own walled-off universe.

The result was that these were things I just could not open up—not to a friend, not to a girlfriend, and not to my first wife, who had been unable to listen and who banished the subject from our home. She was, I sometimes thought, as frightened by it as I was.

As time went by, I found that talking about it at all became harder and harder. When I tried, I felt tremors. The slightest things would trigger them—a movie, a television show, a magazine article. I would read something in a newspaper, and all of a sudden

I would begin to tremble inside. The more disturbing it became, the more I needed to express it, the less I was able to.

At times I even considered seeing a psychiatrist, if only to be able finally to talk it out. But I always thought: No, how can I pay somebody to listen to my troubles? The person will be listening, writing it down, because that is his job. But for me the situation wouldn't be sincere. It would give a context of artificiality to what was deepest inside me. I couldn't bring myself to do it.

But when I married Ruta, something happened. I still could not mention my family or anything that had to do with that time. But she had the courage to ask. She was not repelled or afraid or closed off. On the contrary, she was so open and secure in herself that she had the strength to hear. And she wanted to hear; she wanted to know everything—about my family, my parents, all the details of my past. She would see me shaking about something and she would tell me that we had to talk about it. She refused to leave me alone with my demons.

At the beginning, every time the Holocaust was mentioned, I would burst into tears. But one by one the layers of concrete that I had poured down over the years began to peel back. Slowly she opened me up. This was beyond love, I thought, and more than friendship. This was a person who wanted to be next to me—no matter what I had gone through. We were connected, not two separate individuals who happened to be living together. For the first time in my life I was truly joined with another human being. And slowly I began to talk. Little by little, these things that had been hidden in the darkest recesses began to emerge. When I woke up screaming at night, she listened to my dreams. She wanted to see what I had seen, feel what I had felt, be where I had been.

Still, how could I tell her about lying in the hiding space above the kitchen listening to Fania's hysteric, muffled sobs and Berko's stricken fear, or about Grandfather Freydovicz sitting in the living room with his arms around their baby and the two others, waiting for the SS to come? But somehow I discovered I could.

With Ruta next to me in the bed crying quietly herself, I began to choke the words out.

The pain didn't fade. If anything, as I found my voice it became sharper. But I could sense the tension relaxing its steel grip. It was as if I were emerging from an emotional straitjacket. I began to feel almost normal.

We also talked about children. She was only forty when we were married, and even though I already had three wonderful children, I was ready for another if she wanted. But Ruta decided against it. We were sharing each other's life, and that was enough. Besides, she said, now she had three ready-made children, which was right. Despite some tense times at the beginning, Gisele, Ariele, and Marc all took to her warmth and grew closer and closer to her.

I found, too, that Ruta was an excellent sounding board for my thoughts about Vishay. She was not trained in business, but she was an excellent judge of people, and I learned quickly that she had first-rate instincts. What I was finding was that I had a true partner. Ruta's presence gave me optimism and strength; it encouraged me. As time passed, I began to look at the world without some of the fears that had always dogged my steps.

It may not have been a complete coincidence that after we had been married a few years Vishay began to flourish. Now I had someone with whom I could sit down and talk through problems, someone who had no ax to grind but who would be my support. I may have been a stranger at someone else's table, but my inner life was growing less fragile, less haunted. That could have been one reason why in the early 1980s I found myself looking at my business and my industry in a more aggressive way.

•

From 1962 into the 1980s Vishay had grown strictly through research and development. Our two main products were foil resistors and high-precision strain gages. I had also acquired the rights to my original Photostress process, which had been bought first by Budd, then sold and resold. We did well, slowly getting bigger, until we were up to about $50 million a year in sales. We were careful; I husbanded our money and paid off all the debt. Our balance sheet showed a surplus of $35 million.

All this was more or less according to plan. I had started Vishay with a particular vision. My company would be a high-technology leader that would expand by dint of its own excellence through internal growth. Alfred Slaner and I would also hold the company closely. Vishay would be a reflection of my own ideas and principles—not a faceless corporate entity that I just happened to manage. Even when we went public in 1972, we issued only about 20 percent of the outstanding shares, leaving the rest in Alfred's hands and mine.

But by the early 1980s I was thinking seriously about shifting gears. Among other things, I was learning that having a lot of cash on hand did not excite the stock market. We had originally issued stock at $8 a share. But despite our conservative management and growing sales, the price had dropped to less than $3. What I was realizing was that even though the company was building assets and equity, investors were looking not at the equity itself, but at the return on equity and at future earning potential. We were rich in cash, but in effect our cash surplus was bringing in only whatever the current interest rates were. In that sense Vishay was acting like a bank, and investors were not in the market for bank interest rates of return on their money.

Recognizing that having a lot of cash was not necessarily a good thing shook my innate sense of thriftiness a bit. It spurred me into thinking about different routes we might take that would make more effective use of our assets. As an alternative to my original concept of internal growth, I began to consider the idea of more rapid expansion. Vishay's products were at the high end of the market; we made the most precise resistors available. But there was no inherent reason why we could not produce garden-variety resistors as well. After all, we already had the technical expertise and management ability. Moving in that direction would give us a broader range of customers, so we could make more money and a better return. Moreover, we could synergize our efforts, using our current sales departments and administration for the new products as well as the old.

If we did make such a move, there were essentially only two ways to go about it. We could copy products whose technology was in the public domain, building production facilities and hiring the people. Or we could acquire other companies that already had a share of the markets that interested us. Duplicating is done all the time; it is a standard approach to expansion. But I didn't like the idea. It went against something in my character. On the other hand, I had nothing against acquisition, which had the added advantage of being faster than gearing up for a new type of production ourselves.

But once I had decided on this path, I moved warily. Because I didn't know how to do it or what problems might come up, I wanted to probe it out. Among a number of potential acquisitions we looked at, an English company named Mann Components seemed ideal. Mann Components was small—about $2 million in sales—and they were competitors of ours. They produced a well-made wire-wound resistor one step below Vishay resistors—although they claimed theirs were as good. Mann's owner had recently died, and his widow was running the company with a partner. They were interested in selling. In early 1983 we bought them out, though we brought the partner, Norman Comfort, in to continue managing the company.

Mann was a first test. All the elements looked right; they had a good reputation, and their products complemented our own. At the same time, they were small enough so that if merging the companies didn't work out, Vishay would not suffer any significant damage. This situation would allow me to find out how to manage an acquisition, how to work the synergies and mesh the cultures. As we brought Mann into the fold, few problems arose that we hadn't anticipated, partly due to the efforts of Norman Comfort. There were no clashes. It went like a letter in the post.

Because we had been active in England for years through

our licensee, we were familiar with the market. Now, with Mann working smoothly, we began looking for a corresponding situation in France, another region we knew well. One of our competitors there was Geka, a highly regarded smallish company that our sales people felt might be available. After some preliminary investigation, I decided to approach them. But before I had a chance, they contacted me.

Geka's founder, Dr. Jack Gingold, was a renowned physicist who had developed the carbon film resistor in Berlin during the 1930s, then had fled to France when the Nazis came in. Later, during the German assault on France, he had taken refuge in the United States. Like me, Jack Gingold was a Polish Jew. With the same background and similar professional interests, we hit it off instantly. He had a fine technical mind, and I found talking with him a pleasure.

One day Jack Gingold invited Ruta and me to lunch with his wife and his son, who was the company sales manager. "I'd like you to buy Geka," said the father. "I'm already in my eighties. I know that my son would find a place with you, and you would see that he is taken care of."

I hadn't been quite prepared for that. "Wait a minute," I said. "I would take care of your son. But does your son want to sell the company?"

"That's not your business," he said. "It's my company."

"Yes, but I'm not going to do this unless your son really wants it," I said. "I don't want you giving me someone to look after who doesn't want to be in the situation." When I talked to the son directly, he said, "Absolutely not. This isn't my idea, and I don't want it."

As a result, I let our acquisition discussions drop. Six months later Jack Gingold died, and the son took over the business. Not too long afterward I got a call from the son. "I'm having problems," he said. "The business isn't going well, and the banks are putting pressure on me. Would you consider taking the company over? I want you to know that if you do, I will be loyal and work with you." According to the son, Sfernice wanted to buy Geka, too, and we soon learned that the French government wanted Sfernice to get it rather than an American company. That complicated the picture, but the son was adamant. Despite the government pressure, he would not sell to Sfernice. "I hate them," he said. "I'd rather go bankrupt."

I was more than interested. By this time I knew the company rather well, and I was sure that we could remedy most of the problems. Geka also had an extremely good chief engineer, Yannick LeVacon, whom I was sure would facilitate the kind of technical changeovers I had in mind. The final result was that in July of 1984 we bought the company, a year after we had acquired Mann. The turnaround took no more than several months. From being on the verge of bankruptcy, Geka emerged as a profitable company.

The next acquisition was in the United States. Angstrohm Precision was a small American company on the East Coast that had started to make a foil resistor that was more or less copied from ours. Hoping to capitalize on the federal court's decision in favor of Sfernice, Angstrohm had also brought suit against us for antitrust violations. Their hope in this action was to throw enough of a scare into us so that we would settle. But after the long-running and costly Sfernice litigation, I found the prospect for another suit disturbing.

But Avi Eden, our young corporate counsel, whose advice I had come to value highly, had other thoughts. After examining Angstrohm's financial statements, he asked me for a budget to buy the company that was less than the anticipated cost of a suit and settlement. When we made our approach, it turned out that Angstrohm was amenable to being acquired. At the same time we also bought Elliot, a small component manufacturer on the West Coast. Under Avi's increasingly practiced hand, these two acquisitions went flawlessly.

In all this activity I was probing. I regarded these various small takeovers as trials that would show us if we could successfully incorporate outside companies into Vishay, if we could handle the geographical and cultural difficulties, exploit the synergies, and bring our technical and marketing expertise to bear where they were needed. If it didn't work, I was prepared to accept the losses. Whatever the outcome, Vishay would not sustain major damage. (As a matter of fact, Elliot did not work out, and eventually we lost the business. Elliot and Angstrohm both had facilities in Mexico that we wanted to merge, but we had no experience in dislocating plants and people. The move was improperly planned, and we lost customers. The whole thing was a lesson in what not to do; fortunately for us, a relatively cheap lesson.)

By 1985 I felt ready for something more substantial. I was confident that we had profited from our experiences. With practice we had learned how to analyze potential acquisitions quickly. We knew how to incorporate them into Vishay's operations and how to take advantage of cost-cutting opportunities. In the past several years our core business had become increasingly profitable. Our debt was still zero and, despite the acquisitions, our cash surplus had not diminished. For Vishay it was an opportune moment. I had my eye out for a bigger fish.

In 1985 a very big fish, maybe the biggest out there, was on the verge of being caught by somebody, if not us. Dale Electronics of Columbus, Nebraska, was on the market. At $120 million a year in sales, Dale was the largest wire-wound resistor maker in the world outside of Japan, or maybe even including Japan.

Dale was a subsidiary of the Lionel Company, formerly manufacturers of children's electric trains and now owner of the Kiddie City chain of toy supermarkets. Years earlier Lionel had needed transformers for its trains and had bought Dale, a small manufacturer. Over the years Lionel had more or less left Dale alone, and under aggressive management the little maker of transformers had eventually grown into a giant, with a hefty share of the market for various types of wire-wound and metal-film resistors.

But in 1984 Kiddie City had failed, which dragged its parent company into bankruptcy. The only good asset Lionel had on hand was Dale Electronics, which they now were being forced to sell. With a plum like Dale on the auction block, buyers flocked in, among them DuPont, AVX, Emerson, Square D, and Dynamics Corporation of America. But even though the bankruptcy judge was pushing for a sale, for one reason or another the deals never worked out. Dale's management, used to operating autonomously and unhappy with the idea of being absorbed, even tried to buy the company itself. But they were unable to raise the money.

Eventually Dynamics Corporation, which was an especially aggressive suitor, reached an agreement with Lionel for $55 million. But as luck would have it, before the deal could be closed, Dale's sales figures began to skyrocket. The year 1984 saw a tremendous boom in the electronics business, which lifted Dale far beyond where it had been during the negotiations with Dynamics. Now, regardless of the fact that they had already signed a contract, Lionel wanted more money. Lawsuits ensued.

I watched all this from the sidelines. In addition to being huge, Dale was a profitable company with an excellent name; from the moment I learned it was on the market, I had wanted to buy it. But it seemed a forlorn hope. I couldn't begin to afford it. After all, we had only $35 million in cash available. Our annual sales were in the neighborhood of $55 million, while Dale's were $120 million. Despite the small takeovers we had done, I knew very little about acquisitions games. I was so new to that world that I was unclear how I might possibly leverage our resources into a reasonable offer. I was about to find out.

LEVERAGE

DALE was enticing, and not just for the addition it would make to Vishay. I thought I saw a way of linking Dale and Vishay Israel that would allow me to open a second plant in Israel and put our operations in that country on a rock-solid footing. If I could get the Israeli government to go along with some ideas I had, I would be able to bring hundreds more jobs to Israel and at the same time generate very substantial amounts of cash for future growth. Unfortunately, Dale seemed out of reach. But I was casting around.

In early 1985 Ruta and I were on an El Al flight back from Tel Aviv. I had dozed off while Ruta was talking to the gentleman sitting next to her. Sometime later, she nudged me awake. The gentleman was Dr. Yehuda Shinhav, she said, an economics professor. "I mentioned something about Dale to him. He'd like to talk to you."

It turned out that Dr. Shinhav was involved in the Tel Aviv stock market. He was knowledgeable about leveraged buyouts. When I told him a little more about Dale, he said that it seemed to him a way could be found to acquire it. He might be able to help me with the arrangements. When I mentioned that I had another purpose in wanting to buy Dale—to open a second plant in Israel—he said, "Even better. More power to you. I know Cohen-Orgad, the minister of finance. I can arrange for you to meet him."

In New York I introduced Shinhav to Avi Eden and Alfred. For a time we worked with Shinhav as he attempted to find an investor who would be our partner in a bid for Dale. Unfortunately, Shinhav's efforts didn't bear fruit. But in the course of looking for an appropriate partner, I learned about leveraged buyouts. This was my first real exposure to the concept that in buying a company it is possible to pledge the assets of the company itself in addition to the buyer's own assets. Dale, for example, had assets of about $80 million. The right buyer would find banks willing to lend perhaps $40 million or $50 million against Dale's assets. Together with Vishay's own cash resources and borrowing ability, I would potentially be able to call on perhaps $80 million. This meant that if I bid $80 million for Dale, I might only have to actually come up with thirty in cash, or twenty. It depended on how much leverage I could get out of it. From a perspective like that, Dale didn't seem quite so distant a dream.

The problem with this scenario was Vishay's relative obscurity. We were a small company without experience in this realm of financing. If I were to go to a bank on this, they would ask, "Who are you? Have you done deals like this? Can you appraise these things properly? Can you manage a company two and a half times as big as you?" Cogent questions all. I knew that I needed a credible partner.

One of the early suitors for Dale was Charterhouse, a Rothschild company from London. They had fallen out of the bidding, but it seemed to me they might still be interested. When I approached Charterhouse, their response was predictable: "We've never heard of you," they said. But after they examined our corporate references and understood we were legitimate, they were ready to talk.

"We'd like to have a partnership," I told Larry Fagan, Charterhouse's executive vice president. "You may have been concerned earlier about how to manage Dale. But we have experience as managers, and we can handle that end of it. We'll put up half the money and you put up half. How does it strike you?"

Fagan liked the idea. Once we were in general agreement, he suggested that we could put together a strong bid on the basis of $3 million from Vishay and $3 million from Charterhouse. I was skeptical but fascinated. It seemed incredible—$6 million for a $120 million company. "Just see what happens," he said. We would both take loans of $10 million. With the $3 million additional from each of us, that would make $26 million. Manufacturers Hanover Trust, with whom Charterhouse had a good relationship, would give us the rest of the necessary money, the loan secured by Dale's assets. When we went to Manufacturers Hanover and they agreed, it looked to me like we might have the makings of a deal.

But before we finalized the agreement, the fickle economic climate intervened. The year 1984 had been a boom year for electronics. But in 1985 the market turned. First sales of electronics stopped climbing; then they began to plummet. The previous year Dale's profits had risen dramatically (which had led Lionel to cancel the agreement with Dynamics Corporation); now they were on their way down. I began to sense that Charterhouse was getting cold feet. They started asking me pointed questions about the industry and the products—questions they had obviously answered for themselves before they began pursuing Dale in the first place. When I spoke to them I heard doubt and reluctance in their voices. I met with Charterhouse's president, Jerry Katz, trying to revive their enthusiasm. "This is exactly the time to buy it," I said. "We'll get it at a better price." But the response was lukewarm. I could see the desire slipping away.

But I wanted that company. With the Charterhouse relationship hanging fire, I flew to Switzerland to talk to one of Vishay's major investors about coming in with us. He didn't give me a positive answer either, though he did not completely close the door on the idea. There might be some possibility there, I thought, as I flew back to the United States—though I wouldn't have given odds on it.

But a chance was a chance, and I thought I saw a way to turn Charterhouse around. "I have a Swiss possibility," I told Fagan in New York. "I can go with either them or you. Frankly, I'd rather go with you. But if I do, it has to be on a different basis. I'm not interested in a partnership anymore; I know you're not either. So this will be Vishay's deal now. For you it will be a guaranteed investment. First, I'd like you to put three million into the deal. On that three I'll agree to give you a nine-million-dollar profit at the end of five years. In addition, I want a ten-million-dollar loan at ten percent, secured by Vishay's assets."

I knew the kind of return I was offering would exceed Fagan's highest expectations. "If you don't do it, fine," I said. "We'll go to Switzerland." They looked again at our balance sheet and saw $35 million in cash with zero debt. A loan of $10 million would be no problem, said Fagan. Nor would an investment of $3 million. They would be pleased to do it.

So Charterhouse became our partner without being a partner. That was a key brick in the plan I was already pursuing. What was really driving me now was the possibility of expanding our involvement in Israel.

As the deal with Charterhouse was working itself out, I tried to set up a meeting with Yigael Cohen-Orgad, the minister of finance. My position with him would be that I was interested in opening a new plant in Israel that would take over a portion of Dale's production and employ at least several hundred people. That would be good for Israel and good for Vishay—allowing us to take advantage of Israel's relatively low labor costs, liberal grant and tax structure, and high-quality work force. In essence I would be locating an offshore facility in Israel rather than some more typical setting, such as Mexico (to where Dale was already transferring some of its production).

But I wanted something additional from the Israeli government. My intention was to use the profits from a new Israeli plant to pay back the debt I would be taking on to buy Dale. Ordinarily, if a company took money out of Israel in the form of a dividend, it had to pay a high withholding tax. But the money we were planning to take out would go to pay our debt for the acquisition of Dale. In that sense it fell into the same Israeli revenue category as money used to buy equipment, for example, on which there was no tax. The question was: How would the Bank of Israel regard it? Would this money be considered a dividend (and taxed), or would they allow me to use it to repay debt and leave it untouched? I wanted a ruling from the Bank of Israel and a commitment from the government.

If we were able to get this ruling, it would be a tremendous thing. It would put me in the unusual position of being able to pay off my debt in pretax rather than posttax dollars. While a dollar's profit in the United States would mean maybe fifty cents with which to pay off debt, a favorable ruling by the Israelis would enable me to pay off ninety cents of debt for each dollar's profit (the Israeli corporate tax rate was 10 percent). In other words, we would be able to buy Dale more cheaply than our competitors, who would have to figure their debt repayment in posttax dollars. Moreover, our financial studies showed that if the Israelis approved, we would have in our hands a powerful engine for future growth and investments. If I could use this formula with Dale, there was no reason why I couldn't apply it to other acquisitions. In essence I would be acquiring debt in high-tax countries where interest could be charged off against income, and making profits in Israel that would remain taxed at the low rate to the extent I used the money to repay debt.

But try as we might, I could not get a meeting with Cohen-Orgad. When Dr. Shinhav proved unable to set it up, I approached Israel Pikol, Israel's economic attaché for the United States. Pikol proved a most friendly person, and he in turn arranged a meeting for me with Yakov Meridor, a friend of Yitzhak Shamir's and at that time minister of energy. Meridor was encouraging and said we would meet in Israel. But when I got there, Cohen-Orgad still proved elusive.

Finally one night I was at Israel Tal's house and I told him my problems. "What do you think's going on?" I said. "Why in the world can't I meet the minister of finance? Isn't he interested in such things, or what?" It was twelve o'clock at night, but Tal picked up the phone and called Moshe Arens, the minister of defense. "I have Felix with me," he said. "You know him. He's trying to open a plant here, but he's blocked for some reason. Why can't he get to see Cohen-Orgad?"

In short order a meeting with Cohen-Orgad materialized. Yakov Meridor was also there, and Moshe Shamir and I came in and presented the entire plan to them. Cohen-Orgad showed absolutely no enthusiasm for it, but afterward Meridor told me, "You should continue to fight for this. I'm telling you, don't give it up."

I wasn't about to, though it was hard to see right off what path might get us around the finance minister. But, as luck or fate would have it, shortly afterward Cohen-Orgad decided to leave the government, and when he did, Yitzhak Modai stepped in to replace him.

As soon as Modai heard about what I had in mind, he allowed negotiations to move forward. "I want to build this plant," I told him and his people. "I'll put it anywhere you want me to." They thought about that. "How about Dimona?" they said. "There's a suitable building there. You can rent it."

Dimona, unfortunately, was a distant backwater in the middle of the Negev. A small community of Moroccan and Tunisian Jews lived there, but it was dwindling away because there were no jobs. Unemployment was astronomical. Nor were there any technical people in the area, except for those working at the Dimona nuclear plant, and they were not available. It was a little daunting to think about locating there, but if that was where they needed it, I was ready to go along. "All right, I'll do that," I told them. "Within five years I'll try to give you a plant doing $30 million in export and employing five hundred people."

Still, the Israelis were reluctant to let anyone take dollars out of the country. With their need to buy petroleum and armaments they had severe balance-of-payment problems, which meant that they closely guarded the flow of hard currency out of Israel. They had seen all sorts of ruses to get money out, so they weren't immediately overwhelmed when I explained that the reason I wanted to do this was to buy assets that would benefit Israel as well as Vishay. Yes, I would be moving money out, but I would be doing it in a way that would bring money back in terms of jobs, secondary industries, and so on. But it was a hard sell. The Israelis had been burned more than once, and they were sure there must be a catch somewhere. Eventually, to resolve all their objections, I agreed to use only after-tax profits generated from export sales arising from new investment and to make Dale a subsidiary of Vishay Israel. This would give the government the ability to monitor the flow of jobs and money.

But even while I was agreeing to everything, the Bank of Israel was opposing our request to be exempted from the withholding tax. It wasn't policy and the regulations were unclear, so they decided to play hardball with it. Listening to them arguing and creating one obstacle after another practically brought tears to my eyes. This country needs things like this so much, I thought, and here a few bureaucrats are standing in the way. If an ordinary American experienced problems like this he would never think about investing here. But if I was frustrated, Moshe Shamir held on to his optimism. "Felix," he said, "this is so good for the country. It is impossible for them not to accept it. It can't happen."

Finally the issue was brought to Prime Minister Shimon Peres, who met with Shamir, myself, and two officials from the bank. The bank spokesman made his argument. "It is not the policy of the country," he said, "not the *medinyut*." Peres turned to them and answered, *"Ma li medinyut im lo tihyeh medina."* "What's the point of having a policy if you don't have a country? We're not going to have a country here if we don't have industry."

But in those days of the Labor-Likud coalition government even the prime minister couldn't okay something like this by himself. He needed the approval of Finance Minister Modai of the opposition Likud Party. Fortunately, Ariel Sharon, the Likud minister of trade and industry, was extremely supportive. Sharon ran his ministry the way in earlier days he had run his tank divisions, decisively. His intolerance for pettiness and time-wasting rivaled Israel Tal's. At one point when we needed a permit from Sharon's department, one of his directors told him that such things took three weeks to prepare. Sharon looked at his watch and said,

"You've got thirty minutes. Zandman isn't going back to Philadelphia without the permit in hand. Do it now!" Half an hour later, Sharon signed the permit and gave it to me. Shortly afterward, Modai, too, accepted the idea and called off the bank's opposition. I had my commitment.

Meanwhile, in the United States I was pushing our pursuit of Dale forward. We had done our due diligence and I knew the company was good. Their products were excellent, as was their reputation. Though their profits were sensitive to fluctuations in the business climate, by any long-term standard they were making good money. The employees out in Nebraska had a strong work ethic and high productivity. We checked the plants and machinery and found they were up-to-date and well maintained.

The only risk was the management. With an acquisition this size I felt I needed to have the Dale managers on my side. The top people obviously knew what they were doing; they were running a large, first-rate company. But I didn't know them personally and I didn't know the second-tier managers at all. I did know that the management group was unhappy about the forced sale and had tried to buy the company themselves. If Dale's highest-level managers turned out to be hostile and I started having to fire and rearrange people, I could find myself in trouble. That prospect was the source of more than a few qualms. I badly wanted this to be a friendly takeover.

But though the Dale management posed the biggest problem, I delayed going out to see them before the last possible moment—actually until a week before the formal bidding. I was doing everything I could to keep our interest in Dale quiet, because news that Vishay was involved would inevitably excite other resistor manufacturers. But a week before the bidding, none of them would have time to muster the resources to enter the play. So from the beginning the only face anyone saw was Charterhouse. In the financial press Charterhouse was the only name mentioned.

One week before the bidding I went out to Dale to visit, basically to say, "Here I am. This is who I am. This is what I'm planning to do." My initial meeting with Dale's president, Carroll Novicki, was less amiable than I would have liked. "If you want to come in here," he said, "I can't oppose it. The board of directors at Lionel wants to sell. But we will not collaborate unless we're satisfied with the relationship and the conditions." That struck me as a little arrogant; I wasn't quite expecting it.

"Why wouldn't you?" I asked. "I want to do this in as friendly a way as possible. I think that what you'll find is that since you're bigger, you will end up managing Vishay rather than the other way around. I'm prepared to let that happen." Before long it was quite clear that Novicki had thought about what he might be able to push for, and he was very straightforward about it. To him a reasonable relationship meant being given 3 percent of Vishay's stock— 2 percent for him personally and 1 percent for the rest of the Dale management. I didn't particularly like his aggressive approach, and his proposition was higher than I had expected. But it wasn't altogether unreasonable.

"Fine," I said. "We'll do that. But you will have to perform certain things."

"What things?"

"One of our plans of synergy is to open a plant in Israel, which should significantly enhance profits. If you succeed in meeting my expectations there I'll be willing to give you what you are asking for." In the end we agreed that half of Novicki's bonus in shares would be based on success with the second Israeli plant; the other half would be guaranteed.

"But that isn't enough," I said. "You've been talking for yourself here, and I think you've worked out a nice deal. But whether I go ahead with this or not depends on all the top management. I want to talk with them."

That evening I had dinner with Dale's twelve top managers. I described what we planned to do with the company and how we intended to make it stronger. Between Dale and Vishay we would have the entire line of resistive components. We would have sales synergy. We would build an offshore facility where we would have lower taxes, premiums, grants in equipment, good people, and an excellent opportunity for research and development. That in turn would mean that Dale in Nebraska would become healthier. If we did this right, the company would grow even more competitive; we'd beat down competitors, save jobs that were capable of being saved, and build the home base, too.

"And after all," I said, "one way or another Dale is going to be sold, as you know. You will not be able to remain independent. I understand you would prefer that, but you know it's impossible. Would you like to be sold to DuPont or somebody like that? Or would you rather be with a company that is committed to resistors? Would you rather go to a company that the next day might sell you to somebody else, like a football, from one place to another, just to exploit your assets and milk the cow? Or would it be better to get organically involved with a company like Vishay, which would sink or swim with you?

"As a matter of fact, I will even let you manage Vishay. Whoever can manage better will end up managing. We will become bigger and stronger. Between us we will have the means to acquire other companies. We have the potential to become the biggest power in this market. If we get together, these two companies are going to be integrated in a way that will bind our souls together. We will become one. The fact is that I could do this without you. But though you don't have any power to stop me, you tell me now that you don't want us, and I'll go home. That will be it. The game will be over with Vishay. But think about who will eventually take you over—that's the other side of the coin. So make up your mind. If you say yes, I expect loyalty, and I expect that we will do good work together. Remember, it's not Vishay taking you over. You will take over Vishay. It doesn't matter who the shares belong to, to me or to Joe Blow. What's the difference? It's a public company anyhow. The question is, who's going to manage it? You are going to manage it. I can't manage here—you're twice as big as I am, three times as big. Because of synergies, you'll be managing Vishay, not Vishay you."

They liked this speech. And I meant it; I poured out my heart. Of course, they really didn't have any choice. In their eyes Vishay might have been bad, but their other options were ten times worse. At least I was not a Wall Street tycoon who would buy Dale to cannibalize the assets. On the contrary, they understood that I was a production man whose motive was to build for the long term. The only question I got was from one manager who wanted to know where the money for the acquisition was coming from. I told them that we had a partner, Charterhouse. But I couldn't divulge exactly how it was structured; that was a confidential matter. It didn't go any farther. They knew Charterhouse. They knew that with Charterhouse's backing we could buy ten Dales.

Overall I was pleased with the results of my visit. I came away feeling that the managers believed the acquisition would be a good idea. If I was successful in the bidding, at least I wouldn't be stepping into a hostile environment.

But as the bidding date approached I still had a lot of doubts to iron out. My partner in this process (as usual) was Ruta, who was finding it hard to get a good night's sleep. I would wake her up at two in the morning to help me face the questions. "Look," I would say, "we're putting the whole company in play now. It's complicated. This can go wrong, and this and this. But look at the other side. This is the amount of money we can make. This is what we can do in Israel. But if it doesn't go well . . ." Yes or no, yes or no. Questions and doubts.

During the day I felt strong, but at night the fears came out. Maybe I really wouldn't be able to manage it—with Dale, Vishay would be more than three times as big as it was now. Maybe the Dale management would not support me, despite my meeting with them and the arrangements we had made. Maybe there would be opposition to investments in Israel. After all, we were Jewish; they were midwestern Christians. Here comes this Polish Jew from the East Coast who speaks with an accent, who looks like a Jew and says he's a Jew. Of course they would be civil, but what would their reaction really be? Maybe the cultural clash would be too much. Then again, 1985 was a bad year for components. Maybe the product would become less and less attractive and we wouldn't be able to reinvigorate it. Then I'd have a giant losing proposition on my hands. If this deal did go bad, Vishay would be crippled, if it didn't disappear altogether. God only knew what might happen.

But Ruta would not acquiesce to this kind of talk. "Nothing will happen," she said. "You'll know how to manage it. It's very big, but so what? You'll be able to do it. You're capable of much more. This won't begin to test your limits." I said, "But Nebraska is so far away. How will I handle it?" "Just go for it," she said.

At bottom, of course, it was a matter of risk assessment. I had already decided that this risk was worth taking. But I was scared, which I suppose was natural. Ruta helped allay the fears. So did Alfred Slaner. Their support strengthened my resolve.

Deciding on the price I would be willing to pay was a complex calculation based on a series of assumptions. What would the new plant in Dimona do for me? What about Dale's Mexican facility? What kind of synergies were possible, and what were they worth? What level of sales could I project? How soon would I want to recoup my investment? After the assumptions, the rest was arithmetic. I drew up my assessments based on minimum, average, and maximum scenarios, checked my figures a dozen times, and gave them to my financial people to run through for themselves. Finally I came up with my number.

Only Ruta and I knew what the figure was. My people were eager to hear what I had decided, but I would not tell them. Avi Eden was asking—my lawyer and by now a close friend. "Avi," I said, "you don't have to know." Bob Freece, our treasurer, wanted the number. He had been with me almost from the beginning. "Bob, why do you have to know? What do you care? I'm even afraid to know it myself." I felt it was an atomic bomb. "Maybe by telepathy it might go from your mind to somebody else's mind. Leave it alone." I was going to tell Alfred, but he didn't want to hear. "Don't tell me," he said. "You may want to change your mind. I don't want you to feel bound. Whatever you decide, I trust your judgment." I said, "Look, Alfred, you stand by. If I run into a problem, I'll come back to you."

Finally it came down to the bidding. Ruta and I flew to New York from Europe. At the Regency Hotel that night I slept an hour or two, then woke up with figures running through my head. I felt compelled to work through the numbers again. "Ruta," I said, "put on the light. Let's talk."

"What do you want, Felix?"

"Look, do we or don't we buy Dale? Tomorrow is judgment day."

Ruta had an excellent general sense for these things, and she had been through this so many times she knew the numbers, too. So we went over them again. And at each step she not only supported me, she also incited me to go ahead with it. She wanted no hedging. She felt I had it in me to take on much more than I was doing. As always, she gave me reassurance and reinforced my optimistic side. If she had said, "Felix, we have a nice company. It's growing nicely. It's doing well. What do we need this for?" I would not have done it. Had I felt that she was frightened, or she wasn't interested, I wouldn't have gone ahead with it. I wanted this, but if my real partner was not completely for it, I wouldn't have taken the plunge.

There were two parties at the Dale bidding: ourselves and Dynamics Corporation of America. The bidding was complicated by the results of the lawsuit Dynamics Corporation had brought after Lionel reneged on the original sales agreement. The settlement had stipulated that the new round of bidding would start at $70 million, $15 million over the earlier agreed purchase price. If Dale were sold to somebody other than Dynamics for $70 million, then Dynamics would receive $15 million. If the company were sold to someone else for a higher figure, Dynamics would receive $15 million plus 28 percent of the purchase price above $70 million. Just to enter the room, the rule was that prospective bidders had to bring a certified check for $5 million and an irrevocable letter of credit for $70 million, the figure at which the bidding was to start.

The bidding was held in the offices of Lionel's law firm. We all met there: Alfred, Ruta, Avi Eden, our banker Tim Talbert, and myself (though Alfred and Ruta stayed outside the bidding room so that if needed they could give advice without being influenced by the atmosphere), Larry Fagan from Charterhouse, the Dale management, and the contingent from Dynamics Corporation, led by Ed Vosniak, the Dynamics president.

Our bank was Manufacturers Bank of Detroit, a holdover from the days when Jim Starr had started up the plant in Romulus, Michigan. Tim Talbert, our account manager there, was not very high up in the bank. But he had fought for us like a lion, and eventually, level by level, he had won over the opponents of this deal at Manufacturers. If it weren't for Charterhouse, he told me, he would never have been able to swing it. His bosses had more faith in Charterhouse than in Vishay.

The bidding did not start smoothly. We had our check for $5 million with us, but somehow the letter of credit for $70 million had not arrived, and Lionel did not want to begin until the letter was actually on hand. Tim Talbert was on the phone with one bank officer after another to get the thing sent out. Eventually it arrived and we were allowed to enter the bidding room.

As I opened the door, smoke billowed out of the room; the people inside seemed shrouded in it. At the head of a large oval table sat the judge who would be conducting the bidding; on the left side sat Mr. Vosniak and his colleagues. As I walked in, Vosniak stood up to shake hands, looming over me and everyone else. He looked like a giant.

The bidding started at $70 million, $100,000 at a clip. "Seventy million, one hundred thousand," I said.

"Seventy million, two," said Vosniak.

"Three hundred thousand."

The clerk looked at Vosniak. "Four hundred thousand."

"Seventy-one million," I said.

When it got to $80 million, I asked for a recess. "I need to caucus with my people," I told the judge. "I have to call my board of directors. We've reached our limit."

So we walked out, though not in fact to do any caucusing. Larry Fagan did not care in the least what I bid. Charterhouse was sitting there with a guaranteed profit of $9 million against an investment of $3 million. Alfred, the chairman of our board, was there with me, and I had his implicit trust. We had a cup of coffee, and then I went back in. The smoke seemed not to have cleared in the least. The room was enveloped in a haze.

"Eighty million one hundred thousand," I announced.

Mr. Vosniak had a dilemma. Each additional $100,000 I offered meant $28,000 in Dynamics Corporation's pocket—if they let me win the bid. Of the $80 million that was bid already, their share was $15 million of the $70 million opening price plus 28 percent of the $10 million additional. But that windfall would be theirs only if Vishay won the bidding. If I walked away and they took the company for $80 million, they would be sacrificing $17.8 million in cash. And every increment of $100,000 was costing them an additional $28,000.

Vosniak wanted Dale, but this complicated his decisions. The Dynamics people had a big computer printout with them that contained all their calculations, and as the price rose, they worried the numbers. It was obvious they were torn. Dale was a plum, but $17.8 million and rising in cash had its attractions. My problem was simpler: I only had to know how much I had chosen to afford.

I walked out once. I walked out a second time. As the bidding reached $85 million and kept going up, I began to show signs of stress. I ran nervous figures on the calculator. I leafed through the booklets on Dale I had brought along. The tension in the room had become as thick as the smoke. Then I walked out again.

At $94 million Vosniak got up and said, "We want to

caucus now." The Dynamics contingent got up and walked out. An eternity later they came back in. "Okay," said Vosniak, "you've got the company."

The words brought a vast relief. I looked over at Tim Talbert, who had wanted this so badly for us and had fought so hard to make it happen. He had tears in his eyes. To Tim, $94 million did not sound like too high a price tag. He had not known my cutoff number either. The price I was ready to pay, the figure only Ruta and I knew, was $120 million.

I SRAEL I S O UR S AVIOR

T HE champagne was barely drunk when problems started with
Dale. In the first week I got a letter from Novicki that told me
this might not be the harmonious relationship I had envisioned.
I'm going to put out a memo, he wrote, that we have been acquired
by Vishay and that Dr. Zandman will come to visit our plants
whenever he is invited.

I called him up and said, "What the hell is that? Strike it
out instantly. You're not going to publish language like that. I'm
the CEO of the company. How can you think of doing such a
thing?" "Well," he said slowly, "maybe you're right."

I understood this for what it was, an opening move to
test my limits, to see how far Dale might push its independence. I
didn't let him do that. But other things I did allow. Novicki did
not think that in the company name "Vishay" ought to appear
with "Dale." I wanted it to read "Dale, A Company of Vishay."
But he didn't. "What do you need it for?" I recall he asked. "It will
just cause confusion in the field." "Look," I asked, "what are you
hiding? Are you a part of Vishay or not? "Yes," he said. "So what
do you have against saying so?" But he was adamant about it, and
I told him we'd give it six months. "Your marketing and sales people feel uncomfortable with it? Fine, we'll leave it alone for six
months. You'll change your mind."

In the meantime, I followed through on my promises. I
put Dale in charge of all the resistor business, so that they were
managing Vishay instead of the other way around. "I'm not even
going to sit in on the meetings," I told them. "I don't want to in-
hibit you. I want you to get friendly with the Vishay people and
feel comfortable with them."

But in a dozen ways Novicki seemed to me to be pushing himself forward. His name and picture appeared in many pub-
lications, with no mention at all of Vishay. That in itself had no
importance, but it wasn't a good sign. What disturbed me far more

was that I believed he was taking advantage of the room I allowed him to favor his own people at the expense of those in the Vishay operation.

Ruta's judgment was that Novicki was a negative force. "He's for Dale," she said. "Not for Vishay." But I stood behind what I had told the Dale managers, and what I thought was the right way to go. "What's happening now is because he is unsure of himself," I told her. "This isn't Lionel. At Lionel he had a management that didn't understand resistors, so they gave him a completely free hand. Whatever he said there was *kadosh,* sacrosanct. Here he knows that we understand these things very well, and it makes him insecure. This is just a shakedown period; let's give him some time. After all, it is a takeover. He'll adjust. He's been doing an excellent job running a major company. I'm sure he'll turn out to be a good man for us." "You are dead wrong," said Ruta. "Open your eyes."

I wasn't overly worried. I hadn't expected that Vishay could digest a giant like Dale without a few problems. A little tension between myself and the top man was to be expected. The main thing was that they were in the fold and I could move ahead with my program. Already we were renovating the facility in Dimona, expanding it into a huge, three-hundred-thousand-square-foot structure. Soon I would begin moving some of Dale's production lines over to Israel.

I was also actively considering even more expansion. Once Dimona was on line, Vishay Israel would have a substantial production capacity. I planned to start there with a few hundred workers, but there was no reason the new plant couldn't employ a thousand or more. I watched the construction work, and every brick that went down sharpened my thoughts about what I might be able to accomplish in Israel. Dale was about to make some of my deepest hopes come to life. What I needed now was a mechanism that would give me the resources to continue down this path I had embarked on.

My original concept of Vishay's evolution had been

based on internal growth. In a sense that was tied in with my proprietary feelings about the company. Vishay had come about as a realization of my ideas; in certain ways it was an extension of who I was. The company, I felt, was linked to me, and I to it. Against this background I had been at home with the idea that Vishay should grow by means of its own success, as it was able to finance growth out of revenues. The corollary advantage, of course, was that my ownership (and Alfred's) would not be diluted by the need to raise money through selling stock.

Now I had reshaped my thoughts about Vishay's future. I had seen how the Dale acquisition went, and despite the problems I was eager to pursue expansion. But leveraged buyouts meant raising capital aggressively to finance borrowings. And raising money through the standard channel of issuing stock meant that growth would increasingly dilute Alfred's and my control.

We wrestled with this dilemma for a time, and eventually Avi Eden formulated a plan to create a special class of stock. In addition to ordinary common stock, we would issue a "Class B" stock that could not be traded but that would carry with it ten votes per share. All current stockholders would have the right to convert their stock to "Class B," but if they ever wanted to sell, they would have to convert it back. That meant that once Alfred and I converted our shares to "Class B" we would be unlikely to lose control of the company no matter how badly diluted the common stock were to become or who might at some point start buying it up with an eye toward a takeover. Those who chose not to convert would receive a stock dividend of 2 percent.

Some of the legal opinions we got suggested that since Alfred and I owned such a large percentage of the stock, we would be within our rights to change over to the two-tier system regardless of the other shareholders, that we could find technically correct ways to accomplish it. We would need only the approval of the Vishay board, which was how companies often handled matters like this.

Avi and I both felt differently. If we didn't go to the shareholders now, he argued, whatever we did would always be in danger of a challenge somewhere down the road. It would be far better to fight the battle now than later. That sounded like wisdom to me. It also fit with my general approach. I had confidence that once I delineated it properly, the outside shareholders would go along. One by one I called the major stock owners, mostly institutions, and explained the problem to them. And one by one they told me that they had a history of opposing attempts by management to make special arrangements along these lines. But I was persistent. I went to see them and explained that Vishay was at a juncture. We still had the option of allowing the company to expand slowly through internal growth. Or we could take the path of leveraged buyouts and see what Vishay could really do. The choice was theirs. By the time we convened a shareholders meeting, the majority of them had made up their minds to go full speed ahead.

With the financial resources provided by a new stock issue, I started looking actively for additional acquisitions. It wasn't many months after Dale that a good possibility presented itself, this time in Germany. Our old licensee there was Draloric, which had been called Rosenthal when we first started doing business with them in 1964. Since then Draloric had been sold to AEG and then to Corning Glass, which now was interested in selling the company again.

Draloric was attractive for a number of reasons. They were the largest resistor maker in Germany, one of the world's leading markets. Buying them would bring the full line of Vishay's products to Germany. In effect, we would be making ourselves German, which would give us the ability to sell to the local market as a local company. Draloric was also at a crucial moment of its history. The company had not done well at positioning itself in the emerging global marketplace. Though it still had great strength, an objective observer could see that it was poised at the top of a downward slope. According to my calculations, restructuring Draloric under the aegis of Vishay Israel would not only arrest a slide toward oblivion, it also would make the German company extremely competitive.

The sale was complicated by the fact that Draloric was a large producer of capacitors as well as resistors, and I was only interested in the resistor component. It so happened that AVX, an American capacitor company, wanted the capacitor unit, but not resistors. AVX's president, Marshall Butler, called me just as I was about to call him, and the two of us decided to go into this together. Meanwhile, Corning appointed Goldman, Sachs to negotiate on their part, and involved, three-way talks got under way.

· As this was happening, I met with Draloric's CEO, Werner Statler, and then with the rest of the top management to present myself and lay out my assessment, much as I had with Carroll Novicki and the Dale people. At subsequent meetings I explained my assessment in detail. "It's inevitable that you are going to go down in time," I said. "Prices are continuously eroding, and your labor costs keep going up. It will be harder and harder for you to compete. Your competition is offshore already. Philips is producing in Taiwan and India and Brazil. You have got to have an offshore facility, and you don't have one." Then I laid out the effect that moving some of Draloric's production to Israel would have. Between that move and restructuring the remaining functions in Germany, Draloric was likely to experience a dramatic turnaround.

As I described my plan to Statler over lunch, I scratched out calculations on the back of an envelope. "Let me have that envelope, will you," Statler said when we were walking out to the parking lot. The next day he called to tell me that the numbers looked terrific. "Let's do it," he said.

Dr. Oskar Paul, the former CEO, was also in favor. He was one of the breed of old-style physicist entrepreneurs who had done so much to father the electronics industry; we had been friends now for more than twenty years, ever since I had first decided to license the Vishay resistor in Germany. He was relieved that Vishay was buying the company because he understood that I was not looking at Draloric in terms of short-term gain. On the contrary, I was someone from inside the industry who was going to build the company. From Dr. Paul's perspective, that meant Draloric would be in good hands. "You know," he said, "my son is working in the company. Do you think he has a future with you?" "I don't know him at all," I said. "But if he works well, he definitely will. He only needs to show what he can do." (The postscript to this conversation is that the younger Dr. Paul [also a physicist] eventually succeeded Statler as CEO, then became head of all of Vishay's European operations. Unfortunately, the father died a few months after we acquired Draloric and never got to see his son sitting in his chair.)

This was the second situation where I found a son involved in his father's firm (Geka was the first). But it wasn't to be the last. In fact, the father-son phenomenon was an indication of how the industry had matured. The electronics industry had been started up seriously in the 1920s and 1930s, often by scientist-inventors who created small companies around their inventions. The good managers among them eventually built large companies out of small ones. In the course of time the originators grew old and turned their businesses over to their partners or sons. Some did well, but many didn't, and distressed companies were put up for sale. With the aging of the first generation, a swell of sizable electronics companies began coming onto the market.

That started happening in the 1960s, a time when two of the buzzwords in the business world were "conglomerates" and "electronics." Conglomerates, huge companies that owned many businesses, were emerging as economic powerhouses, and electronics companies were among their favorite acquisitions (it was this climate that had brought me to the United States in the first place). Electronics had high visibility and appeal, much as computers and biotechnology were to have at later periods. Giants such as TRW, Corning, and Litton were paying good money to buy out the manufacturers.

But more often than not, these acquisitions turned out

to be relatively short-term. The conglomerates were buying companies that were not part of their core businesses, which meant that they didn't understand how to manage them. They didn't have the experience, and it wasn't easy to focus their attention. In fact, they weren't really that interested. It was hard even to say that they were "owners," at least in the older sense of the word. The conglomerates were run largely by teams of professional managers who changed from time to time. They had little self-identification with the electronics businesses they had acquired. The result was that the big companies took their new acquisitions and milked them. They didn't put any money into R&D. They stripped their assets for cash. They were an entirely different breed from the people who had loved the industry, whose lives were in electronics and who aspired to accomplishment in their fields. Now it was a question of a numbers game, manipulating the companies for a stock market advantage and then selling out and getting out. The founders and builders had given way to the short-term moneymen.

By chance, I had begun to look for acquisitions during this period when electronics companies were being sold off for profits (Draloric had already gone through several hands before I bought it). To someone in my position, such a company was worth considerably more than the sum of its assets. I looked at it in terms of the synergies I could achieve and the potential for transferring production to our lower-labor-cost Israeli operation. My intention was to acquire products that would help me compete for world markets, then to make the products more efficiently.

The state these companies were in by the time they had been through two or three owners typically made them excellent candidates for the kind of restructuring my plans called for. As I examined Draloric and other potential acquisitions, I found that typically they had evolved according to a certain pattern. During the years when the companies had had decent management, they had stayed competitive by raising productivity.

When they were sold, most often the new owners—those who weren't simply stripping the assets for cash—made an initial effort to increase competitiveness. More machinery came in, and costs were reduced from the bottom by cutting back on the work force (almost never were costs reduced from the top). Eventually all the production levels of these companies were functioning efficiently. The work force had been pruned back. Machinery was up-to-date. The company's products were of high quality, and their customers were happy. Still, the profitability went down, and from year to year they grew less competitive. Something was wrong. But what?

The answer was that the companies were upside down. Management had become bloated. Thirty years ago a company might have employed 1,000 workers and 200 managers. As pressure increased to make the product more and more cheaply, better equipment was installed and the work force scaled back. By the second or third generation the 1,000 workers might have become 100. But now there were 250 or 300 managers, because more managers had been brought in to oversee the automated production. An inverse pyramid had been formed. There was no way to squeeze the number of workers farther, and management would not touch itself.

But for me the heart of the company was its production, not its bureaucracy. The line workers and the first-level supervisors were the people who brought the product out and put it on the market. The support staff, including management, was the support staff. It wasn't the fruit of the enterprise, and it didn't exist for its own sake. Draloric and others presented tremendous opportunities to slash back entire levels of management. Combined with shifting production work to lower labor cost countries such as Israel, management reduction could reduce costs dramatically.

When we moved some of the operations to our new plant in Dimona, a Draloric management team went in to oversee the transfer of production (some of them brought their wives along to Israel). They were highly organized, and they lived there until they had completed their jobs. They set up operations, trained the Israelis, and held their hands until everyone was comfortable that things were working smoothly. (Unfortunately, Dale did none of this, and to my considerable distress Dimona was still tied in knots trying to get the Dale lines of production right.) The Draloric line worked like a charm from day one.

While I was still having serious problems with Dale, the Draloric takeover went like a textbook. Those operations that could remain profitable in Germany we kept in place; the rest we transferred. As I had projected and hoped, the company turned around, and over a period of time it became far stronger than it had ever been. Statler, the CEO, had seen that potential from the beginning, and in time the entire management came to understand that without the Israeli connection Draloric would have fallen on serious times. At one meeting a Draloric manager even projected a slide during his presentation that read ISRAEL IS OUR SAVIOR.

When I saw that, my first thought was, what an irony. But I don't know that anybody else read it the same way. The Germans had quickly developed tremendous respect for the Israelis, which the Israelis reciprocated. The two groups worked together like a close-knit team. In a way I expected it; after all, that was what I had planned for. But it also left me with a kind of bemused fascination.

•

The Draloric acquisition was completed in November 1987. In France, 1987 had been a recession year, exacerbated by the American stock market crash in October that had brought all the other world markets down with it, including the French Bourse. Sfernice, our old antagonist, saw its stock drop from 800 francs to 200. We were told by our auditors (who also audited Sfernice) that they might respond positively if we offered to buy them. I had actually made an inquiry about this the previous year but had met with a refusal. I was willing to try again.

A year had passed and the company had taken its hits, but Sfernice's chairman, Jean-Claude Tiné, was as hard a negotiator as ever. Yes, they would entertain an offer, he said, but I shouldn't bother if I was considering anything less than 800 francs per share—which would have come to about $65 million.

Sfernice was doing about $110 million in sales, but in terms of their profitability the price looked high. But when we looked closely at synergies we were able to identify substantial potential savings. We could move their foil resistor business to Israel and drastically reduce production costs. We also saw ways to reorganize their other divisions.

As I had at Dale and Draloric, I undertook talks with Sfernice's management to persuade them of the benefits an acquisition would have. I spoke at length with Sfernice's new chairman, Philippe Gazeau (who succeeded Tiné shortly after our initial discussions), trying to excite him about Vishay—who we were, where we were going, and how Sfernice could be part of it. Gazeau's basic response was positive, and eventually he agreed to my proposals.

But he had a problem. He had just hired a new CEO from Texas Instruments' French Division, a powerhouse of a manager, and he was quite unsure about whether he would go along. I said to bring him over and let me talk to him, too.

When I met the new CEO I picked up vibes I didn't particularly like. He played his cards hard, pushing for a two-year contract in case I might be thinking of reorganizing in a way that would put him out of a job. While I wasn't happy about his approach, I also felt that if I didn't go along I would not get any support from him in my effort to win approval for this acquisition from the Department of Industry. And I knew I was going to need all the help I could get. After all, the French government was probably not going to be too happy anyway that an American corporation was coming in and buying a large French public business, especially one that sold to the military.

Nevertheless, I didn't think the contract demand was too out of line, so I agreed to it. Afterward I told Gazeau, the chairman, that it wasn't fair that I would give this Texas Instruments manager a contract and not him. "Felix," he said, "it's not necessary. I trust you." But I told him I wouldn't feel comfortable otherwise, and I insisted on writing him a contract as well.

Once Gazeau was convinced, he persuaded his management people and talked to the workers and got their approval. But the permit from the French government was a different story. The French government had to approve any acquisition of a French company by foreigners, and Lazard Frères, our bankers in this situation, thought our chances of getting an approval were almost zero. That was Jean-Claude Tiné's opinion, too. Few if any French public companies had been taken over by foreigners, and no foreigner had ever before purchased a publicly owned French company that was connected with national defense. "If you want to pay us to represent you," the bankers said, "we'll take your money and we'll do our best. But we have to tell you in advance that the chances are not good. We want to warn you because we don't like to be involved with failures."

They may have really believed the chances were zero, or, maybe, I thought, it was just a standard Lazard Frères tactic to paint a bleak picture. In either case, I had prepared my strategies and I was ready to approach the French. "You know," I told Lazard Frères, "I am a Frenchman also. I have the Order of Merit for Research and Invention. I was educated here, I wrote books here, I taught here. I took my first patents here. I speak French. I may not be a typical Frenchman, but I'm certainly not a typical American either."

We first went in to see the president of the French stock exchange. It so happened that just before this the president of the stock exchange had had a very bad experience with English lawyers and, to his chagrin, the news had come out in the press the day before. As a result, he was feeling aggrieved and hateful toward lawyers in general. Our group consisted of three people from Lazard Frères; myself; and Avi Eden, who was, of course, a lawyer. The first thing the president did was go around the room and pointedly ask us one at a time if we were lawyers. He was seething.

One after another, we answered that we weren't. I was wondering somewhat apprehensively how Avi was going to handle this when the interrogation got to him, but to everyone's relief he stopped after he heard my own heartfelt denial.

At the Ministry of Defense we spoke—in French, of course—and I convinced them that the buyout would be good for Sfernice and good for the country. In view of the trends in the industry, I argued, it was inevitable that if we did not buy Sfernice, that company would perish. Not today or tomorrow, but two or three years down the line. Their main problem, in addition to their costs, was that they had no real access to markets outside of France. In this business climate, where everything was global, a producer could not exist on such a basis. But through Vishay's name and distribution network they would have near worldwide access—especially to big markets in the United States that they had tried hard to penetrate, though with little success.

The Defense Ministry was convinced. "All right," they said. "We know you, and you have our approval to go ahead. But what we do want from you is a guaranteed minimum one year's notice before you discontinue any product that we are currently using." That was fine with me, and we signed a memorandum of agreement.

The Department of Industry was a tougher nut. But after a good deal of argument back and forth, the director general and I came to an agreement and signed a letter. When it was all done, he said, "After all, we are not selling out to Americans here. Vishay might be an American public company, but you yourself are a Frenchman." Lazard Frères was enchanted. So was I. The director general may have been indulging in a little face-saving, but he was also saving the company.

In the three or four months that these various negotiations took, Sfernice's stock price started to rise, from 200 French francs to 300, then to 400 and 500. All our discussions were super-secret, but obviously rumors were spreading. By the time we settled on a price of 840 francs, the market price had climbed to 820. Fortunately, in the end the run-up in the price of the stock did not hinder the deal, and in October 1988 we took control of Sfernice.

Like Draloric, Sfernice came into Vishay as a subsidiary of Dale, which in turn was a subsidiary of Vishay Israel. And as I had with Draloric, I immediately undertook to transfer some of Sfernice's production to our Israeli facilities. According to my calculations, this move alone would triple Sfernice's profits and strengthen the company's French base at the same time.

But here we ran into a huge problem. Now that we had reached this stage, the new CEO decided that he was unalterably opposed to any production transfer. No matter how clearly I demonstrated the profitability of it, no matter how evident it was that in the midterm this move would preserve French jobs, he took the opposite position. He believed it wouldn't work, that we'd have a strike, that neither the workers nor management would accept it. The accountants too came out against the transfer. One of the top financial managers said, "Do you want to do this just to make more profits for the company? It's not right." I said, "Aren't you an accountant, a businessman? Who are you? I don't understand you. If Sfernice were making a lot of money, you might have a point. Not a good point, but some kind of point. But you are just barely making a profit. Barely. And I have to pay the interest on the debt we assumed to buy the company." He said, "You wanted to buy the company. You pay your interest. That's not our business." The arrogance was astonishing. This is us, and that's you. They would take care of Sfernice, and Vishay would take care of itself.

Despite what I thought had been a clear presentation of my plans and expectations, I found myself bargaining with the CEO over each step I wanted to take. His approach was consistently different from mine. There was continuous haggling about everything from issues of vital interest, such as the transfer of production, to trivia, such as whether the business cards would be printed vertically, as they were throughout the rest of the company. "No," I heard. "In France one must only print them horizontally."

Ruta thought that he was completely unmanageable. In all my experience I had never met anybody who loved to argue and bargain like this man did.

But I had learned a lesson with Dale (though I still wasn't sure how I was going to resolve the Novicki situation). Before too long I laid down the law. "Look," I said, as I recall our conversation. "I'm sick of bargaining. This is what we are going to do. This, that, and the other."

He said, "No, I can't do this, that, or the other either."

"Well, if you can't do this," I said, "then you are fired."

"What do you mean, fired?"

"That's what I mean. Fired. I'm going to fire you."

"But I can't do it."

"Did you hear what I said?"

"But I just can't do these things."

"Okay, now there are no more discussions. You are fired."

"Fired?"

"Yes. Fired. As of tomorrow you do not have a job. You have no job."

"Well, maybe we can change some of these things."

"No. The discussions are over. I'm tired. I've given you every chance possible. Now even if you want to do it, I cannot work with you. I gave you enough time to adapt to my style. Maybe this is your style. It isn't mine, and I'm the boss. You are fired."

He was shocked. I said, "You pick up your things and go."

"Well, we have to work out the contract."

"You can work that out with Gazeau. I'm not interested in it. Whatever we owe you we'll pay you."

So he was fired. At that moment, Yannick LeVacon, our manager at Geka, was working at Sfernice to try to resolve some technical problems. Yannick was a man I knew I could trust, so I made him general manager. Along with the CEO I also wanted to get rid of the financial manager who had been so intransigent. But Yannick started to argue that he wanted six months to work with him. I saw red flags immediately; Yannick obviously had a certain mental inclination (similar to my own) that people could be converted if only you approached them the right way. What I didn't know at the time was that Yannick had been trained by the Jesuits, so this notion of the possibility of conversion was second nature to him. By now, of course, I was hypersensitive to it, but I had put Yannick in charge, and there was nothing to do for it but let him make his own mistakes and learn his own lessons—which he did. After six difficult months, he ended up firing the man anyway. With Yannick on top we transferred the Sfernice foil resistor business to Israel and began restructuring the company. He had some struggles with the management—the same story: yours and mine, Sfernice and Vishay. But eventually he mastered the situation and brought Sfernice wholeheartedly on board.

As this was going on, I found myself growing closer to Jean-Claude Tiné, Sfernice's former chairman. I knew from long experience that he was a hard-nosed negotiator, but as I got to know him better I was more and more taken with his general business wisdom and high standards of honesty. After discussing the matter with Ruta, I decided to invite him onto our board of directors. I also invited a friend of Tiné's, Guy Brana, a well-known industrialist who was executive vice president of the French Manufacturer's Association. Tiné and Brana gave a European dimension to our board, which we had not had previously but which was becoming increasingly significant as we continued to expand.

•

By the end of 1987 Vishay had been radically transformed. When I stopped to catch my breath I found myself looking at a company that had gone from $55 million to $400 million in sales in a year and a half. We owned businesses in England, Germany, France, and Mexico in addition to the United States and Israel—where we were now employing more than seven hundred people in two plants. Vishay was still digesting Dale, but now Dale was digesting Draloric. Sfernice too was aboard. The whole thing was growing by leaps and bounds, as I had wanted it to and foreseen that it could.

In one way the acquisitions were consonant with the spirit of the day; this was the great moment of the takeover firms and leveraged buyout specialists. But Vishay's growth was of a fundamentally different character. We weren't in this to chop up companies and destroy them, making money by buying and selling. We were in it for the possibilities I believed were inherent in this industry that had absorbed my professional life. I had overarching goals in mind, and none of them was short-term.

All this growth was not without problems, but the only one that troubled me deeply was Dale CEO Carroll Novicki. Because of the way we had structured the takeovers, Novicki was the man on top of the organization. Novicki had had a proven track record at Dale, and I still felt he could manage on a large scale, even though he had not done the job I wanted in shifting Dale production to Israel. I was not happy with his work there. Machinery had been installed, but Dale had provided little support; the Israelis had been more or less left to sink or swim. The result was that at Dimona the Dale lines of production were in trouble. I was struggling to come up with an answer to that.

Even more importantly, time had brought no improvement in the personal relationship between Novicki and myself. To me, he had always seemed closed off and uncommunicative. I still felt the antagonism, the resistance to my direction. Vishay had been a close company that had given many of its employees a feeling almost of a family. Now our intramural relationship was one of adversaries, of distance, even of vague hostility.

Through all the growth I never felt I had a partner in Novicki. I also had the growing sense that my own people were intimidated by him. I picked up hints about it from Avi Eden, and one day Dick Grubb, our accounting officer, asked to see me at my home. Dick was a completely dedicated longtime employee whose opinions I valued highly. "Felix," he said, "I want to tell you that I don't feel the company is going the right way."

"What do you mean?"

"We have problems at Dale, Felix. Our people aren't happy; in fact, there's a lot of unhappiness. In some of the foil product line sales have been dropping because of what I consider improper behavior on Dale's part. I think the whole culture over there is wrong. It doesn't fit with what you've done at Vishay. It's always us and them. It's not one company. I'd like to know what your thoughts are about it."

I told him. "Dick, I know that you are right. I haven't discussed it with anyone yet, but I'll tell you that this will all be taken care of in good time."

Dick Grubb was the first to talk to me. I understood well enough the message behind his words. He did not know where this situation might lead; it looked to him as if Novicki might be the heir apparent, that he was positioned to replace me if and when I retired. I certainly had not signaled that anything different might be in the works. Dick worked on my headquarters staff right under me. If that was his sense of it, others were no doubt getting the same feeling.

I wasn't sure how to handle this. I talked with Alfred and Avi about it to a certain extent, but not in depth. In a way, I was a little ashamed in front of my close colleagues. I didn't want to acknowledge that there was a schism here, at least not while I was still trying to work it out. But with Ruta I had no such compunctions. Finally, the two of us went off to a spa in Fort Lauderdale, Florida, primarily to get away and talk about Dale. And talk we did. We spent the entire three days immersed in conversation.

THE great problem was that Dale operated as a kind of fiefdom; they had run their business more or less independently of Lionel, and they had taken steps to do the same with us. As a result, I was not intimately knowledgeable about Dale; I didn't know the managers and their relationships well, I wasn't familiar with the details of the company's daily life. In a way it was a black box. Taking a chance that Novicki might leave was a risky business. He had worked at Dale in various capacities for twenty-five years and had been managing the company for ten. What would happen to the organism if all of a sudden the head were removed? I couldn't say, but at a minimum I would be creating a dangerously unstable situation. Nevertheless, after three days with Ruta I was convinced that if I didn't clear the air and assert myself, worse would follow. I felt clear about what was required. I had to put the house in order.

When we got home from Fort Lauderdale I called Jim Starr in North Carolina to review the situation with him. Jim's Measurement Group was completely separate from Vishay's component business, so he had more of a detached perspective. Jim was also one of the bluntest people I knew; he had absolutely no respect for persons—which was one of the reasons he had always been my favorite business sounding board. After I talked with him I decided it was time to call in Novicki from Nebraska.

Over tea at my home in Philadelphia, Novicki and I had our discussion.* I recall it as follows: "I have a problem with you," I said. "You know that since I acquired Dale I've been asking you to accommodate me on changes I've wanted to make, things that I've felt would be best for the company. But you have resisted me on most of these issues. I've felt all along as if I've been unable to get anyplace with you. Now the time has come to change all that.

*See the author's note on page v.

"Here's what I want for starters. Number one, Vishay has to be mentioned whenever Dale is mentioned. So as of now the name Vishay has to appear with Dale."

He said, "You know we discussed this and I'm not in favor of it."

"I know that, and I know I told you that we would do it in six months [it was now two years later]. You still don't like it; that's too bad. I like it. So that's the way it has to be."

He said, "Is that an order?"

"Yes, that's an order."

"All right. What else?"

"If you want to put your name and picture in paid advertisements, which I don't consider very elegant, you'll have to ask my permission first. Maybe I'll agree and maybe I won't. But you have to give me the option when you want to aggrandize yourself. So as of now, that's taboo."

"Is that an order?"

"Yes, that's an order."

"I also want you to know that as of now I intend to be more involved with the everyday work at Dale. I feel as if I'm an outsider, and I didn't buy the company to be outside it."

I remember we discussed several other issues in the same way, and at the end he left, not very happy. But he did not quit.

Right after my discussion with Novicki, Ruta and I flew to Europe. We had just arrived at the Inter•Continental Hotel in Paris when Yannick LeVacon, Sfernice's general manager, called and told me he needed to talk to me immediately. "Let's have lunch today, Felix," he said. There was no mistaking the agitation in his voice.

As soon as Ruta and I sat down with LeVacon, he attacked me. "Felix," he said, "do you know that Martin Park has a company that is competing with our company?" Park was general manager of Dale in Europe, Carroll Novicki's direct subordinate and close friend. "Are you aware that he has his own company, called Talema?"

"No."

"Do you know that this Talema is competing with Vishay in transformers?"

"No, I don't know that."

"Felix, are you a part of this?" LeVacon was really upset. He was interrogating me. Ruta and I just stared at each other.

"Yannick, what's going on? We're friends, aren't we? What are you saying?"

"Felix, here's what's going on. I have proof of it. Talema is owned by Park and his family. His wife and others. And they are making transformers that I think are competing with ours. They're even using some of our reps. The reps are in cahoots with them. It's not clean, Felix."

"Of course I don't know that, Yannick. I haven't heard anything about it until this moment."

"Do you know that people in the company suspect that you are part of this? It looks that way because you haven't done anything to clean this mess up."

"What? Why hasn't anyone told me?"

"Because they're afraid to talk to you. They're afraid of Novicki. They don't want to go over their boss's head. But I'm telling you here and now that I am not afraid. If this is the case, I refuse to be a part of it!"

I said, "Yannick, calm down. Let's finish lunch. Give me a couple of weeks to find out what's going on and I'll tell you."

"Fine," he said.

"By the way, how did you find out about it?"

"I heard it from Werner Statler [our German manager]."

"Why didn't he tell me?"

"He's scared. Besides, he has a loyalty problem. Novicki's his boss. When he found out what was going on, he went to his lawyer, who told him he had to divulge it. He's physically sick about it, Felix. He had to take time off, but before he left, he told me the whole story."

As soon as LeVacon left I called Statler on vacation and he said, "Yes, it's all true."

"Do you have documentary proof?"

"Yes. I have all the proof. I didn't open my mouth to Yannick before I had it."

"Fax it to me now."

A half an hour later I received a fifty-page fax: catalogs, Register of Commerce, P and Ls—everything that was public information. Martin Park and his wife owned 96 percent of this company while they both worked at Dale—that is, at Vishay.

I called Park and told him I wanted to meet with him in Paris. "I can't come," he said. "I'm leaving this evening for Nebraska, and I already have the tickets. Can we do it in the States?"

"Fine," I said, "we'll do it there."

A few days later I came back to the States and called in Jim Starr, Avi Eden, and some other close colleagues and told them what I had found. We all thought that when I confronted Novicki he would say that he had authorized it, that there wasn't much in the way of competition, and that it had been approved a long time ago. He had just forgotten to tell me. A minor matter that had been in place for many years (seventeen years, as it turned out). That's what we all thought.

I called Novicki and Park in to Malvern and had Avi and Jim Starr sit in. As I recall our discussion, I asked Novicki first, "Do you know anything about a company called Talema in Germany?" He said, "No."

"Do you know that Park owns Talema?"

"No."

"Did you authorize him to do that?"

"No, I don't know anything about it."

This we didn't foresee. I turned to Park. "Did Novicki know that you own Talema?"

"No, he didn't."

Jim Starr got up with disgust on his face and walked out of the room. "Jim," I said, "come back."

Then I asked Novicki and Park to leave for a moment and think about what they were telling me.

When they came back I asked if they wanted to change what they had said. "I'll forget everything that's been said up till now. Do you want to tell me something else?"

"No," said Novicki. "There's nothing to change. I didn't know."

"Who authorized you to do it?" I asked Park.

"Nobody authorized me."

"Nobody at Dale authorized you to do it?"

"No."

"Why did you do such a thing?"

"Well, I thought it was no real competition. Besides, I'm only an investor. I don't have anything to do with running it."

"Wasn't it your duty to get authorization if you wanted to do such a thing?"

Martin Park was vice president of Dale's international sales, with his offices in Frankfurt. Talema was located right across the street.

"How can you have a full-time job with us, and your wife, too, and meantime be owning and managing another company?"

"Well, I told you, I don't manage it. I just own it."

"You own ninety-six percent and you are a passive owner? The company is across the street? And you're not managing it?"

"Well, I'm not. And Novicki didn't know."

Meanwhile, Novicki was defending Park. After all, it wasn't that much competition, and no great harm was done.

"Novicki," I said, "if I were in your place, if my best friend had done something like this to me, I would spit in his face. I would say, 'You are no friend of mine forever. I don't want to talk to you. Look what you've done. You've betrayed me.' How can you defend him?"

At that point it was noon and I told them to go out for

lunch, that we would meet directly afterward. When Park and Novicki got back, their account had changed.

"Yes," said Park. "In fact I was authorized to do it."

"Who authorized you?"

"Mr. Stinson authorized it, and he was at that time the president of the company."

"Great! That will exonerate you right now. Because if you had authorization from your board, then I can understand. Though I can't understand how come Novicki didn't know about it. You're best friends. You went to school together. Your wives went to school together. You're close all the time. You have a company for seventeen years and he doesn't know it exists? That's not very believable, but . . . let me have Mr. Stinson's address. I want to verify this."

Park smiled at me. "He's dead."

"Oh?"

"But there was someone else who knew: Gates. He was the sales manager at the time, my direct superior."

"Gates is good enough. Give me Gates's address."

"Unfortunately, he also died."

"Come on. Now you give me two witnesses who are dead, and nobody else knew?"

"No, nobody else."

"So the only witnesses we have that you were authorized, verbally, not in writing, are two guys who are dead. And the present manager, who has been your superior for ten years and is your best friend, he doesn't know about it?"

"Yes, that's the way it is."

Park could see I didn't believe him for a minute. "Do you want me to resign?" he asked. I said yes and he wrote out his resignation on the spot.* Then I told Novicki that I wanted him to write to me reconfirming that he had not known.

A few days later I received a letter from him saying ex-

*In a subsequent suit we filed against Park for breach of fiduciary responsibility, the court found that he had, in fact, been given authority by Dale's former management and that Talema was not a direct competitor of Vishay.

actly that. I didn't expect it. Given how close they had been in their personal and professional lives, I was sure in my own mind that Novicki knew all about it, and it seemed to me that he might come clean in a letter after rethinking it. Perhaps he would say, "Felix, I lied. I was frightened. I'm sorry about it and I am going to do whatever I can to make amends for it."

But he didn't budge. He adamantly denied knowing about Talema, and I was never able to prove that either he or Park wasn't telling the truth. But to me the facts hardly mattered anymore. Either way I had completely lost confidence in him.

When I asked Jim Starr how he thought I should proceed, he said, "it's obvious the man can't remain in the company. But give it six months. In six months you'll prepare yourself to manage the whole thing properly."

"I can't do that," I said. "I can't work one more minute with him. I have to get rid of him."

Jim said, "You're risking a hell of a lot. Who's going to manage Dale? You don't know the people well enough. In six months you can build yourself a structure."

"I can't wait," I said. "I'll take the chance."

Once I had made the decision, I talked it over with our board members on the telephone, and they all gave me their support. Then I flew to Columbus, Nebraska, with Avi Eden, Glynn Smith, Bill Spires, Bob Freece, and Dick Grubb from my corporate staff. Bill, Bob, and Dick went to the plant and had all the managers report to a conference room so they could keep an eye on the office. Meanwhile I had Novicki come over to see me in my hotel room. I wanted Avi with me, and I had Glynn Smith wait in an adjacent room. I told Novicki, "Look, I can't work with you anymore. I want you to tender your resignation."

He said, "I'm not tendering my resignation. You'll have to fire me."

"Okay, in that case we'll pay you whatever we owe you under the contract and you're fired."

Novicki's departure caused a tremendous turmoil—in

the company, in the newspapers, in the city of Columbus. Dale was one of the largest employers in town, and the shock waves spread. To calm the situation, I called in each of the managers separately and explained what had happened. They should make their own judgments, I told them, but I expected loyalty and continued hard work. Some things were going to change at Dale, and I was confident that they would be for the better.

I was especially intent on getting Dale's production in Israel straightened out. The main problem was that Dale was providing such poor support. There was little communication between the Dale people and the Israelis; one could even see an element of antagonism. I wasn't so sure that was Novicki's fault, although he was ultimately responsible. He might not have been overly eager for this project to move forward, but he did not oppose it either (I had set it up so he had had a sizable financial incentive in making it work). But he didn't seem to know how to do that, or how to handle some of the people under him who were throwing up roadblocks. They liked their operation in Mexico all right, but Israel seemed too distant, too difficult to control, the Israelis themselves a bit too intimidating. The result was a mess. If we didn't turn it around, we might even have to close down production in Dimona, which would have been a disaster. I couldn't bring myself to think about it.

But once I got Novicki out I said, "Now I am going to make it happen." In his place I appointed William Gaines, the executive vice president. We were going to run this as a triumvirate, I told him: Gaines and two others from Dale. Glynn Smith from Malvern would come to meetings to represent me. Gaines and others from Dale didn't like that at all, and they told me about it. But I was in no mood for compromise. Dale was going to put itself in order, and if Gaines and his colleagues weren't up to it, I was ready to get rid of them, too.

•

Two weeks after I fired Novicki, Carl Fritz came into my office with scarifying news. Carl had been with Vishay for twenty-five years. Starting as a technician, he had worked his way up to vice president of applications engineering. For years he had been intimately involved in Vishay's quality control program; he was, among other things, our primary contact with the Pentagon's Defense Electronics Supply Center (DESC), which oversaw the military's purchase and testing of electronics components. Carl had just been speaking with one of his colleagues at DESC. Did I know, Carl asked, that the Pentagon was on the verge of removing Dale from the list of qualified military suppliers? A "debarment" order was about to be issued.

When I called Dale I was told that yes, there was a problem, but it wasn't anything serious and they were taking care of it. But when I had Carl explore it further with his contacts in the Department of Defense (DOD) he was told, "It's very serious. The debarment is proceeding. There is ample evidence that Dale has been violating testing requirements." DOD was saying that the company had been cheating on the rigorous self-testing procedures mandated by the Pentagon of all its suppliers. In their opinion Dale was engaging in criminal fraud.

I felt numb. At this point Dale was doing about $180 million a year in sales, of which maybe a third was military-related. That third, though, brought in almost 50 percent of the profits. If Dale were disqualified ("debarred" was the technical term), we were looking at the likely loss of all of that for three years, the usual term of debarment—that is, about $180 million. And debarments typically had devastating collateral effects as well; commercial customers almost always got nervous and started shifting business to competitors. Beyond that, fines for violations of government regulations could be stupendous. Big companies had been mortally wounded by such exactions. As I mentally raced through the potential consequences here, I was in a state of shock. If the government stopped doing business with Dale, it could kill the company. Without the military business, and with Dimona losing money, we would be headed directly toward a catastrophe, for Dale and Vishay both.

As I gathered my composure, I remembered that a few years earlier I had gotten a call from Carroll Novicki telling me that the FBI had come in and taken some of Dale's military quality control files. There had been some accusation of cheating, he had said, but it wasn't true. A disgruntled employee was trying to make trouble, but there was nothing to it. Everything was fine.

I hadn't paid any further attention. Dale was running its own show, and there hadn't seemed any reason to look deeper.

After some additional investigation, Carl Fritz, Dick Grubb and I went to the military—in this case to Janet Cook, the head of the DOD's Office of Contract Integrity. I wanted to know in person exactly what the problems were. We were all shaken (a year or two later, when I better understood the massive testing fraud of military products that went on, I wouldn't have been so surprised). Vishay had been doing business with the Pentagon for a quarter of a century and we had never had a single difficulty of this sort. As a matter of course we had always complied with the Pentagon's testing specifications to the letter. Now we were embroiled in a potentially devastating case of cheating—not by us, exactly, but by one of our subsidiaries. I felt tarred. I was determined to understand this in all its dimensions.

The lawyers wanted to go with me to see Janet Cook, but I said, "No, no lawyers." I didn't even let Avi come. "But they are lawyers themselves," my people said. "They'll kill you."

"No. I want to sit face to face with them and find out what this is."

At the Office of Contract Integrity I said, "Look, you know us. You know our record, and you know that we would never knowingly be involved in such a thing. I would like you to tell us exactly what happened. I promise you that we are going to investigate this ourselves and get to the bottom of it."

They told me. The FBI had examined Dale's quality control papers and had found discrepancies in one of the manufacturing units between the testing reports provided to the government and the internal records. Numbers had been altered to indicate that the failure rates of Dale resistors were less than they actually were. In fact, there had been few field failures of Dale components; the company had maintained a good reputation for reliability. But they were purposefully misrepresenting their test results, and that was the basis for the debarment.

Then Janet Cook started quizzing me about Novicki. In particular, why had I fired him? She was suspicious that I might have let him go because I had known about this improper testing situation. I told her that the firing had had no connection whatsoever with these problems. She said, "You mean you didn't know what was happening there before?"

"If I had known," I answered, "I would have fired everyone involved right off." She looked at our twenty-five-year track record, and she believed me.

Once we heard Janet Cook's account, we undertook our own investigation, which was far more thorough than the military's. I sent Carl Fritz to Dale and told him to find out what was going on and root it out. I wanted him to talk to everybody and anybody; I didn't want a stone left unturned. Carl was just the person for this job. Rigidly honest, uncompromising, and thorough, I knew I could trust him to turn Dale inside out.

What Carl found was not good at all. Some employees were highly reluctant to talk about what had been going on, but others were open and even eager to discuss it. They had bad consciences about the cheating and felt they had been pressured into it. Dale was in rural Nebraska. Out there, if you didn't work for Dale, you worked on a farm, or you moved somewhere else.

Behind the cheating Carl was uncovering lay two prime factors: the fierce competitive pressure of the industry, and the unusual approach the Department of Defense takes to military testing. In the United States (as opposed to France or England), suppliers are required to test their own products. Testing specifications are extremely strict, but the Pentagon expects manufacturers to apply them to themselves (in that sense it's like an honor code). As a result, producers have a powerful incentive to cheat. The club

Defense holds is that anyone caught cheating is liable to crippling penalties. Many of the largest names in the defense industry—Teledyne, Northrup, and others—have been subjected to sometimes immense fines, and violators have seen whole levels of management swept away. As we ourselves continued to acquire companies, we found in our preliminary investigations (Dale sensitized us to this subject) that in almost every instance there were irregularities that had to be cleaned up. Testing fraud and negligence permeated the components industry.

In Dale's case, one of their divisions was finding a higher number of failures in their resistors than was permitted by the qualifications for the highest reliability rating. Had they reported this they would have had to notch back their rating, which would have put them at a competitive disadvantage. To avoid that, they were taking failed parts off the test rack and replacing them with other parts. What Carl Fritz found was a conscious pattern of fraud—far more serious than the number-fudging the government had noticed.

Once we knew, we went back to the military and reported it. "This is what our investigation found," we told them. "You were correct, but it went deeper than you knew."

Despite our forthcoming response, the government decided that penalties were in order. "First," they said, "you have to reimburse the Defense Department for its expenses in removing the resistors in question from the military's inventories." Restitution for that, plus interest and associated costs, came to $3 million. "Fine," I said, "we will pay that."

But in addition, Dale had pleaded guilty to fraud charges in the parallel criminal case that had been brought by the Department of Justice. And there we were assessed a fine of $1 million.

That was not in Janet Cook's jurisdiction, but I asked Avi to take the matter up with her anyway. "Ask her not to do that to us," I told him. "We'll pay the three million reimbursement; I'm even willing to pay more. The government will end up with more money. But they shouldn't give Vishay a fine. They'll be sending the wrong signal. In effect they'll be saying that Vishay has acted wrongly, whereas the truth is that we didn't know anything beforehand and we've bent over backward to clean it up."

But Janet Cook was not moved. "That isn't the way it works," she said. "If you had truly been involved in this and we caught you, the fine would have been more like fifty million dollars. This is an absolute minimum."

"But we're not guilty," we argued.

"I know you personally are not guilty, but Vishay is the owner. Vishay owns the Dale stock; therefore you assumed the responsibility. You don't want to accept it, get rid of Dale; it will become the next owner's responsibility. You want to keep Dale? Then pay the fine."

I was extremely upset about this $1 million, but it was hard to find fault with her logic. In the end I said, "You are right. We'll pay."

So we paid. We also got rid of a whole string of managers at Dale. We cleaned out the affected line, and we fixed it. In fact, when we first learned about what had gone on, we were able to rectify 90 percent of the problem in fifteen minutes' worth of discussion (though the rest took a half year to understand fully and undo).

•

The Dale situation was unfortunate. First of all, only one division had been involved. The rest of the company was clean. And even the components that division made rarely created problems in the field. In fact, by and large American military equipment works better than any other country's. Occasionally there are accidents, but overall the equipment functions superbly. So how does this happen if there is widespread cheating on testing?

The answer is that the design of components is generally excellent. But the regulations governing military equipment are draconian. To make sure equipment is 100 percent reliable, the Pentagon imposes such heavy testing requirements that it becomes extremely expensive and difficult to conform. Producers are prone to feel that in any event they know their components are working properly, so why should they perform these excessive and redundant tests? And then they find some way to short-circuit them, whether it is making up numbers, substituting tested parts, or some other device.

Of course, in doing these things they are guilty of fraud. Even though the parts themselves may be performing well, the producers are breaking the law. Instead of going to the military and saying, "Look, this requirement is stupid," then fighting for a year to get the testing procedures revised, they take matters into their own hands. It is easy, and the pressure to do it is enormous. Often top management's attitude is, "I don't need to know what is going on in testing, but I certainly don't want to lose sales because of the quality control program." The message they send is, "Do whatever you have to do." Over time the dishonesty is rationalized and gets embedded in the company's modus operandi.

The Dale cheating story was a case in point. Though the origins happened before our acquisition and the denouement didn't come till later, this is what we were eventually able to piece together. In 1980 Mepco, a Philips subsidiary, came out with a metal film resistor that had extremely high reliability. All the competitors in this particular area (including Dale) were already at a high reliability level: one failure per sixteen thousand parts tested for ten thousand hours. But suddenly Mepco announced a component that tested at zero failures per sixteen thousand parts. They guaranteed this product and put it on the market at the same price as the less reliable components of their competitors.

Dale started losing business to them right away. They badly needed to find a way to regain their competitiveness. But instead of working to match Mepco's performance, they decided to do it on paper, by cheating on their testing.

Then we stepped into the Dale cheating scandal. Carl Fritz and I and some of our other engineers took a careful look at the Dale product for which this reliability was being claimed, and we thought we could achieve the standard without cheating. We would have to improve production techniques in a number of specific areas, but we thought the reliability could be matched honestly. Of course, if we were not able to do it, it would be hard to understand how Mepco was doing it.

So we went to work and we found out that we could indeed match the higher standard. It took us a year, during which we suffered losses in sales—all of it to Mepco. But in that time we managed to equal the performance and we began winning customers back. Then came the shock: The government launched an investigation of Mepco's resistor division for cheating and suspended them, which put them out of business.

To me, the true moral of the story was not only that honesty is good policy. It also was that the American military's policy of self-policing should be changed. Self-policing may be less expensive for the military, but I do not think that is the reason we have this system. The government rarely looks for the cheapest way to do something. On the contrary, they typically love to create additional bureaucracies, and a bureaucracy to test electronics would fit right into this tendency. But I think that in this instance the rationale is a philosophical one. Somehow, the underlying American devotion to self-reliance got itself manifested in this arcane area of the nation's economic life.

But while the honor system may be commendable philosophically, in practice it is destructive. The system incites people to cheat. Controls are necessary in this industry, but we are not practicing an effective method of control. In France, the military tests components. In England, testing is handled by independent laboratories. My sense is that cheating is far less common in those countries. I cannot speak for the military industry as a whole in the United States, but I can say that in the electronics components sector almost every company that we looked at during acquisition or due diligence examinations had violations problems. From what I could see, cheating looked endemic.

For ourselves, as part of the Dale resolution we established an ethics program. At Janet Cook's urging we looked at other companies that had been down this road, then we set up procedures. Vishay had always had a strong ethos of integrity, but the company had grown eightfold in the past few years. It was time to institutionalize that ethos.

Janet Cook was utterly uncompromising when it came to enforcing the law. But she was also considerate and helpful, especially in light of our ignorance about these matters. With her advice, the first thing I did was establish an ethics committee that would operate independently of any production unit and independently of me. I put Avi Eden and Bill Spires (Vishay's chief of human resources, another individual I trusted implicitly) on the committee along with Carl Fritz, whom I appointed corporate vice president for ethics. Together they wrote a code of business conduct that was read by every employee in all our companies. The last page was a personal sign-up card on which employees had to agree to conduct their business lives according to our standards. We also installed an 800 number ethics hotline that went directly to Carl's desk. Employees knew that he had direct access to me and that he had no numbers to make and no ax to grind. If they didn't feel comfortable going to their supervisor or personnel manager, they could call him directly with their concerns. That gave people who might be under pressure from superiors a chance to air problems confidentially.

Once all this was done, Carl gave talks in every division of each of our companies. Every employee from managers down heard him explain the ethics program and describe the kinds of sins that had been committed in the past. He told them why it was important to the company and why the company wouldn't tolerate cheating on any level. "We don't want it, we don't need it, we'll fire you if you do it"—that was the short form, that and "we will help the government bring criminal charges against you." (Since then, all new employees have received the same presentation, as have all employees of new acquisitions.)

I wanted to send two strong messages. One was that we were eager for military business. Vishay had established a record of integrity, and we would bend over backward to maintain it. The second was the message it sent inside the company. When a company is caught cheating, it is a signal that this is the way the management does business, this is what their ethics are like. In effect, management is telling the employees that they are part of a corrupt culture, and this in turn has consequences for their own sense of doing things right or wrong in their work. When a manager acts improperly, it infects the entire organization.

This was a subject I had been thinking about for years, ever since I had worked for the Budd Company. While I was research director, Mr. Budd himself had taught me a sharp lesson along exactly these lines.

The Budd company was a giant, doing $600 million a year thirty-five years ago, the equivalent of $6 billion or so today. At one point I had been studying a contract we had with another company, and I had noticed that under one particular interpretation Budd could make an additional $2 million. What I saw was not within the spirit of the contract, but nevertheless, there it was in black and white. When I checked my reading with our attorneys, they confirmed that I had discovered a loophole that could legitimately be exploited.

I went in to see Mr. Budd, armed with the contract and the lawyers' opinion. I was excited. In my view I had just made an additional $2 million for the company. But when I explained it to Mr. Budd, his face clouded over. "Felix," he said, "we aren't going to do that."

"Why not? It's two million dollars."

"Please, I'm not going to discuss it. We just aren't going to do that!"

When I pressed a little more, Budd got angry. "This subject is closed," he said.

Afterward, I thought about that a great deal. How should I have approached it, and what did it mean? How was it that a big businessman like Mr. Budd would turn down an absolutely legal $2 million?

After a while I began to think that Mr. Budd was right.

One danger for him was that taking that money under false pretenses (my interpretation was definitely not within the intent of the contract) would have been bad for his reputation. Avoiding that was no doubt worth a good deal more than $2 million to him.

But after a lot of reflection I began to understand that there was a greater danger. Suppose he had taken up my suggestion. What would I myself have thought of Mr. Budd? I would have thought that in fact this is what you should do, this is how the Budd Company operates. As a result, I would have been looking for more situations of that sort. I would have had my eye out for how to take advantage of those with whom we did business. And in doing that I would have corrupted those around me.

Mr. Budd had not said that in so many words. But I came to the lasting conclusion that the first and most significant danger of a situation like that is that a superior will corrupt the people under him. They see that he will take advantage under false pretenses. They will believe that is the company's ethos, and before long they will be looking to take advantage for themselves. For the so-called good of the company, the superior will corrupt the whole organization. As the Yiddish proverb had it, a fish stinks from the head down.

Mr. Budd's approach to this question struck me deeply, in part because I had never considered questions of business ethics in such a light. I came out of the ghetto, out of the German occupation, out of Poland, where the operative rule of conduct was *a qui vive*—who will survive. I did whatever I could to save my life. If I had to steal, I would; if I had to cheat, I would. After the war, I smuggled. Sender smuggled for a living; that was how we fed ourselves. Life was of primary importance. We did what we had to.

That had nothing to do with my early moral training, of course. Tema had been such a powerful model, and my father was without a doubt the single most honest person I had ever come across. He seemed congenitally incapable of seeing shades in the truth. His honesty would sometimes rattle your bones (how often had I wondered why he couldn't have been a little more willing to bend). I was so fortunate to have been brought up in an atmosphere suffused by Jewish moral teaching, where discussion and debate and argument over right and wrong were daily bread.

But that was all before the Nazis descended and the world changed. Nothing I experienced in Poland after that gave me a healthy perspective on business ethics. In fact, it had the opposite effect. Nor had I learned anything different in France, where my business experience had been so limited I had never faced anything I identified as a moral problem. In Poland saving your life might have been primary, but in Philadelphia I was not dealing with issues of life and death. There it was a matter of conducting normal affairs among normal people. Other standards applied. I had to readjust my horizons.

Being exposed to people like Mr. Budd and Frank Tatnall, Jim Starr, and Alfred Slaner, I began to think in a different way. In a sense they brought me back to something like the ethics of my father. They were all businessmen, but each one was also in his own way a strict moralist. At first they seemed a little naive to me. But as I thought about them, I found myself saying, What do you mean, "naive"? These people are not idiots. Look how rich this country is. So much richer, for example, than Brazil, which is almost as big and has better resources. So why is Brazil a Third World country and the United States has developed as it has? That was a complicated issue, no doubt. But to a foreigner getting his first look at American business culture, it was obvious there was something different going on here. Who are the people who have done it? I asked myself. Who are the business leaders, and how do they think? How do they conduct themselves? How should a society function ethically in order to survive and grow?

And there I was, immersed by chance in the Budd Company, part of the old-line Quaker business culture of Philadelphia. Mr. Budd and Frank Tatnall were both practicing Quakers—straight, honest people. But it wasn't just Quakers. Jim Starr, a man

of unshakable integrity, was raised Catholic, and Alfred Slaner Jewish—from the New York apparel trade, no less, but just as rigidly
honest as any Quaker. (Alfred used to tell me that he never lost
sleep over money decisions. But if something he had done might
have hurt someone—that would keep him up at night.)

Their values, like my father's, were the values I tried
hard to assimilate myself, and that I wanted to incorporate into
Vishay. Alfred was a special influence. At one point shortly after I
founded Vishay I was involved in a situation where an independent distributor we hired had paid us $200,000 as a guarantee for
sales. Over the period of our association I had used the $200,000.
But eventually they were unable to fulfill the terms of engagement,
and we terminated the relationship.

Shortly afterward they came to me, trying to get the
money back. Didn't the contract say they would make their "best
effort"? they asked.

"Yes."

"And didn't we make our best effort?"

"Yes."

"Then why did you take the guarantee?"

"Because you weren't successful. You didn't fulfill the
contract."

"But if it was our best effort—and that's in the contract,
too—then please reimburse the money to us."

Alfred Slaner was my sounding board. "Alfred," I said,
"here's the two hundred thousand I owe those guys. We have it. It's
ours. We have them by the balls, but to tell the truth, I don't feel
good about it. I would like to reimburse them. What do you
think?" And he said, "That's absolutely what must be done. Reimburse them." I had no doubt that would have been Mr. Budd's answer, too, and that was what we did.

When Vishay was young, I was invited to a talk given to
the Israeli military by renowned archeologist and former commander in chief Yigal Yadin. The subject of Yadin's lecture was: Given
that Israel will always be a tiny country surrounded by enemies

who are bigger and richer, what doctrine should the army follow to best ensure the nation's survival?

Yadin used as his jumping-off point the biblical story of Gideon's battle with the far more numerous Moabites. He talked about the rigorous selection process Gideon used to choose his fighters. Then he discussed Gideon's timing, organization, tactics, and weaponry. It came down to five key elements, he said: leadership, motivation, special weapons, coordination, and one other factor: clean hands. That was of special importance. To function at its best, the army had to have ultimate pride in itself, which came from understanding that it was part of a moral endeavor.

I was impressed. I thought it was deep and well done. While Yadin was talking I was thinking, I have a similar situation in business. Vishay is a small company surrounded by large companies. Competition is fierce. Of course, it's not a matter of life or death, as it is for Israel, but nevertheless there are similarities. And strangely enough, everything that Yadin developed was applicable to Vishay, down to and including his emphasis on clean hands.

What we saw at Dale (and with our later acquisitions) was that as soon as we cleaned out the improprieties, the entire company became stronger. I took pleasure in watching that happen, and our people took pleasure in it. The ordinary people at Dale—the line workers and first-level supervisors—had hated the cheating and dishonesty. They knew that what they were doing was wrong, and they were sick about it. It was a tremendous relief to them that we were able to rectify the situation. It was like opening the window and letting the fresh air in.

Before it was all over I let Gaines—Novicki's successor—retire. The Office of Contract Integrity debarred Novicki, Gaines, and three other managers personally—prohibiting them from working for any company that did business with the military. The government did not accuse any of them of personal involvement in the cheating, but it had gone on during their watch and they were considered responsible whether or not they had known about it. (Novicki appealed his debarment and succeeded in having it overturned.) In Gaines's place I took Don Alfson, the youngest of the Dale executive staff, but exceptionally capable, someone I had found to be highly trustworthy as I got to know Dale and its people better.

Alfson turned Dale around. He restructured the rest of Novicki's staff. Other people resigned left and right. The entire top level was replaced, and Dale became a different company. He gave a straightforward, no-fooling-around tone to the endeavor, and the whole spirit at Dale changed.

Alfson was able to do that because he knew the company intimately. It was something that would probably have been beyond my ability when I bought Dale. If I want to analyze the mistakes I made initially, it was that my assessment of the Dale staff was incorrect. If I had had a clearer understanding I never would have bought the company; it would have seemed too difficult to change the whole upper level of management. If I had said to myself—to manage Dale properly I will have to fire the entire top level of management, I would have had to think it over a hundred times. After all, the management had made Dale a major player. At least that was what it looked like. But the fact was that they had not made Dale the power it was. The workers had done that, the workers and the middle management. Not understanding that, I probably would not have bought the company, which, of course, would have been to Vishay's great detriment.

Among his other accomplishments, Don Alfson was able to turn around the problems at Dimona. He went to Israel and stayed there until he understood the situation; then he did what was necessary to coordinate the two operations. He showed the Dale managers how Israel would work to their advantage and made them understand that it was their responsibility; he forged a new relationship. Very quickly the Dale lines at Dimona started to function smoothly. Dimona began to achieve an entirely new level of efficiency, which was especially fortunate, because I was already exploring moves that would put a far greater burden on the Israelis.

WITH Novicki gone and Dale straightened out, I found myself with plenty of energy. By now we had had substantial experience in takeovers. Avi had become a master at structuring deals, and we had developed close friendships on Wall Street. It was a time when junk bonds were the financing method of choice for leveraged buyouts, but I had no interest in that market, with its high interest rates. All of our financing was solid and conservative.

By this time we were closely involved with the Wall Street house of Bear, Stearns. My dear friend Philadelphia stockbroker Jack Hirsh had originally taken us public, in 1972. Jack had been on our board and he and his wife, Sophie, were among the people we felt closest to. Sophie was an unusual person in her own right, warm and cultured as well as strikingly beautiful. She and Ruta had taken to each other instantly and had become almost like sisters.

At first Jack had worked at Drexel Burnham; then he had switched over to Bache, and we had gone with him. In 1980 we went to the market again, this time with an issue of convertible bonds. As a stock salesman, Jack was not involved in this offering, so Alfred and I decided to split it between Bache and Bear, Stearns, where one of Alfred's contacts was Ace Greenberg, Bear, Stearns's president.

When the evening of the offering came, Bache's bond people were obviously unhappy with the way the pricing was shaping up. Before long it became clear that they wanted either to postpone the issue or cancel it altogether, which was making me increasingly nervous (a failed offering has terrible consequences for a company). When Ace Greenberg saw what was happening he turned to me, his face flushed with anger. "What the hell is this?" he said. "They don't want it? Forget it. I'll take the whole issue myself." With a few words we made a deal and Bear, Stearns bought the entire offering. "Ace," I said, "I have the memory of an elephant. This is something you will not regret."

Since then Ace Greenberg had handled all of our public offerings (he still does). Our relationship quickly developed to the point where we could and did take care of everything over the phone; I had found him a person of utter trustworthiness as well as great professional acumen. With his backing and advice, and with our own growing expertise, we were positioned for more acquisitions.

By this time Vishay had achieved a strong place in the worldwide resistor market. With Draloric, Sfernice, and Dale, we had about a third of the American market and 40 percent or so of the European market. Given the strength of our position, I felt there wasn't much room to expand. We could maintain our share and perhaps increase it some, but if we were going to continue to look for rapid growth, it would have to be in another field where we could bring our expertise to bear.

The other field that beckoned was capacitors, one of the three major types of passive electronic components. Capacitors constituted the largest market in passive components, and also the fastest-growing market. For some time we had been under pressure from customers looking for broader ranges of products from our vendors (resistors, capacitors, and inductors were typically used together in circuits). If we had capacitors, we could utilize many of our skills in producing resistors. We could use the same marketing and the same sales force. It seemed a natural direction to move in, and in 1990 we decided to make a major move. From now on Vishay would not be just a resistor company, but a passive components company as well.

When we began assessing likely capacitor companies, two caught our attention: Kemet and Sprague. Both were for sale, and both were good candidates. We finally decided to pursue Sprague, primarily because Kemet already had a large offshore operation in Mexico, while Sprague's manufacturing was still located entirely in the United States. With Sprague there would be a significant opportunity to cut costs by relocating certain production lines in Israel. To combat the lower labor costs of Kemet and other competitors, Sprague had invested heavily in the very finest machinery and automation. Even without an offshore facility, they were doing an excellent job of maintaining their share of the market. How good would they be, I thought, if in addition to what they were already doing, they also went offshore?

It was interesting to see how our offshore operations were working out, especially in light of the attention that movement of jobs away from the United States was getting. Before we acquired Dale, they had opened a large plant in Mexico, and subsequently we had moved several production lines to Israel. Yet Dale's employment in Nebraska and South Dakota was rising. In fact, in the regions where Dale was the largest employer, the unemployment rate was approaching zero. The same thing had happened at our Malvern plant. After we moved production to Israel, employment there had doubled.

This apparent paradox wasn't really a paradox at all. In the first place, the jobs that were lost in the United States were jobs that could not be held here in any event. They were jobs that had to do with older products that were not competitive, that were a drain on resources. Transferring that production offshore turned those lines into moneymakers that strengthened our companies and allowed us to apply heavy pressure to our competitors. As we squeezed out the competition, we had greater resources available to open new product lines and develop or acquire the most up-to-date equipment, which made us even more competitive. What was good for the offshore companies was also good for the United States, though perhaps not so good for our Japanese and other adversaries.

•

Before we opened our pursuit of Sprague, though, Vishay was shaken by a piece of terrible personal news. One day I got a call from Ray Fridley, senior vice president at the Measurements Group in North Carolina and a close friend of Jim Starr's. Ray was crying on the phone. He had gotten a call from Jim's wife, Brenda, he said. Jim had just died of a massive heart attack.

A number of years earlier, Jim Starr had gone into semi-retirement in the town of Little River, California, not far from Mendocino. His health, unfortunately, was deteriorating, and he had no longer felt able to run the business. Aware of the severity of his problems, Jim had groomed a successor, Hank Landau, who was running the Measurements Group skillfully. Now emphysema was ravaging Jim's lungs, slowly swallowing up the relentless energy he had always brought to everything he did. In a beautiful house overlooking the Pacific, he carried on with his research and took charge of special projects. The ocean air had helped him breathe.

The next day, Ruta and I flew to California, where we joined Ray and a few of Jim's other good friends. Jim had wanted any funeral to be small and private. Though he had been raised Catholic he had left the church and wanted no religious observances. He had asked to be cremated. His ashes he wanted strewn into the Pacific.

I found it unnerving, sitting in the fishing boat we rented holding the urn with Jim's ashes in my hands. Jim had been with me at the beginning of Vishay, almost three decades before. Although technically he had worked for me, I had always considered him a partner. I remembered that at the beginning he had signed a one-year contract, but neither of us had ever looked at it after that. He was brilliant technically, and despite our differences in approach he had given the Measurements Group wonderfully effective leadership.

But the real inspiration he provided went deeper than that. Jim had an utterly independent mind; he was extraordinary in that way. He had been my sounding board on many issues, so much so that when I was faced with difficult problems, I regularly thought about what his assessment would be. My solutions weren't necessarily his solutions, but he had made a place for himself in my mental world. I was thinking about that when we scattered the ashes overboard, then dropped roses into the choppy sea after them.

•

Sprague had been, and in some ways still was, a remarkable company. It was no exaggeration to say that they were the biggest name in components; the entire electronics industry knew Sprague's products well. As much as anyone, R. C. Sprague, the founder, had given the electronics business its start.

In 1926 Dr. Sprague had invented the ceramic capacitor, a component that, like the resistor, was invaluable for the fine tuning of electric circuits. Among other things, capacitors allowed for filtering wave frequencies, which made radio tuners possible, also telephone receivers, and later television receivers. He invented the multilayer technique for capacitors; then he invented the tantalum technique. Almost anything that had to do with the technology of capacitors had been invented by Dr. Sprague. Then he had started to produce resistors, too, then transistors. He went everywhere. If there was a market that had to do with electronic components, he was in it.

But more recently the company had seen its share of trouble. When R. C. Sprague retired, he was succeeded by his son John, a physicist who had also acquired an M.B.A. But despite his training, John Sprague had made mistakes. In the mid-1960s he invested heavily in semiconductors. Competition from both American and Japanese manufacturers was fierce, and the company was not adequately capitalized to withstand the pressure. Losses mounted into the hundreds of millions of dollars.

Staggering under successive financial blows, Sprague was sold to General Cable, which was itself subsequently acquired by the Penn Central Railroad. Penn Central then spun Sprague off as a separate entity controlled by Carl Lindner, a financier from Cincinnati who controlled a major block of shares. As Sprague underwent its changes, the company shed resistors, then transistors, then inductors.

But they were still the world's largest producer of tantalum capacitors. Made from a rare earth metal, tantalum capacitors are the most expensive, yet the smallest as well as the best in performance within certain limits. They are used widely in automobiles, computers, radios, telephones, televisions, and a large range of other electronic equipment. Sprague was still huge: They were doing about $230 million per year in sales and had four thousand employees. When we began analyzing their production lines, it became clear that moving five hundred jobs to Israel would simultaneously improve Sprague's profits, make the company more competitive worldwide, and strengthen its American operations.

But already our Dimona plant was operating at near capacity. Transferring some of Sprague's production would mean building a second plant. That was an exciting prospect by itself—especially since now the immigration of Soviet Jews to Israel was under way in earnest. Dimona had always had a problem getting trained technical employees. But the new Soviet immigrants were looking for work, and I would have good jobs to offer. I could almost see the bricks being laid.

Five years earlier, our discussions with the Finance Ministry and the Bank of Israel about opening our first Dimona plant had been protracted and sometimes rough, despite Finance Minister Yitzhak Modai's quick grasp of the issues. But now we had years of success behind us. Originally I had promised Modai that in five years we would be providing five hundred jobs and doing $30 million a year in export. Now, five years later, we had five hundred employees and were doing slightly over $30 million. With that as background, Modai was eager to smooth the path for this new facility.

"But this time I'd like to ask you to do something different," I told him. "We plan to buy Sprague, and if we do, I will want to hire an additional five hundred people in Dimona. What I would like from the government, in addition to the usual thirty-eight percent grant for equipment, is a ten percent reduction in taxes. If you could do that, I could guarantee the five hundred jobs."

Modai was amenable. We would be bringing in capital from abroad, investing the money in Israel, providing employment. All that was positive. He also knew that our approach wasn't as risky as the more typical Israeli venture into research and development and the creation of new products, which then had to find new markets. Vishay was in the business of buying existing markets—in this case, the worldwide tantalum capacitor market. Sprague already had its products and distribution networks, just as Dale and Draloric had theirs. That's why I could guarantee jobs. Nor would I be competing against homegrown industries for the local market, which is so often a problem for foreign firms coming into new countries everywhere. "That's fine," said Modai. "I agree. What you're proposing makes tremendous sense for us. But doing it the way you're proposing would be difficult because the standard equipment grant is tied by regulation to the tax structure. To give you a tax reduction, we'd have to amend the regulations. We could do that, but it might be a lengthy process." It would be easier, he said, to substitute a jobs grant for the standard equipment grant. The cost to the government would be the same, and that way the regulations wouldn't preclude a tax reduction.

•

With the way cleared in Israel, I moved the Sprague negotiations toward a conclusion. But before signing anything, I was determined to do a thorough quality control audit. The close call over Dale's testing violations had made me a skeptic; after that, I had sworn never again to touch a company without first making sure they conformed completely to the military's requirements. When I told Sprague's management I wanted to examine their procedures, they had no objection. "You're welcome to look at whatever you want," they said.

Until the Dale surprise broke, the very idea of cheating on government testing had been outside our scope of vision. We knew it happened in the industry from time to time, but if we thought at all about the incidents that became public, it was to dismiss them as anomalies. Before Dale we had been strangers to the Pentagon's machinery of enforcement and judgment. But we had become veterans fast. By the time Carl Fritz went into Sprague's plants in Maine and New Hampshire, he knew just where to look. And looking, he found. In some divisions he uncovered a pattern of misreporting that went back decades and was so pervasive it had even been built into the quality control computer programs.

When I got Carl's report I went back to Sprague and told them that the operation wasn't clean. "You've got serious problems," I told Ed Kosnick, Sprague's president. "It's not right, and we aren't buying. The deal's off."

"I don't believe you," he said. "What you're saying isn't possible."

"You don't have to believe me. Send your lawyers with Carl Fritz to take a look, or send whomever you want. I don't care; I know my man. If he tells me he found something, you can believe he found it."

A few days later, Carl went back into the plants along with Gus duPont, Sprague's attorney. They were planning to take two days together and make a thorough investigation. But toward the end of the first day duPont called. He had seen all he needed. "It isn't good," he said. "There's no point in spending any more time on it."

Sprague's management was in a panic. It looked to me as if they had not been aware of what had been going on; most of them were professional managers from Penn Central who knew relatively little about components in the first place. The misreporting that we found had been going on since long before they arrived—it had become an unremarkable standard operating procedure. Now all of a sudden they had been hit by this bolt from the blue (I knew the feeling), and a $120 million deal was slipping out from under them. "Tell us what to do," they said. "We'll do anything you want."

One procedure we had learned about through Janet Cook's office was called "voluntary disclosure," whereby companies that brought violations to the Pentagon's attention were given a chance to rectify them without being subjected to criminal prosecution.

"You have to go to the military and disclose everything up front," I told the Sprague managers. But even in their state of shock, that sounded extreme.

"That's crazy," they said. "We have lawyers. We'll have them look at it and come up with the best way of handling this."

"You do that with your lawyers. Do what you want. But you will not see Vishay. We will go away. If you do what we tell you to do, you have a chance that nothing will happen. Do it your way and God knows what the outcome will be."

I gave them a detailed description of Mepco, the resistor division of Philips that the government had accused of fraudulent reliability claims. Mepco was deeply immersed in penalty and debarment proceedings. They were on the verge of being wiped out. "That's exactly what's likely to happen to you," I said, "if you don't do what I'm telling you."

After some consideration, they agreed to do it. We laid out the procedures for them, and they went to the Special Agency for Criminal Investigation at the Pentagon. "We have found after internal investigation that one of our divisions has been in violation," they reported. And they disclosed everything.

The immediate result was that all Sprague's shipping to the military was suspended. But since they had come in on voluntary disclosure, the Defense Department did not institute punitive action. During the suspension, they were obligated to root out the problems thoroughly. But the Pentagon knew we were behind this, and the situation worked itself out without complications. After the Dale experience, Janet Cook and her colleagues trusted us to do what was necessary.

Because a proceeding of this sort could damage a company's business, the SEC required that stockholders be informed.

As a result, Sprague's voluntary disclosure became public knowledge. Shortly after this happened, the financial press reported that the capacitor division of Philips was also filing a voluntary disclosure. When we saw this in the newspaper we knew exactly what it meant. Philips had never done such a thing before; then suddenly one week after Sprague did it, they turned around and did it, too. It seemed an obvious attempt at damage containment.

Apparently the government thought so, too. Philips's resistor division had been suspended earlier. Why had their capacitor unit not come in on a voluntary disclosure at that time? It threw a questionable light on their intent. And in fact, when the Pentagon regulators looked into it, they found more than was being disclosed.

Philips's problem was that they were assembling components in the Dominican Republic, where it was cheaper, even though the regulations prohibited manufacturing outside the United States. As was often the case in testing violations, their components were good quality. There were no complaints from their customers; no accidents were taking place in the field. But there was also no question that they were cheating, and the government came down hard.

When the smoke cleared, Philips was facing fines in the tens of millions, and the capacitor division was suspended. The annual sales of this $40-million to $45-million-a-year business plunged to $16 million. Not only did they lose their military contracts, but a black cloud formed over their commercial business. In the end only a few customers remained, together with their business in the Far East, which was not affected. In essence they lost their entire American operation.

I was informed about this because as Philips lost customers, their competitors (Sprague among them) picked them up. But my real firsthand knowledge came after a phone call I got from Dennis Horowitz, the Philips capacitor division president, asking to meet me in Atlanta. He turned out to be straightforward and friendly, despite the fact that he was suffering the tortures of the damned as he watched his company plunge toward oblivion. Philips had brought him in from another unit to straighten out the situation. "I cleaned it up," he told me, "but look what happened." Because of the past, all his efforts hadn't mattered. He wanted to sell the division.

I had our evaluation teams look into it. The situation was interesting, but I told Horowitz I couldn't make an offer just then. I was too busy with Sprague, and another very large possibility had just come up in Germany. He mentioned that a potential Japanese buyer was looking at it. He'd get back to me later.

The Sprague acquisition went smoothly. After our analysis, we realized we would be able to make use of the line managers but not the top-level management, and we told them that up front. We unified the sales departments and the computer and accounting operations. We started consolidating everything that could be consolidated.

In order to accommodate the Sprague lines in Israel, we were planning to expand into the unused second half of our 350,000-square-foot Dimona plant. But just as we were preparing the expansion a violent, freak snowstorm hit the Negev. Before we had opened up the first half of Dimona we had reinforced the roof in order to support the air-conditioning equipment. But the unused part of the facility had not been reinforced and under the massive weight of snow the roof of this part collapsed, making the space unusable.

In its place we built Dimona Number Two, an ultramodern, one-hundred-fifty-square-foot facility to which we immediately moved some of Sprague's production. That brought our total employment in Israel to more than a thousand. As we expected, our labor problems in out-of-the-way Dimona were mostly solved by the Russian immigrants. Attracting enough technical people there had been a real problem before, but now we were knee deep in engineers. We hired them and sent them in groups of twenty for two months' training at Beersheba University. When they came back they were ready to specialize in our areas of production.

As production increased in Israel, I also pushed our effort to persuade the U.S. Department of Defense that Israeli-made products should be permitted to qualify for the American military's coveted "ER," or "Established Reliability" rating. As it was, in Israel we were producing components under commercial specifications, but in fact they met the far more stringent ER requirements. To qualify for the ER rating, though, American regulations required that parts be produced and tested entirely within the United States. If DOD would accept Israeli-made parts, it would open up significant new business possibilities for Vishay as well as for other Israel-based companies. So far, our campaign had not borne fruit, but I was determined to press the case.*

I loved Dimona. I loved the fact that it was good for the company and good for Israel. It meant more to me personally than anyone other than Ruta knew. Of course, many American companies were locating offshore, in places such as Mexico, Taiwan, and Korea. But I didn't speak Spanish, Chinese, or Korean; I didn't know the people or the local business cultures. Most often, American companies going into foreign lands bring in their own American managers. But I didn't like that approach; I didn't feel comfortable with making foreign employees into second-class corporate citizens. Local companies, I believed, should be managed by local people.

But I did know the Israelis. I knew their skills and their mores. I also knew that if you want to succeed you have to be involved personally, and I couldn't see myself getting involved personally in someplace like Taiwan. But Israel was another story

---

*The upshot was that in 1994, after almost fourteen years of effort, Israel was accepted as an Established Reliability supplier. In 1994 also, Vishay contributed to another long-term goal of mine—breaking the so-called Big Eight accounting firms' apparent compliance with the Arab boycott against Israel. While the Big Eight firms never admitted to obeying the boycott, none of them had branches in Israel, although their worldwide networks embraced many obscure countries with business sectors a fraction the size of Israel's. Partly due to our discussions with CEO Phillip Laskowy, Ernst & Young, the largest of the Eight, for the first time opened offices in Tel Aviv. They were shortly followed by most of their competitors, a development that has opened a major conduit of world trade to Israeli companies.

altogether. In Israel I could be happily involved up to my ears. Every time I went there I felt I was going home.

•

In early 1991, while we were negotiating for Sprague, Draloric's Werner Statler and Gerald Paul were talking to me about our competition in Germany. They argued that the time had come to make a strategic acquisition there that would strengthen Draloric's position in the resistor market. As a result, we had begun looking at several possibilities, but nothing had really jelled. Then, in the middle of the year Statler called with news: Roederstein Electronics was in trouble.

Roederstein was a giant, the largest component maker in Europe, a company with a spectrum of technologies and sales of close to $300 million a year. The company, Statler said, was very sick. They had been laying off people and trying to restructure, but apparently without much success. Rumors were floating around that they might be near bankruptcy.

Roederstein had been founded back in the 1920s, at about the same time that R. C. Sprague was starting up his firm in the United States. The founder had died, leaving the business to his son, Dr. Hans Georg Roederstein, who had built the company into a power. World War II had ruined them, but afterward Dr. Roederstein had started up again and had built the company even bigger than it had been before.

One problem, Statler said, was that back in 1945, when Dr. Roederstein was rebuilding, he had promised his workers that if they went along with his plans he would never lay anyone off. All these years he had stuck to his vow, despite the immense changes that had taken place in the company and the industry. In recent times the policy had caught up with him dramatically. He had tried to make changes, opening up offshore operations in Portugal, but it was too little, too late.

In the middle of his desperate attempts to restructure, Dr. Roederstein had become ill with cancer. To help him manage, in the last years of his life the old man had taken his two sons, Jorg and Til, into the business. Til, a lawyer, was given responsibility for production at the German plants. Jorg was put in charge of the plants in Portugal, the facility in the United States, and all marketing.

To compound Roederstein's problems, the two sons didn't get along. They talked to each other no more than necessary. They were also young and inexperienced, vastly unprepared to meet the life-and-death challenges the company was facing. Even while the father was alive, the company's banks were getting nervous. The elder Roederstein had taken on substantial additional debt to pay for start-up costs in Portugal and layoff costs in Germany. With the company in straits, the banks had been unwilling to provide normal long-term financing to meet these costs, and all the new money was in the form of demand loans. Now Portugal wasn't generating the profits the company had needed. In fact, recently Portugal had begun to lose money. Roederstein was in peril.

On that note the father had died. Unwilling to leave the two inexperienced sons in charge, the banks brought in a management consulting firm—Hayek, from Switzerland—to run the company. Then, because there was no one knowledgeable on top of production, they forced the brothers to hire a technical man, Dr. Bauer from ITT. Bauer had a good reputation, but he was not well versed in the components industry. Now, instead of two people who weren't talking, Roederstein was being run by four people who weren't talking. The whole enterprise was going nowhere fast. The products were still first class, and the company's high reputation among customers had not yet suffered, but the top management was a disaster area. Roederstein was hemorrhaging money.

The Roederstein division that was competing with Draloric was called Resista. Resista made metal film resistors and also commercial thick film chip resistors in which they were beginning to compete with the Japanese. This was a technology I was quite interested in acquiring. Roederstein's thick film chips were extremely reliable and precise—better than those of their Japanese competitors. I looked at that and I marveled. I wanted it for Vishay.

Thick film resistor chips were used in masses in all kinds of entertainment equipment, computers, automobiles, telephones, and many other products. They were sold at a very low price— about $4 a thousand—but they were used by the billions, and the market was growing almost vertically. The problem was that Roederstein's high manufacturing costs made their chips just barely competitive. But I knew that if I put the production into Israel they would soon become quite competitive.

Resista looked like an excellent acquisition. At $20 million in annual sales it was a nice, manageable size, and it offered good potential synergies with our other German operations. Roederstein could spin Resista off to us and use the money to shore up their main capacitor business. We on our part could transfer some of the production to Israel and merge the rest with Draloric, doubling, tripling, or even quadrupling profit.

Toward the end of 1991 I went to Germany to talk to the young brothers Roederstein. They wanted to sell and retained the London branch of Lazard Frères to represent them. We negotiated a price, prepared the takeover, and in short order we had the structure of a deal.

I was happy to have done with so that quickly. All the pieces fit. Werner Statler was just in the process of retiring, but I had no doubt that Dr. Paul would handle the consolidation expertly and that Israel could incorporate Resista's lines of production. The whole thing was hardly more than a minor distraction from my ongoing effort to work out a deal with Penn Central for Sprague.

But the smooth sailing ended abruptly. On Friday, shortly after we had reached agreement with Lazard Frères, I received a telephone call from Til Roederstein. Something urgent had come up. Could he and his banker fly to Philadelphia to meet with me? Would Sunday be all right?

On Sunday morning I was sitting down with Til and a

Lazard Frères man at Philadelphia's Four Seasons Hotel listening to them tell me they couldn't sell Resista to me after all.

"What's going on?" I asked. "Didn't we agree on this already?"

"Of course, and we want to go ahead with it. But our banks won't let us."

"What business is it of your banks?"

"They've told us that if we go ahead with this sale they'll call all the demand notes. Resista is the strongest unit we have. They're afraid that selling it off will weaken the company too much. As far as they're concerned, we either sell off everything or nothing. They also say that if we want to sell everything, they have a buyer for us."

The preferred buyer, Til said, was someone named Schoeller. His company was Gesellschaft Synergy Management. I had never heard of either the man or the company. Neither had anyone at Roederstein. I was doubly shocked when I heard the purchase price the banks were dictating: 5 million Deutsche marks, about $3.5 million, for this $300-million-a-year company.

"What?" I said. I hardly believed my ears. "Five million for the whole thing?"

"We have a lot of debt," said Til Roederstein. "But it's worse than that. The banks are saying that if we don't sell to Schoeller for five million, they'll liquidate us."

I listened in silence. "Dr. Zandman," said Til, "please take over Roederstein for the same five million marks. I prefer you to do it rather than them. At least I'm sure you will maintain the name. We know exactly what they'll do. They'll sell off the real estate, then declare bankruptcy. So I'm asking you now to buy the whole company."

I said, "Look, I can't do it just like that. We'd have to go through a complete evaluation. It's a detailed process."

"Please buy the company, Dr. Zandman. Or at least give us an indication that you are going to buy it."

It was obvious he was really suffering. And this was

tempting. Roederstein had tantalum capacitors that were competing with Sprague in addition to resistors, which we wanted to buy
anyhow. They also had film capacitors, another technology I was
interested in. But this wasn't the right time. We were heavily involved in finishing the Sprague deal; there were a host of issues
outstanding. We just didn't have the strength for it. How could I
take over two major companies at the same time? On the other
hand, I thought, maybe our German team could do this takeover
on their own. Gerald Paul was a talented manager. Roederstein was
hugely tempting. If only I could put it off a bit.

"If you can wait another year," I said, "I'll be extremely
interested for sure. But right now I'm only after the resistors."

"Another year?" said Til. "I don't know if I can wait another week."

"Well, if that's really the case, there's not much I can do
about it. The best I can promise is that I'll send our evaluation
teams out to look. If we eventually do decide to buy sometime
down the line, of course we'll pay off the banks, refinance, and
so on."

After some more discussion I borrowed a piece of tablet
paper from the Four Seasons maître d' and wrote out a protocol
saying that we intended to buy the company at some later date
provided we found certain things satisfactory. It left us plenty of
room to get out, and maybe it would give Til Roederstein enough
room to get us in. With this protocol he could at least go back to
his banks and show them that a legitimate buyer was in the wings.
He could ask for time, which was what I needed to give this step
full consideration.

The meeting lasted from Sunday morning until late afternoon, and right afterward Til and the Lazard Frères man left for
the airport. On Monday morning I got a telephone call from Munich. It was Herr Schoeller from Gesellschaft Synergy Management. He introduced himself as the individual who had bought
Roederstein. As I listened in disbelief, Schoeller told me that he
had his arrangement with Roederstein's banks already worked out

and that he had an agreement of sale signed by the Roederstein brothers. Would I still be interested in buying the resistor division?

"Wait a minute," I said. "How can you have bought Roederstein? When did it happen, overnight? I just met with one of the brothers yesterday."

"We know that," said Schoeller. "The other brother told us. But the fact is that we already have an agreement in hand. We're taking it over, with the debt, of course. By the way, the debt is enormous. But do you still want Resista? We'd like to sell it to you."

"Look," I said. "I can't answer you. First of all, I don't do business over the telephone. Second, I don't know you. Besides, there's something not right here. I can't do business like this."

"Well, we need the answer right now, because after to-morrow it's not going to work. The price will be going up. Right now you can pay us the same thing you were going to pay them. We can make the deal by fax."

"Look, I just told you: I don't do deals like that. I don't understand what's going on. I talked to Til Roederstein yesterday. How could he propose something like that to me without telling me what's going on? Let me investigate. I'll let you know."

"I have a signed agreement of sale!" said Schoeller.

"I'll get back to you," I told him.

As soon as I hung up, I called Til Roederstein. "Did you sign an agreement with this person Schoeller?" I asked.

"Not really," he said. "It's not an agreement; it's a proto-col. We didn't do it in front of a notary public, so it's not binding in any way. It's just like a letter of intent. It's worthless."

I was boiling. "But why didn't you tell me about it? I mean, I saw you yesterday! I don't want to play around with you anymore. I'm washing my hands of the whole thing. You sat in front of me and you incited me to get involved in this, to sign a protocol. You were crying that you were going to be sold out. And here you already signed an agreement? This really stinks!"

"But it's not binding. It's not valid. It's just the beginning of negotiations."

"Even not valid. If you signed it, you should have told me about it. I can't deal with people who hide things behind their backs like that. How do you expect me to trust you?" And I hung up.

A moment later he called back, almost crying on the phone. "I'm sorry," he said. "I made a tremendous mistake. It was wrong of me. I'm a lawyer myself, I should have known better. But I'm inexperienced at these things. Please forgive me. This wasn't right. I understand it, and it's the last time anything like this will happen. Please. You can trust me."

"How about that banker from Lazard Frères, the stinker? He knew about it and he was sitting right next to you."

"Well, it wasn't his fault. He was there, but I was the boss. Please, I want you to continue as we discussed yesterday. Will you do that?"

"I'll give it some thought, but I have to tell you that from now on we're on a different footing. You're going to have to prove yourself."

"I promise you," Til Roederstein said, "from now on everything will be absolutely up front." And he was as good as his word. Then and later.

I also called Lazard Frères to give them hell. But despite all the shouting, within a few days our evaluation teams in marketing, manufacturing, and finance were on their way to Germany to join Werner Statler, Gerald Paul, Bob Freece, Dick Grubb, Avi, Hank Landau, and Glynn Smith. They moved fast, examining each of Roederstein's fifteen plants. In a week and a half we were absolutely sure we wanted this company.

But it wasn't a simple situation. Although Roederstein had not yet gone into bankruptcy, it was already insolvent. Their demand debt was $115 million, plus debt to suppliers who hadn't been paid in months. Creditors were knocking down the doors.

The company was losing money hand over fist. Their situation was so desperate they were now borrowing to meet payroll. Not surprisingly, their banks, led by the Bayerische Vereinsbank, wanted out. They saw an avalanche roaring down at them, and they were right. The only one at Roederstein they had any faith in was the Swiss consultant from Hayek they had forced the boys to take on. But as far as I could see, he wasn't making himself of much use either.

Once our evaluation was complete and I was sure we wanted the company, I decided to make a personal presentation to Bayerische Vereinsbank. First I sent Avi to prepare the way, then I went myself, to let them know about Vishay, give them some idea of our strength, and persuade them that we were the right people to take over the company. On the given day, I presented myself at their main office in Munich. I explained that we wanted to buy and that the Roedersteins did not want Schoeller, they wanted us. I expected them to say something like, "We don't care who it is, as long as our loans are secured," then maybe give some indication of their willingness to look at our refinancing plans. What I actually heard was, "You are Americans. We don't know you at all. We do know Schoeller, and we know they understand how to manage something like this."

"What?" I wasn't sure I had heard them right.

"Look," they said, "if Schoeller takes over the company, we aren't going to call the debt. You want to take over? Go ahead. We'll want the entire debt paid off at the same time."

I looked around the room. All I saw were set jaws and expressionless eyes. I had been in hostile atmospheres before, and there wasn't much question I was in one now. "You know I can't do that instantaneously," I said. "Give me some time."

"Okay," I heard, "take one week."

"You mean you are giving me one week to come up with a hundred and fifteen million dollars? I'm a new kid on the block. I only know this company from a professional point of view. We can't possibly restructure the debt that fast."

But not a word I said had the slightest discernible effect. Nothing doing. One week. That was it. I went back to Roederstein's headquarters and had them call the bank asking for a meeting the following Thursday, nine days away instead of seven. That was fine with them, they said, provided I brought a letter of credit along for $65 million (Bayerische Vereinsbank's share of the total debt). If I didn't have that, there would be no need for a meeting. They would be foreclosing the company.

After treatment like this, I suspected there was some kind of deal between Schoeller and the bank. Bayerische Vereinsbank was much too eager for Schoeller to take over instead of us. The way I saw it, it almost seemed as if the bank and Schoeller were mounting a raid on Roederstein.

Now I had a few days to come up with a letter of credit for $65 million. I had the resources at Vishay to back that amount, but putting such an encumbrance on Vishay's books would have ruined the balance sheet. What I needed was a letter of credit against Roederstein. But who would give me such a thing against a failing company? No one was about to commit money to Roederstein. The minute we showed the balance sheet, they'd jump back in fright.

I called Moshe Shamir in Israel and explained the situation to him. "We can make a gold mine out of this," I told him. "It will work beautifully, no question. We'll be able to bring jobs to Israel, we'll restructure Portugal. There are a dozen things we can do with this company." I laid out a whole reorganization plan. "But I need to call on the banks. I need a letter of credit for sixty-five million. And I need it right now."

"That's not a problem for Vishay," he said. "I can get that anytime."

"Not against Vishay," I said. "Against Roederstein, with no Vishay guarantee."

Moshe might have been a little stunned when he heard that, but this kind of situation was grist for his mill. It called all his political and financial talents into play. He went to work, and by the end of the week he had managed to get a commitment from Bank Hapoalim and FIBI, the First International Bank of Israel, not for a letter of credit, but for a letter of intent to provide the funding. In essence the letter said that they knew and trusted Vishay and that they were ready to loan the funds to Roederstein provided certain conditions of sale were met.

It wasn't exactly what Bayerische Vereinsbank was demanding, but it was something. It demonstrated our seriousness and the level of our backing. And since the German banks knew the Israeli banks, I was sure they wouldn't be able just to dismiss it, much as they might have liked to.

When I presented the letter to the bankers on Thursday, they were taken aback. As soon as they saw it they knew they wouldn't be able to foreclose. To make sure they got the message, I put it explicitly: "You can see that something positive is going to happen here," I said. "If in spite of this you do keep pushing, you'll leave me no choice. I'll take you to court immediately. Besides, I'm positive you don't want to foreclose and put four thousand people out into the street. Or am I wrong?"

"Now that you have this [the letter], what I'd like from you is a few months to reorganize the whole debt situation." They were amenable to that, though there wasn't any enthusiasm in the room. But when I broached the subject of buying out the debt at a discount rate or getting them to forgive the interest for a time, they were cold as ice. There was zero give. They agreed to an April 1 date (it was now February 19), but at that point they wanted to be reimbursed completely. "And before that," they said, "we'd like you to sit down with Schoeller. Maybe you can work out a three-way deal."

"Fine," I said. "I have nothing against sitting down with him. But I have to tell you that I can't see what he might have to bring to the table. He doesn't know resistors. He doesn't know capacitors. He doesn't have management expertise (by then I knew that Schoeller's company was a paper organization). What does he have? Money? We also have money. And besides, who is this Schoeller? Nobody's ever heard of him."

"Don't worry," they said, "he has impeccable credentials."

The next day I was sitting down with Mr. Schoeller in a Munich hotel. When I asked him about his background and his company, he told me something about his family. His company had been set up specifically as a vehicle for acquiring other companies.

"Is your family backing you?" I asked.

"No, I have other backers," he said, but neglected to tell me their names.

The rest was equally vague. He mentioned a lot of people he knew, but not in a way that had any bearing. His company understood German law intimately, he said, they were expert at operating in Germany—the implication being that they would be better at handling the acquisition.

"Look," I told him, "we own a German company that's been doing business here for seventy years. We're familiar with the territory." Before long it was clear he had nothing tangible to offer, so we adjourned the meeting.

When I came back to the United States I got a telephone call from a certain Mr. Alan Patricof. Very friendly. "Felix," he said, "do you remember me? I'm a friend of Alfred Slaner's. You and I have been at a couple of meetings together." I wasn't sure I remembered meeting him, but I certainly knew him by reputation. "You know, Felix, we have an investment arm in Germany. Our people there have put a hundred million out to this fellow Schoeller to acquire Roederstein. In effect Schoeller is really our agent there. Why don't we make a deal? You buy this Resista division and we'll take the rest of it. Or we do it together, or whatever you'd like."

At least now I knew why the banks were so comfortable with Schoeller. He did have impeccable credentials. His backer was a venture capitalist on the grand scale; to Alan Patricof $100 million was little more than a drop in the bucket.

But I told him the same thing I had told Schoeller. I'd be happy to talk further, but what could he provide us with that we could use—other than capital? "Would your money be less expensive than the bank's?" I asked. "What return would you want?"

He wanted an enormous return. Not much different from other investment banks. But we hardly needed money at those rates. The discussion was cordial, but in the end I told Patricof that we could find our own funds, which put an end to any idea of a joint deal. That left us alone to face what was still a complicated situation.

One big problem was the German metalworkers' union, the toughest group of organized labor in the country. To bring Roederstein back from the brink and make it profitable, we were going to have to lay off a lot of people. Many of the cuts would come from management—Roederstein's upper levels were bloated. But we'd also have to cut a thousand or more line workers. First of all, we would have to get the union to go along with that. Second, even if we succeeded, the substantial layoff costs along with all Roederstein's other debts would show on Vishay's books, which would badly affect the balance sheet.

After wrestling with that difficulty for a while, Avi Eden came up with a plan. Instead of buying the entire company outright, we would buy only 19 percent of it while taking a two-year option to buy the rest. At a purchase price of 5 million Deutsche marks, 19 percent would come to just under 1 million Deutsche marks. If at the end of two years we didn't buy the whole company, we would forfeit the million.

If we did it this way, from an accounting standpoint we would not have to consolidate the Roederstein and Vishay balance sheets. Roederstein would be listed as a simple investment until we exercised the option. This arrangement would also put us at an advantage when we went to talk to the unions. If they knew we had the option of sacrificing a relatively small investment and walking away, they'd have that much more incentive to cooperate.

When we approached the metalworkers, we hid nothing. We laid out the restructuring plan in detail, the cash flow, the mathematical necessity that lay behind our thinking. We told them how many workers we would need to lay off and described the extent to which moving some of the production to Israel and some to Czechoslovakia (just across the border from Roederstein's plants in the city of Selb) would strengthen the company and help secure the jobs that remained. Then we asked them to go along with our plans. "If we can't find a common ground with you on what we are proposing here," I said, "we'll take the million-mark loss and walk away. I'm ready for that. If it does work, though, we'll pay off the debt and look at where we can upgrade plant and equipment. There will be a lot of money invested here. We need your okay. But we're also open to your suggestions. If you have ideas that make more sense, I want to hear them."

I knew that our proposal was cogent, but with the metalworkers' reputation I wasn't at all sure what the outcome would be. They examined the books and they listened. Finally they said that they didn't have a better plan. Of course they didn't like the layoffs, but they could see we were treating them fairly, and it seemed clear that we knew how to manage. With Vishay they had faith that the company (and the bulk of the jobs) would be saved. By that evening they had agreed to our entire proposal.

The next day the union went to the press with the announcement that Vishay was saving Roederstein. The publicity was wonderful. The agreement also gave me a large step up in trying to reach some kind of solution with the banks. We had the letter of intent, and now we had an agreement with the unions as well. Already Gerald Paul was moving in with his team to take over day-to-day management.

With all this, the German bankers were becoming much more relaxed. I assured them we would have a letter of credit to supersede the Hapoalim/FIBI letter of intent, and that we were in the process of forming a consortium of other banks to buy out the loans. I even came to them with another German Bank, BHF, who said, "Yes, we are going to run the consortium that will finance the takeover. We know Vishay, and we have no problems at all with this. We know the assets. [In fact, the real estate, plant, and equipment value was equal to the debt. Schoeller had known exactly what he was doing.] We know Vishay is guaranteeing up to nineteen percent. That's plenty—more than enough to reimburse you completely. So if you don't want to join the new consortium, we'll pay you out."

Hearing this, the hard-faced men at Bayerische Vereinsbank became quiet. And when they saw that BHF was bringing in a French bank and two Israeli banks, they suddenly wanted a portion of the new financing themselves. So Roederstein's banking crisis was finally deflated.

There was still one aspect of the deal I wasn't comfortable with: the price of 5 million Deutsche marks. I knew that almost the whole of that sum would have to go toward the Roedersteins' inheritance taxes and that the family would be left with next to nothing. It was a stark situation, tragic in its way. The father had built the company into an empire. Landshut was a fairly large city, and Roederstein was for a long time the largest employer; in Landshut the family was royalty. Then the father died and the empire crumbled, leaving the family with one or two apartments around the city and nothing else. One day they were lords of the place; the next, everything had disappeared. (Was there an echo here of Grandma Tema's admonition about who owned what?)

I didn't feel exactly right about taking advantage of this situation. I found that I was listening to arguments in my head. If you find a man in the street who has a gold watch, Felix, and he needs bread and is willing to give his gold watch for the piece of bread—would you give him the bread and take the watch? No, you wouldn't. You'd give him the value of the watch, or maybe a little less. Okay, maybe even much less. But you'd give him some value of the gold watch, right? You wouldn't just give him a piece of bread, would you? You wouldn't do to him what was done to you in Losossna, when the mayor gave you that loaf of bread for Bass's gold wedding ring, would you?

This was the same situation. Here was a family that needed a piece of bread but had only a gold watch. Somebody wanted to give them a piece of bread for the gold watch, but they didn't want to give it to him, they wanted to give it to me. I couldn't really do that (though the investment community had a hard time understanding my feelings on this point). But it wasn't only personal. From a strictly self-interested point of view, I thought, if I do this, how will I be perceived by our own management and people? They have consciences, right? What would they say? They would say that for a piece of bread I took a gold watch, right? I didn't like the sound of that at all.

So I raised the subject with Til Roederstein, and he suggested that maybe I could provide another 5 million Deutsche marks to him and his brother and his two sisters as pensions. I agreed to that, and Til arranged a dinner meeting for the family and me. Around the table I told them what I had agreed to do. "And in addition to that," I said, "if this deal turns out really very well—that means not contractually, and at my option—when and if I decide, you may get as much as ten million more. But at a later date. If all the plans come out as we hope and I have your full cooperation, then you will deserve more and I will do it." They were very grateful and I felt better also. By the time dinner was over I felt as if I was not committing robbery.

Once the acquisition was settled, Gerald Paul went into Roederstein with a five-man team—his accountant, sales, personnel, planning, and manufacturing managers—and began reorganizing in earnest. The first thing he did was release the Hayek and ITT men. Then he went to work on the top level of management.

"We don't need any of them," he told me. "Can I let them all go?" I had promised the Roederstein brothers that they could stay, but with those two exceptions the entire top level disappeared. (Shortly afterward, Jorg resigned anyway. Til Roederstein stayed on as legal counsel and board member.)

When Paul investigated the second layer of management, he found it enormously bloated. Where they needed one person they had at least five and often seven. Over the previous year and a half Hayek had split the company into seven distinct units; each product line had been organized as a separate business. There were seven business heads, seven sales departments, seven accounting departments, right on down the line. The idea was that if the units were independent, each would do better because the people would have more incentive to run it as if it were their own business. That seemed to me utter nonsense, since in any case the businesses did not belong to the people, but to the Roedersteins. Or maybe Hayek had believed that the seven-part organization would make it easier to sell the company off piecemeal.

Whatever their thinking might have been, we immediately began slicing away the excess. In fact, though Roederstein may have been more bloated than most, in almost every company we had taken over we had found an astonishing inflation in management. In a way it was shocking to realize that we could eliminate entire layers of management and watch production actually improve. Here we started at the top and proceeded downward. We consolidated back and forth, restructured Roederstein with Draloric, and saved tens of millions of Deutsche marks.

Then we began looking closely at the individual divisions. We found that one of the aluminum capacitor plants was irretrievably obsolete. So we had to close it. We told the unions, and, of course, we had to pay for the layoffs. The unions agreed. There were no strikes and no threats. We had just gotten rid of two thirds of Roederstein's management, so it was hard for them to complain about closing down a factory that was impossible to run profitably. As a result of this closure the sales went down to a certain extent, but what remained was sound. Then Paul went into the Portuguese facilities and knocked them down from 1,200 to 750 employees. The production took a 20 percent jump upward.

Gerald Paul did with the top layer of Roederstein's management what I should have done at Dale. Had I handled that situation the same way I could have integrated Dale into Vishay in three months. But I had not had the right approach. With hindsight it seemed to me that underneath I had wanted Dale's management to love me; as a result, I tried to reform them and wean them to me. But there is no love involved in these things. You have to get rid of the superfluous and the uncooperative; the remainder will love you anyway because you have kept them in the company and have improved their working environment and their lives. My initial approach was too romantic by half. But with time I had recognized my mistakes. Gerald Paul's sweeping reorganization of Roederstein embodied the principles I had had to learn the hard way.

The Roederstein takeover was essentially flawless. Within nine months this company, which had been teetering on the brink of dissolution, became a clean, efficient, profitable operation. By this time we had had sufficient acquisition experience so that we avoided almost all the mistakes. We knew not only what to do, but also what not to do. Our sales agreement gave us two years to decide if we wanted to exercise our option and acquire the company formally. But we were ready to do it in nine months. On January 1, 1993, we took Roederstein into Vishay.

A few months after we incorporated Roederstein, I got a call from Dennis Horowitz, the head of the Philips capacitor division. When we last talked, he had been negotiating with a Japanese company for the sale of his division. Now, he said, he was ready to close the deal with them. Was I by any chance still interested?

The next week I flew to Florida, examined the Philips business closely, and decided to buy it. The division had been vastly reduced by losses following its debarment, but the potential synergies made it an attractive acquisition. So the Philips division, too, was folded into Vishay.

With all the acquisition activity, this also seemed like a good time to pursue a company I had been watching for years. In 1975, at one of the industry exhibits, our booth had been located next to that of a company named Vitramon. Talking with their president, I learned that Vitramon made a multilayer ceramic capacitor that performed far better than those of its competitors. Looking at their specifications, I was impressed. Afterward, even though I wasn't particularly interested in capacitors, I made it a point to look at how Vitramon was doing from time to time.

When we began talking about moving Vishay into the range of electronic components beyond resistors, Vitramon immediately came to mind as a possible acquisition. Multilayered ceramic capacitors would add the right kind of additional dimension to Vishay, and the company had an outstanding reputation. But when I asked Carroll Novicki to make inquiries, he came back with the report that Vitramon had just been sold—to Thomas and Betts, a major producer of electrical products for the construction industry.

Now that we had completed the Sprague and Roederstein acquisitions, we had made ourselves substantial players in the field of capacitors. But we did not have the multilayer ceramic technology; that was the one glaring hole in our product line. Moreover, multilayer ceramic capacitors were the fastest growing and largest segment of the capacitor business. Again I looked longingly toward Vitramon. The deeper our investigations went, the more I was convinced of how beneficial Vitramon would be to Vishay. I wanted to buy it.

On the other hand, Thomas and Betts had given no indication that they wanted to sell. I didn't know the Thomas and Betts chairman, but I thought that if I could talk to him I would

NEVER THE LAST JOURNEY

be able to convince him that Vitramon belonged not with them but with us, that it would be to both our advantages for the company to change hands. I was given confidence in this conviction by the fact that since they acquired Vitramon, Thomas and Betts had not bought anything else in the electronic components industry. They had, however, bought out another company in their core business and had grown quite substantially in the field of electrical construction products.

To me, this suggested that when Thomas and Betts had bought Vitramon they had been planning to expand into electronic components. But along the way they changed direction and were now concentrating on their original field. I guessed that they could use capital for further investment in their own industry, and that at this point they probably were looking at Vitramon as a business that, although profitable, wasn't within their main sphere of interest. If that was the case, and I was willing to bet that it was, why should Thomas and Betts want to keep Vitramon? Wouldn't it be better for them to sell it to Vishay? I would get a company that I needed, and they would get money they could use for what they needed.

In addition, I knew that Vitramon would soon require a very substantial capital investment. Their capacitors were in such demand that Vitramon plants were working three shifts, seven days a week. They desperately needed more capacity, and to build it would take an investment of close to $100 million. Kevin Dunnigan, Thomas and Betts's chairman and CEO, was reputed to be a first-class businessman. I did not think that he had any intention of making such an investment in what was for him an essentially extraneous business. But I was quite prepared to do what was necessary to see Vitramon flourish. In my mind, I was already clear about how to go about it.

Mark Hassenberg, one of the analysts who covered Vishay for the Wall Street house of Donaldson Lufkin and Jenrette (DLJ), also covered Thomas and Betts, and knew Kevin Dunnigan. When I suggested to him that a meeting between myself and

Dunnigan might be in order, he agreed instantly. "That's absolutely right," he said. "It makes perfect sense."

A week later I was sitting down with Dunnigan in the DLJ dining room. He had come prepared, with a stack of documents and figures. To sell Vitramon, he said, he wanted $225 million.

Dunnigan was an organized man, straight-thinking and to the point. But the figure he mentioned took me by surprise. "I can't believe it," I told him. "The sales are only one hundred twenty million dollars. You want us to pay almost two dollars for every dollar of sales? Never mind how much for every dollar of profit?"

But he had made his calculations, and he demonstrated how Vitramon was growing and how he had arrived at what he needed, the chief reason being that selling for less than that would dilute Thomas and Betts's earnings per share. "I'm not going to go backwards," he said. His number was $225 million.

When we made the calculations together on a slightly different basis, though, I was eventually able to show that $200 million was a more reasonable figure. That, he said, was possible. At that point, we decided to go home and study it further, which meant that the game of cat and mouse could now commence in earnest.

The second time we met I made a proposal of $165 million. At first I thought he was going to throw me out of his office. But I had made the proposal based on certain assumptions. In our first meeting, we had spent a lot of time making calculations for each other. "But look," I told him now, "when you made your calculations for us, you didn't count the fact that your assets had already been written down completely. But if we buy Vitramon we have to revalue the assets. That puts a different value on the company. On that basis the right number has to be one hundred sixty-five million."

"No," he said. "Absolutely not. Good-bye."

But it wasn't good-bye, because the fact was that the

deal was too good for either of us to back away from. After exchanging more papers and proposals, I eventually invited him to my office. When he came, I said, "Look, you want two hundred. I want one hundred sixty-five, right?"

"Right."

"You want to sell the company, but you don't want to sell it for nothing. I want to buy it, but I don't want to overpay. Let's be reasonable. Let's split it at one hundred eighty-five." With that, we looked at each other, shook hands, and I opened the bottle of champagne that I had brought in for the occasion. We had an agreement.

It was only then that the trouble started. The problem was that we had offered to buy only Vitramon's assets. But Dunnigan wanted us to buy the company's stock as well, which would have made us responsible for whatever hidden liabilities there might have been. The result was an extended war between the two teams of lawyers over who would take responsibility for what and at what price. After three months of fruitless negotiations, Dunnigan and I decided to meet in New York to try to resolve the issues ourselves, though to my dismay I was not successful in excluding the lawyers from our meeting.

Before I knew it, the room filled up with smoke and the lawyers were off and running, even more eager to prevail over each other now that they were performing in front of their principals. At one point an interminable, savage argument developed over a fifty-thousand-dollar issue. Finally, I said, "Look, you take the fifty thousand. Have it. Let's move on."

"No," said the Thomas and Betts attorney. "I want to show you that we're right in this, that the fifty thousand actually does belong to us."

"Stop already," I said. "Take the money. We're wasting too much time. I agree. You've convinced me."

"No," said the lawyer. "Let me show you why we're right."

My lawyer wanted to talk, too, but I said, "You be quiet. You I control. Let me talk with these other lawyers myself."

Eventually, I succeeded in convincing the Thomas and Betts attorney to take the fifty thousand. But after that, other sticking points arose to plague us. Finally, exasperated, Kevin Dunnigan and I walked out into the corridor together and resolved everything in a couple of minutes. When we came back into the room, he told his lawyers what we had decided. They were outraged; there was so much more to be squeezed out of this situation. But in the end they had little recourse but to accept.

Altogether, the Vitramon situation was one of the most complex I had ever been involved in. Because of the need to keep our negotiations hidden (to preclude any media attention and avoid other offers that would begin to develop as a result), we had to do our due diligence secretly, examining the Vitramon plants in four countries without being recognized. At the same time, we did not have the $184 million the company would cost (the $185 million price had been reduced by one million during the subsequent negotiations), so we had to muster our consortium of twelve banks to restructure our old debt and wrap the new debt into it. As part of the total financial package, we also planned to go to the market with a $100 million stock issue.

But all of these things had to be done quickly and simultaneously. We gave ourselves a firm date in July 1994 to bring our entire agenda to a conclusion—the negotiations with Thomas and Betts, the due diligence examinations, the debt restructuring, and the stock issue. We knew that to let it go longer would put the entire deal at risk. Once July deepens, vacation time begins in Europe (where many of Vitramon's plants were), and it becomes impossible to get anything accomplished. Nor can anyone be sure what the stock market might be like after vacations; before they start is the right time to float an offering.

On the tightest of timelines we proceeded in each of the four areas. In each one of them, hurry brought risks. But we were aware of what they were, and by now we had acquired considerable experience in doing what we were doing. We knew, though, that nowhere was the risk greater than in the stock offering.

Normally, a company that wants to make a stock offering gets approval from the SEC prior to launching the roadshow that will promote the offering among investors and fund managers. Theoretically, one could begin promoting the stock before the SEC acts. Approval is needed only immediately before the stock is actually put up for sale. But, in fact, nobody actually does anything without approval because of the possibility that the SEC will find something they want changed.

In all of our previous stock offerings we too had exercised this normal prudence. But now we did not have time to wait. Besides, in none of our earlier offerings had the SEC made any changes at all. We decided to take the promotional show on the road. If by some stroke of terrible misfortune the SEC decided that we had to change some aspect of our offering, we would do it in midstream.

Here luck deserted us. For reasons completely unrelated to the stock offering, the SEC had started to examine Vishay's 10K, a random examination that was of no real significance except that it was going to take time. And while the SEC was examining our 10K, they would not approve a new offering.

The examiner was in no hurry and the examination dragged along. Then the examiner went on vacation. We begged her to expedite it. Every hour was important, and once the appointed time for the offering had passed we would be dead. We couldn't postpone. Once an offering is delayed, Wall Street senses something is awry and the stock plummets. Disaster waits in the wings.

Stock prices for new offerings are set at four o'clock, right after the market closes. At 10:00 A.M. Eastern Standard Time the morning of the offering I finished up a stock presentation to a group of Los Angeles portfolio managers and got on a plane at LAX bound for Philadelphia. We still did not have SEC approval. Airphones had been installed on the plane, but as I quickly found out, they were not yet working. At 3:45 P.M., we landed in Philadelphia. In desperation, I looked around for a free pay phone, but they were all taken. By the time I got out to my car, I was sure that what was left of my hair was standing on end. It was exactly 4:00. My driver had a message. One hour earlier the SEC had given us its blessing. On the car phone, I dialed Ace Greenberg at Bear, Stearns, and we set the price of the offering. On my way home I stretched my legs and relaxed in the back seat thinking of the hundred-million-dollar factory we were already planning to build in Israel's Migdal haEmek and the additional new Vitramon space we would soon be adding in Virginia. Before long Vitramon would have the capacity to enter markets the company had only dreamed about before.

•

Several years earlier, the Dale, Draloric, and Sfernice acquisitions had brought us from a $50-million-a-year company to a $450-million-a-year company that was a major player in the world's passive components market. That had been a whirlwind. Now I was looking back on a second cycle. With Sprague, Roederstein, Philips, and now Vitramon on board, we were suddenly doing a billion a year. We had plants in the United States, Israel, Germany, France, England, Mexico, Morocco, Portugal, Brazil, Czechoslovakia, and Japan. In one capacity or another, more than sixteen thousand people were working for Vishay. Our stock had gone up substantially; we were able to convert bonds into shares and restructure our debt. We had emerged from this round of takeovers as the largest passive components maker outside of Japan, or maybe even including Japan.

When *Fortune* magazine published its 1993 issue on the nation's largest industrial corporations, I had found Vishay listed for the first time among the top five hundred. Our return to investors, they noted, put us at number fifteen. When I looked us up in the electronics industry listing, which included such behemoths as General Electric, Intel, and Motorola, we turned out to have been first in total return to investors for both the year and the decade. It was a wonderful surprise to see in black and white that our efforts had borne such fruit. It made me proud to think that we had been able to perform so well among the giants. That wasn't so bad, I thought, for a company named after a vanished Jewish shtetl.

I KNEW that much of this considerable growth was due to the skill of the people I had managed to gather around me at Vishay— Avi, Don Alfson, Gerald Paul, Moshe Shamir, Abe Inbar, Gad Negbi, Jim Starr, Philip Gazeau, Yannick LeVacon, Dick Grubb, Bob Freece, Bill Spires, Carl Fritz, Glynn Smith, and Hank Landau, among others. To a large extent it was their talent that had brought the takeovers and growth to fruition. But in my heart I understood that the strength I needed to undertake these challenges in the first place came from Ruta. Over the years her love had enabled me to look directly at my past, to face it, even examine it. The pain hadn't grown less piercing, but I no longer had to frantically shift my defenses around to keep it buried. It didn't threaten to overwhelm me from the depths, as it had for so long.

One consequence was the change in my outlook on Vishay. It wasn't that I was less careful in business than I had been earlier, but I had become more aggressive, more eager to search out opportunities and grasp them. In my personal life, too, the changes were evident, at least to me. They brought on a series of events I could never have imagined without having Ruta by me.

In Israel a week before Independence Day comes Yom ha Shoah, the Day of the Holocaust. Throughout the country at twelve noon the sirens begin to wail, and all activity ceases. Cars stop where they are on the streets, and drivers and riders get out. In businesses, stores, schools, and homes, people stand, observing a long minute of silence.

At Yad Vashem, the Holocaust memorial on the hills outside Jerusalem, a ceremony is held, attended by survivors, their children and grandchildren, and others who take time off to commemorate the destruction. I had never even considered visiting Yad Vashem; the very thought of it made me shake. But two years after we were married, Ruta and I decided to participate in Yom ha

Shoah there, together with our daughter Gisele, who was then in medical school at Tel Aviv University.

I approached this visit with foreboding. We parked our car and walked up through the glades of trees that surround the heavy stone building. But as we neared the door I felt the anguish crushing my chest. I had the old sensation of not being able to breathe. I just could not bring myself to open that door and walk inside to the names that I knew were engraved on the floors and the candles burning there for the dead. I felt Ruta putting an arm around me from one side and Gisele from the other. The three of us turned and walked slowly down toward the parking lot.

I knew that as part of its work Yad Vashem honored non-Jews who had saved Jews—"righteous persons." For years I had wanted to initiate that honor for the Puchalskis, but I could not face entering the place, let alone taking part in a ceremony there. So even while the thought gnawed in me, I kept pushing it away.

Then Ruta began talking to me about it, urging me to do it. Janova had passed away fifteen years earlier, Jan five years before that. They had never received any recognition for what they had done, certainly not from Poland, and not from the Jewish people either. I knew the family would feel good about it; Krystyna and Irena and Sabina had been part of what had happened back then. They had shared the danger every moment of those seventeen months that Sender, the Basses, and I lived beneath their floorboards. So had the two younger ones, Wladek and Wanda, even though they hadn't been aware of it at the time. I knew that in the Puchalski family those days had remained as a powerful memory. The story was known by all the children and grandchildren, and they revered Jan and Janova for their compassion and heroism. I badly wanted to do this for them.

Yad Vashem's recognition of those who saved Jewish lives does not happen quickly or easily. A thorough investigation takes place. Researchers establish a dossier and gather testimony, then look for corroborating witnesses. A year passed before they had finished all the work, but in the spring of 1987 approval was given for the Puchalskis to come and be honored.

All of Janova's children traveled to Israel for the ceremony except Sabina, the second oldest. Sabina's son Zdzislaw had come to live in the United States some years earlier—a strong-minded young man who had had his problems with the Communist government and had fled. He had first lived in Atlanta, where he got a job at the University of Georgia as an electrical technician. Then I had invited him to Philadelphia to work for Vishay. Sabina had visited him and us the previous year and had overstayed her visa. Now the Polish government refused her request for a passport to go to Israel. I pulled every string I could think of, but it was no use. This was her punishment. She was not to be allowed out of the country.

So Zdzislaw came to Israel in Sabina's place. He, Krystyna, Irena, Wanda, and Wladek toured the country with Ruta and me; then on June 15, 1987, we arrived at Yad Vashem for the ceremony. Outside the memorial building is a small forest, where each tree commemorates a "righteous person" who had saved a Jewish life. There a tree had been planted in honor of the Puchalski family; we took turns watering it in the warm June sunshine.

Inside the building, it was cool. Serge and Beate Klarsfeld had come from France for the occasion, and all of us listened as Judge Beisky, a member of the Israeli Supreme Court, made the presentation in Polish. Beisky himself was a Schindler's list survivor; this was, he said, the first time he had given a public address in Polish since the war. Then Mordecai Paldiel of Yad Vashem made a speech in English, and I spoke in Hebrew. People like the Puchalskis, I said, had saved Poland's soul. And it was true; the name plaques on the trees outside were mostly Polish. That was mainly where Europe's Jews had died, and that was where some Poles had risen above the hatred and fear to risk everything—themselves and their families—to save the lives of innocent people.

When I was finished, Wanda, Janova's youngest, came up to the front spontaneously. She had not prepared a speech; she had no notes, but she spoke magnificently—straight from the heart. She talked about the Jews, about Israel, about how Israel must be strong, and how she felt so good to be there. We were, she said, like one family. By the time she finished, everybody in the room was in tears.

After the presentations, we moved to the chapel for a brief religious ceremony. In the middle of the floor burned an eternal flame, around which the names Auschwitz, Buchenwald, Treblinka, Sobibor, and the others were carved into the dark stone. There a cantor led a small choir in prayers for the dead, and in the middle of it I saw Zdzislaw walk up to the rabbi and talk to him briefly. When Zdzislaw returned to his aunts and uncle he said a few words to them, then all of them sank to their knees with their hands clasped and began a prayer in Polish. With the Hebrew chanting in the background, I could just barely make out the words: *"Ojcze Nacz Ktorys Jest w Niebie . . ."* "Our Father, Who art in heaven, hallowed be Thy name . . ."

Afterward I had a hard time speaking. Paldiel said that nothing like it had ever happened before at Yad Vashem. These are extraordinary people, I thought, on their knees in a Jewish sanctuary, the men in yarmulkes, praying a Catholic prayer in Polish. Strength of character shone in them, just as it had in Janova.

There was one Pole there that day who had not prayed with the Puchalskis. In 1987 the Polish Communist government had not yet formally recognized Israel. They had no embassy in the country. But they did have a small diplomatic delegation there, and when the consul heard about the ceremony at Yad Vashem he sent an observer. When the prayers and presentation were finished, this man invited us to the consulate in Tel Aviv.

We went there, but I asked Zdzislaw not to come in.

Knowing the anger he felt toward Communists in general (and how furious he was at their treatment of his mother), I really thought he might attack someone physically and end up getting arrested. So Zdzislaw waited outside.

It was good he did, because inside the consul was trying to feed us a line of propaganda, expounding over coffee on the brotherhood of the Polish and Jewish peoples. It was shameless, which was what I told him outright. I was as angry as Zdzislaw. "If you invite someone," I said, "don't give him this kind of propaganda. What do you have to tell me that falseness for? Who is forcing you? What kind of brotherhood was there?" I felt my temper give way completely. "There was no brotherhood! But your honor, your soul was saved by people like these sitting right here. The trees out there at Yad Vashem are covered with Polish names. They rescued your honor because they risked their lives to save fellow human beings, Jews. But the Polish people in general? The huge majority did nothing! And you, the Polish government, you don't even honor them. For years these people here had to hide the fact that they had saved Jews. So nobody would know about it and retaliate."

That put an abrupt end to the conversation, and a few minutes later we walked out—an emotional conclusion to what had been an emotional day for all of us.

•

We saw the Puchalskis the following year in Poland under equally emotional circumstances. Nineteen eighty-eight was the forty-fifth anniversary of the Warsaw Ghetto uprising. Ruta and I decided to go, and to visit Auschwitz and Treblinka at the same time, although this was something that had always held the greatest terrors for me. Still, I thought I had to make the visit, and for the first time in my life I felt strong enough to deal with it.

My son, Marc, came with us. By then he, like Gisele, had chosen to live in Israel. He had graduated from Philadelphia's Drexel University in 1984 and had gone to work for Vishay. Initially he had come to Israel for a year's stay, but now it was apparent he had decided to remain in the country. I still had not talked much to my children about the past, though they knew the outlines of the story well enough. But the old inhibitions were still there, for me to tell and them to ask, even now that they were adults. The silence on the subject that had been the rule when they were young had transformed itself into a kind of mutual reticence. Marc and I were tender about approaching this area, as if afraid of intruding on each other's emotions. Yet now, as we went through this together, it seemed almost as if words were superfluous.

We traveled to Auschwitz by train with a large group that had come to Poland to commemorate the uprising. Several thousand young people had brought Israeli flags and conceived the idea of marching from the train siding to the gas chambers. So it was with a sea of blue and white Stars of David waving above us that we passed through the portal whose inscription read *"Arbeit Macht Frei."* A plaque inside the gate announced simply, "In this place four million men, women, and children were killed between the years 1940 and 1945." The text was repeated in dozens of languages, including Hebrew—but it said not a word about Jews. Reading that, I felt as if someone had kicked me in the stomach. Here was the place where the Germans had killed us, and in this same place the Communists were doing their best to wipe out our memory. When we marched into the building and entered one of the gas chambers, I had time to see many young people inside, praying. Then the tears blacked out everything, and I felt myself reeling.

Later that day we traveled to Gdansk (World War II's Danzig) to see the Puchalskis. Sabina lived there with her family, as did Krystyna and Wladek with their families. Sabina, in whose house we gathered, lived in very modest circumstances, and people crowded the small rooms for the beautiful dinner that had been laid out. We kissed and held each other and spent the night talking about our memories. They felt closer to me than sisters and brothers.

The next day we all went to Warsaw for the Uprising

ceremony. There the rest of the family met us, Irena with her husband and daughter, and Wanda, who had come in from her home in Germany. Now Janova's five children were all together with Ruta and me and Marc. We took part in the commemoration, then walked to the Sejm, the Polish parliament. Poland was now in the middle of rapid political changes that had begun with the Solidarity struggle. One result was that as the Communist grip weakened, the Sejm had decided to recognize formally the Polish heroes who had saved Jews. There we watched as the Puchalskis and a hundred others were honored for the things they had done forty-five years before.

In Warsaw I met with Viktor Voroshylski, my old Grodno friend who had graduated from high school with Leon and me in 1946. Viktor's father had wanted him to become a doctor, and Viktor had done that, giving up his poetry that Leon and I had thought so remarkable. But in later years Viktor had left medicine for writing and had become one of Poland's best-known poets and literary figures.

Viktor had stayed in Poland after the war. "I feel like this is my country," he told me when I urged him to join me in leaving. "I'm going to help rebuild it." Viktor had been a committed Communist. But in 1956 he had been in Budapest as a journalist when the Soviet tanks rolled in. That experience had radicalized him, and when the Solidarity movement started, he had become one of Lech Walesa's advisers. Several years earlier I had seen Viktor in Paris, where he was giving some lectures. Since then he had been in prison for a year when the government had cracked down on Solidarity, part of that time with his wife and daughter. The French press had created a scandal over the Polish regime's jailing of Solidarity members' families, and after three months Viktor's wife and daughter had been released. Viktor and several other leaders were the last to get out.

The next day we traveled with the Puchalskis to Treblinka, the death factory where the majority of Grodno's thirty thousand Jews had ended their lives, my own parents and grandparents among them. Auschwitz, where we had been the previous day, has been preserved. The railroad siding is there, where Jews were herded off the trains, the gate they marched through, the gas chambers where they took their last breaths, the crematoriums that spewed out their bodies as ash. But at Treblinka there is nothing except the railhead; a monument; and a field littered with large, jagged rocks, each one bearing the name of a slaughtered Jewish community. The monument marks the great pit that received the bodies, and there the Puchalskis and other visitors laid their flowers, the colors lovely against the harsh gray stone. Everyone in the crowd was crying and praying—Poles and Jews weeping together over the death of Polish Jewry.

•

Not long after our trip to Poland, Ruta and I were back in Israel, where one day we were visiting Moshe Shamir. Moshe's aunt Hadasia from Mexico also happened to be visiting. She was part of a branch of the Kelmer Maggid family that had fled Poland just before the war and had tried to get into the United States across the Mexican border. When they failed at that, they had settled in and made lives for themselves in Mexico City. Over the years, Ruta and I had become quite friendly with my cousin there, Jack Wiener and his wife, Doris.

Another visitor was also there that day, an old boyfriend who had been courting Moshe's aunt Hadasia when they were eighteen, before the German invasion.

When I joined the conversation I found that this man had survived the war as a partisan. His home had been in Lida, the town where my uncle Grishka had died and where my dear friend from liberation time Solomon Polachik had come from. "I had a friend from Lida who was a partisan," I told him. "He was killed at the front after the liberation of Grodno. Might you by some chance have known him—Solomon Polachik?"

"Solomon Polachik?" he said. "What do you mean, Solomon Polachik? Solomon Polachik is alive! He lives in Minsk! I write to him regularly."

I couldn't believe it. I had last seen Solomon in the fall of 1944, when he left to join the Red Army. I remembered as if it were yesterday when the notice came announcing his death. That had been such a terrible, terrible blow. Now, after forty-four years, Solomon was alive?

I wrote to him immediately, and before long I had a letter back. It was true, he wrote, he had not been killed, though he himself had thought he was dead. In November 1944 he had been fighting in eastern Prussia after having been trained as an artilleryman. In one battle against a German tank assault, his crew had not had time to dig their gun in properly, and a tank had scored a direct hit on them. Their gun was destroyed, and most of his crewmates were killed. It had been a bloody mess, with bodies flung all over the place. Solomon himself had been knocked unconscious with a bad head wound, and his identification had somehow gotten entangled with one of the bodies lying around him. When he awoke three days later in a hospital he had already been reported dead, though he wasn't aware of it.

When the war was over Solomon had stayed in the army, eventually retiring from the Soviet missile forces as a major. Not long after he left the military, a wave of official anti-Semitism swept the Soviet Union in the wake of the Six-Day War, which had ended so badly for the Soviets' Arab allies. Jews with Zionist sympathies were specially targeted. Solomon Polachik, who had never retreated from a fight in his life, publicly declared himself against the anti-Jewish persecution.

In the face of this offense, the fact that Solomon was a war hero with a jacketful of medals did him no good whatsoever. He was thrown out of work, and for twenty years he had been unable to get a job. Fortunately, the army had sent him to many technical courses over the years, and he had become knowledgeable in engineering. Now he taught himself English and became a translator of technical literature, from English into Russian—work he could do under the table.

My visits to the USSR had halted when scientific contacts were curbed after the Soviet invasion of Afghanistan. But when Gorbachev came to power the ice melted, and exchanges started up again. In October 1989 I arrived in Moscow as chairman of a scientific panel, and while I was there, I telephoned Solomon. I made arrangements to fly to Minsk to see him, and we also talked about the possibility of driving back to Grodno, which was still a closed city, off-limits to foreigners. Seeing Grodno was another of those things I had needed to do for a long time but had been dreading. But with Ruta I had managed to visit Yad Vashem and even Auschwitz and Treblinka. Now I wanted to take her with me to Grodno, to show her all the places I had been filling her head with for so long.

Solomon was waiting for us at the Minsk airport. We recognized each other right away and hugged each other close. He took us home to meet his wife, Elvira, who had prepared gefilte fish and other specialties. Over dinner he told me the details of his time in the army and his struggles to survive since then. He had even saved his old partisan jacket, covered with medals and ribbons down one side from collar to belt and halfway down the other. Solomon was as direct and honest as ever, as straight as an arrow— exactly the same person at sixty-two as he had been in the old days, except without the hair. What was right was right, and what was wrong was wrong.

Since Grodno was not on the Intourist approved list, getting a hotel room there wasn't permitted. The only possibility was to rent a car and drive to and from Minsk in a day—a four-hundred-mile round trip—providing you could find a car. I couldn't, but Solomon's son-in-law volunteered to loan us his and to come along with us as the driver.

At five o'clock in the morning we set out in the tiny Fiat, like conspirators—Ruta and I, Solomon and his wife, with the son-in-law behind the wheel. Through the window we watched the devastatingly poor countryside roll by, an unrelieved landscape of stark forests dotted with broken-down farms and dilapidated houses. On this road there were no amenities—no gas stations (we brought jerry cans of gasoline along in the trunk and jammed into the car with us), no places to eat, no rest rooms (we used the forest). Nor were there any other cars; except for an occasional truck, the roads were empty.

When we arrived in Grodno we found Salomon Zhukovsky and Gregory Hossid, the only two survivors I knew of who had remained in the city. Hossid I didn't remember very well, but Salomon Zhukovsky had been a teacher and a friend of our family. We embraced each other for a long moment. Zhukovsky was an old man now, living in a tiny, one-room apartment overflowing with Hebrew books. He had stayed in Grodno partly because he was a committed lifetime Communist. Even now his political passions were close to the surface. He still hated Zionism. He had a sister in Israel who sent him books and magazines. "Whenever I read something about Grodno written in Israel, how come they never mention the workers and the Communist movement?" he demanded, as if he expected me to defend the injustice. He was right, of course: Jewish Grodno had been filled with Socialists and Communists as well as Zionists. But he was really upset. "Calm down, Salomon," I said, "it's a political thing. But you and I are friends, so let's relax."

When I took Ruta to our old house at Brygidzka 28, we found that it had been divided into many apartments. The first-floor quarters where I had lived with my mother and father and sister had itself become three apartments, and when we knocked on one of the doors we were told the owner wasn't at home, we could not come in. Standing in front of the house, we looked at the balcony where Grandma Tema had once held me by the hand and told me that wealthy as we might have been, nothing was really ours, that it could all slip away in the blink of an eye. Across the courtyard were our old shops, and on the other side of the courtyard stood the barns and storehouses that once had been stacked high with Freydovicz goods.

Around back I showed Ruta the window of what had once been my room and where our kitchen had been. "And where was that hole?" she asked, walking down toward the other end of the building, "the one you and Sender and your mother escaped through that time?" "Somewhere around there," I said, pointing, and a moment later Ruta shouted, "Here it is!"

And there it was, partially hidden behind the weeds and high grass that grew along the back wall. I was flabbergasted. We both bent down to look; the hole in the foundation stones was precisely the same as it had been that morning in early November 1942 when Sender had finally managed to push Sarah through in our mad rush to get away from the Germans. Forty-seven years, and no one had bothered to repair it. Not a thing had changed.

That was more or less the way the city was, too. New buildings had gone up on the outskirts, but the old city looked the same as it had, except more run down. The offices, stores, and apartment buildings were as I remembered them. So was the entranceway to the ghetto, and Chasna Street, where Sender had run for his life while Wiese tried to gun him down.

With Polachik and Zhukovsky we drove out to Losossna, still a wooded suburb, but more built up than it had been. Where there had once been only Janova's house, now several houses stood. Still, I easily made out which had been hers. The house had been renovated and slightly enlarged, but there was no mistaking it. One of the neighbors was standing in his yard, and I asked if he knew whether this was where the Puchalski family used to live. The Puchalskis? he said. He thought he had heard of them, but as far as he knew, their house had been a little way off from there. He heard it had been torn down years ago.

There was nothing to do but go back to town, but I promised myself I would come to Grodno again in a more organized way. I wanted to take a look inside our Brygidzka Street house, and the Puchalski house, too (I knew we had been to the right place). I wondered if it were possible that underneath the bedroom floor I might still find our pit. I also wanted to drive to the village of Vishay, about thirty miles north of Grodno, but time was running out. We'd have to leave that till the next trip.

Back in Grodno, we sat down again with Salomon Zhukovsky in his overcrowded room. He had gone to the mayor many times, he said, to ask if the city would not at least put up some kind of plaque on the entrance to the ghetto to mark what had happened there, to say, "This was a Jewish town, this is where the Jews were concentrated, this is where the annihilation began." The mayor had refused. "After all," he told Zhukovsky, "how do we even know that Jews lived in Grodno? Where's the proof?"

"Look at the synagogue," Salomon had answered.

"Maybe," the mayor said, "but that's not proof that any- thing actually happened here. Where's the proof that something happened? We don't know anything about things like that."

After the war Grodno became part of the Soviet Union, and by the second generation the memory of what had taken place in the city had been swept away. Not only were thirty thousand human beings eradicated from the face of the earth, but their memory, too, in the place where it had happened, was wiped clean.

I knew that already. In my library at home I had several post–World War II Soviet books about Grodno, and I also had looked up the city in the Soviet encyclopedias. None of them men- tioned the destruction of the Jews. They described the glories of communism and the triumphant patriotic struggle against fascism, but about the Jews who lived and died in Grodno there was not a word. One of the history books even had a picture of Lisa Chap- nik, my old friend who had worked as a maid for the SS and run intelligence and arms for the underground. In the books she was described as a Soviet partisan hero. There was no mention that she had escaped from the ghetto, that she was Jewish, that she was a survivor. The Soviets had erased history.

Before we drove back, Salomon gave Ruta and me a sil- ver Torah pointer and Torah mantel he had somehow saved from the Great Synagogue. He said he had a chance to get them out to Israel, but the people who could have taken them had gotten scared. It was illegal to remove "historic items" like these from the country.

Ruta and I did manage to get them out, but not without a scare of our own. At the Moscow airport we had them in one of our suitcases, and we watched with increasing nervousness as the customs officials looked into bag after bag of the people in front of us. By the time our turn came, we were sweating. But the inspector didn't even get to our luggage. Instead he began asking pointed questions the moment he looked at our papers. Our certification for the $3,000 in currency we had brought into the country had not been stamped. Where was the stamp? And where was the money? We had most of the $3,000 still with us. He inspected it. This was something we could go to jail for, he said. Did I know that?

In Hebrew I told Ruta that we should just give him the money—anything to quiet him down and keep him from opening our bags. "Not a penny!" Ruta was telling me as a senior official came over. What did we mean, not getting a stamp? Did we have any friends in the Soviet Union? Who were they? Fortunately, two of the physicists from the panel I had chaired had accompanied us to the airport. They were still there. When the customs inspector started haranguing them, too, they gave him the number of the senior science official who had organized the conference. After a moment on the phone with this individual, the customs inspector's tone abruptly became almost reverential. He sincerely hoped, he said, that my wife and I had enjoyed our trip. He hoped we would visit the USSR again. Wouldn't we please pass through the gate and make ourselves comfortable in the waiting lounge. We sat down, but we weren't that comfortable. I couldn't wait to get on the plane.

After we got back to the United States I made sure the pointer and mantel got to Salomon Zhukovsky's sister in Israel (eventually they ended up at the Holocaust Museum in Washington, D.C.). Earlier I had sent Zhukovsky a set of the six-volume *Documents Concerning the Destruction of the Jews of Grodno,* which we had published after the German courts had finally released the Nazi trial documents. He told me later that he had taken the books to the mayor. "You wanted proof?" he had said. "This is the proof. Read it." And he had left them on the mayor's desk. A month later he was invited back and told that the city government was looking into his request for a memorial.

•

They looked into it for several years, during which time I thought about Grodno often. But I didn't visit again. Ruta and I did get to see Vishay, though, on a trip I made to Riga to give lectures at a Soviet conference of stress scientists. After the conference, Professor Milov, head of Riga's airplane test center, arranged for us to travel from Riga to Vilno and from there to the little wooden village of Vishay.

As much as Vishay had been part of my family's background, I had never actually been to this shtetl where Grandma Tema and her brothers and sisters had been born and had grown to adulthood. I knew that, as in the other villages in this region, Vishay's Jews had been wiped out by the Nazis. But I wanted at least to look at what was left and see if there was any memory at all of the people who had once lived there.

Though Vishay's Jews had disappeared, the village itself was still there, looking much as it did in the old painting Joe Szwarc had hanging in his office at our Holon plant (I had made a copy for my own office). Ruta and I walked along the lakefront and through the town, stopping in front of a stone marker that commemorated Vishay's most famous citizen, Ludwik Zamenhof, the creator of the artificial language Esperanto. Jewish himself and a firsthand witness to the hatred of Russians, Poles and Lithuanians, Zamenhof had dreamed that a world speaking one language might be a world free of prejudice. His huge efforts in the late nineteenth century to spread his universal language were a leap toward that vision.

Zamenhof's monument was there, and his house had been preserved, too. It was a kind of horrible irony—that these memorials to an eccentric visionary of universal harmony were the only intact remains of a Jewish community that had been extinguished by racial hatred. Not even the cemetery had been left standing. A young man Ruta and I struck up an acquaintance with at first didn't want to show us where it had been, but in the end he led us to an overgrown hillside littered with bits and pieces of gravestones. Engraved Hebrew letters poked up from the earth, and here and there on a few half-buried, toppled markers we could even make out whole words and the names of families.

Our young guide didn't know what might have become of the thousand or so Jews who had lived there in 1941, but he introduced us to his grandmother who he thought might remember those days. I told her that I was a Solnicki, great-grandson of Sender and Chaya Solnicki, grandson of Tema, who moved to Grodno, and son of Genia, her daughter. She remembered the Solnicki family and was even able to point out the house they had lived in. After we had talked a while, I asked her what had happened. She remembered that, too.

She would never forget what the Lithuanians had done, she said. When the war started, Lithuanian fascists, not Germans, had come to Vishay. First they had found the Jewish houses, then they had herded all the Jews inside the school building. For a while they had made the Jews work, but afterward they had taken them away. She didn't know where they had gone, but none of them had ever come back. "It wasn't the Germans," she repeated, "it was Lithuanians. Murderers, murderers, murderers."

•

But we didn't get back to Grodno. I was too taken up with all the hectic activity of acquiring, then incorporating, our new companies. Events seemed to pile on top of events, inside the company and outside, where after forty-five years the Cold War was rapidly losing its grip. By the time 1991 came around, the Americans and Soviets were exploring a tentative friendship and even talking about military cooperation.

That was fortunate for everyone, because in August of that year, when Saddam Hussein invaded Kuwait, he did it without a Great Power patron. In December George Bush issued his ultimatum. If Iraqi troops were not out of Kuwait in thirty days, the coalition would take action.

Everyone knew that war was coming. Bush had set a deadline, and Iraq was doing nothing to meet it. In Israel there was widespread apprehension. Saddam had vowed that if the United States attacked him he would retaliate against Israel. It was known that he had medium-range Scud missiles that could reach every part of the country. It was also known that the Iraqis had been developing poison gas warheads for the Scuds. For the Israelis, the idea of being gassed had a special meaning.

I got to Israel the day before the deadline. Ruta wasn't able to come instantly, but she would be joining me soon. I knew I had to be there while Israel was undergoing this latest danger. But in the face of the potential attack by Saddam Hussein's missiles I was also experiencing the deepest fears about my children and grandchildren (Marc was still unmarried, but Gisele now had three children and was pregnant with her fourth). In a way I was responsible for them being in Israel; where else had they gotten their Zionist feelings from? So I was also responsible for exposing them to horrors like this.

My heart was stopped by anxiety for their safety. I begged Gisele to leave, just for now, to go back to the United States, where she and the children would be safe. She could come back right afterward, but now, while this was going on, she should just go. But she wouldn't have any part of that. "Daddy," she said, "I understand how you feel, but I'm not in Israel to please you. I'm here because I believe in it. It's my country, and I'm staying. So just forget it."

"At least send the children," I said. "If you don't want to send them to the States, then send them to a kibbutz, or to Ruta's family in Hadera. At least get them out of Tel Aviv." But the answer to that was the same: Absolutely not. They would all stick it out together.

I went to Marc, who was not even an Israeli citizen. "Marc," I said, "there's a directive from the State Department ordering all Americans to leave. Please do it. You should pack up and go until this is over."

He looked at me. "You're joking," he said.

"I'm not joking. There's a State Department directive."

"I'm not quitting. I'm staying, and I know you don't mean it."

"Marc, I mean what I say. I know I can't make you go, but there is this directive. Consider going. Please. I think you should at least do that."

"I wouldn't even consider it," he said. "I'm not running anywhere."

That evening I visited Ruta's family in Hadera—her brothers Yitzhak and Ya'akov; their children Ziv, Roy, Ron, and Shai; and Ya'akov's wife, Erela. I arrived carrying my gas mask, which Marc's girlfriend Orit (soon to become his wife) had shown me how to use, along with the syringe of nerve gas antidote. We looked at the masks and discussed what might happen. Even among these strong people, apprehension ran deep. Israel had never before faced a situation like this. The entire population was exposed to missile attack, and there seemed to be no way to fight back. The United States was putting the greatest pressure on the Shamir government to stay out of the war, even if the missiles did come. I felt almost as if I were in the ghetto again, trapped and with no way to fight back.

In the middle of that night, the missiles did come. The warning sirens went off, and people got their gas masks on and crowded into the sealed rooms. I was with Marc at the time, and when the sirens started, I began getting dressed very deliberately. While I was putting on my tie, Marc started yelling, "Dad, we're being bombed. There may be gas. What are you doing?"

A few minutes later, Gisele was on the phone. She had been called into the hospital; could we come to stay with Eli and the children? At 3:00 A.M. Marc and I drove through Tel Aviv's darkened streets, deserted except for a few roving army patrols and roadblocks set up around areas where missiles had hit. Shortly after we arrived at Gisele's, Ruta telephoned from Philadelphia. They had CNN on and were watching Israelis in their gas masks and plastic-wrapped rooms. They were frightened. Ariele; her husband, Steve; and their son Daniel had come over so they could all spend the night together.

Families were grouping together. People instinctively felt more secure with their loved ones next to them. In the following days, more missiles hit. A sense of powerlessness sapped people's reserves. At least in 1967 and 1973 the army had been fighting. Units were at the front engaging the enemy. Now there was nothing to do but wait for the Scuds to fall out of the sky. Gisele had the advantage of working. She was now an established internist, and she spent her days and often her nights at the hospital. But her husband, Eli, was having a terrible time. He was a lawyer, but his firm had closed during the emergency. A strong man, a fighter, now he felt useless. As a reservist, Eli was in a combat unit, but as of yet, at least, he had not been called up. So he stayed at home, sleeping a lot and keeping the children close around him.

Like Eli's office, almost all of Israel's businesses were shut down. At Vishay, though, Moshe Shamir, Abe Inbar (our chief of operations), and I decided to open the plant for anybody who felt comfortable coming in. We had production obligations, and we were going to do everything we possibly could to meet them.

The first attack was Thursday night. On Friday and Saturday we were closed as usual, but on Sunday the engineering and managerial people came in. That day we called all the employees to inform them that the plant would resume operations. No one was obligated to come (schools were closed, and the government had announced that it would be better if parents stayed with their children), but we were open. We were setting up day care for young children and organizing school classes for older ones. Transportation would be available to anyone who needed a lift to and from work.

The next day something remarkable happened. Eighty

percent of our employees showed up for work. The following day we had 100 percent (we ordinarily had 5 percent absenteeism). Through the rest of the emergency, everybody made it a point to come in. Productivity went up. Even though El Al was the only airline flying, shipments went out continuously. On each box going to America, a white and blue ribbon was affixed with a label that read, "To America with Love." The missiles were coming down, but American support was helping buoy spirits, as was the constant flow of messages and news from Vishay operations around the world.

The day Ruta flew into Tel Aviv, three attacks hit the city. When the first sirens went off we were at Gisele's, where everyone crowded into the sealed room, hurrying to put gas masks on and get the children into their equipment. The masks themselves were macabre; the black rubber facing, the head straps and bulbous cannisters gave people an alien, frightening look. Gisele got Yam, her baby, into the airtight plastic cage the government had provided for infants while Eli encased their three-year-old Shir in one of the special plastic bags for toddlers. As the sirens wailed, Maya, Gisele's fourteen-year-old daughter, struggled with her mask, but it wouldn't go on right and she started to panic. Taking my own mask off, I helped her with hers, chin-piece first, as the television instructors had demonstrated, then tightening the head straps.

When we got it on, a wave of despair suddenly washed through me. It seemed only a moment ago that I was in the hole pleading with Sender to let me escape to the river before the Germans found us and killed us. During the previous days newspapers had run stories about the German companies that were helping the Iraqis make their poison gas. Now my family was huddled around me in this chamber, waiting for the gas to come—Ruta, Eli, Eli's father, my three grandchildren and Gisele, pregnant with her fourth. Looking at them, I realized I was crying silently, my face hidden behind the plastic and rubber of the mask.

Over the next few days Ruta and I spent our time with

our families, waiting for it to stop. Despite the fear, I had never felt so proud of my children. I drew strength from Gisele and especially from Marc, who at first had been too nervous to put his mask on, but who had demonstrated so much determination and courage. Although neither Marc nor I were official citizens of this country, we both felt very Israeli.

•

Eventually the city of Grodno did decide to erect a plaque at the entranceway to the old ghetto, identifying the place. The unveiling was set for March 12, 1991, the day that had been adopted as the anniversary of the ghetto's destruction. It had been on March 12, forty-eight years earlier, that the Germans had transported the last remaining survivors to their doom.

I received a telegram announcing the unveiling on March 8, four days before it was to take place. The Soviet embassy in Washington rushed me a visa, and I flew via Moscow to Grodno. Avi Eden met me there, along with his two sons and his father, Nachum (who had left Grodno for the United States in 1938). When we arrived, we toured the city. We saw the old Tarbut school and the Grand Synagogue—which had become a kind of co-op and practice space for artists. This time we were able to go into the house on Brygidzka Street, and also to the Puchalski house out in Losossna (unlike the hole in the foundation, the pit under the second room had been filled in).

While I was in Grodno I was invited to speak to a small group called the Cultural Association for the Restoration of Historic Grodno. In this group were Jews, Poles, Russians, and Belarussians (Grodno has now become part of Belarus). It was the first time I had ever seen non-Jews interested in restoring the Jewish roots of Grodno. They were decent people, very fine, and they talked about the distortion of history and what might be done to correct it. The Communist mayor wasn't there, but the deputy mayor was, a young Belarussian nationalist with an open mind and a direct manner.

Later I met with the mayor. I asked him about the synagogue and about the cemeteries that had been razed. He agreed to allow a stone marker at the place where the main cemetery had been. "But for the synagogue," he said, "that I can't give you. The painters are using it. Where will they go? Will you build them a house?" "No," I said. "This is your problem, not ours. You build them a house. This synagogue is not your property. This property belongs to the Jewish community. This is what it was before, and you are desecrating it. You must give it back to us."

He was a little tense at this. I told him about the falsification of history. "Well," he said, "now we know that Jews lived there. So where's the falsification?" I said, "Take down your encyclopedia and show me what it says about the Jews of Grodno." He opened the encyclopedia, but there were no Jews there. "You are falsifying what was," I said. "Is that the way you want it to be?" "Let me think about what you're asking," he said, and the meeting ended as stiffly as it had begun.

March 12 was bitter, with a freezing rain falling from the leaden Grodno sky. At the entrance to the ghetto on Zamkowa Street a crowd of people stood, some holding candles in their hands. Many were Jews, members of a new Jewish community of about a thousand people who had come to live in Grodno since the war. Mounted on a house next to where the Gestapo checkpoint once stood was a large plaque. In rough, beaten bronze one could see the outlines of the ghetto and an endless stream of men, women, and children marching forward. In Hebrew and Russian the text read, "In memory of twenty-nine thousand martyrs of the Grodno Ghetto." Several town dignitaries gave speeches. So did Lisa Chapnik, who had come from her home in Razan, deep inside Russia. Lisa's speech was a sharp evocation of what had been and what we had lived through. Although in her mid-sixties now, she still had the innocent sweetness of the young woman I remembered.

When my turn came, I was full of rage. I spoke about the ghetto and the Jewish community of Grodno. But I also spoke about the Soviet-made Scud missiles that had fallen on Tel Aviv less than a month before, during the Gulf War. Soviet missiles were killing Jews, I said. I appealed to them to put an end to the animosity toward Israel.

Finally Salomon Zhukovsky said Kaddish, the prayer for the dead. His rough old man's voice broke through the icy air and battered down the city noises in the background. Every word seemed a hammer blow. He chanted slowly, emphatically, this old man who was a continuous living link to the Grodno that had been vibrant with Jewish life when I was a child and whose existence had stretched back in uninterrupted vitality almost six hundred years before that—mourning our dead. *Yiskadal v'yiskadash Shmay rabAH, b'almah deevrah keertzoSAY, v'yamleech malkooSAY, bhayaykon oovyomaykon oovhayay deekol bays YisraEL, b'agahlah ooveezman kahreev, v'eemroo ahMAYN!*

On March 11, 1994, I took out papers as an Israeli citizen. It was something that had been in my mind for a long time. When I finally did it, I had the feeling that I had at last come to the end of a long journey.

That journey had started when I first arrived in France as a student in 1946. At the police station where I went to fill out the required forms I was asked what nationality I was. When I hesitated over the answer, the police officer looked at my visa and said, "You're Polish." "What do you mean, Polish?" I said. "I can't be Polish. I'm not Catholic, I'm Jewish." "Just write down where you were born," he said. I wrote "Poland," and on the line for nationality, he marked me down: "Polish." "Wait a minute," I said. "Cows and horses are born in Poland, too, but that doesn't make them Polish." But the officer had no interest in this logic. As far as France was concerned, I was *"Polonais."*

Some years later, I became French. I was deeply grateful to France. In France I had filled my lungs for the first time with free air—something no one born in freedom can adequately appreciate. The French had provided me with a place to live and opened the doors of their great universities. In France I had finished my studies, written books, taught, and worked; it was there that I made my first inventions. The French had given me the basis for my intellectual life. So I became an official Frenchman.

But inside I didn't feel French. Among other things, I couldn't bring myself to vote. It didn't seem to me that I really had the right. I wasn't born there; my ancestors and parents hadn't built the land or fought for it. No one ever said anything like that to me, but that was how I felt. So while my passport now read "French citizen," my "Frenchness" was an adopted thing, a suit that didn't quite fit.

In 1956 I came to the United States, and though I hadn't exactly planned it that way, I ended up staying and making my career here. In the course of time I became an American citizen, too (though I never lost my French nationality; a Frenchman never does). In the United States I had a different feeling. Here I voted. I felt I had the same rights as everyone else. After all, who other than the Indians is actually a native here? They're all from somewhere else, as I am—even the Philadelphia Quakers. In other words, it was just a matter of time, and not biblical time, either. Talk to an American at random and chances are that he's second- or third- or fourth-generation at most.

But though I love America and owe her more than I can say, in my inner recesses I have always felt like a man apart. Some time ago I was given a business award in Philadelphia. I felt honored, but in private I told the committee, "Fellows, I'm not really a Philadelphian." "But you've been here almost forty years," they said. Yes, I thought, physically I have been here almost forty years, but I still don't belong. I love you and I know you love me. There's no question about that. But essentially we have different interests, we have different understandings.

The fact is that I am Jewish in my heart, which for me means Israeli. To most people Israel conjures up the image of a particular country, with its national conflicts, border problems, and domestic difficulties. But it is not that to me. I was Israeli before there was an Israel. Israel was in my heart at birth. It was my father's country and my grandfather's country. For me to become Israeli was a natural act, a normal thing, a simple statement of who I truly am. It was a way to come home.

Ruta felt it wasn't necessary. "You are an Israeli," she said. "Whatever nationality you are, you have always been an Israeli." But I had arrived at a point where that was not enough. I felt somehow that not doing it was a way of hedging, something less than a full acknowledgment of who I was, and I was tired of it. In a way, becoming an Israeli citizen was like having a bar mitzvah at the age of sixty-six: I had declared myself a full member of the community.

Strangely, being Israeli, I do not feel less American, or

even less French. These places have given me so much of what I am that I am irrevocably bound to them. But I have found my greatest satisfaction in building Israel and being part of Israel. Not that what I have done has been in any way grand. But it's my little brick. That is how Trade Minister Ariel Sharon put it when we dedicated our factory in Dimona. "This is just one brick, but each one should lay one brick after another, until we have built our country." And that's the way I feel about it every day. Every day that thought fills me with tremendous inner strength.

How many problems does the government of Israel have? They seem endless. And doing business there has its own full share of difficulties and frustrations. Many businessmen don't go to Israel because of them. But in essence those are all excuses. It's such a wonderful thing that the country exists, such a wonderful thing that we can do something for it. Just think: Before Israel existed, anything we Jews did was empty. We were building on sand, for others. This is the first time in two thousand years that we can do something strong and stable for ourselves, something we can identify ourselves with. We live in a tremendous historic time for our Jewish people. I live in this story. I feel it internally.

I talk to my children. I tell them, look how extraordinary it is. How terrible it would have been to have lived eighty or a hundred years ago. And who knows? Maybe after a hundred years people will be blasé about Israel, as so many Americans are about America. But we are living through this period of bringing the country into life and building it. And we have a role in that. That I, a survivor of the ghetto, who should have been dead in 1943, can put a hand to that? This is the biggest thing in my life. It is just not comparable to anything else. And that's what makes me so grateful. That's what drives me.

And at the same time, this is good for the company. I am, after all, the CEO of Vishay. I am supposed to do everything possible for Vishay, and I do. If you look at it on a long-term basis, the company does not only mean results for tomorrow, or the next quarter. It also means building a team for the long run. It means building a community. In Israel we have built a wonderful group of people, more than two thousand strong now, who are linked with the rest of our people throughout the world and are contributing to Vishay everywhere.

Perhaps I could have done that in Taiwan or China or Indonesia. But my heart has been elsewhere. Interesting as such places are, I would have begrudged the time it takes to plant and nurture a thriving business. But every day I set my foot on the land of Israel, I know I am at home. I feel completely free, completely welcome. It gives me the feeling that I am going back to the womb of my mother.

Sender Freydovicz became a successful importer of business machines in Paris. In 1953 he remarried, and he and his wife, Roma, had a daughter, Antoinette, and a son, Michel. Sender died on May 22, 1973, and is buried in the Bagneux cemetery. Roma passed away in 1993 and is buried next to him.

Leon Trachtenberg is an air-conditioning consultant and contractor. He lives with his wife, Dziunia (also a survivor), in New York and Miami. They have one son, Avi. Leon's parents and brother Julek also immigrated to New York, where they lived until their deaths.

Viktor Voroshylski is a prominent Polish literary figure. He was formerly adviser to Lech Walesa, Poland's president. Viktor and his wife live in Warsaw, where they had two children. His younger sister immigrated to the United States.

Mottl and Goldie Bass moved to the United States after the war and owned a small store in Atlanta, Georgia. After Goldie's death, Mottl moved to Pittsburgh to be near his son. Mottl also has a daughter, who lives in New Jersey.

Boris Shulkes, the Farbindungsman who was with us in the hole for the first few days, survived the war in hiding and later immigrated to Australia.

Meir Zamoszczanski, the Jewish policeman who was also with us in the hole at the beginning, fought with the partisans through the remainder of the war. Afterward, he and his wife moved to Canada, where they owned a lighting fixture factory. They now live in retirement in Florida.

Josef Weiss remained my uncle Sender's close friend and business partner in Paris. He died there in 1991, never having married. In his will he left the whole of his small estate to the Israeli Army.

Ania Klempner and Bolek Shiff, Sender's close friends, married and immigrated to the United States. They live in Los Angeles.

Zaydl Asch, who fought with the partisans, moved to the United States and owned a grocery store. He lives in New York.

Frumka Halpern, my mother's schoolmate who visited me in Oklahoma, now lives in Florida.

Mesha and Pela Byelodvorski, who lived with us after liberation, moved to Paris where they lived until their deaths. Their son Dan became a Ph.D. engineer.

Jonah Zaretsky, who had saved himself from the SS by jumping into a cesspool, earned a diploma in film in Paris and subsequently moved to Israel. He married there and became a highly regarded documentary maker.

Lisa Chapnik and Anja Rud, the two Grodno girls who gathered intelligence and smuggled arms for the underground, moved to Razan, USSR, after the war. In recent years they both immigrated to Israel. Lisa lives with her husband and son in Beersheba. Anja, whose husband (Lisa's brother) was killed by the Nazis, never remarried. She lives in Tel Aviv.

Haschia Bielitzka, Lisa and Anja's colleague in the underground, worked for the Bricha organization after the war. In 1946 she led a group of a hundred children to Israel, smuggled them in, and was among the founders of a kibbutz in the North, near the Golan Heights. She later married and had children and grandchildren. Haschia still lives on her kibbutz, Lehavot haBashan—Flames of Mount Bashan.

Esther Heidemak and her husband the Polish underground operative moved away from Grodno after the war. Despite our efforts, we have never been able to locate them.

Josef Szwarc, who fought with Stalin's Polish Army, became an engineer in France, immigrated to Israel, and works at Vishay, where he is chief engineer and chief scientist. He is married and has three children.

Jascha Jonas, who fought with Stalin's Polish Army alongside Joseph Szwarc, married in Poland after the war and had two children. Eventually he immigrated to Israel, and worked at Vishay until his death. His wife and one of his sons also worked at Vishay.

Noah Berezowski, my Tarbout classmate who became a partisan, emigrated in 1990 from Russia to Israel. He now works in Vishay's quality control department.

Solomon Polachik immigrated with his wife, daughter, and son-in-law to Israel at the end of 1990, just prior to the Gulf War. He now works at Vishay's Holon plant as a materials manager.

Hillel Seidel, the Bricha organization leader for whom Leon Trachtenberg and I bought guns after the liberation, came to France with me in 1946. He subsequently immigrated to Israel, established a political party there, and served as a member of the Knesset. His wife, Ola, is also a survivor.

Bella Hirschorn, whom I had first met in Slonim at the age of fourteen, spent the war as a partisan. She now lives in Haifa with her husband and two sons.

Franye Braude, the girl who was pregnant in Slonim, immigrated to Israel with her husband, Hillel. Now widowed, she lives with her children on Kibbutz Kfar Menachem in southern Israel.

Alex Blumstein, who deposited Franye Braude's baby on the doorstep of a childless Polish couple, became a Ph.D. chemist. He worked at Budd with me, and subsequently became a prominent professor of chemistry at the University of Lowell, where he lives with his wife, also a professor of chemistry.

Hela Tarlofsky, my schoolmate at the Tarbut, married Kolek Blumstein, another Grodno survivor. They lived in Paris, where Helen still resides after her husband's passing.

Josef Rakoch, who helped organize our escape from Poland in 1946, studied dentistry in France. He married another student in our group and immigrated to Israel, where he opened a practice in Hadera.

A Note on Names

Throughout this book we have used the spelling "Freydovicz" for the name of Felix Zandman's maternal family as being closer to the pronunciation than the original "Frejdowicz." Janova Puchalski's Christian name was "Anna." In accord with prevailing Polish rural custom she was called Janova, deriving from her husband's name, Jan.

Acknowledgments

Among the survivors whose lives intersected with mine before and during World War II are a number who lent me their memories of events to check and amplify my own: Leon Trachtenberg, Nachum Eden, Mottl Bass, Lisa Chapnick, Anja Rud, Solomon Polachik, Josef Szwarc, Joseph Starowolski, and Lisa Starowolski. To them I owe special thanks, for their continuing friendship as well as for their help during the writing of these memoirs. I am deeply grateful as well to Sabina Kazimierczyk, daughter of Janova Puchalski, who was able to recall many of the details of life aboveground at the Puchalski household while we were under the floorboards. Her son, Zdzislaw Kazimierczyk, also provided a wealth of knowledge about those times. Thanks go as well to Hanna Kazimierczyk for her skill as an interpreter.

In Israel I would like to express my gratitude to Israel Tal, Elisha Roih, Abe Inbar, and Moshe Shamir for their contributions to this book. To my great sorrow, Moshe Shamir passed away as we were nearing completion. Had he been able to read the finished work, he would have known something of my feelings for how central his magnificent efforts were to the success of Vishay-Israel, which he served as president for more than two decades.

Various other individuals at Vishay have also been generous in giving their time and filling in essential parts of the story. Among these, I would especially like to thank Avi Eden, Don Alfson, Gerald Paul, Carl Fritz, Sharon Vinette, Bill O'Connor, and Ray Fridley. My thanks also go to my secretaries, Mercedes White and Betty Henry, who handled the logistics and details with their usual efficiency. I wish to mention as well several members of Vishay's board of directors who, while not having participated in the writing, have served as a source of strength during the process: Professor Edward Shils, Mark Salomon, Bob Freece, Dick Grubb, Guy Brana, Jean-Claude Tiné, and Eli Hurvitz. Those at Vishay will also know how significant the memories of former directors

Milton Scofield and Gerald Frank are to me—most especially now that I have been telling the story of the company's life.

I would also like to express my gratitude to Serge and Beate Klarsfeld for sharing their memories of events surrounding the Bielefeld and Cologne Nazi trials and to Fritz Wald, Raphael Bouganim, and Anne Lapidus for their help in translating documents from German, Hebrew, and Yiddish.

In more ways than one, a memoir is a family affair. My wife, Ruta, has participated fully in this project, as she does in all my undertakings. Only she knows how much I owe her. My children, Gisele, Ariele, and Marc, have given me their support and love during the writing (as they always have). In many ways they served as the inspiration for this book. Luella Slaner and Marcia Burnham were able to shed light on areas of the family's past where my own knowledge and memories were less complete and vivid than theirs. My debt to them is gratefully acknowledged.

Finally, my cousin and partner, Alfred Slaner, has been a constant presence in my mind as I have been working on this book. As readers will know by now, it is literally true that much of what they have read would never have happened had it not been for his faith, support, and wise guidance from the moment I arrived in the United States. It is another immense sorrow that for a number of years Alfred has been incapacitated by Alzheimer's disease. I would so have loved to have shared the experience of writing with him, as we shared so much else.